MAKERS OF THE
RUSSIAN REVOLUTION

MAKERS OF THE RUSSIAN REVOLUTION

Biographies of Bolshevik Leaders

Georges Haupt and Jean-Jacques Marie

Translated from the Russian
by C. I. P. Ferdinand
Commentaries translated from the French
by D. M. Bellos

CORNELL UNIVERSITY PRESS

ITHACA, NEW YORK

This translation © George Allen & Unwin Ltd 1974

First published 1974 by Cornell University Press

Translated from the French *Les Bolchéviks par eux-mêmes*

© 1969 Librairie François Maspero

International Standard Book Number 0-8014-0809-1
Library of Congress Catalog Card Number 73-20814

Printed in Great Britain
in 10 point Monotype Plantin
by W & J Mackay Limited, Chatham

Authors' Note

As the original French title of this work (*Les Bolchéviks par eux-mêmes*) was meant to suggest, the documents themselves form the major part of the text. Selecting which documents to include was a difficult but challenging task. The main difficulty was that the dimensions of this book obliged us to limit ourselves to a small number of characters.

The first and essential criterion of selection we used was the importance of the role played by the character in the Russian Revolution. We do not restrict the term 'revolution' to mean only the year 1917, but consider it to cover a whole process which started well before the birth of Bolshevism and continued through the early years of Soviet power. Thus we have included not only members of the political general staff of the Bolshevik movement in 1917 and the military leaders of the October uprisings, but also men who were in the foreground during the Civil War, in the building of the Soviet State and in the internal struggles of the Party. Thus Bogdanov has his place in this volume, for although he retired from the political scene in 1913, he was important in the history of Bolshevism as the leader of a whole group of 'dissidents' who joined the Party in 1917 and formed a considerable contingent of its general staff; for the same reason we have included Kirov, a minor militant in 1917 who became a figure of the first importance as Stalin's team became established in the 1920s.

The second criterion – which flows naturally from the first – was that of political representativeness. The third criterion was, where possible, to use original documents, that is autobiographies, rather than other sources. The three criteria of selection, taken together, account, for example, for the inclusion of Stasova and the exclusion of Lashevich and Lutovinov.

A second problem was the manner in which the documents were to be presented. Our aim was not to compose a biographical dictionary. Therefore we decided, out of the many possible ways of grouping the documents, on that which seemed least bad. We rejected classification by membership of the various post-revolutionary splinter groups and tendencies, particularly since neither the groups nor their members were very fixed. Bukharin is a case in point—a 'left-wing' communist until 1919, and then leader of the 'right' from 1924. The same problems occur in attempting to classify these documents by the occupations or achievements of their authors, using categories such as 'political leaders', 'Party men', 'theoreticians', 'military chiefs', etc., since each in fact took on, in turn and according to circumstances, extremely diverse tasks and positions.

The classification adopted in the end derives from our introductory essay: considering 1917 as a point of arrival, not as a starting-point, we have taken as our framework the political origins and allegiances to pre-revolutionary splinter groups of the selected militants.

The presentation of this material involved some technical problems which call for comment. Though we hope to have obeyed the rules of historical science, we intended to provide not a work of scholarship but a book that could be useful to anyone who might wish to have reliable documentation on the Bolsheviks and the 1917 Revolution. Footnotes seemed inadequate to this task, and we have therefore employed a different technique. Each biographical document is followed by a more or less lengthy note, in which we have sought to correct whatever errors there may be in the text, be they involuntary omissions or deliberate distortions, and to draw a portrait of the character concerned—and especially to sketch in his life after the composition of the autobiography. We have used numerous sources for these complementary notes, but provide no bibliography of them.

We are well aware that these notes are incomplete and may contain errors: Soviet archives are to this day almost totally inaccessible. Many of the victims of the purges are still 'Unpersons', on whom it is extremely difficult to obtain information. To fill these gaps, researchers often have recourse to second-hand sources: there is a great body of erroneous, not to say fabricated, information of that currency. We have tried, not always successfully, to avoid falling into this trap. Lack of fact, as well as the desire to make these notes more readable, accounts for the anecdotes in our commentaries.

As a general rule these autobiographies are complete; but we have indicated in the usual way [. . .] the suppression of minor episodes from overlong or overwordy biographies, and the omission of otiose or familiar details.

The reader will find a glossary at the back of the volume, containing short notes on the organisations, institutions and newspapers quoted in the text.

We must express our sincere thanks to Claudie Weill, who gave us valuable help in composing this volume and compiling the glossary; and to Marie Bennigsen who took on the task of checking a number of documents.

For the help that was afforded us in our research for this book we must thank the USSR and Slavic Documentation Centre of the École Pratique des Hautes Études, Paris, and the librarians at the Bibliothèque de Documentation Internationale Contemporaine.

Georges Haupt
Jean-Jacques Marie*

* Each commentary is signed with the initials of its author.

Translators' Note

In translating the Introduction and the commentaries, we have attempted, not always successfully, to locate and check quotations against their original language, in most cases Russian, but sometimes English or German.

The transliteration of Russian names in this volume follows the usage of British historians, and not any 'standard' convention.

All dates follow the modern calendar except where the abbreviation NS (New Style) follows in square brackets. In such cases the first date given follows the pre-revolutionary calendar, the second the modern calendar.

D.M.B.
C.I.P.F.

Contents

Introduction

I

When news of the October Revolution reached the West, most newspapers both failed to recognise the significance of the *coup d'état* and mistook the characters of its protagonists. Who were these men who had triumphed, and who were their real leaders? To such questions the newspapers had no answers. The names of most of the members of the new Bolshevik government in Petrograd did not mean much even to the best-informed journalists, and the press provided its news-hungry public with completely fictitious biographies. The names of Lenin and of some of his comrades, such as Trotsky or Lunacharsky, were known to only a small circle of socialist leaders who had attended congresses of the International. They had been scarcely interested at that time in these revolutionary Russian *émigrés* who had given so much trouble to the International before 1914 with their divergences and internal struggles: and so their lives had remained unknown.

Not much more was known inside Russia about the makers of the October Revolution. In May 1917, Lenin had been obliged to answer a smear campaign launched by the press and had an article, giving the main outline of his life as a militant, written by Krupskaya and published in the newspaper *Soldatskaya Pravda*.[1] In Russia, nevertheless, in the years 1917–18, the image of Lenin and of his immediate entourage was a stereotype of exiles, of banished men, of revolutionaries baptised in the camps and jails of Tsarist Russia. There was no sly calculation behind this discreet lack of information—it derived from the very principles of the Bolsheviks. The information on Lenin published in 1917 was considered an exception necessitated by circumstances, and the rule was expressed thus by Olminsky: 'In principle, we Bolsheviks do not write a comrade's biography until he is dead.'[2] Each individual militant was subordinated to the collective will of the Party—and history

[1] 'Stranitsa iz istorii russkoy sotsialdemokratii' (13 May 1917).
[2] *Sotsial-demokrat* no. 65 (26 May 1917).

in the making hardly left time to consider him as a person. By this rule the Bolsheviks expressed above all their contempt for the way in which leading bourgeois politicians polished up their image and their careers: for the Bolsheviks had no *careers* as such.

This was the original stance. Progressively thereafter, however, the intransigent line taken by Olminsky was relaxed, particularly since the Soviet authorities of the 1920s accorded great importance to the evocation of the revolutionary past; they thus brought the leaders of October 1917 out of their anonymity. Names and faces that had become familiar were given personalities by numerous collective dictionaries of biography. These works included not only the leaders, but all professional revolutionaries of any importance. Most frequently, the collective biographies contained the autobiographies of militants. Normally intended for the Party *cadres* or for the archives of the Association of Former Political Exiles and Prisoners, these documents were not confidential: contemporary reviews, dictionaries and encyclopedias reproduced them extensively. But none of these publications had more than a short life. From the 1930s on, they were withdrawn from circulation, shut away in the secret sections of libraries or pulped down. For after he had eliminated the Old Guard of the Revolution and secured his own power, Stalin imposed his own version of history. He disposed of its actors and principal witnesses, and the same fate befell the printed or unpublished documents that might contradict or belie his claims.

It is well known that Stalin attached great importance to this transformation of history into myth, and especially of the history of Bolshevism and the October Revolution. One looks in vain for the names of the members of the Central Committee of 1917, or of the political and military leadership of the October Revolution, in any of the innumerable works published at the time of the 'cult of the personality'. Stalin carefully erased from history the names and evidence of his opponents—while frequently attributing their deeds and their merits to himself. The history of the Revolution became a means of self-glorification which put Stalin at the root, centre and summit of everything, and submitted his Old Guard opponents to systematic and rhetorical denigration.

Thus after the twentieth Congress, 'ghosts' began to reappear. In fits and starts, a good number of the Old Guard who had been victims of the purges were rehabilitated. On some anniversary a biography would appear in a newspaper or a specialist review, and end with the set phrase: 'Fell victim to the cult of the personality.' Thus in the course of the last ten years, formerly banished names have been gradually reappearing in the history of Bolshevism, sometimes in the form of stereotyped articles and sometimes as biographical studies shaped according to the political requirements of the moment. For even if the Soviet historian is no longer restricted to the propagation of myth, even if progress has been noted in research, there are still certain legends which he is in no way permitted to shatter.

Though dozens of books have been written in the West on Lenin and Trotsky, as a group the leaders of the October Revolution remain unknown. A faceless history still prevails, in which only the great men have any features. Militants' names may be mentioned; sometimes the traits of Lenin are projected onto all revolutionaries; or there may be hasty and inaccurate portraits taken from unverified sources. As a result, the Bolsheviks of 1917 have a group image of men with no profile, no personality. For non-specialists, the authors and actors of the 'ten days that shook the world' remain after fifty years mere names. The names may be well known, but considerable research is required in order to obtain any precise biographical information. Biographical knowledge, however, is of especial importance in the historical study of an organisation which consisted of a relatively small group of professional revolutionaries; it was far from being a mass party like the European social-democratic movement of the period.

This book would be valuable even if it simply filled a gap in our knowledge and gave life to those who made up the Old Guard of the October Revolution. But it has another point: we have sought to resurrect, to exhume, either *autobiographies* or the so-called *authorised lives*, written by the men whose actions and ideas have moulded events. These sources are of unique and paramount value for any serious research or documentation on the Bolsheviks. For the interested lay reader seeking to understand the men and the spirit that moved them, these autobiographies, full of personal detail and up to 1917 of political detail also, provide a unique source of material. For the historian, they form a group of rare and exceptional documents which will enable him to escape from 'Congress-history' and to grasp events that have been 'tailored' according to later needs, and see them in their proper light. The autobiographies allow us to appreciate more accurately the role played by each of the protagonists in preparing and carrying out the Revolution; and beyond this, these sources put the Bolsheviks of 1917 in the context of their social milieu and of the circumstances that had shaped their minds, and thus allow us to go deeper than the events themselves and to undertake a political analysis of this group of men.

II

First, a few words about our sources, about the origin of these autobiographies. The great majority of them were reprinted in the famous

Granat Encyclopedia.[1] The three fascicules of volume 41 of this publication, prepared for the tenth anniversary of the October Revolution but written in 1924 and 1925, contained three appendixes with the biographies of some two hundred leaders of the October Revolution. In keeping with the spirit of their times, the editors of the Encyclopedia published mainly autobiographies or the so-called authorised lives—which were really a kind of impersonal autobiography. As a rule the Encyclopedia invited contributions from all who had played an effective part in the Revolution (the term being taken in a wide sense, to include its prehistory, that is the history of Bolshevism, the revolutionary year 1917, and the Civil War period), without regard to position and official status within the Party. Almost all the important men in the Soviet Russia of those days were included. (The most notable and inexplicable absentee is Podvoysky.)

In content and in style these autobiographies are quite different from most memoirs and recollections. Their style is less artificial, more direct: few concessions are made to fine writing. Their content is sharper, usually missing out cumbersome anecdotes or generalities, and they often reflect later experiences or political situations. All this makes these documents less readable, but frequently more reliable. It is useful in this respect to compare an autobiography or authorised life written between 1922 and 1926 with the later memoirs of the same person. Where the autobiography traces the author's life and shows his real personality, the memoirs often tend to highlight the part he played by placing him either at the centre of events (even if he had in fact been only a minor figure) or in the immediate entourage of Lenin. The autobiographies are free from conscious or unconscious substitutions—especially those which were written immediately after the Revolution. The 'hero' had not yet been sanctified.

There are also disadvantages deriving from the nature of these documents. Sometimes, a story as rich as the life of a revolutionary, moving from underground work through a major role in the Revolution to participation in the destiny of the Soviet State, is reduced to a few dates and a succession of official positions. These autobiographies are not easy to approach for readers unversed in the internal history of Russian socialism: but their brevity can be an advantage for the historian. Facts are

---

[1] 'Deyateli SSSR i Oktyabrskoy Revolyutsii', in *Entsiklopedichesky Slovar Russkogo Bibliograficheskogo Instituta Granat*, seventh edition, Moscow, 1927–9. Dzerzhinsky's autobiography is taken from the first issue of *Materiali dlya biograficheskoga slovarya sotsialdemokratov vstupyvshykh v Rossiyskoe rabochee dvizhenie za period ot 1880 do 1903*, edited by V. I. Nevsky.

here reduced to their bare reality, and attitudes are stripped of grand-iloquence and questionable motivations.

The major defect of these autobiographies, more circumstantial than intrinsic, is the rapidity with which they pass over the period after 1917. (Sokolnikov's autobiography presents a notable exception.) All they provide is a dry enumeration of functions and titles. From the Revolution on, it becomes increasingly difficult for the reader to grasp an evanescent past, for the present speaks a new language; and with a few exceptions there is nothing behind the lists of titles but a realm of silence. Why such discretion? There are many reasons. Those given by the men in question are all of a kind: their lives after 1917 merge with public life, with the supposedly well-known history of the Revolution. But even if the reader of 1927 could accept this explanation, which really evades the issue, such is not the case for the present-day historian. It is obvious that the particular political circumstances of the time at which these autobiographies were written determined their defects and their discreet lacunas.

In order to undertake a deeper analysis and to provide a better understanding of the texts at first reading, their exact dates of composition must first be established. These documents were not all drawn up at the same time or for the same purpose. The first group of texts originates from 1921–4, the time of the weeding-out of Party membership. This group was written for the attention of the Party's Membership Control Commission. The second group of texts was drawn up between 1924 and 1926 for the archives of the Association of Former Political Exiles and Prisoners—an association which enjoyed considerable authority (with the help of Nevsky and Yaroslavsky), and which undertook enormous investigations in order to assemble the documents and biographies of its members. The third and final group of texts was written during the same period, but specifically for the Granat Encyclopedia. Into this category come, firstly, the lives of militants who were already dead (Lenin, Sverdlov, Frunze, Kamo, etc.), and who had not apparently left any auto-biography; and secondly, the authorised lives of the major protagonists of the period (Stalin, Zinoviev and Rykov, glorified by their secretaries, Trotsky, denounced by a supporter of Stalin, etc.).

Lenin's life was related by his sister Anna, who had been his confidante and close collaborator from youth. This text is considered by most of Lenin's biographers to be a useful source for the study of the milieu in which the leader spent his youth, in which he was shaped and took his first revolutionary steps. On the other hand, this biography is quite inadequate on and gives no insight into Lenin's development, on the ripening of his theoretical views, on his strategy and tactics in the 1917 Revolution and after the establishment of Soviet power.

As for the authorised lives of Stalin and Zinoviev, one needs only to glance at them to realise that they were directly inspired, if not partly written, by the leaders in question, and were certainly scrutinised by them. Zinoviev comes over as he really was, full of himself and self-appointed heir to Lenin; and the major concern of the lives of Stalin and Rykov is to dispute precisely that.

The editors of the Encyclopedia did not impose, as a general rule, any form of censorship or constraint, and were able to use the texts listed in the first two categories in almost their original form. The great differences between the texts reproduced – differences of form, content and length – indicate that these biographies were not made to fit any schematisation of history. Very probably the parties concerned imposed on themselves, by some unspoken convention, a kind of 'censorship'—either avoiding mention of events in which they had been involved, or, as is the case with the authorised lives, providing the editors with a *curriculum vitae* and allowing them to write the biography and put it in its final form.

III

It is not easy to give a general assessment of the nature of the errors contained in these documents. The omissions can be imputed, in general, not to the editors, but to the authors, and what one tries to hide another reveals. Thus Krasin, in his autobiography, is silent on his differences and break with Lenin between 1908 and 1914, and on his membership of the left-wing opposition group *Vperyod*. However, in an autobiography in the same volume Bogdanov mentions this break and counts among its members the same Krasin.

Speaking of historical evidence, Marc Bloch used to say that there were many gradations between pure and simple dishonesty and totally involuntary error.[1] To reveal these gradations in the Bolsheviks' autobiographies, the date of composition must be taken into account, for some of them were written at a time when the Party's internal struggles were at their highest pitch. When they were composed, the opposition had not yet been beaten and the enemy camp respected certain rules of the game in most cases. The autobiographies are marked by this. Since the struggle between the leadership and the opposition was still contained within Party ranks, current political disagreements had to remain internal Party matters.

This discretion over contemporary divergences, however, was also projected backwards onto past events. Motivations for these silences differ, to be sure, from one militant to another. There were many who

[1] *Apologie pour l'histoire, ou Métier d'historien* (Paris, 1964).

agreed with Trotsky's view in December 1921 that it was politically harmful to revive old polemics and to use earlier chapters of history in current political struggles, to wield the debates of the past as an arm in new, fundamentally different, divergences. At one time these considerations were tacitly accepted by the editors of various publications and biographical dictionaries—and all the more since no one, save a very few old militants, had not had in the past his own differences with the Party and its general line, and since the life of any militant of the Bolshevik Old Guard was stained with 'errors' with which he could be reproached. Hence deliberate omissions, and hence also a certain political caution which creates a definite lack of precision in the human documents that these autobiographical accounts most certainly are: they fail to deal more than superficially with major political problems, and devote more space than necessary to striking rather than significant past exploits, to suggestive but subjective and superficial descriptions; or they take cover under a dry and monotonous listing of facts.

At the same time, our general considerations must not obscure other aspects and explanations. When this Encyclopedia appeared the time was long past when Trotsky could reply to Lenin's proposal that he should join the Bolshevik Party on definite terms in the following manner: 'I cannot define myself as a Bolshevik. Sticking old labels on oneself is undesirable.' That was in June 1917. Shortly afterwards Trotsky himself accepted the 'old label'. Seniority of membership of the Bolshevik Old Guard weighed heavily in the balance as early as 1925; and as soon as Lenin had suffered his paralysis the triumvirate commenced the fight against Trotsky in the name of the Bolshevik succession. Political *curricula vitae* became important, if not essential, and previous allegiance to a different branch of socialism, to one of the Menshevik splinters, although not yet constituting a chapter of accusation, could already do a lot of harm to a man. When the volumes of the Granat Encyclopedia appeared, the struggle against the left opposition was at its height. On 13 January 1925, *Izvestia* proclaimed that 'the great masses and even many young Party members have no very clear idea of the Party struggle which occurred between Bolshevism and one of the forms of Menshevism, namely 'Trotskyism', and the paper appealed to propagandists to 'fill this gap in the educational work of the Party'.

The bitter political battle that divided the Party ranks at all levels and in all four corners of the State did not at that time affect all sectors of cultural life; and publications as 'respectable' as the Granat Encyclopedia were not at first considered as weapons in ideological or political struggles. The majority of the autobiographies and authorised lives that appeared in the first two fascicules of our basic sources had been written well before the start of this campaign, and did not therefore comply with the demands of *Izvestia*. Things changed with the third supplement of winter 1929, which included the biography of Trotsky. It had been written by Nevsky, a Bolshevik of the first hour and at the time the official (and best-known) historian of the Russian workers' movement (though a few years later he too was purged). The biography of Trotsky is a fighting article and culminates in a rabid denunciation.

These documents, then, are not wholly marked with the stamp of political censorship; but the spirit and tendency of the autobiographies (even of those written before the defeat of the opposition) were profoundly influenced by the political origins of their authors. And in many of them, of course, there are wordy passages inserted solely to camouflage (though too transparently!) vain boasts or falsifications.

There were indeed many who wished to appear what they were not— that is to say, Bolsheviks of the first hour and without failings. Crudely speaking, one can distinguish two separate groups here: the first consists mainly of the 'old' Bolsheviks who had been for all that notorious adversaries of Lenin between 1908 and 1914. In the second group, some are 'illegalists', or 'underground workers' (revolutionaries who had worked inside Russia, often as obscure militants up to 1917), and some are characters who came to the forefront after obscure, unverifiable revolutionary careers, and who used these circumstances to tailor a past to fit themselves and the tastes of the times. Stalin's biography is the most characteristic of this group.

The biographies of those who wavered between one side and the other before and after 1917 are characterised by discretion concerning the political aspects of their lives as militants. Men like Lozovsky say little or nothing about their political changes, and Kamenev does likewise with respect to his frequent oscillations at decisive moments. In the same way, Lunacharsky and many others gloss over both their theoretical and political differences with Lenin, and the sharp criticisms he had addressed to them. Their silence is not hard to understand. The deification of Lenin and the proclamation of Leninism as a body of dogma raised his critics to the status of blasphemers. Those who had joined the Bolsheviks after being active in other socialist tendencies preferred to keep quiet about the question of their relationship to the Bolsheviks— without necessarily wanting to reject or denounce their past. The autobiographies of Rakovsky and Ioffe, to cite but two examples, are of the greatest dignity.

In short, the lacunas of these texts are dependent on the narrator, his milieu, and the date of composition. It must not be forgotten that we are dealing not with general rules, but rather with particular cases. Personal motivations turn out to be more important, very often, than obedience to some tacit code. The USSR had not yet been Stalinised: ideological and political imperatives did not yet spin the web of memory. That is why these autobiographies can reveal both personality and character: on the one hand, for example, one can see the sincere, honest modesty of Krupskaya or Bukharin in the brevity of their texts; or in similar brevity, the quiet confidence of Preobrazhensky, or the more lyrical certainty of Sosnovsky, taking pride in his past. On the other hand, there is Radek, verbose and complaisant, using his autobiography as a convenient means to distort and 'improve' certain aspects of his earlier activities, or simply to re-invent them. The most insidious kind of distortion is also to be found, namely deceit, which gives the reader not easily checked untruths but either a sharp-minded re-ordering of facts or a crafty interpolation.

These bare and simple autobiographies, lacking story line and elegance, lack also, and in consequence, those embellishments that make for 'readability'—but in compensation and in consequence also, they have very great authenticity. It is not always the fullness of activity that lends fascination to an autobiographical tale, but the talent, intelligence and depth of its author. One may compare, in this connection, the profound and sharp analysis that Chicherin made from his *curriculum vitae* with that of Voroshilov—rhetorical and empty, larded with stereotyped figures of speech and meaningless anecdotes; or one may put the sober, discreet but none the less gripping evocations of Skrypnik beside the strangely contrasting, colourless naivety of Molotov.

The list of lacunas could be lengthened substantially, and each autobiography requires, in fact, its own explanations. We have tried to fill the lacunas, at least partially, in our commentaries: and the most flagrant errors and omissions in each document have been corrected, irrespectively (and in ignorance) of whether they were conscious attempts at deception or involuntary mistakes.

The historian's craft makes a critical analysis of that sort obligatory. In general, however, the many gaps do not play, fundamentally, a more than marginal role. Less importance will be attached to these defects than to the details these texts provide, and to the frequently new light that they throw on the makers of the Russian Revolution.

IV

Beyond the facts, these documents allow us to set aright the whole perspective. The 246 lives and autobiographies of the Granat Encyclopedia, including those that are reprinted in this book, give us a picture of 246

different characters, of 246 very different fates, which explode and
diversify first the confused and simplistic notion of the 'Bolshevik Old
Guard', and secondly, the apparently monolithic, uniform term of
'Bolshevik'.

The notion of the 'Bolshevik Old Guard' is a confused one, since it
is used to qualify a large number of militants whose revolutionary activities go back well before 1917, but who only joined the Party in the year
of the Revolution. The term has gained currency in ordinary usage and
in historical works to designate the protagonists of the October Revolution. Historians, apparently, have merely conformed to a usage that
dates back to the 1920s. In general terms, in the Soviet Russia of that
period, a 'veteran' was a man who had joined Lenin's Party before
October 1917, irrespective of whether he had worked with the Bolshevik
ranks before the fall of Tsarism or had only joined after the February
Revolution. From the time of the struggle against the left opposition in 1923, the notion of the Old Guard becomes more precise:
the Old Guard were those Bolsheviks who had remained at Lenin's
side ever since 1903-4. Stalin remarked ironically that Trotsky was
wrong to worry about the fate of the Old Guard since he did not
belong to it. The term 'Old Bolshevik' or 'Bolshevik Old Guard' gained
particular importance at the time of the purges of the 1930s, as a
term denoting the revolutionary old guard that Stalin had eliminated
and which included the great majority of the leaders of the October
Revolution.

The term 'Old Bolshevik' used in this, strictly speaking abusive, way
can be a source of historical confusion, and may mask a number of
historical problems: it distorts and obscures the fundamental changes
that occurred in the history of Bolshevism before the October Revolution, particularly in the leadership of the Party after the February
Revolution, when its ranks were swelled by revolutionaries of some
consequence who had been, up till then, bitter enemies of Lenin,
opposed in particular to his organisational methods. To be sure, the
influx of new members from one side or the other had been a continuous
process before the Revolution, but it had been made up of individual
acts and had had no organisational consequences. Even on a rapid reading of these 246 lives, one cannot help being struck by their political and
ideological heterogeneity: only one part of the front leadership was made
up of Bolsheviks of long standing. Almost half of them were not among
Lenin's supporters before 1917: they came from different socialist
splinters, against which Lenin and the Bolsheviks had waged a bitter
campaign for many years.

Now it is clear that these revolutionary forces were not simply absorbed by Bolshevism in 1917. The early supporters of Lenin, the born Bolsheviks, may have forged the Party, may have constituted its middle ranks and apparatus, but the newcomers, either rallied dissidents or long-standing opponents, provided a large part of the leadership and general staff of the Revolution:[1] they contributed often decisively to changing a style of life inherited from the years of withdrawal and defence, to modifying methods and mentalities, and thus helped the Party to find the masses and facilitated the seizure of power. Moreover, one must not exaggerate the monolithic character of the 'old nucleus' itself. In 1907, for example, Lenin had been outvoted by the boycott supporters; Tomsky had never ceased to be to the right of the Party; the 'conciliators' (Nogin, Dubrovinsky, Frumkin, etc.) were the majority in the Party between 1909 and 1911; and during the First World War, Bukharin, Pyatakov and Bosch were opposed to Lenin on the national question; and so on. . . .

The composition of the first Bolshevik government already reflected the changes that had taken place in the leadership of the pre-revolutionary Bolshevik Party. The autobiographies allow us to go further into this question and to identify with greater precision the political origins of the first generation of the leaders of the Soviet State. The framework consisted of Lenin's lifelong supporters, the only ones entitled to carry, *stricto sensu*, the name of 'old Bolsheviks'. Among them we find Lenin's old team of the emigration years: Zinoviev, Kamenev, Litvinov, and the 'young Eagles'—Bukharin, Pyatakov; as well as professional revolutionaries and illegalist Bolsheviks such as Sverdlov, Stalin, Kalinin, etc., who had led the underground organisations in the heartland of Russia; and another 'nucleus group', some of whom, such as Skrypnik, Kossior and Voroshilov, had come to prominence in the Revolution itself, while others, like Kirov, only rose later, after the Revolution and the establishment of the Party and of Stalin's group.

Other militants might, but only just, lay claim to the title of 'old Bolshevik'—namely, the heterogeneous group of Bolshevik dissidents who had risen against Lenin in 1908, had left him and had campaigned against him for years. They consisted, first, of the former friends of Bogdanov, members of the first 'left' opposition—Lunacharsky, Manuilsky and many others; secondly of the right-wing dissidents—

---

[1] A large part of the newcomers of 1917 had been members of the *Mezhrayonka* since 1913. This organisation, which had 4,000 members in July 1917, existed only in Petrograd. It formed such a reservoir of leaders, agitators, and journalists that in May 1917 Lenin wanted to get Trotsky (not yet a member of the Bolshevik Party) to set up and run a big, popular Party paper with his own staff of supporters.

Rykov and his friends. All had left the Bolshevik Party before the 1912 Prague conference, all had been bitter opponents of Lenin, all had belonged to various groups or groupings hostile to Bolshevism, and all joined the Bolshevik Party after the February Revolution. Only a few returned to the fold as individuals; most rallied to the Party in virtue of their membership of *Mezhrayonka*.

A third and fairly large group of leaders was composed of former revolutionaries belonging before 1917 to various splinters opposed to Bolshevism, to which they rallied at the outbreak of the Revolution: Trotsky, for example, and his political associates of various periods, Ioffe, Uritsky, the internationalist Mensheviks, Chicherin, and so on.

The Russian Revolution was seen by its protagonists as the starting-point for a world revolution, and it included in its ranks many foreigners, recruited by chance, particularly from among prisoners of war, who were to play a part in the Civil War. Those, however, who were members of the revolutionary leadership were accredited militants, some of whom – Radek and Rakovsky, for example – enjoyed an international reputation. Most of them came from the ranks of Polish social democracy, like Dzerzhinsky, Unschlicht and many others who were connected, by their historical situation, to the Russian revolutionary movement. In general, all these 'international revolutionaries' had been active in Russian social democratic circles or had established contacts with Lenin well before 1917.

Lastly, the February Revolution itself caused Bolshevik Party membership to swell rapidly. Some of the newcomers, such as Tukhachevsky, were to play roles of the first importance in the October Revolution and Civil War.

At first sight the Revolution appears to have succeeded where ten years of effort had failed: it reunited around Lenin a large part of the left wing of the Russian social democratic movement.

The First World War had brought new splinters in the Russian workers' movement, but also new alignments. The choice between internationalism and 'socialist patriotism' destroyed some former divergences and gave the first impetus towards unity. Nevertheless, mistrust of Lenin and his supporters remained strong even among left internationalists. The pro-Bolshevik tendency on the editorial board of *Nashe Slovo*, led by Manuilsky, accused Lenin's group of 'narrow sectarianism'. From 1916 on, however, the articles in *Nashe Slovo* laid the groundwork for unification by providing the necessary element of understanding. Thus in January 1916 there appeared a long article explaining that the group known as 'Leninists', placed at the very heart of Russian political action, was 'losing its sectarian traits', and that the various groups in touch with Lenin were 'the only complete and coherent international force in Russia today'. This point of view remained, of course, a minority opinion until the Revolution. As late as February 1917 Trotsky did not hide his hostility towards Lenin and warned the leftwing Zimmerwald group away from him. Thanks to recent research work, we now know how the process of *rapprochement* came about and what platform these new partisans of Bolshevism used to effect the merger.

They were all well aware of the significance of this merger. In January 1916 the supporters of the merger declared in *Nashe Slovo*: 'Of course, in coalescing with the Leninists we run the risk of losing some of our own characteristics, which are not without their value.' But the Revolution brought changes that tended to clear away divergences, and to channel all the streams into the same river—all the more so since Lenin posed no conditions, did not ask them to reject a past of which they were proud, as indeed their autobiographies testify.

V

Are these 246 autobiographies representative?—or to be more precise, do they give a sufficiently large sample of the social origins of the Bolsheviks?[1] The answer is yes, even if the survey is limited to the leaders. The character of a party of the sort that Lenin's was on the eve of the Revolution must be taken into account: it was a party of the *avant-garde*, of professional revolutionaries—former outlaws, moreover; the Party was considerably weakened by the War and in February 1917 had no more than 5,000 active members.

It is a fairly common cliché to view the Bolshevik leadership as dominated above all by the intelligentsia, and to see the Revolution as having been stirred up and led by intellectuals. These biographies allow certain corrections to be made to this sterotype. Of course, the Bolshevik *cadres* originated from every class of Russian society, even from the high aristocracy (Chicherin), from the higher ranks of the civil service (Kollontai), from the landowning classes (Smilga) and from the upper industrial bourgeoisie (Pyatakov). The educational level of Party militants was in general higher than the national average, and the intelligentsia and the liberal professions, which traditionally provided the *cadres* of the Russian revolutionary movement, were strongly represented. But the striking thing is that the proportion of militant *workers* - not only men

---

[1] For a detailed sociological analysis of these 246 autobiographies and lives, see W. M. Mosse, 'Makers of the Soviet Union', *Slavonic and East European Review* XLVI (1968), pp. 141ff.

of working-class origins, but active production workers – was at least equal to if not higher than the proportion of workers in the leading *cadres* of the great European social democratic parties of the period. This phenomenon is all the more significant as the microcosm of the *cadres* was not recruited from the macrocosm of a mass party with high working-class membership, as was the case, for example, of the German Social Democratic Party, but in the dangerous and delicate conditions of an underground movement.

There was only a small percentage of women among these 246 *cadres*, as in all the social democratic parties of the period. On the other hand, the age range bears witness to the youth and vitality of the Party.

An analysis of national origins is of particular importance, considering the tenacity of the thesis that the October Revolution was the work of 'foreigners and Jews'. Revolutionaries descended from non-native stock were greater in number, proportionately, than in the national average (119 in all, of which 16·6 per cent were Jews), but this is explained by the situation of the minorities in Russia. Nevertheless, the Russian contingent in the revolutionary leadership was in the majority (127 out of 246). If the Russians did not always appear predominant, it is because the Bolsheviks, internationalists by leaning, took no account of national origins but solely of competence and devotion.

Through these autobiographies one can draw a whole stratification of the Russian social democratic movement in general and of Bolshevism in particular: first the veterans, who had been active since the end of the nineteenth century, the pioneers of Russian social democracy, the agents of ISKRA, such as Krasikov and Krupskaya; then the groups that were formed after the split that occurred at the second Congress of the RSDRP; then the generation of 1905; and lastly the recruits of the period of the new revolutionary leap in Russia, immediately before the First World War. These successive waves reflected the growing implantation of Bolshevism in Russia, which gave rise to an increase in working-class recruitment just before 1914. Lenin considered this to be a period 'when the Russian workers' movement was going through an era of mass agitation' and when 'the Bolsheviks were in the process of gaining a majority in the workers' movement'.

Despite the diversity of the personalities and their social and political backgrounds, the constellation of 1917 does have its own characteristic features, as a group. Keen and full of faith in the Revolution, unconditionally devoted to the Party's aims, in general very young – the average age was thirty-five – but also very experienced, the great majority of these militants had behind them years of prison, of clandestine activity, of propaganda and organisation.

The Revolution not only brought fruit to the years of apprenticeship, but above all revealed individuals' vocations. These 'agitators', to use the Okhrana's term, showed themselves in turn to be soldiers, military organisers, then State-builders and professional economists. For with a few exceptions, such as Antonov-Ovseyenko, who had formerly been an officer, or Chicherin, a former diplomat, most of these men were not professionally qualified for the tasks they took on. For example, a former typographer turned organisational technician, Pyatnitsky, turned out to be a gifted economist; the theoretician Pyatakov made an outstanding practical man, a really great 'technocrat'. They were characterised by fearsome energy, will and a passion for work. Talking of Sverdlov, Lunacharsky remarked that 'the Revolution threw up a great number of indefatigable workers who appeared to exceed the limits of human capacity'.[1]

VI

The historian, like the reader, cannot but be sickened by the final chapters of these lives. Their ends, mostly, are tragic and uniform, differing from one other only in chronology. Where the Okhrana had failed, Stalin succeeded—in eliminating politically, or more exactly, in physically liquidating the flower of the Bolshevik movement. For apart from a handful of survivors, mostly supporters of the General Secretary, the men of October, the acknowledged *cadres* of 1926, all ended their days before a firing squad, or in prisons and concentration camps. The opposition was dealt with first, and then the embarrassing witnesses, and finally, from 1936, it was the turn of Stalin's supporters themselves. Many of those who thought they had escaped the purge had been granted but a stay of execution. They were to be disgraced after the Second World War.

Are we to accept the explanation given by the victims themselves, that 'Stalin-Bonaparte' first eliminated the opposition as an obstacle to his acquisition of power, then liquidated the old party *cadres*, that is to say his own team, in order to establish his personal dictatorship?

The transformation of the Soviet Union 'from Lenin to Stalin' overlay a deep split among militants which was the immediate consequence of the problem of 'socialism in one country'. Most of the militants who gathered around Stalin and formed the group which allowed him to take power were former internal revolutionaries, men like Molotov, Kossior, Kirov and so on, who had spent almost the entirety of their militant lives as underground workers. The opposition was largely composed of

[1] A. V. Lunacharsky, *Revolutionary Silhouettes* (London, Allen Lane, 1967), p. 106.

former exiles, militants who had lived abroad for many years—either to escape arrest or to ensure the essential continuity of propaganda.

The struggle between the left opposition and the partisans of 'socialism in one country' appeared to be the expression of an antagonism that Stalin and his supporters made out to be the conflict between the realities of the Russian workers' world – whose spokesmen were the former 'internal revolutionaries' – and the isolated, gossiping world of the former *émigrés*. This demarcation is true only in the crudest sense, since some of the leaders of the left opposition (Preobrazhensky, Muralov, Smirnov and so on) had been 'internal revolutionaries'. But it is also doubtless true that the former *émigrés*, educated, polyglot theoreticians, steeped in the European workers' movement and made by their past more inherently aware than the internal *Komitetchiki* of the links between the Russian Revolution and the international class struggle, were from the start reluctant to envisage the desert island utopia that the building of 'socialism in one country' appeared to them to be. That is why Stalin chose his men from the ranks of former 'internal revolutionaries', assuming that they had seen the October Revolution as a Russian phenomenon. Stalin thought them prepared, from Brest-Litovsk to Vladivostok, to withdraw from the course of world events— by a decree of the will.

Paris, September 1967

Part I

THE MAJOR FIGURES

NIKOLAY IVANOVICH BUKHARIN

(autobiography)

I was born on 27 September 1888 in Moscow. My parents were teachers in the same primary school. My father was a trained mathematician (he had graduated from the Mathematics and Physics Faculty of Moscow University). I received a normal intellectual upbringing. By the age of four and a half, I could already read and write, and thanks to my father's influence, was passionately interested in books on natural history—Kaigorodov, Timiryazev and Brehm were my favourite authors. I eagerly collected beetles and butterflies, and was constantly keeping pet birds. I was equally keen on drawing. At the same time, I gradually adopted an ironical attitude towards religion.

When I was roughly five years old, my father was appointed tax inspector in Bessarabia. We lived there for approximately four years. Spiritually speaking, this period in my life was one of impoverishment. There were no books and the general atmosphere was typical of an out-lying provincial town with all its charms. My younger brother and I were now a good deal freer from systematic education and spent much of our time outdoors. We grew up in gardens and fields, knew literally every tarantula hole in the garden, hunted death's-head butterflies, caught ground-squirrels, and so on. My greatest dream at that time was to be given the *Atlas of the Butterflies of Europe and the Central Asian Territories* and other similar works by Devrien. Then we moved back to Moscow and my father was without a job for two years. We lived in great poverty. I often collected bones and bottles to sell for two or three kopecks, and I would carry old newspapers round to the shop on the corner for half a kopeck. It was at this time that I entered the second form of the municipal primary school.

Although my father led a very dissolute life, he had an excellent knowledge of Russian literature, and among foreign writers held Heine in greatest esteem. At that time I read absolutely everything. I could recite pages of Heine and I knew the whole of Kuzma Prutkov by heart. I read all the classics whilst still very young. Strangely enough, I read almost all of Molière at this age, as well as the *History of Ancient Literature* by Korsh. This unsystematic reading of whatever came to hand sometimes produced odd effects—for example after reading a few absurd Spanish novels about chivalry, I became a passionate supporter of the Spaniards during the Spanish-American War. Under Korsh's influence, I became infatuated with antiquity and looked on contemporary life with a certain contempt.

At the same time, I was often to be seen in the company of the so-called 'street urchins', for which I have no regrets whatsoever. Knucklebones, skittles, scuffles—these were the vital ingredients of their life. Roughly then or a little later, I underwent my first spiritual crisis and parted company with religion for good. This was shown in, amongst other things, a mischievous prank I played: after an argument with some lads who still had some respect for holy things, I brought the 'host' out of church hidden underneath my tongue and victoriously deposited it on a table. Here, too, there were some bizarre moments. Quite by chance I came across the famous *Lectures on the Antichrist* by Vladimir Solovyov, and for a while afterwards I was unable to decide whether or not I was the Antichrist. Also, I read the Apocalypse (for which I was hauled severely over the coals by the school chaplain). From it I knew that the Antichrist's mother must be a whore, so I kept asking my mother whether she was one. Being far from stupid, of rare honesty and diligence, virtuous beyond doubt, and doting on her children, she was of course greatly embarrassed by this, since she could never understand what put such questions into my head.

I left school as top pupil, was unable to enter the First Moscow Gymnasium for a year, and then went directly into the second form after passing an examination and doing some preliminary work for Latin. At the Gymnasium, I was almost always given top marks, although I never made any great effort, never had dictionaries, always hurriedly cribbed words from classmates and 'prepared' lessons five or ten minutes before the teacher arrived. In the fourth or fifth forms we began to organise 'circles' and 'journals', at first completely innocent ones. As one might expect, we also went through a Pisarev phase. For me this was followed by reading illegal literature, membership of circles and 'student groups' which included both SRs and SDs, and final commitment to the Marxist camp. My studies of economic theory at first left a painful impression: after sublime beauty, I was confronted by commodity – value – commodity. But after plunging into the thick of Marxist theory, I became aware of its exceptional, logical shapeliness. It was undoubtedly this feature which influenced me above all else. SR theories seemed to me no more than a hotchpotch. And my liberal friends had turned me violently against liberalism.

Then came the 1905 Revolution with its meetings and demonstrations. Of course, we all took the most active part in them. In 1906 I officially joined the Party and began clandestine work. During my school certificate examinations I led a strike at the Sladkov wallpaper factory with Ilya Ehrenburg. When I entered the university, I used it mainly for secret rendezvous or for challenging some respected liberal professor during a seminar.

In 1908 I was co-opted on to the Moscow Party Committee, and in 1909 I was elected to the new committee. At that time I felt a certain heretical attraction towards Empiriocriticism, which led me to read everything that had appeared on the subject in Russian. On 23 May 1909 I was arrested at a meeting of the Moscow Committee, only to be released and arrested again. Finally I was freed on bail, but in 1910 the whole Moscow Party organisation was smashed and I too was arrested, although I was working only within the law. I was imprisoned for several months, deported to the Onega region and then, to avoid a sentence of hard labour (I was charged under Article 102 of the Criminal Code), I escaped abroad. Throughout my Party work in Russia, I was an orthodox Marxist (that is I was neither an *otzovist*[1] nor a 'conciliator'[2]).

Emigration marked a new phase in my life, from which I benefited in three ways. Firstly, I lived with workers' families and spent whole days in libraries. If I had acquired my general knowledge and a quite detailed understanding of the agrarian question in Russia, it was undoubtedly the Western libraries that provided me with essential intellectual capital. Secondly, I met Lenin, who of course had an enormous influence on me. Thirdly, I learnt languages and gained practical experience of the labour movement.

It was abroad, too, that my literary activity began in earnest (correspondence in *Pravda*, articles in *Prosveshcheniye*, my first printed work – about Tugan-Baranovsky – in *Neue Zeit*). I tried to take an active part in the labour movement wherever I could. Before the [First World] War I was arrested in Austria, where incidentally I heard Boehm-Bawerk and von Wieser, and was deported to Switzerland. From there I made my way with great difficulty (including temporary arrest in Newcastle) to Sweden, where I worked intensively in the libraries with my closest friend Pyatakov until I was arrested (in connection with the Höglund case). Then I lived for a while in Norway (where I was very closely involved in publishing *Klassekampen*, the organ of the 'Youngsters' group). Finally I was obliged to travel in secret to America. There I was the editor of *Novy Mir*, and I participated in the formation of the left wing of the socialist movement.

After the Revolution, I reached Russia via Japan, being arrested by the Mensheviks in Chelyabinsk for agitation among the troops. On arrival in Moscow, I became a member of the Moscow Committee and

---

[1] An *otzovist* urged the 'recall' (*otzyv*) of Bolshevik deputies from the State Duma and thus a boycott of it.

[2] The 'conciliators' were Bolsheviks who wished to see an SD Party reuniting the Bolsheviks and Mensheviks, and were prepared to make concessions to the Mensheviks to achieve this.

the *ispolkom* of the Moscow Soviet, as well as editor of *Sotsial-Demokrat* and the journal *Spartak*. I was always on the left wing of the Party (and whilst abroad had proclaimed the inevitability of a socialist revolution in Russia). At the sixth Party Congress I was elected to the CC [Central Committee], and I have retained my seat on it ever since.

Of the most important stages of my political career, I consider it necessary to mention the Brest-Litovsk period when, at the head of the 'left communists', I made a colossal political blunder. The feature of the whole of the ensuing period was Lenin's growing influence on me, and I am indebted to him as to no other person for my Marxist education. Indeed, I was fortunate enough to be not only on the same side as him, but to be close to him both as a comrade and as a man.

The most important of my theoretical works are:

1. *The World Economy and Imperialism.*
2. *The Political Economy of the Rentier* (a critique of the theory of value and profit of the so-called 'Austrian School').
3. *The Economics of the Transitional Period* (an attempt at a theoretical analysis of the fundamental laws of capitalist disintegration and social reorganisation under the dictatorship of the proletariat).
4. *The Theory of Historical Materialism.*
5. A collection of theoretical articles entitled *Attack* (directed against Boehm-Bawerk, Struve, Tugan-Baranovsky, Franz Oppenheimer, etc.).
6. *Imperialism and Capital Accumulation* (an analysis of the process of reproduction, a theory of market crises in the light of the theories of Rosa Luxemburg and Tugan-Baranovsky).

The most widely read of my popular works are *The ABC of Communism* (written with Preobrazhensky) and the *Programme of the Bolshevik Communists*. Two works which stand rather apart are the historical work *From Tsarist Dictatorship to the Dictatorship of the Proletariat* and *On the Question of Trotskyism* (a collection of articles containing a theoretical analysis of the correct and incorrect lines of economic policy under the conditions of Soviet power with regard to the relationship between town and country). In addition, I have written a series of works of secondary importance—pamphlets, articles in journals, etc. Many of them, chiefly pamphlets, have been translated into European and Asian languages.[1]

The career of Bukharin – 'the Party's favorite son', as Lenin called him in his *Testament* – is without doubt the most enigmatic and at the same time the most significant of the careers of all the Bolshevik leaders.

[1] For a full bibliography of Bukharin's works, see Sydney Heitman, *Nikolai I. Bukharin, a Bibliography* (Stanford, Hoover Library, 1969).

Neither theoretical inconsistency, weakness of character, nor self-seeking opportunism are enough to account for Bukharin's evolution from the far left of Bolshevism in 1918 (and in preceding years) to the Party's extreme right wing from 1924 on. Bukharin's consuming passion for ideas kept him distinct from Stalin, even at the time of their closest association; and his personal honesty and rigour separated him from Zinoviev, for example. Through the prism of his individual character traits, Bukharin's development reflects the transformations of Bolshevism between 1917 and 1924-5 as well as the changing milieu and situation in which the movement evolved.

Bukharin had in all senses of the word a systematic mind: he sought to understand political, economic and social problems by fitting them into a coherent global system; and at the same time he took this system to the extreme limits of its *internal* coherence. He was satisfied and enchanted by harmonious abstractions. He did not therefore bother himself with tactics, and when he 'manoeuvred' as any politician must, tactical concerns came as an adjunct to his politics, not as their consequence. That is what Lenin explained in his *Testament*: 'Bukharin is the Party's most eminent and most valuable theoretician [. . .]. Nevertheless, his views can be described as Marxist only with considerable reservations, for he has something of the scholiast in him (he has never studied and, I think, never fully understood dialectics).'

Bukharin's career began like the careers of all the other Bolshevik militants of any stature who lived in the West. One amusing detail: Bukharin made Lenin's acquaintance in Krakow, in 1912, and then left for Vienna, where in 1913 Lenin asked him to show a young militant around the libraries. The young militant, whom Lenin had commissioned to write a pamphlet on *Marxism and the National Question*, was called Joseph Stalin.

Bukharin was a defeatist by conviction from 1914, and in his utter consistency he was the embodiment of the far left. In 1915, with Eugénie Bosch and Pyatakov, he stirred up opposition to Lenin's views on the national question. Bukharin considered national self-determination to be utopian and harmful. In 1918 he opposed national self-determination, in favour of self-determination by the workers: 'We recognise the right of a national majority of workers, but not of the nation as a whole, to dispose of itself' (*The ABC of Communism*, written in collaboration with Preobrazhensky). In 1916, there was a polemic with Lenin on the State, which Bukharin denounced as a 'new Leviathan'. Stalin was to accuse him in April 1929 of the crime of *lèse-majesté* in claiming to have had the better of Lenin on this point.

The atmosphere of the Revolution intoxicated Bukharin and transported him: he spent the years of the Civil War in the expectation of a

European revolution and in a state of permanent enthusiasm. At the sixth Congress in 1917 he called for a 'holy war in the name of the proletariat'. Like the great majority of Bolshevik leaders he saw the Russian Revolution as one moment in a larger world revolution. The peace of Brest-Litovsk appeared to him, therefore, as both a betrayal of the European proletariat and an unacceptable, dishonourable compromise. The state of continuous exaltation that accompanied Bukharin's ideological systematisation brought him to consider every question as a question of *principle*. Moral strictures and heroic purity involve the rejection of tactics and compromise which are considered acts of moral capitulation, not political acts, even if they look like the latter. 'In order to preserve our socialist republic,' he stated, 'we shall ruin the chances of an international movement.' This doubtless deeply felt persuasion came to the surface when Bukharin replied to Trotsky's information that Franco-British proposals of support had been made conditional on the war against Germany being restarted. 'It is not permissible to accept support from imperialists,' he said, and made 'concrete proposals: to accept no treaty from the French, British and American missions concerning the purchase of arms, or the services of their officers and engineers.' The left-wing communists then founded a splinter newspaper, *Kommunist*. The editorial of its first issue, signed by Bukharin and Radek, proclaimed: 'We ought to die in a fine gesture, sword in hand, declaring Peace is Dishonour! Honour is War!' When the decision was taken, he collapsed in Trotsky's arms and cried: 'We are turning the Party into a dung heap.'

When Lenin mentioned the possibility of sacrificing the Russian Revolution to a German revolution, it was as a political possibility based on the size of the German proletariat. For Bukharin crises of enthusiasm and despair were resolved, in his rigorously but formally logical mind, by a *gesture* or by *verbal* politics. This attitude is, of course, but the exaggerated translation of Bukharin's deep feeling for the world unity of the class struggle and for the common bond of destiny between proletarians the whole world over. But at that time these feelings gave rise to no practical strategy, apart from the idea that occurred to Bukharin and a few of his comrade dissidents: to force Lenin's resignation and to put Pyatakov in his place over a coalition government of left-wing communists and left-wing SRs. The idea went no further. Four months later, the left-wing SRs staged a rising in Moscow: Trotsky crushed them on the streets, and in the pages of *Pravda* they were crushed by . . . Bukharin. It was in the same newspaper that he later recounted the story of this shadow of a conspiracy. Vyshinsky used this story in 1938 to accuse Bukharin of having planned Lenin's assassination in 1918.

The Civil War created a pragmatic system which Bolsheviks later called 'War Communism': it subordinated all political, economic and and social life to a tentacular State machine. Early in 1918 Bukharin objected to compromising with private capital, demanded the total nationalisation of the means of production, and constructed a theory which made 'War Communism' a stage in the march towards socialism. This no doubt explains why at the time of the union quarrel in spring 1921 Bukharin first formed a 'buffer group' between Trotsky's line on 'union militarisation' and Lenin, who supported the idea of relative independence for the unions, and why he then moved to Trotsky's position.

The NEP (New Economic Policy) and the downfall of the German Revolution in October 1923, which showed unmistakably that the tide of European revolution was on the ebb, shattered Bukharin's views. His heightened awareness allowed him to perceive and to live Russia's transformations and isolation. He transferred to Russia the passion he had had for world revolution. Incapable of shilly-shallying and unsuited to gradual change, Bukharin performed a violent about-turn, of which the first signs could be seen in October 1922, when he opposed the retention of the monopoly on foreign trade, as did Stalin and a majority on the Central Committee. With foresight remarkable for a man in serious ill health, Lenin wrote: 'Bukharin is taking the side of the speculator, of the *petit bourgeois* and of the higher peasantry, against the industrial proletariat.'

Up to then Bukharin was very close to Trotsky, who declared that the relationship was 'typically Bukharinian, that is to say semi-hysterical and semi-infantile'. The 'scissors crisis', resulting from the NEP, and the failure of the German Revolution in October, threw them to opposite ends of the Party. They scarcely met again until 1925 and then only to compose jointly a Central Committee resolution on literature and the arts. With the struggle for the 'new course' and the crystallisation of the left opposition (winter of 1923), Bukharin came to defend the criticised Party machine, by explaining that Soviet Russia faced two dangers: the *kulak* and the 'politico-democratic' danger; and he denounced the opposition as a potential anti-Party group.

Bukharin then maintained that capitalism had reached a 'stabilisation' period, which put off into the distant future any prospect of world revolution. Soviet Russia, he continued, should build socialism in isolation and by her own efforts. Stalin discovered 'socialism in one country' and put the notion forward: Bukharin demonstrated the idea, and elaborated the complementary theory of 'building socialism at a snail's pace', based on the integration without force or coercion of the only producers of surplus – the *kulaks* – into the socialist system. It was therefore necessary to avoid any moves which might frighten the peasantry in general, and the *kulaks* in particular; and consequently Bukharin became opposed to rapid industrialisation. From the end of 1924 he became engaged in a violent polemic with his former literary collaborator Preobrazhensky and his theory of 'primitive socialist accumulation'. As always, going the whole hog, he declared on 17 April 1925: 'We must tell the peasants, all the peasants, to enrich themselves.'

For four years he was Stalin's ideologist and stooge. He was even at times his inquisitor. At the fifteenth Congress he gave a flamboyant speech directed against the expelled opposition, whose members were soon to be deported: 'The iron curtain of History is about to fall'.

Taking Zinoviev's place as President of the International from 1926 on, Bukharin began to decline precisely when the victory of the right appeared complete. Almost as soon as the left opposition was expelled from the Party, the peasants refused to hand over their grain. Hunger haunted the cities. The threatened system answered back with a political turn against the *kulaks*, towards collectivisation and industrialisation. As early as July 1928, Bukharin, terrified, confided his fears to Kamenev: 'Stalin will have the heads of all of us.' He counted up his aces and expressed repugnance at using them before being certain that the Central Committee would understand and follow. As Stalin dismissed his supporters one by one, or corrupted them, as he began to fight the right wing, demoralised but still the majority in the Party and in the country, Bukharin had a stirring of resistance—and capitulated. In July he was relieved of the presidency of the International, after Stalin had made him chair the sixth Congress which promulgated an ultra-left ('third period') policy, opposed to Bukharin's own; in November he was expelled from the Politburo, and he made his self-criticism the same month, together with Rykov and Tomsky: 'Our opinions have been shown to be wrong. We acknowledge our errors.' Stalin left him his perch on the Central Committee.

In 1933, Stalin appointed him Director of *Izvestia*. Bukharin paid homage to the General Secretary at the sixteenth Congress, but, passing through Paris the following year, confided: 'He's the devil', adding: 'We all rush into his jaws knowing that he'll devour us.' He was a member of the drafting commission for the 'Stalin Constitution' of 1936. Made suspect, together with Rykov and Tomsky, by the defendants in the first Moscow trial, he got off with an acquittal, but was then arrested and sentenced to eight years' imprisonment. Brought before the Central Committee, he attempted to defend himself but the decimated, terrified Committee booed until Bukharin became inaudible. He was the main defendant in the third Moscow trial: he was supposed to have wanted to assassinate Lenin in 1918, and to be working for Trotsky and the Gestapo to restore capitalism in the USSR. In his final, ambiguous statement he said:

We rose up against the joy of new life, using highly criminal methods. I reject the accusation of having attempted to kill Vladimir Ilyich, but I led a band of counter-revolutionary accomplices, who attempted to kill Lenin's work, carried forward with such remarkable success by comrade Stalin [. . .]. Only Trotsky can still go on fighting. It is my duty here to show that in the balance of forces that forged counter-revolutionary tactics, the driving force of the movement was Trotsky.

Accused of having taken part in the assassination of Kirov, of Kuibyshev, of Menzhinsky, of Gorky and his son Peshkov, Bukharin signed an ultimate, ironical and ambiguous confession in which each word meant its opposite: the dialectics of cat and mouse.

Bukharin was strict, but Bukharin was weak, 'lachrymose' according to Trotsky. His lack of self-control, his passion, his tenderness for those he reckoned his superiors (Lenin at all times, Trotsky during the Civil War) allowed more calculating minds to take advantage of him. Stalin's companions called him 'Bukharchik' ('our little Bukharin'). To get a congress moving, what better means is there than the one employed by Stalin against the New Opposition in December 1925?—'So you want Bukharin's blood? Well we shan't give it you!' He was often thus the puppet of those he thought he was leading: calculation was for him but an instance of exaltation. Both Trotsky and Lenin have emphasised this trait of character.

This man's nature is such that he must always lean on someone, be dependent on someone, be attached to someone. He then becomes nothing more than a medium through which that someone speaks and acts. (Trotsky)

We are fully aware of comrade Bukharin's gentleness, which is one reason why he is so much loved, and why he cannot help being loved. We know that he has often been jokingly nicknamed 'soft wax'. It appears that on this 'soft wax' any 'unprincipled' individual, any 'demagogue' can inscribe whatever he likes. It is comrade Kamenev who used these brutal terms between inverted commas [. . .] and he had the right to. (Lenin)

One day in 1918, Lenin asked Trotsky: 'If the White Guards kill us,

you and me, do you think Bukharin and Sverdlov could manage things ?'
Contrary to the opinion of E. H. Carr, Bukharin was therefore a possible
'heir' and Lenin gives him greater space and importance in his *Testament* than he gives Zinoviev, Kamenev or Pyatakov. But Bukharin could
not have become a Machiavelli or a Bonaparte.

J.J.M.

LEV BORISOVICH KAMENEV
(authorised biography)

Lev Borisovich Kamenev was born on 18 July 1883 in Moscow, where his father was an engine driver on the Moscow–Kursk railway. Both his parents had risen from a *petit-bourgeois* background. His father had completed his education at the St Petersburg Technological Institute, his mother had followed the higher Bestuzhev courses.[1] Both had belonged to the radical student movement at the end of the 1870s. His father had been a fellow student of Grinevitsky, one of the assassins of Alexander II. Kamenev's father soon changed his job to become chief engineer at a small nail factory in Vilno province, near the Landvorovo station. Kamenev spent his childhood in the factory settlement. His playmates were the workers' children. Nor did his links with the factory cease when he was sent to the Second Gymnasium in Vilno. During his holidays, his father encouraged his wish to learn a trade in the factory workshops. First he learnt joinery and then metalwork. In 1896 his father was given a post on the Transcaucasian railways in Tiflis and moved there with all the family. In 1901 Kamenev completed his education at the Second Tiflis Gymnasium. During his last years at school, he was already in touch with Marxist circles in Tiflis and had read illegal literature. The first illegal pamphlet he read was Lassalle's *Programme of the Workers*. This gave shape to his general interest in the labour movement, which had been formed by childhood impressions of the factory atmosphere and contact with workers. He was further influenced in this direction by what he read in legal journals of the conflict between Marxists and populists.

The arrests of 1900, which affected a number of Kamenev's acquaintances, did not touch him. Nevertheless, he left school with a bad mark for conduct, which would have prevented him from going to university. He had to make out a special case to the Minister of Education, Bogolepov, before he was allowed to do so. His father's pleas that he should follow an engineering career were rejected and Kamenev chose the Law Faculty in Moscow, having already decided to devote himself to revolutionary activity.

At Moscow University, Kamenev immediately associated himself

[1] The Bestuzhev courses were founded in St Petersburg in 1878 by a group of intellectuals to provide a higher education for young women. They were named after the first director, Professor K. N. Bestuzhev-Ryumin. There were two faculties, one catering for philology and history, the other for mathematics and physics. Graduates were entitled to teach in educational establishments. Despite strict governmental restrictions imposed in 1890, there were 6,996 students in 1914.

with radical students, and after a few months he was elected the representative for his year at the union council of students' friendly societies (*zemlyachestva*). He defended the need for a political line in the student movement and took part in the famous gathering of 8 February 1902, when the university was surrounded by police.

After the arrest of the then leaders of the Moscow student movement (Tseretelli, Aleksinsky, Budilovich, etc.), Kamenev and a group of comrades organised the second council of friendly societies to carry on the work. He was entrusted by the council with the task of travelling to St Petersburg to make contacts among the student leaders there. He wrote a series of proclamations with clear political overtones, calling for a united movement of students and workers, and was one of those who arranged a counter-demonstration on Tver Boulevard on 13 March, the day when the Zubatov organisation had called for a demonstration by workers in front of the monument to Alexander II. The counter-demonstration was surrounded by police, Kamenev was arrested and put first in the Butyrki and then in the Taganka jail.

After a few months there, he was escorted back to Tiflis to live under police supervision, and he was deprived of the right to return to university. He immediately began to work for the local social democratic organisation as a propagandist among the railway workers in Nakha-lovka, and the shoemakers at the Officers' Economic Society. In autumn of the same year, 1902, he went to Paris with the aim of studying revolutionary literature, and quickly joined the *Iskra* group. There he met all the leaders of the Paris *Iskra* group (Lindov-Litaizen, etc.), contributed accounts of the student movement, and after a few months met Vladimir Ilyich Lenin, who had come to Paris for the first time to give a paper.

Kamenev's acquaintance with Lenin and the impression made by the series of lectures and papers the latter gave during that visit, had a decisive influence on his further career. Learning that *Iskra* would in future by published by Lenin in Geneva rather than London, Kamenev left Paris for Switzerland, where he spent several months on a detailed study of revolutionary social democratic literature, and where he made his first report to the *Iskra* circle, which was directed against the then fashionable criticism of Marxism made by Struve, Berdyaev, Bulgakov, etc. His opponent was Martov, who, incidentally, used Kamenev's passport during his lecture tours in Europe. In September 1903, immediately after the second Party Congress, Kamenev returned to Russia. Whilst still in Paris, at a meeting commemorating the fifth anniversary of the Bund, he had met his future wife, Olga Davydovna.

He returned to Tiflis, where he became closely linked to the local SD leaders (including D. S. Postolovsky, M. A. Borisova and V. I.

Neneshvili), and helped prepare a strike on the Transcaucasian railways. After being searched during the night of 5/6 January 1904, he was obliged to leave Tiflis for Moscow, where he worked under the direction of the Moscow Party Committee (leading propaganda circles, distributing proclamations, storing print, etc.). At this time the social democratic organisations were in the throes of the arguments between Bolsheviks and Mensheviks. Kamenev became a determined ally of the Bolsheviks and found himself in agreement with the Central Committee representative in Moscow, Comrade Zemlyachka.

To prevent the planned demonstration of 19 February, the Okhrana carried out arrests among the Moscow leaders. Victims included B. Knuniants (Radin) and Anya Shneyerson, as well as Kamenev. He was detained for five months, and on 15 July was deported under open police supervision to Tiflis. Whilst in prison he wrote a pamphlet containing a vigorous criticism of the line of the new *Iskra*, which was passed from hand to hand among the inmates but was then lost and did not find its way abroad.

Kamenev's attempt to acquire legal status by enrolling for Yuriev University ended in failure when the following note was sent by the Police Department to the university:

> According to our information, the ex-student of Moscow University, Lev Borisovich Rosenfeld, on his return from abroad in November last year, settled in Moscow, where, after the arrest of prominent leaders of the Moscow social democratic organisation, he occupied himself with the training of a group of propagandists experienced in social democratic ideas. This group adopted the name of a social democrat group and began to conduct intensive propaganda among workers for a street demonstration of a political nature on 19 February of this year. This information about Rosenfeld served as the basis for an interrogation about the above-mentioned anti-government group by the Gendarme Department of Moscow province. During a search of Rosenfeld's room, correspondence was seized of a politically incriminating nature. Under interrogation, Rosenfeld would not admit guilt and refused to give any explanation.

When Kamenev returned to Tiflis, he was included on the committee of the Caucasian Union (together with Mikha-Tskhakaya, Stalin, Knuniants (Radin) and Khanoyan), which directed the whole labour movement in the Caucasus. He collaborated on the committee's organ *Borba Proletariata*, wrote items of propaganda, and spoke to railway workers at large meetings in connection with a strike prepared by the social democrats in the Caucasian railways. He also toured local organisations in Batum and Kutais. This committee strictly defended the Bolshevik viewpoint and waged a fierce campaign against the Georgian Mensheviks (Zhordaniya, Tseretelli, Khomeriki, etc.). At the same time, Kamenev corresponded with Lenin's paper *Vperyod*.

After the formation on Lenin's instructions of the Bureau of Committees of the Majority in the north, the Union Committee wholeheartedly affiliated itself to this All-Russian Bolshevik organisation, and delegated Kamenev to be its representative. He went to St Petersburg and there was given the task of visiting a number of local committees to urge them to support the summoning of the third Congress. So he toured Kursk, Oryol, Kharkov, Ekaterinoslav, Voronezh, Rostov and the Caucasus. Kamenev himself received a mandate to attend the Congress on behalf of the Caucasian Committee. He slipped illegally across the frontier and reached London (in the minutes of the Congress he appeared under the pseudonym 'Gradov').

When the Congress was over, the newly elected Central Committee appointed Kamenev as its agent and sent him to a number of organisations to drum up support for the Bolshevik tactics: a boycott of the Bulygin Duma and preparations for an insurrection. Between July and September 1905, he visited almost all the large towns of central and western Russia, defending the Bolshevik position at meetings of local committees, in propaganda circles, and at popular gatherings and meetings.

The general railway strike and the October Manifesto found him participating in the demonstration in Minsk which was fired on by the army under orders from the governor Kurlov. Kamenev returned to St Petersburg on the first railway engine leaving the city. He took up local work in the capital and became one of Vladimir Ilyich's closest collaborators on all Bolshevik literary undertakings. From the end of 1905 until 1907, he was extremely active as a propagandist and agitator in the capital, and defended the Bolsheviks at electoral meetings. In April 1907, he was instructed by the CC to conduct a pro-congress campaign in Moscow, and this city elected him as one of its delegates to the fifth Party Congress. After the dissolution of the second Duma, he remained in St Petersburg as a member of the Bolshevik 'centre' (together with Zinoviev, Meshkovsky and Rozhkov).

Following Vladimir Ilyich's departure abroad and a number of searches, Kamenev was arrested on 18 April 1908 and accused of preparing a leaflet for May Day. When he was released in July, Vladimir Ilyich sent for him in Geneva, conveying the message through Dubrovinsky who had just arrived in Russia. When Kamenev arrived abroad at the very end of 1908, he was appointed editor (with Lenin and Zinoviev) of *Proletary*, the central organ of the Bolsheviks. He attended all the Party conferences of *émigrés*, and for a while was the Party's representative on the Bureau of the Socialist International. He participated in the International Socialist Congress in Copenhagen (1910), and spoke on behalf of the Party at the Basle Congress (1912) and the Chemnitz Congress of German social democracy.

Whilst contributing from abroad to all Bolshevik legal and illegal publications, he also published a book edited by Lenin entitled *The Two Parties*, which signalled the final break with Mershevisk, and in his spare time he undertook an analysis of problems of the Russian revolutionary movement, in particular of the period from Herzen to Chernyshevsky.

In 1913, he followed Lenin and Zinoviev to Kracow so as to be nearer the frontier, and at the beginning of 1914 he was ordered to St Petersburg by the CC to take charge of *Pravda* and the Bolshevik 'fraction' in the fourth Duma. He carried on this work until 8 July, when the closure of *Pravda* obliged him to go to Finland. He was still there when war began, and he called a successful conference of the 'fraction' and local activists in Finland to discuss the war as a preliminary to a larger conference. All those attending the latter (including Badaev, Petrovsky, Muranov, Shagov, Samoilov, Yakovlev, Linde, Voronin and Antipov) were arrested on 4 November in the village of Ozerki on the outskirts of Petrograd. The trial was held in May 1915, and the Petrograd Court of Justice condemned Kamenev, several deputies, and other accused to deprivation of all rights and deportation to Siberia. The prisoners were first escorted to Turukhansk, then to the village of Yalan, near Yeniseisk, and finally to the town of Achinsk. Then the February Revolution broke out, and those in Yalan – Kamenev, Stalin and Muranov – immediately set off for Petrograd, where they arrived a few days before Lenin's return from emigration.

At the Party Conference in April 1917, Kamenev was elected to the CC. At the same time he became an editor of *Pravda*, and right up to October was a Party representative on the Petrograd Soviet and its Executive Committee. Later he was also included in the TsIK.

After the July Days in 1917,[1] the Kerensky government arrested him and detained him in prison until Kornilov's advance. Whilst under arrest, Kamenev was subjected to the vilest accusations by the Mensheviks and SRs. Prior to October, disagreements began to manifest

---

[1] Between 3 and 5 July, an abortive rising took place in Petrograd in an attempt to force the Petrograd Soviet into seizing power. The Bolshevik leadership had opposed it, but some Bolshevik agitators, particularly from Kronstadt, were involved.

themselves between Kamenev and Zinoviev on the one hand, and Lenin and the majority of the CC on the other. These provoked a determined rebuff from Lenin, and they were completely resolved before the rising. Following Lenin's nomination of him, Kamenev was elected Chairman of the Second Council of Soviets, which carried out and consolidated the October Revolution, and then first Chairman of the new Bolshevik TsIK. Kamenev soon relinquished this post in favour of Ya. M. Sverdlov to become a member of the delegations which concluded first the armistice and then the peace treaty at Brest-Litovsk.

After a temporary interruption in negotiations with the Germans in January 1918, Kamenev was assigned by Lenin the task of going to England and France to acquaint their peoples with the Revolution and the aims of the Soviet government. After one week in London, he was deported by the British government. Returning via Finland, where a heated civil war was in progress between the Reds and the Whites, he fell into the hands of the Whites, was arrested on the Ahvenanmaa (Aland) islands, detained for a while in Mariehamn prison, and then transferred to solitary confinement in the Oulu (Uleaborg) fortress, being released in August 1918 in exchange for Finns arrested in Petrograd.

On his return, he was elected Chairman of the Moscow Soviet. In 1919, when the republic went through its darkest hours, he was sent by the Council of Defence to the front with special emergency powers. In 1922, during Lenin's illness, he was appointed Deputy Chairman of the Sovnarkom and the STO, and after Lenin's death, Chairman of the latter. In January 1926 he was released from this post and appointed People's Commissar for Trade.

During his political career, Kamenev has shown himself a consistent Bolshevik and Leninist. He inherited a great deal from his teacher, Lenin. As early as July 1917, when Vladimir Ilyich went into hiding, he wrote to Kamenev: 'If I am killed, I beg you to publish my notebook *Marxism on the State*.'[1] Whilst Lenin was still alive, he gave Kamenev permission to publish a collected edition of his works. During his illness, he entrusted Kamenev with his personal archives, which later grew and developed into the V. I. Lenin Institute, of which Kamenev is the present director.

Throughout his public career, Kamenev has devoted a great deal of energy to writing. Selected articles of his on social and political questions before 1917 have been collected in the book *Between Two Revolutions*. It does not include articles on questions of literature, for example

[1] This was what Lenin thought of calling the book which appeared under the title *State and Revolution*.

the large-scale studies of Chernyshevsky, Herzen and Nekrasov, which appeared in the collection *The Literary Decay*. He is also the author of *The Economic System of Imperialism and the Tasks of Socialism*, *The Two Parties*, and *The Struggle for Peace*. A collected edition of his works is at present in preparation and the first volume has already appeared.

F. Muzyka

Commentary: see pp. 100–106.

VLADIMIR ILYICH LENIN

Vladimir Ilyich Lenin (Ulyanov) was born at Simbirsk on 10 April 1870 [. . .].

He grew up in a happy family atmosphere, where ideas and hard work were encouraged. Apart from the influence of his parents, he benefited greatly from the example of his elder brother, Aleksandr Ilyich. He was the favourite elder brother, an ideal to be emulated. As Aleksandr had been noted since early childhood for a strong interest in ideas, a firm will, self-discipline, fair play, and high moral qualities in general, this emulation stood Vladimir in very good stead. Right up to the time when he left for St Petersburg, they lived either in the same room or in adjacent rooms, and Vladimir could see what his interests were, what books he read. And for the last two summers, Aleksandr brought home books on economics, history and sociology, including Marx's *Das Kapital*. Aleksandr's execution was a tremendous shock for Vladimir and of itself strongly impelled him towards the path of revolution.

At that time there was no other direct revolutionary influence on Vladimir Ilyich in Simbirsk apart from books and his brother. The Gymnasium, directed by F. I. Kerensky (father of the former head of the Provisional government), was devoid of any liberal tendencies, and in any case the years of Vladimir Ilych's education belonged to the period when the school was kept under close supervision, when any at all free-thinking teachers were strictly dismissed and, apart from toadies, there remained only the more colourless individuals who more or less adapted themselves to the regime and kept their lips severely sealed. So an interest in social questions was only kept alive by conversations with school friends. According to contemporaries, Vladimir Ilyich always took the lead in these talks and was never under anyone's sway.

Every summer, Vladimir Ilyich went with his family to the village of Kokushkino in Kazan province. His mother had spent her youth there. She had maintained very cordial relations with the local peasants, and Vladimir Ilyich had the opportunity of observing at close quarters the life and mentality of the backward Russian countryside. He heard complaints of the shortage of land and he heard his parents lament the fact that the Kokushkino peasants resisted all exhortations to change to the quit-rent system from their own private plots.

He was awarded a gold medal when he left the Gymnasium in 1887. There had been some uncertainty as to whether it should be given to him since the school had received a reprimand for awarding a gold medal and top marks to such an important state criminal as his elder brother.

But Vladimir Ilyich's successs throughout his school career had been such that even a school of that time could not deprive him of his due reward.

After leaving the Gymnasium, Vladimir Ilyich entered the Law Faculty of Kazan University. There had been no direct ban on his going to Moscow or St Petersburg universities, but the Director of the Police Department had hinted to his mother that it would be better if he applied to one of the provincial universities, and better still if he lived with her. The headmaster, Kerensky, had groomed Vladimir Ilyich for the Philological Institute or the Philology Faculty of the university, for which he would have been fitted by his brilliance at Latin and philology, and was greatly disappointed by his choice. But by then Vladimir Ilyich had already developed a definite leaning towards law and political economy. Moreover he was not attracted to the teaching profession, and in any case he knew that this career would be closed to him. So he veered towards a freer profession—that of a lawyer.

He cannot be said to have had time to be influenced by university and student life, for he was sent down three months later. During that autumn, a wave of student 'disorders' swept through all universities in protest against the new statutes, against intensified police control of students and against the expulsion of numerous students whom the police suspected of the slightest political 'unreliability'. These repressions followed directly on the attempted assassination of the Tsar on 1 March 1887, when almost all those involved were students. Vladimir Ilyich had always had a very independent mind. He had always been very sensitive to personal insults and had reacted strongly to them, and in addition had been very critical of the established order. Now, therefore, he was shocked by the execution of his brother into violent opposition to the government. At the same time, although he was prevented from establishing close friendships at university, the very fact of his being Aleksandr's brother meant that he was treated differently from other freshmen by the rest of the students, particularly the revolutionary ones.

All this helps to explain the report by sub-inspectors that he had been seen in the company of students under suspicion, and that, it was alleged, he had been 'whispering' to them. On the other hand, it must not be forgotten that police supervision had for obvious reasons always been much more eager to find fault with Vladimir Ilyich than with many other students. However that may be, when the Inspector of Students was set upon by a mass of excited young people, he later asserted that Vladimir Ilyich had been in the vanguard and had almost raised his fist against him. As a result, Vladimir Ilyich was one of the forty students arrested that night and taken to the police station. Adoratsky tells of Vladimir Ilyich's conversation with the police officer escorting him:

'Why are you rebelling, young man? After all, there is a wall in front of you,' said the policeman.

'That wall is tottering, you only have to push it for it to fall over,' replied Vladimir Ilyich.

All those arrested were banished from Kazan to their place of birth, but since none of Vladimir Iliych's relatives were still living in Simbirsk, it was agreed that he should be deported to Kokushkino, twenty-five miles from Kazan, to join me, his sister Anna, who was living there under open police observation following the affair of 1 March 1887. He remained there until autumn 1888. He read a great deal—in a wing of the house there was a bookcase which had belonged to his uncle, a very widely read man, and Vladimir Ilyich devoured all the books in it on social questions, in addition looking for valuable articles in old journals. Then he would go hunting, take long walks in the area round about, and of course he had many opportunities for observing the life of the peasants. He had no company except for his cousins, who came to Kokushkino for their summer holidays, but they were colourless people devoid of social concern, and could contribute nothing to Vladimir Ilyich's evolution. In autumn 1888 he was given permission to return to Kazan where he spent all the following winter. Here he looked up old acquaintances and made a few new ones. He met a woman called Chetvergova, a member of *Narodnaya Volya*. He was greatly in sympathy with her ideas. Indeed he always had great respect for the old *narodovoltsy* (as is witnessed by the memoirs of Krupskaya, Zinoviev and others), and he never denied being their 'inheritor'.

It was during this winter that he began to elaborate his social democratic convictions. He undertook a passionate study of Marx's *Das Kapital*. He started to frequent a circle of young people who were hammering out their own convictions and exchanged views on the works they read. They had no recognised leader; they sought their own way quite independently. The main organiser of Marxist circles in Kazan at that time was N. E. Fedoseyev, of whom Vladimir Ilyich had heard but whom he did not have occasion to meet. It was only later that they became acquainted through letters and exchanging articles. They were roughly of the same age and equally outstanding in their youth, so that it is impossible to determine the influence of the one on the other.

In spring 1889 Vladimir Ilyich accompanied his family to the farm of Alakaevka in Samara province, and in the autumn he went to the town of Samara. There he spent a little over four years. He devoted himself to a study of Marxism, reading all the basic texts of Marx and Engels in

Russian or foreign languages, and he explained some of them to a circle of young people which he organised there. They were younger and less well read than he so that they considered him an authoritative theoretician. Generally speaking social democracy at that time, particularly in the provinces, was only just springing up and found support solely among young people. Throughout this period, Vladimir Ilyich came across (in 1891 or 1892) only one convinced, mature Marxist—P. I. Skvortsov, who was on his way to Nizhny Novgorod. This acquaintance was of great interest to him and he later took pleasure in recounting their conversation, but he emphasised that Skvortsov was only a theoretical Marxist and that he would never make a revolutionary.

Among the revolutionary-minded groups in Samara, there were many former Siberian exiles who were now living under supervision. They were all of course Populists or *narodovoltsy*. Our family was on more or less good terms with all of them. Vladimir Ilyich saw N. Dolgov and the Livanovs more often than the rest. The latter were typical *narodovoltsy*, full of integrity and idealism. He loved chatting with them, and whilst they were following a different path, he benefited from their revolutionary experience. He studied the history of the revolutionary movement with the aid of their stories, since there was a complete lack of illegal literature in our province. But when it came to fundamental beliefs, he conducted ever more heated arguments both with them and with Populists of every ilk. In the process, his views were sharpened and he learnt to argue them better. One of his opponents was V. V. Vodovozov, who was spending one year under supervision in Samara. The more respectable members of his audience were shocked by the irreverence of this young man's arguments but they often deferred to him. Vladimir Ilyich also had many discussions with M. I. Yasneva (Golubeva), a representative of Russian Jacobinism who was living under supervision in Samara and who became a social democrat under his influence.

Besides the elaboration of his views on revolution, Vladimir Ilyich also made progress in conventional learning during these years in Samara. He was not permitted to re-enter university and his petition to be allowed to go abroad to study was rejected. It was only in 1890, three years after his expulsion, that his mother was able to obtain permission for him to be allowed to sit the examinations as an external student. Then Vladimir Ilyich immersed himself in work and within eighteen months he had done all the necessary preparation without outside help. He sat the St Petersburg University examinations in spring and autumn 1891 and was given excellent marks. Thus he had kept abreast of students who had begun their course at the same time as him and had remained at the university.

During his visits to St Petersburg to sit the examinations, Vladimir Ilyich met a few Marxists, and from one of them, a teacher at the Technological Institute called Yavein, he received Marxist literature which he brought back to Samara—it included the journal. *Neue Zeit* and the weekly newspaper *Für soziale Gesetzgebung und Statistik*.

After being awarded his degree, Vladimir Ilyich became a pupil of a lawyer called Khardin, a prominent representative of liberal society in Samara and a very intelligent man whom Vladimir Ilyich respected. On a few occasions he took cases himself, but they were of minor importance, requiring little preparation. Pupillage was the first step towards entering a profession in which he could earn a living, but his chief energy and strength were directed to a study of Marxism and Russian society, as well as to preparations for revolutionary activity. It was in this period that Vladimir Ilyich's first literary works were written: a paper on Postnikov's book *Peasant Economy in Southern Russia*, which was only recently printed, thirty years after it was written, and the notebooks of criticisms of the Populist writers, V. V. Yuzhakov and Karyshev, which later grew into his first major work, *Who the 'Friends of the People' are and how they fight against the social democrats.*

In autumn 1893 he moved to St Petersburg where he entered the chambers of a lawyer called Volkenstein. This provided him with a position and a living. In the capital, too, he appeared on a few occasions as defence counsel, but only in cases to which he was appointed. He came into contact with St Petersburg social democrats, as well as the circle of Krasin, Radchenko and some technical students including Starkov, Krzhizhanovsky and Zaporozhets. In addition he made the acquaintance of the Marxist writers Struve and Potresov. He wrote a reply to Mikhailovsky's outbursts against Marxists in the legal Press and this formed the first chapter of his book *Who the 'Friends of the People' are*. This work was first typed and then mimeographed by a group of Moscow social democrat students. Later, Vladimir Ilyich issued a criticism of Struve's book.

This criticism was printed (under the *nom de plume* 'Tulin') in a collection of Marxist articles entitled *Materials to Describe Our Economic Development* and was called 'The Economic Content of Populism and the Criticism of it in Mr Struve's Book'. But the book was burnt by the censors, chiefly on account of Vladimir Ilyich's article, and only individual copies survived. In this article, Vladimir Ilyich agreed with Struve's criticism of Populism but came down firmly against the liberal deviation which could already be discerned in the latter's views.

Thus the period from September 1893 until December 1894 which Vladimir Ilyich spent in the capital was employed not only in opposing Populism and elaborating a correct Marxist point of view, but also in revolutionary social democratic activity. He developed links with some workers (Shelgunov, Babushkin, etc.). He participated in workers' circles beyond the Nevskaya Zastava. And he wrote leaflets both on broad political topics, for example for May Day, and on particularly requested subjects at individual factories.

It was during this period that he made his first trip abroad (in spring 1895) and became acquainted with the Emancipation of Labour group (Plekhanov, Vera Zasulich and Akselrod). All this group, and in particular Plekhanov, had a great influence on Vladimir Ilyich. Whilst still in Russia, he had become familiar with Plekhanov's main writings. He greatly respected him and considered him his teacher. Their personal meeting strengthened his links with the whole group and, as he himself admitted on his return, taught him a lot. He mentioned that both Plekhanov and Akselrod had found a certain narrowness in his attitude towards other classes in society as expressed in the 'Tulin' article. Both considered that as the Social Democratic Party entered the political arena, it could not confine itself solely to criticism of all parties as it had done during its formation; and that whilst becoming the most progressive party, it must not lose sight of a single opposition movement that betokened an awakening of social concern and the enlargement of the struggle against the autocracy by various classes and groups.

Vladimir Ilyich recognised the justice of this point of view and his discussions with Plekhanov and Akselrod undoubtedly hastened his entry in to the vast revolutionary arena with the founding of the League of Struggle for the Emancipation of the Working Class. Members of the Emancipation of Labour group also encouraged him to publish a political organ for Russian social democracy. He wrote the main articles for the first edition of this underground paper, called *Rabochaya Gazeta*, and had passed it for printing, when all the material was seized during the arrests of 9 December 1895, which made almost a clean sweep of the circle.

During the fourteen months he spent in prison Vladimir Ilyich never ceased working. Firstly, he took advantage of the St Petersburg libraries and book repositories to collect material for his planned book *The Development of Capitalism in Russia*. Secondly, he never abandoned his illegal activity. He made use of codes and invisible ink to smuggle out leaflets, pamphlets, and an outline Party programme with appended explanations. On his release in February 1897, he and some other comrades were given three days by the Police Department 'to settle their affairs' in the capital. During that period he met social democrat activists and spoke vigorously against the 'economist' deviation which was beginning to manifest itself in the movement. He was allowed to make his own way into exile without escort. So he travelled by the newly built Siberian railway as far as Krasnoyarsk, where he was sent on to the village of Shushenskoye in Minusinsk district. He was to spend three years of his exile there. After one year his fiancée, N. K. Krupskaya, arrived there with her mother—she had received permission to leave her own place of exile, Ufa province, for Shushenskoye, in view of their forthcoming marriage. The only other exiles in that village were two Polish workers, but in neighbouring villages lived some comrades whom Vladimir Ilyich was occasionally permitted to see, for example on holidays and at his wedding. He maintained an extremely vigorous correspondence with all comrades in exile. He was also very meticulous in his correspondence with the Russian and *émigré* centres. Most of his letters, both ordinary ones and in invisible ink, were forwarded by me. I took out subscriptions to journals on his behalf, sent him the latest books as far as possible, and also brought back many books he wanted from abroad.

In exile Vladimir Ilyich wrote *The Development of Capitalism in Russia* on the basis of material he had gathered in prison. In addition he wrote articles for short-lived legal Marxist journals. These were collected and published under the title *Economic Studies and Articles*. Both these books, for which I did the proof-reading, appeared in 1899. Besides this, he and his wife, Nadezhda Konstantinovna, translated from English *The Theory and Practice of Trade Unionism* by Sidney and, Beatrice Webb, and he wrote a short book called *The Tasks of Russian Social Democrats* which was published abroad, as well as several articles and papers to be read by comrades in exile. It was in Shushenskoye that he composed a protest against the so-called *Credo* of Kuskova and Prokopovich, which was printed abroad as *The Protest of Seventeen Social Democrats*, but was known by the shorter name of *Anti-Credo*. In it Vladimir Ilyich analysed and demolished this profession of faith by the most prominent so-called 'economists'.

Returning from exile in February 1900, he visited his parents and then went to Pskov where he had elected to reside (all university and large industrial towns were out of bounds for returning exiles). A. Potresov, Lepeshinsky and Tsederbaum (Martov) also arrived from exile to join L. N. Radchenko and other social democrats who were already living there. The indispensable task of uniting circles in separate towns into a party was made more difficult by constant arrests. After the first Party Conference in 1898, almost all the delegates were arrested. A second Congress was planned for 1900 by the southerners—chiefly the Ekaterinoslav Committee which published *Yuzhny Rabochy*. But in spring of that year, this group too was uncovered. Then the idea came to Vladimir Ilyich of attempting to unite the activists not by a congress, which under those conditions would be too costly, but around a newspaper published abroad and out of reach of the police. This paper would serve, to use his own image, as the 'scaffolding' around which the Party would be built up. He advocated this idea at the so-called Pskov Conference of social democrats. It was decided that, to carry it out, he should go abroad with Potresov and Martov. All three applied for exit passports—at that time the Police Department issued them quite readily since experience had shown that people, particularly writers and intellectuals, were swallowed up abroad and rendered more or less harmless from the point of view of revolutionary activity.

This plan, however, almost came to naught as a result of the arrest of Vladimir Ilyich and Martov during a clandestine visit to St Petersburg. Fortunately they only spent three days in jail and were released without the matter being taken further. Following this Vladimir Ilyich decided to advance his departure. Before he left, he travelled only to see mother and myself in Ufa, where his wife was due to spend the last year of open supervision. Of course, both in Ufa and Samara, where he stopped on the way, he met social democrats and expounded his plan to them.

When he arrived abroad, it was decided to co-operate with the Emancipation of Labour group in publishing *Iskra* ('the spark') with an epigraph from a poem about the Decembrists: 'The spark will kindle a flame'. The other *émigré* group, which published *Rabocheye Delo*, were not invited to participate as being too close to 'economism'. For the sake of greater independence and remoteness from the swarms of *émigrés* in Geneva, it was agreed that the paper should come out in Munich. Vladimir Ilyich, Potresov and Vera Zasulich moved there, and were later joined from Russia by Martov. Apart from *Iskra*, it was also decided to publish a scientific Marxist journal called *Zarya*.

Vladimir Ilyich set to work with a will. Given the limited number of collaborators, he had at first to shoulder most of the tasks himself—deal with correspondence, compose codes, arrange means of smuggling copies into Russia and maintain contacts both inside Russia and in *émigré* colonies. [. . .] *Iskra*, and even more *What is to be done?* which he wrote at this time and which insisted on the necessity of creating an organisation of professional, underground revolutionaries, greatly contributed to this cause. Most Party committees supported *Iskra*, and at the second Party Congress it was declared the Party's official paper.

At this congress, however, there occurred a split between the majority and the minority [. . .] and *Iskra* fell into the hands of the Mensheviks. At this time Vladimir Ilyich wrote *One Step Forward, Two Steps Back*. He found himself denied the leadership of the Party, but this situation could not last for long. The majority of the organisations and the overwhelming majority of workers inside Russia were on the side of the Bolsheviks and they demanded their own paper. Vladimir Ilyich, too, saw this as essential, and roughly one year after leaving *Iskra*, the Bolsheviks began publication of *Vperyod*. The editorial board also established links with organisations inside Russia, started sending professional revolutionaries to various localities and called for greater militancy in preparation for a revolutionary uprising.

By that time, Vladimir Ilyich was already living in Geneva. In 1902 the editorial board had been forced to leave Munich, where police attention was becoming too conspicuous, for London, and from there it made its way to Geneva. During all these years Vladimir Ilyich lived extremely modestly. Party funds were meagre and he took as little as he could for himself, earning extra money with his writings. The immense amount of work and the accompanying strain very seriously affected his health. During his journey from Geneva to London for the second Congress, he fell ill with a nervous disorder. Every summer, particularly after congresses, conferences or major disagreements over editorial policy, he tried to go away into the country, to the seaside or into the mountains—and he always selected a remote and wild spot, and the simplest and cheapest guest-house. Throughout his life Vladimir Ilyich loved nature and knew how to relax in the countryside.

The waves of revolution were rising at that time, particularly since January 1905. This spurred both the *émigrés* in general and Vladimir Ilyich in particular to even more intense work, and also led to an uncontrollable longing to return to Russia. Vladimir Ilyich's perspicacity was seen in late summer 1905 when he wrote to me, apparently in reply to my complaints about the difficulties and delays in receiving literature from abroad: 'Soon we shall open a newspaper in St Petersburg with offices on the Nevsky Prospekt.' I laughed at it then as something wildly improbable, but within three months the sign of the editorial offices of *Novaya Zhizn* was indeed hanging in splendour on the Nevsky.

Vladimir Ilyich arrived immediately after the outbreak of our first revolution and the proclamation of the manifesto granting release from prison or the opportunity of returning from abroad to a whole series of people. This concession immediately proved to be in doubt as far as he was concerned. After spending just one night in a room belonging to a family of friends and taken in his name, he realised that he was being followed, so he began moving from one room to another and using false papers. He also made speeches under assumed names, for example his famous speech at Panina's house when he called himself Karpov [. . .]. He went to Moscow twice during the winter of 1905–6, once before the December rising and once afterwards. He corrected the attitudes towards the first Soviet of Workers' Deputies, which the Bolsheviks were inclined to ignore and disparage, thus showing for the most part a *petit-bourgeois* approach. He realised the significance of an institution genuinely elected by the masses and could foresee its role in the future.

While it was possible to think that the waves of revolution were still rising, Vladimir Ilyich advocated the most revolutionary tactics. Thus he defended the slogan of a boycott of the first State Duma and proclaimed the necessity of partisan warfare—the so-called 'groups of three' (*troiki*) and 'groups of five' (*pyatki*). When the movement was on the wane, however, he changed fronts, speaking of the necessity of participating in the Duma and of using it as a platform for propaganda when the people were progressively being denied all other opportunities for spreading their views. The Bolshevik papers were closed one after the other: *Novaya Zhizn* was followed by *Volna*, *Vperyod* and *Ekho* [. . .].

But the scope for propaganda became more limited and attention increasingly turned to underground work. Vladimir Ilyich was obliged to settle in Kuokkala in Finland, from where he went to St Petersburg on visits, but more often people came to him for manuscripts and consultation. Apart from a whole series of small-scale conferences, a full Party Conference took place in 1905 in Tammerfors, and a congress in Stockholm in 1906. This was the so-called 'Unification Congress,' so named because it was attended by both Bolsheviks and Mensheviks, whereas the Mensheviks had not attended the third Congress of 1905. The attempt at unification, however, came to nothing.

After the dissolution of the second Duma in 1907, repression became steadily more intense, and in the autumn of that year Vladimir Ilyich was warned by the Finnish Social Democrats that an order had been issued for his arrest. Then amidst strict precautions he made his way abroad via Abo and Stockholm.

After the temporary freedoms of 1905–6, this second period as an *émigré* was more difficult than the first. A mood of despair and disillusion gripped large sections of the intelligentsia and the younger generation, and it infiltrated itself among the workers. Broad social concerns gave way to personal ones, questions of sex, quasi-mystical philosophy and religious searchings. The disillusion also took a grimmer form: an epidemic of suicides broke out among the young, that most sensitive barometer of social life. Among the Mensheviks appeared the 'liquidators', who preached the confinement of activity to what was strictly within the law. All these deviations were particularly marked among the *émigrés*, but Vladimir Ilyich never lost heart and was always a source of comfort for the others. He indicated the reasons for the suppression of the 1905 Revolution and said that the movement must be prepared for the next one. Just as before he had taken advantage of exile for research, so now he devoted the darkest part of his second spell of emigration to the study of philosophy, for which there had been no time previously, and to his philosophical book *Materialism and Empiriomonism*, which appeared in 1909. It was directed against all varieties of idealism, and in it he made a critical analysis of all philosophical theories, both in Russia and abroad, and in particular of Neo-Kantianism.

It was partly on these grounds and partly by reason of political disagreements that Vladimir Ilyich broke with the group of *Vperyodovtsy* or *otzovisty*, so called because they proposed 'recalling' the social democratic representatives from the Duma. He demonstrated the necessity of making use of all legal channels, for example the Duma and the legal press, at a time when it was impossible to rely on an immediate revolutionary struggle. I happened to speak to him in 1911 about the mistrust of militants in clandestine provincial circles towards the one modest, legal newspaper which managed to be published for a while in Saratov, and he sharply condemned their unwillingness to support it.

I saw him indeed towards the end of this period of reaction and, if I remember rightly, he said: 'I don't know whether one will live to see the next revolution.' In summer 1911 he founded a Party school at Longjumeau near Paris and gave a series of lectures there to workers from Russia. In 1912 he was elected to the International Socialist Bureau.[1]

But the strength of the masses was growing and the massacre of workers on the Lena in April 1912 called them to action. First of all, despite all the difficulties and restrictions, a legal workers' press began to flourish. The workers' daily newspaper, *Pravda*, made its début in St Petersburg, the very centre of autocratic power, and could in no way be silenced. A new front had been opened and all energies had to be concentrated on it. Vladimir Ilyich moved from Paris to Krakow. St. Petersburg was only twelve hours away by express train, so articles could arrive in time to enable the newspaper to be distributed the day after it was printed. It was easier to arrange meetings with underground activists and members of the Duma – by now the fourth – for whom Vladimir Ilyich wrote speeches. It was also easier to direct illegal work inside Russia. Thus although Vladimir Ilyich did write for the illegal press as well, in particular the central Party organ *Sotsial-Demokrat*, his main

[1] In fact, Lenin had been delegated to the ISB as early as 1905.

energies were directed to the newly opened window of the legal workers' press: apart from *Pravda*, he also wrote for the weekly *Zvezda*, and the Marxist journals *Mysl* and *Prosveshcheniye*. The onset of war, however, shook things up. All workers' newspapers were banned. The Bolshevik deputies in the Duma were arrested, tried and exiled to Siberia. At the very outbreak of war, Vladimir Ilyich was arrested by the Austrian authorities and spent three weeks in prison. Although his whereabouts were completely unknown and he was thus in a very vulnerable position, he remained as cheerful as ever, which greatly surprised a few intellectuals who found themselves in the same straits. Thanks to the intervention of the Austrian social democrats, he was released and went to live in Switzerland. Amidst the upsurge of patriotism that gripped the whole Party, his voice was almost alone in calling for no departure from internationalism and in emphasising that the only way of combating the imperialist war was by turning it into a civil war inside each country against each government. Nadezhda Konstantinovna tells in her memoirs to what extent Vladimir Ilyich was alone in this struggle and how much he was distressed by the utter incomprehension around him.

He composed theses on the attitude of revolutionary social democrats towards the war. Smuggled into Russia, they were found on arrested Bolshevik members of the Duma and were used by the prosecution as one of the main pieces of evidence against them. They affirmed quite definitely that every consistent socialist must apply all his energies to the struggle against his own government and that the best outcome of the war would be the defeat of the Tsarist government as the most reactionary one. He also gave papers on this theme in Switzerland and rallied all those he could around the idea of consistent internationalism.

At the Zimmerwald and Kienthal conferences, he was the representative of the left-wing internationalists. They were then an insignificant minority abroad—the vast majority of socialists were patriotically inclined. Communications with Russia and the shipment there of literature were also greatly hindered by the war. A large number of activists had been sent to the front. Patriotic hysteria was also strong inside Russia, and the notion of 'defeatism' was accepted exclusively by the Bolsheviks, or their allies. This was a difficult period for *émigrés* and their isolation from Russia was unbearable.

In 1916 Lenin wrote *Imperialism as the Highest Stage of Capitalism*. With the Revolution of 1917 he immediately began to move heaven and earth to return to Russia; but this was not so easy to arrange. Trotsky had been detained by the British authorities in his attempt to return. After discarding a few more or less impracticable schemes,

Vladimir Ilyich decided to travel via Germany in a 'sealed' coach. Great play was made of this at the time: Vladimir Ilyich and his companions were denounced as traitors who had made a pact in wartime with the hostile German government. In fact all that was agreed was that they should travel through Germany and that they would absolutely refuse to see or speak to anyone in that country. This was why the expression 'sealed coach' was chosen.

During the journey Vladimir Ilyich was completely uncertain as to whether he would be arrested by the Milyukov government—indeed, he was almost convinced that this would happen. But after reaching Stockholm safely, he travelled equally safely through Finland as far as Beloostrov station on the Russian frontier. There he was met by a few Party comrades who accompanied him to Petrograd, arriving in the evening of 2 April [Old Style]. Here a triumphal welcome had been arranged at the Finland station by the Central and Petrograd Committees, who had also invited crowds of workers from all districts.

Vladimir Ilyich made a short speech to them from an armoured car, urging them to fight for the socialist revolution. He also spoke on the same theme at a meeting of representatives of Party organisations that same evening. With his natural dislike of high-sounding phrases and ovations, he immediately turned to the practical tasks of the morrow. He sharply castigated the shameful behaviour of international social democracy during the war and persuaded the RSDRP(b) Party to change its name to that of Communist Party so as to dissociate itself from their behaviour. He remarked that the revolution which had swept away the Romanov throne had still brought no benefit to the workers and peasants, and that the Provisional government of the Kadets, and also later of the SRs, was incapable of doing so and must be overthrown. He wrote pamphlets and vigorous articles in *Pravda* to this effect. The first attempt at insurrection, in June, was unsuccessful. Although the Bolsheviks had taken no part in it, many prominent Bolsheviks were arrested by the Provisional government. To escape this fate, which for Vladimir Ilyich might have proved fatal, he and Zinoviev went into hiding.

At that time, as Vladimir Ilyich subsequently remarked, only workers would shelter a man of his convictions, and both were concealed at first in workers' flats in Petrograd, then in Sestroretsk, and finally in Finland. They had recourse to all the techniques of clandestine life—wigs, disguises and false passports. They had to change rooms frequently, pass for the fireman on a locomotive, and hide in huts. But even from there Vladimir Ilyich followed the life of the Party, writing articles and letters to the CC. During this period he began *State and Revolution*, which he completed later. Seeing that the authority of the Bolsheviks was growing among the workers, as evidenced by the municipal elections in Petrograd and Moscow, and that the authority of the Provisional government was waning among the masses, he began to insist on the necessity of a rising without further ado. The disagreement over such a determined line on the part of some of his closest comrades could not deter him.

He arrived secretly in Petrograd in time for the second Congress of Soviets and personally took part in meetings of the CC. The rising was decided upon and took place on 25 October. That evening, at the first session of the second Congress of Soviets, it was announced that the Provisional government had been overthrown by the Communist Party. Vladimir Ilyich proclaimed the Soviet Socialist Republic and read out its first two decrees, one on the cessation of hostilities and the other on the transference of all landlord and privately owned land to the workers without compensation. The dictatorship of the bourgeoisie was replaced by that of the proletariat.

The consolidation of Soviet power was begun amid extreme difficulties. All government officials and almost all the intelligentsia declared a boycott. The formation of a government without the co-operation of other parties and groups provoked dissension even inside the CC. But Vladimir Ilyich had set his face against all collaboration. He had a firm belief in the masses, in their ability to manage the State and to learn how to do so at a much faster rate with the benefit of practical experience.

However, the formation of a government solely from Communist Party members, experienced in revolution but completely inexperienced in the construction of a state, placed an immense burden of work and responsibility on Vladimir Ilyich himself, who headed the new government as Chairman of the Council of People's Commissars. It fell to him to direct work in all departments, from military to educational or rationing matters. The civil wars, subsidised and supported by the international bourgeoisie, uprisings inside the country, famine and economic dislocation resulting both from these upheavals and the preceding world war—all this demanded a huge effort from Vladimir Ilyich as the brain and driving force of the government. The attempt on his life by the SR Kaplan on 30 August 1918 in the yard of the Michelson factory[1] was almost fatal and greatly undermined his health.

On his initiative, and again in the face of strong opposition from part of the CC, the so-called 'Brest Peace' was concluded with Germany in 1918. We agreed to the annexation of a whole series of towns and a large quantity of land, as well as the payment of a massive indemnity. The terms were rightly called shameful, but Vladimir Ilyich saw that the

[1] Now renamed the Vladimir Ilyich factory.

peasantry would not go to war. In addition he considered that the revolution in Germany was rapidly approaching and that the most humiliating clauses would be ineffectual. And so it turned out. The outbreak of the bourgeois revolution in Germany annulled the most onerous conditions of the Brest treaty [. . .].

At the end of the Civil War, Vladimir Ilyich realised the iron necessity for a change in policies towards the peasantry. Food requisitions were replaced by a tax on agricultural products that left surpluses in the hands of the peasants as a stimulus for them to help in the reconstruction of the economy. He introduced the so-called 'New Economic Policy' (NEP), which conceded free private trade and granted to the peasantry and broad sections of the population the opportunity of finding for themselves those means of subsistence that the State could not yet provide. He argued that this change was necessary as long as the world-wide proletarian revolution was delayed, and that under the conditions of capitalist encirclement the RSFSR would have to repair its economy with the co-operation of the *petit-bourgeois* section of the population.

At the same time he insisted on the development of State-run enterprises, on electrification, which would put our backward country on the same level as the most civilised nations, and on the growth of co-operatives. He indicated that, whilst awaiting the world-wide revolution, all major industry must be controlled by the State so that socialism could slowly and partially be achieved in one country. In this way, he said, although making concessions to private capital on the one hand, we shall squeeze it until the outbreak of revolution in other countries and the massive rise in productivity in our own permit us to make a fresh and more determined advance towards communism.

Vladimir Ilyich was, however, so immensely overworked that his health began to suffer. He was gripped by attacks of headache and insomnia. The doctors at first only diagnosed general overstrain and recommended prolonged rest. But this was impossible in view both of conditions inside and outside the USSR, which demanded intense effort from the government, and of his own character, his strictness towards himself and his responsbilities, his increasing concern for all that was happening in the country, his inability to relax fully or to rest. He himself complained that during walks he would think again and again about the same things. And the illness began to grow progressively worse. On 25 May 1922 he suffered his first stroke. Complete rest and attentive treatment put him back on his feet by autumn, and in October he returned to work. But although his duties were much lighter than before, he was only able to carry them out for two months. At the end of November he took to his bed. Until March he was still kept informed of events, although only in the most general terms, and he dictated his last articles: 'Better less and better'—about Rabkrin, 'On Co-operatives', and a third article about the work of Narkompros.

In March came a second stroke which deprived him of the power of speech. This never returned despite the efforts of doctors and the fact that he had physically recovered by the summer. He died on 21 January 1924 at 6.50 p.m. Death came almost suddenly as nothing had indicated that the end was so near. The post-mortem revealed complete degeneration in the arteries of the brain, although general arteriosclerosis had only been observed to a very limited extent in him.

His body was embalmed and placed in the mausoleum in Red Square.

A. Ulyanova-Elizarova

In only a few pages it is simply not possible to draw a full political portrait of Lenin, which would involve a consideration of all the political questions arising from his activities as a working-class militant from 1895 to 1923. His entire, complex strategy would have to be examined, from the struggle for a narrow party of professional revolutionaries adapted to the conditions prevailing under the autocracy (a struggle in which for fourteen years he was ceaselessly opposed by Trotsky) to his final battle, fought from semi-paralysis, against a faceless enemy he called 'bureaucracy'.

Only this last moment will be mentioned here, since it is entirely omitted in the biography written by his sister. On 3 April 1922, shortly after the eleventh Congress, Stalin was appointed General Secretary of the Central Committee. Doubtless a purely administrative position: but had not Lenin just emphasised that any administrative question could turn into a political problem? Perhaps it was then that he commented on Stalin's appointment with the phrase, fraught with anxiety, 'This cook will cook us spicy dishes'; in fact, we don't know. But what we do know, on the other hand, is that immediately after the first attack which removed Lenin from public affairs, on 26 May 1922, ever deeper disagreements came between him and Stalin, who was filled with self-confidence by the impotence of the 'boss'. Lenin had to fight to save the monopoly on foreign trade, which Stalin and others wanted to make more supple; he had to fight against the chauvinistic, Great-Russian conception of the draft Constitution of the USSR drawn up by a commission of the Orgburo, chaired by Stalin; and he had to fight against the consequences of this Great-Russian policy in Georgia, where Stalin used force to smash the opposition. In September, during a meeting of the Politburo, Stalin passed a note to Kamenev, which reveals the change in his relationship with Lenin, and the extent to which the different bureaux of the State machine had become self-sufficient: 'I think we must stand firm against Lenin'.

On 12 December 1922 Lenin received Dzerzhinsky, whose revelations on the Georgian affair so shook him that he had another attack on the 13th, a third on the 15th and a fourth on the 22nd, which left him paralysed on the right side. It was then that he began to write his various internal documents ('Letter to Congress', the letter 'On Autonomisation', etc.). These turned more and more towards a denunciation of Stalin, whom he finally proposed to remove from the position of General Secretary on 4 January 1923. From 18 December, Stalin had taken over *personal* responsibility for Lenin's medical care, and on 24 December, together with Kamenev and Bukharin, he forbade him any contact with the outside world: 'Visitors are not allowed.' The only contact Lenin had, for a few minutes a day, was with his secretaries and his wife, Krupskaya, who were not allowed to give him any political information. Lenin, allied with Trotsky over the defence of the monopoly on foreign trade, attempted to extend the alliance on the Georgian affair; he prepared an ambush for Stalin, and organised the attack on his domain, the Peasant and Workers' Inspectorate (Rabkrin)—a valuable tool of manipulation for the governmental machine.

This final battle was fought in desperate conditions. For example, Lenin could never get hold of a list of Soviet civil servants, which would have allowed him to grasp the development of bureaucracy. On 12 February his secretaries noted: 'He obviously thinks that it is not the doctors who advise the Central Committee, but the Central Committee which gives orders to the doctors.' On 5 March he wrote two letters, one to Trotsky asking him to take on the struggle over the Georgian affair, and the other to Stalin, threatening to break off all personal relations. On 9 March he suffered a final attack which made him a dumb and paralytic invalid until his death.

A few weeks after Lenin's death, a plenary meeting of the Central Committee voted by thirty to ten against Krupskaya's reading the *Testament* at the thirteenth Congress. The Central Committee simply took note of it and passed on to the next matter on the agenda.

J.J.M.

JOSEPH STALIN
(authorised biography)

Joseph Vissarionovich Dzhugashvili—Stalin—was born in 1879 at Gori in Tiflis province. A Georgian by nationality, he was the son of a shoemaker who worked in the Adelkhanov shoe factory, although he was registered as a peasant from the village of Didi-Lilo.

In 1893 Stalin completed his studies at the ecclesiastical school in Gori and entered the Tiflis Orthodox Seminary. The seminary was at that time a hotbed of revolutionary ideas among the young of Tiflis, both Populists and nationalists as well as Marxists and internationalists. It swarmed with all manner of circles. In 1897 Stalin became leader of the Marxist circles there. He came into contact with the underground Tiflis SD organisation, received illegal literature from it and attended clandestine meetings of workers from the Tiflis railway workshops.

In 1898 he officially joined the Tiflis RSDRP organisation. During this period he distributed propaganda among workers' circles in the railway and factory districts. At the seminary, where detection of 'suspicious elements' was quite efficient, the authorities began to have an inkling of his clandestine activities and expelled him for 'unreliability'.

He spent the next two years on intensive propaganda among the workers. In 1900 the Tiflis RSDRP Committee was established. Stalin had a seat on it and was one of its most prominent leaders. During this period the labour movement began to outgrow the old framework of purely propagandistic work aimed at 'outstanding individuals' from among the workers. Mass agitation by means of leaflets on topical themes, short meetings and political demonstrations against Tsarism became the order of the day. An argument flared up between the 'elders', the supporters of the old methods, and the 'youngsters', who turned their attention to 'the streets'. Stalin championed the 'youngsters'. Here one must emphasise the striking part played in the triumph of the new methods over the old ones, as well as in Stalin's own revolutionary education, by Kurnatovsky, Lenin's closest comrade-in-arms and the first man to spread Lenin's ideas in Transcaucasia.

The wave of economic strikes throughout Tiflis in 1900–1 and the famous May Day political demonstration there led to the wholesale arrest of the Tiflis Committee. The search made in Stalin's flat in 1901 and then a leaked Okhrana directive for his arrest forced him to go underground. He became a professional, clandestine revolutionary and remained so until the February Revolution of 1917, working under the pseudonyms of 'David', 'Koba', 'Nizheradze', 'Chizhikov', 'Ivanovich' and 'Stalin'.

In late 1901, Stalin moved to Batum, founded a local RSDRP committee, led strikes at the Rothschild and Mantashev factories and organised the famous political demonstrations by workers in February 1902. The following month he was arrested, held in custody until the end of 1903 and then deported to eastern Siberia for three years, to the village of Novaya Uda in the Balagansk district of Irkutsk province.

In January 1904, one month after his arrival at the place of exile, he escaped and returned to Tiflis, where he worked as a member of the Transcaucasian regional organisation, then called the Transcaucasian Union Committee. His activities in 1904–5 consisted of impassioned opposition to Menshevism. He made systematic visits to the districts of Transcaucasia (Batum, Chiatury, Kutais, Tiflis and Baku) to spread both oral and printed arguments against the Mensheviks, as well as against SRs, anarchists and nationalists. As early as 1903, when he learnt in prison of the grave dissensions between Mensheviks and Bolsheviks, Stalin had sided firmly with the latter. When the conflict became acute on his return from exile, he took over the leadership of the Transcaucasian Bolsheviks, directed their illegal paper *Borba Proletariata* (1905), and was most active in helping to organise the third Bolshevik Congress. The October Manifesto of 1905 found him in Tiflis with the struggle over the Bolshevik slogans about revolution at its height. It was at this time that he wrote in Georgian the pamphlet *An Outline of the Party Disagreements*. At the end of 1905 he was delegated by the Caucasian Bolsheviks to attend the All-Russian Bolshevik Conference in Tammerfors, where he finally became linked to Lenin.

The year 1906 saw the eradication of the 1905 Revolution, elections to the 'new' Duma and preparations for the Party Congress in Stockholm. The Bolsheviks were in favour of a boycott of the Duma. The arguments between Bolsheviks and Mensheviks flared up with redoubled intensity. Anarcho-syndicalist elements came to the surface and were particularly vociferous in Tiflis. Stalin was at the centre of the struggle against all these anti-proletarian tendencies in Transcaucasia. He gave guidance to the legal Bolshevik daily *Dro* ('Time'). He also wrote at this time the series of long articles in Georgian called *Anarchism and Socialism*. At the Stockholm Congress of 1906, he figured as the Tiflis delegate under the pseudonym 'Ivanovich'.

In 1907 the Baku period of his revolutionary career began. Returning from the London Congress, he left Tiflis for Baku where he undertook a feverish campaign to rally the local organisation around the slogans of the London Congress. Here he directed the illegal paper *Bakinsky Rabochy* and succeeded in having the Mensheviks expelled from the workers' districts of the city (Balakhany, Bibi-Eibat, Chorny Gorod and

Bely Gorod). He directed a large-scale campaign for consultation and a collective agreement between the workers and the oil companies. Finally he achieved a complete victory for Bolshevism in the ranks of the Baku organisation, which from then on became a Bolshevik stronghold.

In March 1908 he was arrested, and after being held in custody for eight months was deported to Solvychegodsk in Vologda province for three years. A few months later he escaped and returned to underground work in Baku. In 1910 he was again arrested and after a few months in prison was sent back to Solvychegodsk.

In 1911 he escaped again and this time settled in St Petersburg on Party orders. This began the St Petersburg period of his career, but he was not due to work there for long. He was again arrested and conducted back to exile in Vologda.

At the end of 1911 he escaped yet again, returned to the capital and took a leading part in the St Petersburg underground movement. By this time, he was a member of the Central Committee, having been elected in his absence at the Party Conference in Prague. He was instructed by the CC to tour all the most important areas of Russia. He made preparations for the coming May Day demonstrations, directed coverage by *Zvezda* of the Lena strikes and was one of the leading founders of *Pravda*.

In April 1912 he was rearrested and, after a few months in custody, deported to the Narym region for four years. That same summer he escaped, spent some time in the capital, and then went to see Lenin in Krakow. He attended a conference there and returned to St Petersburg, where he gave guidance to the Duma 'fraction' and the Bolshevik organs *Zvezda* and *Pravda*. It was at this time that he wrote the pamphlet *Marxism and the Nationality Question*.

In spring 1913 he was caught by the police yet again, and deported to the village of Kureika in the region of Turukhansk, where he remained until 1917.

After the February Revolution, he returned to Petrograd. At the All-Russian Conference of Bolsheviks in April, at which two tendencies came to light in the Party, Stalin doggedly defended Lenin's position. In May, the CC Politburo was set up. Stalin was elected to it and has retained his seat on it ever since. During the preparations for the October uprising, he worked in complete harmony with Lenin. Throughout the period of the 'Kornilov days', the Democratic Conference[1] and Pre-

---

[1] The Democratic Conference took place from 14 to 22 September 1917. It was called by the Mensheviks and SRs in an attempt to frustrate the summoning of the second Congress of Soviets, and was boycotted by the Bolsheviks.

Parliament,[1] the organisation of the rising and the arguments over a 'homogeneous Socialist government' after its success, Stalin unfailingly remained Lenin's closest collaborator at a time when the hesitations of one part of the Party (Kamenev and Zinoviev) threatened the whole undertaking. From the July demonstration right up until October, he was in effect in charge of the Party's central organ (*Rabochy i Soldat*, *Proletary*, *Rabochy*, *Rabochy Put'*, etc.). During the October days the CC elected him a member of the *pyatyorka* (the group of five organising the political leadership of the rising) and the *semyorka* (the group of seven entrusted with organisational control of it).

Since 1917 Stalin has had a seat on the TsIK. From 1917 to 1923 he was Commissar for Nationalities, and from 1919 to 1922 Commissar of Rabkrin. Since 1922 he has been a CC Secretary, and since 1925 a Presidium member of the Comintern Executive Committee.

Most of the Civil War he spent at the front. During spring and summer 1918 he was on the Tsaritsyn Front, organising with Voroshilov and Minin the town's defence against Krasnov's forces. In late 1918, he and Dzerzhinsky inspected the front of the Third Army in the region of Perm in an attempt to halt our retreat. In spring 1919 he organised our attack against Yudenich's first advance on Petrograd. In the summer of that year he was at Smolensk on the Western Front planning the repulse of the Poles. In winter 1919 he was active on the southern Front against Denikin's troops, and he remained there until the latter's final defeat and the capture of Rostov and Odessa by our troops. In 1920 he was directly responsible for the break-through in the Polish lines made at Zhitomir on the South-Western Front, which led to the liberation of Kiev and our advance to the gates of Lvov. Still in 1920, he participated in the defence of the southern Ukraine against Wrangel. From 1920 to 1923 he was a member of the RVS of the Republic. For his military exploits he was awarded the Order of the Red Banner.

His chief pamphlets are: *Marxism and the Nationality Question, On the Paths to October, On Lenin and Leninism*, and *Problems of Leninism*.

I. Tovstukha

This authorised life of Stalin, written by a member of his personal secretariat, draws a fairly dull picture of the future Marshal, but a less pretentious one than those of Zinoviev and Rykov included in the same volume. Nevertheless it is one of the first stones in the delicate elabora-

---

[1] The Pre-Parliament met at the same time and was intended as a permanent consultative body attached to the Provisional government with members drawn from the Democratic Conference. It, too, was boycotted by the Bolsheviks.

tion of Stalin's legend. Khrushchev reminded his audience, at the twentieth Congress, that 95 per cent of them had known nothing about Stalin in 1924, two years after his appointment as General Secretary. The task of establishing the biography of the General Secretary will be the most difficult and dangerous project to be undertaken by official historians. The nascent legend, in this text, mixes exaggeration with fabrication, without for all that giving a fundamentally false picture of Stalin. Everything is made to suggest and to support the idea that is, as yet, only explicitly stated with reference to 1917: 'Stalin was always Lenin's right hand and closest collaborator.' The image of a faithful and irreproachable disciple was necessary to Stalin at that time—it was justification in the struggle against the united opposition (Trotsky, Zinoviev, Kamenev) and a guarantee to his peers, who saw Stalin as their equal and their representative in the fight against Trotsky-Bonaparte.

Therefore almost every 'fact' put forward by his biographer requires correction.

Since Stalin was only co-opted onto the Central Committee in 1912, nine years after the birth of Bolshevism, he had to remodel his youth to make it appear exemplary. No other Bolshevik leader had in fact waited so long. In this text he does not make himself out to have been the brilliant Number Two of Bolshevism from before its birth (as he claimed later to have been). But he does put himself at the forefront of Marxist circles in the seminary from 1897 on, and has himself expelled two years later for 'political disloyalty'—which is probably untrue; in Batum he claims to have founded the RSDRP Committee, which in fact already existed, even if it was inactive: actually, he reorganised it. Tovstukha claims that Stalin inspired the great strikes at the Rothschild and Mantashev works, which ended in a demonstration of 6,000 workers being shot at by the police. Today the journal *Voprosi Istorii KPSS* merely states that 'Apparently the Batum Committee led the February–March strikes'. The committee really only followed a movement which it was not strong enough to lead.

Stalin claims to have been a Bolshevik from 1903. The schism must have seemed fairly obscure in the Caucasus. Moreover, in order to prove his precocious Bolshevism, Stalin had to forge two documents in 1946— the so-called *Letters from Kutais*, dated September–October 1904. But despite the blows struck against the Party's *cadres* in the Caucasus by the police, young 'Koba', a professional underground revolutionary since 1900, was not made a delegate to the third Congress: the delegates were in fact Barsov (Tskhakhaya), Gradov (Kamenev), Nevsky (Leman), Rybkin and Golumbin (Dzhaparidze).

Stalin was deported several times: with the exception of his last deportation, this punishment emphasises that up to 1912 he was viewed by the police as small fry—and of course his biographer does not stress this fact. In 1908 and 1910. Stalin was exiled to Solvychegodsk, Vologda province, about 310 miles from St Petersburg and Moscow. He did not escape. After doing his time he was released on 27 June 1911. Likewise, the Prague Conference, which set up the Bolshevik Party in January 1912, did not 'elect' him 'by default' to the Central Committee. Quite the contrary, for the conference rejected his candidacy: but at its first meeting the Central Committee, at Lenin's insistence, co-opted Stalin and made him a member of the Russian Bureau. Stalin was accompanied in this ascension by leaders of the Baku Committee, a Bolshevik stronghold in 1907–8; of the five members of this Russian Bureau, three (Stalin, Spandarian, Ordzhonikidze) were Baku leaders. He then proposed creating in Tiflis a common Bolshevik–Menshevik centre. At the end of 1912, in charge of *Pravda* with Molotov, Stalin followed a 'conciliatory' policy, that is to say a policy of *entente* with the Mensheviks, and Lenin had to replace Stalin and Molotov by what he called 'an editor of *ours*', namely Sverdlov.

The role that Stalin played during the three weeks (12 March–4 April) when, with Kamenev and Muranov, he led the Bolshevik Party, is distorted in this biography. In his preface to *October Ways* dated December 1924, Stalin still admitted to having been in error 'with the majority of the Party'. In fact he declared himself in favour both of lending critical support to the Provisional government of Prince Lvov 'in so far as' it took progressive measures, and of a Bolshevik-Menshevik unification. For fifteen days he opposed Lenin's 'April theses', which, he claimed on the 6th, were 'a scheme without substance'. As from 1926, this episode was pushed into the shade. Some years later E. Yaroslavsky got his knuckles rapped for bringing it up.

This omission prepared the way for the claim that 'during the entire period of preparation for and consolidation of the October Revolution . . . Stalin was always Lenin's right-hand man and closest collaborator'. In this Stalin was attributing to himself a role usually granted to Trotsky. To do so, Stalin had to silence a number of facts, for example his conciliatory attitude towards Zinoviev and Kamenev when they came out publicly against the nascent insurrection, and his vague response to Lenin's urgent appeals to prepare the insurrection: he proposed, for instance, to send letters for discussion to the provincial organisations so as to delay the Central Committee's decision on the question. He was just beginning to give himself a practical part in the insurrection (participating in the *pyatyorka*, in the phantom 'Revolutionary Military Centre', and in the '*Semyorka,* a political bureau which he claimed had been founded in May—but these bodies never met. Somewhat later on Stalin increased the importance of the Revolutionary Military Centre and diminished the Petrograd Soviet RVS, which was the real leading force of the October Revolution; and twenty-nine years after the event, he fabricated a somewhat tardy but unambiguous statement: 'We must firmly and irrevocably commence the insurrection'. In fact, on 24 October 1917 in *Rabochy Put* Stalin called upon the workers to put non-violent pressure on the Congress of Soviets to ensure their claims were met. . . .

So much for the first layer of arrangements, complemented by the omissions. Only in 1946 did Stalin admit to having been opposed to Lenin on the agrarian question in 1906 (Stalin was against nationalisation, in favour of division). On the other hand, he remained entirely silent on his participation in the terrorist activities of the Bolshevik 'combat groups' in the Caucasus in 1906-7. Stalin was not himself involved in the attacks on the bank coaches and railway wagons, but the very real control he exercised over these 'expropriations' and which helped him enormously in his rise through the Bolshevik Party machine, did not suit his image as General Secretary—an image already taking on the feature of the Statesman and Head of State of the USSR.

In this biography the Civil War legends are only sketchily mentioned. Although Tsaritsyn had by then already been renamed Stalingrad, it was only in 1929 that Voroshilov wrote an article, 'Stalin and the Red Army', which discovered in the General Secretary the great strategist of the Civil War.

The truth is simpler: during the Civil War Stalin, like all the other Bolshevik leaders except Lenin, Zinoviev, Sverdlov and Bukharin, had military tasks thrust upon him. In carrying them out he revealed on the one hand his force and authority, his ability to make others perform, and on the other hand his rebellious, systematically insubordinate spirit, his illwill towards 'specialists' of any kind. 'Be assured that our hand will not tremble,' he cabled Lenin from Tsaritsyn, where his hand, indeed, did not tremble. On the Southern Front and then at the eighth Congress, he supported the so-called 'NCO opposition' (Voroshilov, Budyonny, etc.). Stalin the centraliser thus supported behind the scenes the advocates of a decentralised partisan army simply because the 'professional' army was in the hands of Trotsky, whom he had detested ever since he first met 'this magnificent appendage' in 1907.

Stalin's pride and his insubordinate spirit were shown up by the defeat of the Red Army on the Vistula in 1920. In order to have *his* victory at Lvov, he refused to obey orders to send much-needed reinforcements to Tukhachevsky, and thereby precipitated a defeat (which he could not have really stopped anyway).

But as from summer 1917, Stalin was a central figure in the Party machine: with Sverdlov, he kept the day-to-day running going during the repression of Bolsheviks in July and August 1917; he was co-director of *Pravda*; one of the seven members of the Politiburo, which was set up in October to prepare the insurrection, but never met; and he was Commissar for Nationalities. As such, he became one of the essential instruments of Soviet centralism; and his cleverness in manoeuvring in the conflict over nationality policy explains – for example – why he was chosen by the Central Committee in 1919 to go to fight the left-wing Ukrainian communists. Above all, he was one of the four members of the 'small cabinet' of the Central Committee set up after October (Lenin, Trotsky, Sverdlov, Stalin), and one of the five members of the common Bolshevik-left SR Executive Committee set up in February 1918 (Lenin, Trotsky, Stalin, Proshian, Karelin).

In 1919 Stalin was appointed Commissar for the Peasants' and Workers' Inspectorate (Rabkrin) and made one of the five established members of the first Politburo (Kamenev, Krestinsky, Lenin, Stalin, Trotsky); and in April 1920 he became a member of the Orgburo.

Stalin's political ascent, unhindered by the Civil War, and for which his status as the only Bolshevik leader never to have come into outright public conflict with Lenin was partially responsible, had always aroused amazement. In 1922, when Stalin was still uncontroversial, the Menshevik Sukhanov wrote of spring 1917, when he and Stalin had had much the same ideas: 'During his modest activity on the Executive Committee, Stalin created – and not only on me – the impression of a grey blot, animated from time to time in a dull and featureless way. That is all one can say about him.' Quoting part of this assessment, Trotsky commented: 'Evidently Sukhanov under-estimates Stalin in general.' An understatement, perhaps.

Stalin's comrades made harsh criticisms of his intellectual and moral qualities. Bukharin considered his main feature to be impassibility. Ivan Smirnov and Kamenev thought he was a provincial mediocrity, and for Krestinsky Stalin was 'an unnerving man with his yellow eyes'. The Russian bureau of the Central Committee at first refused in March 1917 to admit Stalin, despite his being a former Central Committee member, 'because of certain moral characteristics'. Trotsky concluded: 'Stalin is the Party's most eminent mediocrity.' His dull outward appearance deceived all who judged a man's value by his visible liveliness. But Lenin left him at the head of the Rabkrin for a long time because he believed him to be not of the intriguing sort, and, in his *Testament* of December

1922, considered Stalin to be, after Trotsky, the most eminent member of the Central Committee.

In April 1922 Lenin either permitted or created Stalin's appointment as the Party's General Secretary. At the same time Lenin declared technical problems to be political problems, and Preobrazhensky denounced the unbelievable accumulation of administrative posts in Stalin's hands. No doubt it was only shortly afterwards that he made the guess, 'This cook will cook us spicy dishes.'

At the very moment when Stalin gained the position that gave him control over the Party machine, Lenin fell ill. In the course of the year 1922, Stalin began to oppose Lenin on several fronts: on the Constitution of the USSR, on the foreign trade monopoly, on the Georgian affair. His attitude to Lenin became less respectful, much sharper, for he realised that the balance of power between the impotent political head of the Party and himself, representing a machine of ever growing weight and requirements, had changed. Lenin's last heart attack, six days after he had learnt the details of the Georgian affair, saved Stalin.

From then the successive stages of Stalin's rise to power run on like chapter headings: liquidation of the triumvirate (Zinoviev-Kamenev-Stalin) after the victory over the left opposition and the double rout of Trotsky; alliance with the right against the united opposition, and then in 1929 the resumption of a number of points from the left-wing programme against the right, now also eliminated. Accompanying these zigzags which allowed him to eliminate his political adversaries, Stalin's ideology was built up from elements that corresponded to the needs of his developing bureaucracy and underpinned his power: first, the invention in 1924 of 'socialism in one country'; then a brutal struggle against Bolshevik egalitarianism (*uravnilovka*), in words at first, at the fourteenth Congress ('You must not play with the idea of equality, for you are playing with fire'), and then in acts, in a great campaign against *uravnilovka* from 1929 to 1932.

Forced industrialisation and collectivisation made the balance of forces between the peasantry, the depoliticised working class and the Party machine even weaker. Thus Stalin could rise above clan and Party. He sensed it very clearly and the following measures are revealing: on 7 November 1929 an article by him launched a speed-up of collectivisation, at a rate five times higher than the top level set down by the Collectivisation Commission of the Politiburo; a Central Committee resolution, decided in reality by Stalin alone, set absolutely fantastic collectivisation rates on 5 January 1930; and an article by Stalin, entitled 'The Intoxication of Success', slowed down the movement only two months later.

The nature of this personal power which set institutions against each other – the Party against the police and vice versa – was only understood by Stalin's supporters when he decided, in 1936, to eliminate them as the final obstacle to his absolute dictatorship; for Stalin remained hidden away in silence behind the Kremlin walls for long periods (1931–3, 1946–50). According to Evgenia Ginzburg, the Tatar Stalinist Sagidulin told her husband Pavel Aksyonov, a member of the Central Executive Committee, in prison in 1937: 'Koba is the 18th Brumaire. The Party's best workers, who either did or could oppose the establishment of his dictatorship, are being exterminated.' Evgenia herself, who remained always within the Party line, asked herself a little later: 'Is this Joseph Stalin's 18th Brumaire? Or what else can you call it?'

The Second World War at first threw Stalin into disarray: but it elevated him from Bonaparte to Napoleon, and in the minds of the millions whose sons he sent to Siberia, he took on the dimensions of a myth. Soon he became Generalissimo, changed the name of the Council of People's Commissars to Council of Ministers, that of the Red Army to Soviet Armed Forces, explained that membership and non-membership of the Party were the same thing, and finally died on 5 March 1953, in circumstances that will continue to arouse discussion for a long time. In 1961, in *Clear Sky*, Chukray symbolised Stalin's death in a suggestive manner: dead branches burst into leaf, the frozen rivers crack and spring waters flow again, the heavy black clouds part and the sun shines forth. Khrushchev's report to the twentieth Congress reflected the fear and terror which the distrustful Generalissimo had inspired in his closest collaborators. With his charming air, heavy eyes and traditional pipe, he looked, in his flattering portraits, like the 'little father of the people' watching over his flock, a strict but just paterfamilias. Khrushchev's report, and speeches by Khrushchev, Shelepin and Shvernik at the twenty-second Congress, drew the portrait of demented tyrant, bloodthirsty and morbidly suspicious, whose personality thus became the scapegoat and explanatory principle of all the convulsions created by 'socialism in one country'. The other side of the explanation was to make Beria the real devil, who was supposed to have deceived the distrustful but also gullible Marshal.

Stalin had cunning, patience, flair, craftiness, force, ferocity, prudence and tenacity—put to the service of a ruling caste and his personal power. But he also scorned ideas, preferred constant pragmatism and opportunism, and cared above all for the immediate. This did not prevent him from putting off any political change for as long as possible, and he had no scruples in sacrificing the supporters of the 'old line' when the change came. Stalin, quite obviously, scorned them as much as he scorned ideas. The solitude of his last twenty years was not just the result of the fear he inspired, but the fruit of this fundamental disdain. . . .

J.J.M.

YAKOV MIKHAILOVICH SVERDLOV

Yakov Mikhailovich Sverdlov was born in May 1885 in Nizhny Novgorod, the son of an engraver from Polotsk. His father owned a small printing-press, and his premises looked out onto the main street of the town. From his earliest childhood Sverdlov was an unusually lively, restless boy, attracted by the most hair-raising escapades, though at the same time he showed quick wits and an inquisitive mind. Often even adults would be hard put to answer his questions.

Despite the burden of a large family and difficult financial circumstances, his father tried to give his children an education. Thus on 30 April 1896, Sverdlov was admitted to the Nizhny Novgorod provincial Gymnasium. There he spent four full years, during which time the family's financial position worsened considerably, and he fell foul of the teachers. He rebelled violently against the school routine and the arid scholasticism. He began to miss lessons, his progress declined and his marks for conduct slowly fell to three out of five. All this made it unsuitable for him to stay on and he left in August 1900 with a certificate showing that he had completed five years at school. His leaving could not halt his cultural development. On the contrary, his thirst for knowledge became all the stronger. He began to read a great deal and as his horizons widened, his dissatisfaction with life around him swelled into a feeling of protest against the existing authorities. Illegal literature began to come into his hands.

Political consciousness was awakened in him at an early age. He developed a growing desire to devote all his energies to the interests of the working class. The first revolutionary seeds were implanted in him whilst he was still at the Gymnasium by three people: his elder brother Zinovy, who was later adopted by Gorky; Drobysh-Drobyshevsky, then editor of *Nizhegorodskaya Gazeta*; and above all the socialist revolutionary V. E. Lazarev, who subsequently proved to be an *agent provocateur*. After the Gymnasium, Sverelov found work as an apprentice in the chemist's shop at Kanavin. Here he came into contact with the working masses for the first time. Near Kanavin were timber works with a large number of workers. Sverdlov made contact with them. He began to visit them regularly for propaganda. Through them he also came into contact with Sormovo workers. He won over the craftsmen at his father's printing-press and thanks to them all the necessary forms and stamps were easily made for the secret organisations. His father's flat already served as a hiding-place for visiting Party activists and as a store for illegal literature and even arms. Jokingly nicknamed 'The Swiss Republic', it supplied clandestine circles in Nizhny Novgorod with leaflets.

Illegal work in the town was greatly stimulated by the creation of the Nizhny Novgorod RSDRP Committee in 1901. Sverdlov's youth was spent amid invigorating revolutionary activity in the bustling labour movement. As he grew, he became more deeply drawn into what had become his 'profession'. At the age of seventeen he participated in the demonstration that accompanied the funeral of the student Ryurikov on 22 April 1902. It was dispersed by the police and most of the demonstrators had their names taken at the gendarme headquarters. Sverdlov managed to hide. But when he made an appearance at home a few days later, he was arrested and imprisoned for fourteen days on a charge of 'behaving in a disorderly manner, and non-compliance with the orders of the police at the funeral of Ryurikov'. Thus he progressed from handing out leaflets and proclamations to active participation in the movement against the existing order. On his release from prison, he was forced to go to Saratov in search of work and he lived there with his elder sister; but police harassment soon compelled him to return. In Nizhny Novgorod he devoted all his time to illegal activity at the Sormovo works where it was imperative that organisation should be improved in the aftermath of crippling arrests.

In spring 1903 fresh arrests took place. Sverdlov increased his activities, obtained money to equip a printing-press and for a long time provided leaflets and pamphlets for agitators at the works. On 14 April 1903, proclamations, illegal pamphlets and books were discovered during a thorough search of his flat. The affair was handed over to the gendarmes and soon after the murder by workers of an *agent provocateur* called Pyatnitsky in October/November 1903, he was put under open supervision by the police on suspicion of complicity.

After the split at the second Congress of the RSDRP, Sverdlov immediately adopted a firm line and was one of the first to raise the question of a Bolshevik organisation in the town. He exemplified all the best qualities of a clandestine revolutionary. Already he exercised great influence among the working masses and enjoyed the affectionate esteem of older Party comrades, including A. I. Rykov, N. A. Semashko and M. F. Vladimirsky, who were active at that time in the province. All paid tribute to this young, but already sufficiently experienced Party worker, to his talent, energy, and excellent organisational abilities.

With the formation of the Northern Committee, Sverdlov settled in Kostroma where he became extremely active. He succeeded in escaping the attention of the police for a long time. On 15 February 1905 he moved to Kazan and joined the committee there as one of its chief organisers. When the autumn term began at the university, he became one of the most popular speakers among the students. Throughout his prolonged and active stay in Kazan, the police did not once succeed in tracing this indefatigable 'Baby' (his code name).

In late September 1905 he moved to Ekaterinburg, where he undertook the unification of all the major Party organisations in the area around the Urals Bureau. Under the name of 'Comrade Andrey', he soon became the favourite leader of the Urals workers. Then he arrived in Moscow before the December uprising and made a few speeches at large meetings in the 'Aquarium'. And only after a trip to Tammerfors to attend the Party Conference did he reappear in the Urals as the CC's special envoy. Later, he embarked upon work in Perm where the Party organisation had been completely smashed. By means of a careful selection of workers and prolonged propaganda he succeeded in raising its standard to the required level. As the organisation grew, it was gradually infiltrated by the police and new arrests came. On 10 June 1906 he was arrested with his wife 'Olga' (Novgorodtseva). It was autumn before he was transferred from Perm prison to the penal battalions in Verkhoturovo district, where an unusually harsh regime was in force, and only in September 1907 did members of the Perm organisation appear before the courts.

Sverdlov was sentenced to two years in a fortress with no account being taken of preliminary imprisonment. There he studied hard to broaden his education. Released in 1909, he went to Moscow and began to collect and rally the scattered ranks of the local organisation. He was soon arrested and deported to Narym for three years. His boisterous nature could not endure this lengthy, enforced idleness. He escaped and by summer 1910 was already back in Moscow, where he became involved in the very thick of the campaign to establish a firm ideological line and organise the Party committee.

All this had to be done under extremely difficult conditions as the organisation had been penetrated by a network of police and *agents provocateurs*. On 14 November 1910 he was rearrested and held in custody until May 1911 when he was sent back to Narym, this time for four years. A few unsuccessful attempts at escape did not break his resolve and only the caution of the gendarmes in keeping him under the closest supervision in Maksimkin Yar – the most distant place of exile – restrained him. Lacking warm clothing, he caught a chill and was ill in bed for a long time, after which he was transferred back to Narym. He recovered and rested a little. Then he escaped again, but unsuccessfully. The boat in which he was travelling down a turbulent river capsized. He covered several miles and spent several hours in the icy water. He was dragged out by fishermen and sent back to his place of exile under gendarme escort whilst still in his wet clothes. The arrival of his wife and child in Narym reassured the gendarmes for a while, but soon afterwards he made a new and audacious attempt at escape which succeeded.

In autumn 1912 he reached St Petersburg and was immediately co-opted onto the CC. He enlarged his work among the Bolshevik deputies in the Duma, and he also helped to rectify the editorial policy of *Pravda* which under his influence became a purely Bolshevik paper.

In February 1913 he was betrayed by Malinovsky and put in the Kresty prison. Three months later he was deported to the Turukhansk region of Siberia. He and Stalin were banished to the remote village of Kureika. From there Sverdlov was transferred to the village of Selivanikha, where he worked intensively at improving his education. He was in constant correspondence with comrades still at liberty and through them he was kept informed of all the events taking place at the centre. The war years dragged on and then the Revolution drew nearer. Immense snow-covered wastes separated Turukhansk from the places where the greatest events in the history of the working class were at hand. February arrived. At the news of the first flashes of revolution, the exiles became delirious with joy, and Sverdlov was one of the first to escape so as to be as near as possible to the Revolution and the work on which he had already expended so much effort and energy. After riding over 1,300 miles on horseback along the Yenisey, he reached Krasnoyarsk where he spent a few days before going on to Petrograd.

At the conference in April 1917, he was elected to the CC. He assumed a large share of the work of rallying the Bolshevik ranks in readiness for October. With victory secure, he was appointed to the vital post of Chairman of VTsIK and he was directly involved in formulating its first decrees. The newly fledged government took its first steps under his guidance and he presided over six congresses as permanent chairman. He was at the head of the Bolshevik Party during the difficult years of the establishment of the Soviet State, but when the demands on him reached their peak he caught a chill after a trip to the Ukraine and a speech to a meeting at Oryol. He returned to Moscow, but after an illness of only a few days he died on 16 March 1919.

V. I. Lenin paid homage to Sverdlov's memory in these words:

If we have succeeded in bearing for over a year those burdens that fell on a narrow circle of selfless revolutionaries, if the leading groups could solve the most difficult problems in such strict unanimity, it is only because a prominent position in them was occupied by such an exceptionally talented organiser as Sverdlov. He alone succeeded in assembling an amazing personal knowledge of the leaders of the proletarian movement, he alone succeeded in cultivating over many years the practical flair, the organisational ability and the indisputable authority which enabled him to direct single-handed the VTsIK, that most crucial branch of the government which would normally require a group of men to control.

Such a man we shall never be able to replace, if by that we mean finding one comrade who combines all these abilities. The tasks which he performed alone will now be entrusted to a group of people who, by following in his footsteps, will continue his work.

G. Sverdlov

Some say it was typhoid, others claim it was tuberculosis, and the official version has that it was Spanish influenza that ended the life of Sverdlov, the first head of the Soviet State and one of the great men of the Bolshevik Party. From 1917, he was a member of the Bureau of the Central Committee, a permanent executive of four: Lenin and Trotsky, acknowledged political leaders of the Party, and Stalin and Sverdlov, its main organisers.

Even before the Revolution he had a great reputation as an illegalist Bolshevik, courageous and efficient in clandestine work: at the age of 27, in 1912, he was co-opted onto the first Central Committee of the Bolshevik Party and onto its Russian Bureau, and in April 1917 he presided at the Party's first legal conference. Nominated by the Conference itself, Sverdlov was unanimously elected to the Central Committee, then composed of nine members. Thenceforth, he seconded Lenin's efforts in the essential task of reorganising the Party and in the elaboration of its machinery. In a few weeks Sverdlov succeeded in creating an efficiently structured Central Committee, which became a true HQ with a large permanent staff, instructors and emissaries. At the same time he transformed the face of the old organisation in the major centres of Russia, and he was one of the main designers of its organisational implantation. Taking in hand all current business, he effectively became the Central Committee's first General Secretary, long before the post existed officially.

Sverdlov was a brilliant organiser; he possessed an enormous fund of knowledge about the Party and its *cadres* (in Lunacharsky's words, 'His memory contained something like a biographical dictionary of communists') and he had an exceptional gift of intuition in dealing with men. The Party's internal life and the working of the Central Committee rested entirely on his efforts. The Petrograd demonstrations of July 1917 (the technical organisation of which was largely his work) brought him out of the anonymity he had sought in order to manage the flow of events at Lenin's side; July 1917 put him in the foreground. The result of the July crisis was the arrest of Bolshevik leaders, and Lenin had to go back into hiding. Sverdlov, who remained free, became the main leader of the Party.

As from August 1917, Sverdlov controlled the organisational bureau of the Central Committee and its five-man secretariat, and with Dzerzhinsky he was at the head of the Central Committee's military commission. In Lenin's absence, in October 1917, it was he who presided at Central Committee meetings.

Lenin's constant supporter,[1] Sverdlov showed in these critical circumstances that his loyalty was absolute. He was indeed the only member of the Central Committee to support Lenin unhesitatingly in the tumultuous and agonising debates of 1917 and 1918, which often put the leader in the minority. During the preparation of the October Revolution, Sverdlov was responsible for liaison between the Party machine and the RVS, of which he was a member. After the victory, he did not enter the first Bolshevik government, but continued to devote himself to the Party, of which he held the reins. Already, at the beginning of November 1917, the Party faced a serious crisis. Kamenev, head of the opposition within the Central Committee, demanded a coalition government. Kamenev was forced to resign and a clever, reliable man was needed to take his place—a man capable of keeping the unstable Soviet Parliament in order. Sverdlov was chosen. While taking on the presidency of the Soviet TsIK, he retained his post at the head of the Central Committee's secretariat and continued to supervise its organisational activity, to direct and control the machine at all levels.

Sverdlov's authority was never questioned, though he held two of the regime's key positions. Honest, always respecting Party orders strictly, he enjoyed the quasi-unanimous confidence of all the tendencies and currents which conflicted so violently in the ranks of the Bolshevik movement. His capacity for work was unequalled, his character extremely firm (he was nicknamed 'the shutter up'). Undogmatic, decisive, naturally straightforward, Sverdlov had no personal ambitions, no pride, and devoted himself to a sort of myth of the cause.

Lunacharsky drew a striking psychological portrait of this short, dark, very Jewish-looking man, who was the first to wear the commissar's uniform of black leather. The characteristic that struck Lunacharsky most in all great revolutionaries – namely their calmness and imperturbability in extremely trying situations – was possessed by Sverdlov to an 'imposing and so to speak monumental degree'. He could keep cool

[1] In 1913 it was Sverdlov whom Lenin put in charge of reorganising *Pravda*, which had infuriated him with its conciliatory attitude towards the Mensheviks under the direction of Molotov, Stalin and Raskolnikov.

in the most heated atmosphere; but his cold, phlegmatic appearance hid a powerful and passionate temperament. As for his role and place in the Revolution, Lunacharsky defined them thus: 'Whereas Lenin and a few others provided the intellectual guidance for the Revolution, between them and the masses – the Party, the Soviet government apparatus and ultimately all Russia – like a spindle on which it all revolved, like a wire transmitting it all, stood Sverdlov.'[1]

On the eve of the sixth Congress he left for the Ukraine to sort out the political situation (left-wing communists had gained control of the Central Committee). It was there that he caught the disease (not a chill, as his brother claims in this biography) that killed him. Lenin's first words in his opening speech to the eighth Congress were about Sverdlov, whom he called the 'principal organiser of the Party and of the Soviet State'. But neither Lenin nor the delegates to the eighth Congress were in a position to realise just how great their loss was. The man who had held the Party together so solidly was hostile to any fractional movement. His control of the machine would without doubt have altered the conditions of the struggle that tore the Party apart from 1923 on. Lenin said it would take several men to replace Sverdlov: he was indeed unsuited to any role other than that of a revolutionary.

G.H.

[1] *Revolutionary Silhouettes*, p. 106.

LEV DAVIDOVICH TROTSKY

Lev Davidovich Bronstein – Trotsky – was born on 26 October 1879 in the village of Yanovka in Elizavetgrad district, Kherson province. Until the age of nine he lived on the small estate of his father, a Kherson colonist. At that age he entered the Odessa Real School, studying there for six years before being transferred to Nikolaev where he completed his secondary education. Recalling his childhood and school years, Trotsky tells us that he was very interested in art, that he would draw with coloured pencils and thought himself a budding artist. But subsequently he failed to reveal any gifts in this direction. At the Real School he even tended to look on painting as a burden, although he was very diligent. His greatest enthusiasm was turned to the writing of essays and he dreamt of a career as a writer. Naturally, he also wrote poetry. He translated Krylov's fables into Ukrainian. He produced a magazine with friends in the second and third forms. All this was quite normal. He was suspended from the second form for a protest about the French teacher, a Swiss called Bernard. He was almost expelled from the fifth form for another protest, this time about the Russian language teacher, but the affair was confined to detention and a mark of three out of five for misconduct. After leaving school, he attempted to enter the mathematical faculty as an external student. It was at this time that his political career began. When transferred to Nikolaev, he came into contact with revolutionary-minded young people, but for a while he considered himself an opponent of Marxism rather than a Marxist.

These students soon established links with the Nikolaev workers. Remembering these events, Trotsky writes:

I was surprised at the ease with which we, a small circle of adolescents, managed to win the confidence of the Nikolaev workers, who lived in a fairly cultured, educated environment, marked by various types of sectarianism among the older generation and atheism among the younger ones [. . .]. The Nikolaev organisation comprised 250 workers in 1897, which was a large number for that time. I was known there as 'Lvov'. We organised circles, held small public meetings in the woods and issued proclamations and newspapers. The political ignorance of the masses was very great. In fact, I had not read a single revolutionary book at that time. I became acquainted even with the *Communist Manifesto* only by reading and explaining it to the circles.

The organisation to which Trotsky refers also spread to Odessa and he had to act as the link between the Nikolaev and Odessa groups. The activities of the circle soon came to the notice of the authorities, and it was infiltrated by *agents provocateurs* and informers [. . .]. Trotsky was arrested and moved from one prison to another—Nikolaev, Kherson and Odessa, spending two years in the latter. Finally he was sentenced to be deported to eastern Siberia for four years, and then followed months in Moscow, Irkutsk and Aleksandrovsk transit prisons. It was in jail that Trotsky became a Marxist. 'The decisive influences,' he wrote, 'were the two studies on the materialist conception of history by Antonio Labriola. Only after this book did I go on to Beltov and *Das Kapital*.' The time in exile opened Trotsky's literary career. 'During my first period of exile, I stepped out on the literary path, so to speak. I began with correspondence, and then progressed to articles for the Irkutsk *Vostochnoye Obozreniye*. I signed myself "Antid Oto", a pseudonym that I used for a long time, even in the legal Russian press.'

After two years of exile in the village of Ust-Kut, Irkutsk province, he escaped in August 1902 and reached Samara by way of Irkutsk, using a false passport in the name of Trotsky, the name under which he subsequently became universally known: 'I personally wrote this name into the blank passport, calling myself after the chief warder of the Odessa prison.' On his way from exile, he made contact with the Siberian Social Democratic Union in Irkutsk and the central *Iskra* group in Samara. After carrying out various tasks for this group in Kharkov, Poltava and Kiev, he crossed the Austrian border and reached Vienna, where he made the acquaintance of Victor and Friedrich Adler. From thence he went to London, where *Iskra* was edited at that time by Lenin, Martov and Zasulich with the collaboration of Plekhanov, Akselrod and Potresov, who were living on the continent. [. . .]

Lenin subjected the newcomer to a detailed 'examination on all policies', being particularly interested in the attitude of the Russian social democrats towards the theoretical argument between Kautsky and Bernstein. [. . .][1] The period of Trotsky's collaboration on *Iskra* coincided with his first reports and speeches to the Russian colonies in Brussels, Liège and Paris. When the editorial board moved to Geneva, Trotsky accompanied them. Here he met the remaining prominent figures on *Iskra*, Plekhanov and Akselrod. His relations with Plekhanov, which were cold and official from the beginning, grew no warmer as time passed. On the other hand, he remembered Akselrod's family with affection, remarking on their simplicity and genuine comradely fellow feeling. At the second RSDRP Congress, Trotsky spoke on

[1] Here we omit five quotations from *On Lenin*. Their basic point is the indication that Trostky believed Zasulich and Martov much more than Lenin and that he did not at first perceive the differences existing on the editorial board of *Iskra*.

behalf of the Siberian SD Union. During the polemics over the Party rules, which split the Party into 'Bolshevik' and 'Menshevik' (or opposition) factions, he sided with the latter. [. . .]

After the Congress, he continued to contribute to *Iskra*, which was now in the hands of the Mensheviks, and he joined the Menshevik 'Centre' which was formed to combat the Bolsheviks. Moreover, he helped to formulate those measures that amounted to the creation of fresh Menshevik bodies at all levels in the Party as a counter-weight to the Bolsheviks. A Menshevik press was also set up in case of need. In 1904, however, he split with the Mensheviks over the question of the possibility of agreements with the liberal parties. During these years, his political views coalesced into the 'theory of permanent revolution' which he and Parvus advocated in a series of pamphlets and articles. He wrote:

> With regard to an assessment of the internal forces of revolution and their prospects, this author did not at that time join either of the main currents in the labour movement. His point of view can be schematically outlined thus: the revolution, beginning as a bourgeois one in its immediate tasks, will soon reveal powerful class contradictions and will achieve victory only after relinquishing power to the one class capable of putting itself at the head of the oppressed masses, that is the proletariat. Having come to power the proletariat not only will not want, but will not be able to confine itself to a bourgeois democratic programme. It will only carry the revolution through to the end if the Russian revolution grows into the revolution of the European proletariat. Thus the bourgeois democratic programme with its national limits will be transcended and the temporary political supremacy of the Russian working class will expand into a prolonged socialist dictatorship.

After 9 March 1905 Trotsky returned to Russia, working first in Kiev and then St Petersburg, where he provided copy for the underground Party printing-press. In that year he entered the St Petersburg Soviet, and after the arrest of Khrustalev-Nosar he was elected its Chairman, sharing the presidium with Zlydiyev and Sverchkov. He and Parvus published *Russkaya Gazeta* and he was very closely associated with *Nachalo*. In December 1905 he was arrested with other members of the Soviet. In October 1906 the St Petersburg Court of Justice sentenced him as chief accused to exile and deprivation of all rights. Trotsky was due to be deported to Obdorsk in Tobolsk province, but he escaped from Berezov on the way. At the London Congress in 1907, he led the 'centre' group which stood apart from both Bolsheviks and Mensheviks. On one of the most acute questions of the Congress, however, namely that of the attitude towards the liberal parties, he drew closer to the views of Lenin. After the Congress, he settled in Vienna, where he maintained close contact with Russian comrades and the left wing of German social democracy. During the Balkan war he travelled as a correspondent to Serbia, Bulgaria and Romania, holding discussions with Balkan socialists. In 1908 he and A. Ioffe brought out *Pravda*. This was the paper of the Ukrainian *Spilka* SD organisation and was published in Lvov. Then publication was transferred to Vienna, where Trotsky organised a group of Menshevik writers to propagate views which he and his disciples described as being opposed to factionalism, but which amounted to support for the Mensheviks. L. B. Kamenev attempted to win over Trotsky to the Bolsheviks and even obtained the agreement of the then Bolshevik RSDRP Central Committee to his becoming Bolshevik representative on the editorial board of the Vienna *Pravda*. Nothing came of this venture, however, and Kamenev was recalled. In 1909 Trotsky gave his unequivocal allegiance to the Mensheviks.

The central question occupying the Party at that time was the move to abandon the Party's illegal organisation in the face of government reaction. This position was supported by the Menshevik right wing. The other extreme was represented by the group of left-wing Bolsheviks and *otzovisty*, who were supported by the main body of the Bolsheviks in their hostility to the 'liquidators'. Trotsky spoke of the need for reconciliation of the opposing groups. In September 1912 the Bolsheviks gathered in a conference in Krakow attended by representatives of the illegal organisations active inside Russia. Here the practical revolutionary experience of these organisations was reviewed and Marxist revolutionary class tactics were formulated. To counter-balance the Bolshevik preparations for the conference which had begun in January 1912, Trotsky and the Menshevik 'liquidators' formed a so-called 'Organisational Committee' to summon an all-Russian conference. It included Trotskyites, Menshevik 'liquidators', Georgian and Lett Mensheviks, *vperyodovtsy* (Bolshevik 'liquidators') and members of the Bund.

The conference opened in August, but despite all the attempts of the leaders of the bloc (Trotsky, Martov and Dan) to gather them into a party, they did not succeed. First of all Plekhanov refused to participate as he opposed the 'liquidators', and then the *vperyodovtsy* departed. There were no representatives of the underground Bolshevik organisations present, and the representative of the Polish illegal organisation who did attend proved to be an *agent provocateur*. The conference was clearly anti-Bolshevik, as can be seen from the fact that instead of demands for the summoning of a Constituent Assembly, it put forward the slogan of a sovereign Duma, and instead of the confiscation of all land, it proposed a revision of the land acts of the third Duma. The newspaper *Luch*, founded by the August conference, was so 'liquidationist' and lacking in principles that even the Georgian Menshevik N. Zhordaniya abandoned it and the bloc, as did the Letts as soon as Bolsheviks were elected to the CC of the Lettish Party in 1914. Then Trotsky himself left and in 1914 founded a new journal, *Borba*, in which he advocated the same 'non-factional' line as he had done in the Vienna *Pravda*, which had supported the Mensheviks.

After the declaration of war, he was obliged to leave Vienna on 3 August. He went to Zurich where he published the pamphlet *Der Krieg und die Internationale*, directed against the policies of the German social democrats. In November 1914 he moved to Paris as correspondent of *Kievskaya Mysl*. Simultaneously he was one of the editors of the SD paper *Nashe Slovo*, which appeared at the end of January 1915. After Martov's departure from it, Trotsky remained in charge and it is all the more characteristic that at that time, in his own words, there were three points on which *Nashe Slovo*, and therefore Trotsky himself, was at variance with the Bolsheviks: 'These points concerned "defeatism", the struggle for peace, and the character of the coming Russian revolution.' The Bolsheviks were the 'defeatists' and Trotsky opposed 'defeatism' with the 'struggle for peace', thus replacing the Bolshevik slogan of 'civil war', whilst instead of the dictatorship of the proletariat and peasantry, he proposed the slogan 'socialist dictatorship'. In September 1915 he attended the Zimmerweld Conference. At the end of September 1916 he was expelled from France. Since he refused to leave France voluntarily, demanding that specific charges be brought, two police inspectors had to take him over the Spanish border. In Madrid he was arrested and three days later it was suggested that he should go to America. He landed with his family in New York in mid-January 1917.

As soon as the Russian Revolution broke out, he set off for Europe. In Halifax (Canada), the British military police detained him and five other passengers, also Russian *émigrés*, on the basis of blacklists compiled by diplomatic agents of the Tsarist Okhrana. After one month in custody in Canada, he was released on the demands of the Provisional government and reached Petrograd in early May. There he joined the Organisation of United Internationalist Social Democrats (*Mezhrayonka*). He described its position thus:

> The relations of this completely independent organisation with the SD Bolshevik Party were entirely friendly. I considered that the disagreements of principle which had formerly set us apart from the

Bolsheviks had been outlived, and therefore I insisted on the earliest possible union. . . . Our political line was in general the same as that of the Bolsheviks. I personally advocated both in my articles in *Vyperyod* and in my speeches the transference of all power to the Soviet of Workers', Soldiers' and Peasants' Deputies.

In July 1917 Trotsky officially joined the Bolsheviks, although this was accompanied by certain reservations. The motive for conversion was, he claimed, the fact that the Bolsheviks were becoming less Bolshevik. He opened declared that he could not call himself a Bolshevik.

He took an active part in the preparations for October. After the July events, he was arrested and spent roughly two months in prison. On 23 September 1917 he was elected Chairman of the Petrograd Soviet, and in October played a leading role in the Petrograd Revolutionary Committee which organised the armed uprising. After the October Revolution, he became Commissar for Foreign Affairs and travelled to Brest for peace talks with Germany, refusing, however, to sign the treaty. Subsequently he held the posts of Commissar for Communications and Commissar for Military and Naval Affairs, and was finally appointed Chairman of the Military Revolutionary Council. At the sixth Congress of the Communist Party he was elected a member of the CC. During his membership of the Party, he participated in a series of all-Russian discussions on the Brest peace, trade unions, the Party apparatus and the 'Plan'.

His disagreements over the Brest treaty represented in essence a deterioration in the position of the left wing and can be summarised as follows: 'Don't make war, don't sign the peace.'

The differences over the trade union question amounted to the fact that Trotsky wanted to apply the techniques of war communism to the field of economic relations. He defended the idea of State control of trade unions, their merging with government bodies and thus their bureaucratisation. In his pamphlet on the subject, Lenin clearly and unequivocally described Trotsky's line as being a factional one, with its own platform and centre.

In 1923 Trotsky took part in the discussions over Party organisation accusing the CC of obstruction and the leading Party organs of degeneration into a Party bureaucracy. He demanded freedom of discussion and faction. To counter-balance the allegedly degenerated 'Old Guard', he put the accent on youth and the young Party *cadres*.

At the same time, the opposition also put forward an economic programme: so-called 'socialist' accumulation at the expense of the peasantry. Instead of the Leninist policy of the union of proletariat and peasantry, the opposition recommended the destruction of the small peasant economy.

In 1924 a collection of Trotsky's articles appeared with a preface entitled 'The Lessons of October'. In it the whole Bolshevik concept of revolution underwent revision and the basis of the opposition platform became the hypothesis of permanent revolution, that is, Trotsky's fundamental error, his disparagement of the role of the peasantry in the revolution. Other incorrect assertions flowed from this. They concerned the role of the trade unions and the tasks of the Comintern in East and West, the role and significance of the Party, the Party apparatus and its leading organs, the nature of democracy, etc. Finally this led to the formation of a second, Trotskyite, party, its struggle with the CC of the VKP(b), and its open demonstrations against the dictatorship of the proletariat and against the Party. The latter could not reply to this in any other way than by expelling Trotsky and the opposition from its ranks.

V. Nevsky

'One can end like Lenin or like Liebknecht.
One must be up to either eventuality.'
(Trotsky)

Organiser of the October uprising, head of the Red Army, then exiled and assassinated by one of Stalin's agents, Trotsky 'began' like Lenin – and against Lenin – and ended up like Liebknecht. He was up to both eventualities. But one can dispute the justification of the second eventuality, and with it the concept of history that condemns Spartacus, Baboeuf, Blanqui, Rosa Luxemburg, Liebknecht and Trotsky because they did not end up as consuls or prime ministers. . . .

He was not at all as his legend makes him out—a missionary and sectarian dreamer where missionary and sectarian complement each other, or a dispossessed tribune-cum-prophet tirelessly reconstructing in solitude the October uprising. For fourteen years he fought Lenin's idea of the Party in the name of a wider organisation, and he only abandoned this conception in 1914, and by weight of evidence. Lenin paid him this compliment: 'Trotsky said a long time ago that unification was impossible. Trotsky has at last understood that, and now he is a perfect Bolshevik.' And immediately after his exile in 1929, Trotsky thus defined the tasks of the opposition: 'We are coming to such difficult times that any friend of ideas, and even any potential friend of ideas, must be precious to us. It would be an unpardonable mistake to reject even one. . . .' But, remaining faithful in this respect to the spirit of

Lenin (accused for a long time of being pathologically inclined to splinter groups), Trotsky could not conceive of a grouping based on equivocation, vagueness, compromise or unformulated agreements.

Was he a missionary dreamer?—that is to say, did he impose on the real world a society based on his personal ideal (Jewish messianism)? Though Trotsky's point of departure was a denunciation of 'socialism in one country', he did not base his denunciation on a *wish* to see the whole world in flames, but on an *assessment* of the facts:

> For many years the productive forces of capitalism have ignored national boundaries. Socialist society should constitute a higher level of evolution, in terms of production and technology, than capitalism; thus if it is proposed to contruct a socialist society *within national boundaries*, than – notwithstanding temporary successes – productive strength will inevitably be weakened, even relatively to capitalism. The attempt to create a self-sufficient and harmonious system, including all branches of the economy, in a purely national framework, is a reactionary utopia.

Only if a politician is regarded as the sum of his speeches or, rather, as nothing more than an agitator, can one accept the traditional and facile attribution of the volitional fallacy to Trotsky. His verbal brilliance reveals a rigorous mind.

We shall not attempt a portrait of Trotsky here. Every scholar has tried to make one, usually by drawing the classical parallel between Trotsky and Stalin, an essay chestnut in the tradition of comparisons between Dickens and Thackeray or Fielding and Smollett. The general tenor of such essays is given by Louis Fischer:

> 'Trotsky was a generalissimo, fighting with crushing political offensives; Stalin was a commander carefully waging trench warfare from a mud-spattered dugout. [. . .] Trotsky was a tormented amalgam of morality and force, of philosophy and fear, of literature and revolution: a divided personality. Stalin was a solid block of granite. His life did not touch the plane of ideas or doubts.

For Deutscher, as indeed the title of his biography suggests – *The Prophet Armed . . . Disarmed . . . Outcast* – Trotsky was the hero of a Greek tragedy reborn into the proletarian revolution, an exemplary hero, a Prometheus, unable to reconcile himself with Zeus but wasting the last ten years of his life in search of a ghost quite out of proportion to his immense talents: the fourth International.

Between 1923 and 1940 Trotsky pursued a single cause in several different forms: first, the struggle against the Party machine and its incarnation in Stalin; then the struggle to reassert the Party and the International, among other things, in face of the rising tide of Fascism in Germany, by defining the policies of a 'Single Workers' Front'; and after Hitler's victory, the abandonment of attempts to reform communist parties which had gone over to the bourgeois social order, and the call for the rebuilding of a new International. He denounced the policies of the Popular Front in France as a liberal caricature of the 'Single Workers' Front', subjected to a bourgeois party programme; and finally, in 1938, there was the proclamation of the fourth international, to be composed, according to Trotsky, by force of circumstances, of *cadres* capable of resisting in 'history's deepest hour of gloom'.

After his expulsion from the USSR in January 1929, Trotsky subordinated his entire activity to this task. He had just spent a year's exile in Alma-Ata, from where he had directed the left opposition, shaken already by capitulations which continued to weaken Trotsky from 1928 to 1934; but he seemed stronger in defeat than in victory. Exiled to Prinkipo from 1929 to 1933, in France from 1933 to 1935, thence to Norway in 1935–6, where the Labour government, harassed by the threat of a Soviet boycott of Norwegian fish, was forced to get rid of him, Trotsky was finally made welcome by President Cardenns in Mexico. The first attempt on his life (by machine-gun), in which the painter David Siqueiros took part, failed; but an agent of Stalin, Jacques Mornard-Mercader, killed him with a pick-axe on 21 August 1942. During all these wanderings, Trotsky pursued the task he had set himself, and took as much care in writing the *Opposition Bulletin*, despite its falling contributions and circulation in Russia, as he had taken in running the Red Army.

The dialectics and irony of history made Trotsky the best upholder of the historical inheritance and of the future of Bolshevism—squashed between the rollers of Stalinism and Fascism. His long struggle against Lenin had equipped him for this role far better than the subordinate positions of Kamenev, Zinoviev, Bukharin and the others could have done, (for they were always won over to Lenin in the end, reluctant or not). Trotsky's awareness of this historical role – which he alone considered indispensable – can be seen in his last conflict with Zinoviev. After the failure of the 'demonstrations' of 7 November, the ex-president of the International told him: 'Lev Davidovich, the time has come for you to have the courage to capitulate.' The former head of the Red Army replied, with the pride that often turned into arrogance towards those whom he regarded as no longer useful to his battle: 'If that sort of courage were enough, the Revolution would have engulfed the whole world by now!' While the old Bolsheviks lost themselves in the maze of Stalin's policetraps, Trotsky's attitude meant that he was never far from the centre of contemporary history. In 1939, the French ambassador Coulondre explained, with fright, that the Germano-Soviet pact was 'playing Trotsky's hand for him'.

Cold and severe, Trotsky had friends but no 'pals'; he took little notice of men's susceptibilities. His surface 'tactics' were always part of an idea, a tool with which to understand. He was not interested in establishing a clique. His first pseudonym was 'Pero' ('the pen'). Like Lenin, he was passionately interested in *ideas*, for action can only result from a clear understanding of the relationship between the opposing sides of a struggle. He constantly wanted to express his thoughts, hence the plethora of his 'theses'; and that is also the reason why his essays are always systematic. In March 1920, for example, the Central Committee rejected his proposal for what was to be called, a year later, the NEP. Defeated, Trotsky accepted his opponents' point of view and took the war communism to which they were hanging on to its extreme limits: he advocated the militarisation of labour, the necessity of force and the advantages of forced labour. If he thinks something, he says so—the opposite of Stalin, for whom any idea must be subordinated to *his* own immediate aim.

The force Trotsky put into the defence of his ideas has nourished the legend of an impenitent romantic, for ever projecting onto the world his views, feelings, aspirations and wishes; and therefore, the legend goes, he was defeated by the more 'realistic' Stalin, all the more crushingly since his pride earned him many personal enemies.

Seventeen years of constant defeat, the capitulation of all his friends, one by one – Sosnovsky, Muralov, Rakovsky – failed to bring Trotsky to his knees; for the 'old lion' (as his comrades called him) was of no ordinary moral stamp. But many of the old Bosheviks who went under had also proved that they too were no cowards. The difference between them and Trotsky is a political one: he never dissociated the fight in the USSR (or elsewhere) from the wider, general struggle of the world proletariat to overthrow capitalism. It was not because of an abstract or moral sense of internationalism, but because he grasped, almost instinctively, the economic, political and social problems and the close links between these problems and a world unified by capitalism and by its supreme 'flowering' in 'imperialism'. The class struggle, like the flow of capital, is international. Thus the 'permanent revolution' arises from the existence of a single world market based on an international division of labour.

It is from this reality that Trotsky drew his self-confidence: 'The laws of history are stronger than the will of a General Secretary,' he used to say. The portraits of Trotsky that have been written tend to illustrate the limits of their authors and of their idea of history rather than to correspond to reality. Lenin, who knew Trotsky well, reproached the so-called 'romantic revolutionary' with an 'excessive liking for the administrative side of things'—which has hardly very much to do with dreams.

To those for whom ideas are mere alibis or provisional excuses, Trotsky appears an impenitent left-winger. His passion for ideas and his surface brilliance suggest to the hasty observer some adventurer of idea and act, a Malraux hero with little taste for metaphysics but whose passion for literature and poetry suffices to prove him lacking in Stalin's healthy realism. That is the general picture that transpires from the sketch by Victor Serge:

> He came in, dressed in a sort of white uniform, with no insignia, and with a big, flat, white kepi on his head; a fine figure of a man, broad-chested, very black hair and goatee beard, flashing eyeglass; less approachable than Lenin, rather authoritarian in his bearing. I and my friends, critical supporters of communism, admired him a lot without liking him. His severity, his insistence on punctuality in work and war, his absolute correctness of behaviour at a time of general relaxation of formalities, led to hostile insinuations of some kind of evil demagoguery.

This so-called 'adventurer' was nevertheless suspicious of adventures; in 1920, for example, he opposed the invasion of Poland by which Lenin hoped to probe Europe with the bayonets of the Red Army. In his autobiography, *The Crimes of Stalin*, Trotsky does not mention this divergence, as he fails to mention the deeper divergences between Lenin and himself on the question of the TSEKTRAN and the union conflict (1920–1), both of which led him to form a splinter struggle against Lenin and the majority of the Central Committee. In 1937 he wanted to set against his 'traitor' image an image of 'lieutenant', which had already led him, in his *History of the Russian Revolution*, to minimise his own importance beside that of Lenin. A rather upside-down kind of 'pride'!

In *La Nouvelle Critique*, someone recently wrote that 'Trotsky was a man of revolution, of times of physical battle, a leader of crowds, but not a builder at all. One could almost say that Trotsky was interested in revolution, not socialism.' Yet Trotsky promoted State planning not in theory but in practice when he advocated the creation of Gosplan—which made Lenin tease him for his 'planomania'; and from 1923 he was one of the most convinced supporters of collectivisation and industrialisation.

It is true, on the other hand, that Trotsky was more a man of the masses than a Party man: the line of his 'career' follows roughly the same curves as the line of revolutionary activity among the Russian and European masses. He was twice President of the Petrograd Soviet—in 1905 and in 1917, and the dates are not mere coincidence. The struggling masses recognised him as their representative, as they recognised the Soviet as their organ. But Trotsky was aware of this feature, which was both a strength and a weakness. It is therefore striking to see the trouble he took, from 1933, over the problem of creating parties 'against the tide'. The patience and flexibility he manifested in this, even if he failed for the time being to achieve anything, are the qualities not of a 'prophet' but of a practical man.

Willingly or unwillingly, Trotsky's enemies as well as his admirers always marked him as a *model*. It was his enemies who invented the term 'Trotskyism', first in 1907–9 to denote a policy of systematic union between the social democrat splinters, then in 1923 to denote the struggle against bureaucratisation, and finally from 1926–7 to indicate the alternative to Stalinism. And thus, like Lenin and Stalin, Trotsky spreads beyond the bounds of his own biography. His name illuminates an entire historical period: Mao Tse-tung and Khrushchev threw his name at each other, a name which from Prague to Mexico, via Paris, rises again at every convulsion of our history.

J.-J. M.

GRIGORY EVSEYEVICH ZINOVIEV

Grigory Evseyevich Zinoviev, Chairman of the Executive Committee of the Comintern, member of the Politiburo of the RKP(b), Chairman of the Leningrad Soviet and Gubispolkom, and one of Lenin's closest collaborators and disciples, was born in September 1883 in the town of Elizavetgrad in Kherson province. He came from a *petit-bourgeois* background—his father was the owner of a small dairy farm. He was educated at home and from the age of fourteen or fifteen he began earning his own living and helping his parents with his small wage. At first he gave lessons and then worked as a clerk in two large commercial enterprises.

At the end of the 1890s he participated in the first self-education circles in the south and became closely associated with the group that organised the first economic strikes by workers there. In 1901 he was one of the first to suffer police persecution and in 1902 he went abroad, first to Berlin, then to Paris, and after that to Switzerland (Berne). In all these cities he joined the *émigré* SD groups and gave papers to small circles. In 1903 he met both Lenin and Plekhanov for the first time in Switzerland. When the split occurred at the second Party Congress, he immediately embraced the Bolshevik cause. Soon afterwards, in autumn 1903, he returned to the south of Russia. He worked in *Iskra* organisations, opposed the 'economists', helped set up a clandestine printing-press and established contact with the *Iskra* bureau in Poltava.

In late 1904 he fell ill and again went abroad, where he passed an examination to enter Berne University to study chemistry. He was a member of the Bolshevik *émigré* organisation and collaborated on *Vperyod*, the first Bolshevik journal. With the beginning of the 1905 Revolution, he returned to St Petersburg with a group of comrades. He arrived when the general strike was at its height. He threw himself into local Party work but soon became seriously ill with heart trouble and was sent abroad by his doctors. A couple of months' treatment, during which time he was forbidden all political activity, proved sufficient to cure him. He transferred to the Law Faculty, but soon abandoned university and in March 1906 was back in St Petersburg. He quickly established himself as a popular agitator with the metal-workers beyond the Moskovskaya Zastava. After a few weeks he was elected to the St Petersburg Party Committee and he remained a member until his arrest in spring 1908. At that time the committee included both Bolsheviks and Mensheviks but they were in sharp conflict, and this flared up particularly after the Stockholm Congress.

In Stockholm, the Party Central Committee had passed under Menshevik control, and St Petersburg became the stronghold and most important organisation of the Bolsheviks. During and after the first Duma, argument raged between the Menshevik CC and the Bolshevik St Petersburg Committee. It was a struggle of concern to the whole of Russia and brought about an equal division in the Party. The Moscow CC was led by Martov, Zhordaniya, Dan, Martynov and Khinchuk. The St Petersbrg Committee was in effect headed by Lenin. All the immediate, practical leadership in St Petersburg fell on the local committee's executive commission, which consisted of G. Zinoviev, N. A. Rozhov and I. A. Teodorovich. This trio was the centre of influence for all the Bolshevik forces in the capital at that time. During the first Duma, Zinoviev led agitation against the Kadets and Mensheviks. He contributed to the legal Bolshevik papers and was editor with A. A. Bogdanov of the illegal *Vperyod* (which came out in Finland). He lectured to meetings of students. He also participated in trade unions. When he moved from the Moskovsky district to the Nevsky one, he began to work among the weavers there. Many times he evaded arrest, although the police were scouring the area for him. After the dissolution of the first Duma, he went to Kronstadt with I. F. Dubrovinsky (Innokenty,) Ramishvilli and Aleksinsky, and on Lenin's instructions organised a rising there. After its collapse he returned to St Petersburg.

He spent the whole of 1907 in many working-class districts of the capital. He participated in the Bolshevik electoral campaign for the second Duma, and he was equally active in the Bolshevik campaign for election to the London Party Congress in spring 1907. At these elections, the St Petersburg workers cast an overwhelming majority of votes for the Bolsheviks. When the Mensheviks came out with the slogan of 'responsible (that is Kadet) ministers', Zinoviev joined other Bolsheviks in the capital in energetic opposition to it. At numerous meetings and in arguments with influential Menshevik speakers, he successfully defended the Bolshevik policy. In addition he conducted agitation among the soldiers in St Petersburg and surrounding areas, he visited the barracks at Tsarkoye Selo and in disguise attended soldiers' meetings outside the palace wall. At the London Party Congress, he was one of the St Petersburg delegates and was elected to the six-man Bolshevik CC (including Lenin, Bogdanov and Dubrovinsky). Since that time he has been a member of every CC. In this capacity he also entered the so-called 'Bolshevik centre', which directed all the work of the Bolsheviks.

He returned to Russia immediately after this Congress, arriving in St Petersburg at the moment of the dissolution of the second Duma. The Bolsheviks were driven underground. The CC proceeded to publish its central organ, *Sotsial-Demokrat*, illegally in St Petersburg, and Zinoviev was one of its editors.

He played a vigorous role in the Party electoral campaign for the third Duma, whilst at the same time being fully involved in all the clandestine life of the Party. In spring 1908 he was arrested during an editorial meeting on Vasilievsky Ostrov. The Okhrana, however, was not fully apprised of his activity. He fell seriously ill in custody and thanks to the intervention of the late D. V. Stasov, he was soon snatched from prison's grasp, being released under police supervision within a few months.

Towards the end of summer 1908 he was summoned abroad to Geneva, where Lenin and the CC were then living. He attended a CC plenum there and joined the editorial board of *Proletary*, which henceforth was to be edited until its closure by Lenin, Kamenev and himself. In December 1908 he presented a report to the All-Russian Party Conference in Paris on 'liquidationism', which was then only just taking shape. The conference approved the creation of the central organ, *Sotsial-Demokrat*, with Martov and Dan representing the Mensheviks on the editorial board, and Lenin, Zinoviev and Warski the Bolsheviks.

Both for *Proletary* and *Sotsial-Demokrat* Zinoviev wrote many editorials on questions of the theory and practice of the movement, whilst at the same time maintaining contact with Russia, in the main with the St Petersburg organisation. In 1910 he represented the Party at the International Congress in Copenhagen. In 1911 *Zvezda* and then *Pravda* were launched in St Petersburg, and *Mysl* in Moscow. Zinoviev was closely involved in all these papers and conducted correspondence with contributors to them in the two cities. In 1912 in Prague the historic All-Russian Conference of Bolsheviks took place, which saw the re-establishment of the Party after years of counter-revolution. Against the background of a resurgence in the labour movement (the Lena strike), it laid the foundation of the present Communist Party. Zinoviev attended it as one of the Moscow delegates, made a report on a series of problems and was elected to the new CC.

Soon after this conference, Lenin moved to Krakow in Galicia so as to be nearer to Russia, and Zinoviev went with him. A CC bureau was set up there consisting of the two of them, and they were visited for consultations by a number of comrades from Russia. From here, Zinoviev wrote speeches for the workers' deputies in the fourth Duma, and Lenin directed the theoretical journal *Prosveshcheniye*.

The outbreak of war found Zinoviev with Lenin in Galicia. From there they both made their way with great difficulty by way of Vienna to Switzerland. Here they resurrected *Sotsial-Demokrat*, in which they heatedly fought against the chauvinism that had triumphed in all parties. 'Against the Current'—that was the slogan of *Sotsial-Demokrat*. The first article printed under this heading was written by Zinoviev (see the collection of articles with the same title). At the same time Lenin and Zinoviev undertook a campaign among foreign workers, published illegal leaflets and pamphlets in German, and smuggled them into Austria and Germany. They both represented the Party at the Zimmerwald Conference, organised the Zimmerwald left wing and joined the latter's bureau, helped establish the German internationalist journal *Vorbote*, and organised circles among Swiss workers. Zinoviev also represented the Bolsheviks on the ISK (International Socialist Commission of Zimmerwald). In February 1917 both he and Lenin were in Berne.

All attempts to reach Russia via allied countries were blocked by the Provisional and allied governments, and it was only one month after the Revolution that Lenin, Zinoviev and a group of comrades passed through Switzerland and Germany to Russia. Although this provoked a furious outcry from all the bourgeois press, they were warmly welcomed by the Petrograd proletariat. From the day of his arrival in Russia, Zinoviev began to prepare the Party and the broad mass of workers for the October Revolution.

Long before the February Revolution Lenin had outlined in close collaboration with Zinoviev the fundamental Bolshevik policy in the period of transition from the bourgeois-democratic dictatorship to the dictatorship of the proletariat. The two basic documents (*A Few Theses* of 1915 and *Outline of the Theses of 17 March*) were written by Lenin after the closest consultation with Zinoviev. The general conference of the Petrograd organisation, at which Zinoviev was elected Chairman, and the All-Russian Conference in April, took place under Lenin's guidance. Together they enlarged upon the most important problems on the agenda, which at the same time were the crucial questions in the preparation of the revolution. Zinoviev became an editor of *Pravda*, a post he held until the paper's closure during the July days, contributing almost daily articles about the war, fraternisation, the secret agreements, the peasantry and land, etc.

In addition to this, he was entrusted by the CC with the task of attending the continuous chain of congresses and conferences hostile to the Bolsheviks and of exposing the Menshivks and SRs who directed them. He also worked in the Petrograd Soviet, mainly in the workers' section. On 3 June this section approved a resolution drawn up by Zinoviev on the transfer of power to the soviets and elected him to the bureau formed to implement this decision. Zinoviev's relentless struggle with the bourgeoisie and the 'social-patriots' earned him widespread popularity among the Petrograd proletariat and soldiers, as well as the violent hatred of his enemies. Mensheviks, SRs and the bourgeoisie took all possible steps to isolate such a dangerous opponent and after the July days spread forged documents which allegedly 'exposed' Zinoviev and Lenin as German spies.

The CC directed that the two of them should go into hiding. At first Zinoviev sheltered in the flats of various comrades in Petrograd, but then on 9 July he and Lenin went by the coastal railway to live in the 'mysterious cabin' with a worker called Emelianov from the Sestroretsk factory. At the beginning of August Zinoviev made his way back to Petrograd to stay with Emil Kalske, a worker at the Aivaz works, where he remained until October. From his hiding-place he sent articles to *Proletary* and *Rabochy*, which were appearing in place of the banned *Pravda*. From the end of August he participated in the work of the CC. On 10 October he was elected to the Politburo formed to lead the rising. On the day of the Revolution, he spoke at a session of the Petrograd Soviet for the first time after a long interval and urged the continuation of the fight. At the beginning of November 1917, earlier disagreements between the majority of the CC and a number of comrades, including Zinoviev, became more pronounced. They concerned the exaggeration by the minority of the influence of the left wing of the so-called 'Soviet parties' on the masses, but these differences were resolved in a matter of days.

Until the middle of November Zinoviev performed the functions of CC member in Petrograd, speaking at the Peasant Congress and at a session of the Petrograd Soviet. On about 15 November he left for the Ukraine with instructions from the CC to organise the struggle against the Rada. He toured a number of the largest centres of the Ukraine, participated in a conference in Kiev which prepared an insurrection against the Rada, during which, just as in Znamenka, he narrowly escaped arrest. After his return to the capital, he was elected Chairman of the Petrograd Soviet on 13 December 1917, which post he has held to the present day. At the beginning of January 1918 he was put in charge of the Committee for the Revolutionary Defence of Petrograd, which was intended to repulse the advancing German army. On 26 February 1918 he was elected Chairman of the Council of Commissars of the Petrograd Workers' Commune. It was at this time that certain disagreements took place inside the Party concerning the Brest talks. Lenin and Zinoviev waged a struggle against the so-called 'left-wing' communists and other Party groups whose position threatened the Revolution with destruction.

On 26 April Zinoviev became Chairman of the Council of Commissars of the Union of Communes of the Northern Region. Subsequently, he was the organiser of the defence of Petrograd (against Yudenich he was a member of the RVS of the Seventh Army), and he mobilised the campaign against famine. In addition to his work inside the country, he followed Lenin's lead in gathering the remnants of the Zimmerwald left wing who had been scattered throughout Europe. And when in 1919 the first Congress of the Comintern could be held, he was elected Chairman of its Executive Committee. Since then his work for the Comintern has occupied the major part of his time. In 1920 he attended the Congress of the Party of Independent Social Democrats in Halle, where he encouraged the split in the party and the assimilation of its left wing into the Comintern. He directed the Congress of the East in Baku. He made reports on fundamental questions at all the Comintern Congresses and almost all the Party ones—at the twelfth and thirteenth Party Congresses he presented the political reports of the CC.

Zinoviev's most important works are *War and the Crisis of Socialism; War and Socialism* (written with Lenin); a collection of articles entitled *Against the Current, the History of the RKP (b); On the Fundamental Questions of Leninism*, articles in the journal *Kommunistichesky Internatsional*; and another collection, *Facing the Countryside*. Zinoviev also wrote a whole series of documents fundamental to Bolshevism, which include: the resolution 'On the role of the Party in the proletarian revolution', and 'Conditions of admittance to the Communist International', both of which were approved by the second Congress of the Comintern; the theses 'On the role of trade unions', approved by the tenth Party Congress; and the theses 'On the Bolshevisation of Parties in the Comintern' adopted by the fifth enlarged plenum of the Comintern Executive Committee in 1925. In his works Zinoviev casts extremely illuminating light on questions about tactics in the class struggle, the role of the Party and trade unions in the Revolution, problems of international and internal politics, the relations between the working class and the peasantry, and the struggle with Menshevism and intra-Party deviations from Bolshevism.

B. Bogdan

The names of Zinoviev and Kamenev have been linked so closely by history since October 1917 that it is well-nigh impossible to consider the two men separately. In his *Testament*, Lenin made personal references to Trotsky, Stalin, Pyatakov and Bukharin, but was content to link Zinoviev and Kamenev in the following short and cynical comment: 'I shall mention only that Zinoviev and Kamenev's October episode was not merely a chance event, but that it cannot be held against *him*[1] any more than non-Bolshevism can be held against comrade Trotsky.'

[1] The original text does indeed read 'him'—'them' is a correction made by editors. This lapsus reveals the inseparability, for Lenin, of these two men.

The name of the one can hardly be without the other. This is rather surprising. Their past, their character and temperament did not on the face of it predispose these two men to a symbiotic existence for twenty years as the Siamese twins of Bolshevism. Trotsky made this point in a brief comparison of the two:

Zinoviev and Kamenev were men of profoundly different natures. Zinoviev—an agitator; Kamenev—a propagandist. Zinoviev was led mainly by his political flair. Kamenev thought, analysed. Zinoviev always tending to get excited. Kamenev, on the contrary, somewhat over-cautious. Zinoviev was entirely absorbed by politics, had neither taste nor interest for the rest. Kamenev—half-epicurean, half aesthete. Zinoviev was vindictive, Kamenev easy-going. [. . .] For the last thirteen years of their lives, they had to live side by side. for ever named together. Despite their dissimilarities, they had not only a common experience of exile, under the personal leadership of Lenin, but also much the same tenor of thought and will. Kamenev's analysis completed Zinoviev's intuition; they groped together towards a joint solution. The more cautious Kamenev sometimes allowed himself to be led by Zinoviev further than he really wanted to go, but they always found themselves in the end on the same line of retreat. Close to each other in their personal qualities, they complemented each other by their differences.

From 1908 to 1914, Zinoviev and Kamenev were Lenin's principal lieutenants, after the split with Bogdanov, Krasin and Lunacharsky. They were in disagreement only once, in January 1910, when Zinoviev supported Lenin against Kamenev who was for conciliation with the Mensheviks. In 1914, Lenin sent Kamenev to take over *Pravda*, but when Kamenev and Zinoviev met again on 3 April 1917, at Beloostrov on the Finnish border, they did not seem predestined to follow the same paths thereafter. From 1914 to 1917, Zinoviev the agitator had been Lenin's faithful helper in the struggle against 'socialist chauvinism' and in the fight for revolutionary defeatism and the transformation of imperialist war into civil war. This close solidarity was witnessed by the publication of a joint volume *Against the Tide* (1915), which contained articles by Zinoviev and Lenin. Faced with war, Kamenev, the 'man of letters', revealed his natural moderation; at the trial of the Bolshevik deputies and militants in February 1915 he declared himself to be hostile to revolutionary defeatism, which Lenin claimed was 'an incorrect procedure, and, from the point of view of a revolutionary social democrat, inadmissible'.

Kamenev's attitude roused the indignation of Bolshevik militants inside Russia. When, with Muranov and Stalin, the three former deportees went back to Petrograd on 12 March 1917, and tried to take control of the Party and of *Pravda*, the Central Committee Bureau declared:

> Considering the conduct of Kamenev at the trial, and the resolutions passed both in Siberia and in Russia by the Bolsheviks on this matter, the Central Committee will accept Kamenev as a collaborator on *Pravda* [. . .], will accept his articles, but without his signature [. . .]. Moscow has stated clearly that if Kamenev were to be given a post of responsibility, there could be a split in the organisation.

Nevertherless, it was Kamenev who, together with Stalin, determined the direction of the Party: defence of the 'revolution' against the Germans, critical support for Prince Lvov's Provisional government. 'In a short time', according to Sukhanov, '*Pravda* became unrecognisable.'[1]

On 3 April, at the Beloostrov border post, Lenin repeated this point to Kamenev, who was emotionally overwhelmed by the meeting. Kamenev ran to fetch Zinoviev from his railway carriage, and, pulling him along by the hand, introduced Zinoviev to the young Bolsheviks, who only knew him by name. This gesture was to take on a symbolic significance.

A few days later, Kamenev began his fight against the *April Theses* which had been published in *Pravda* over Lenin's name alone. Zinoviev at first remained silent, and then joined the majority gained by Lenin. The July days brought Kamenev and Zinoviev together in calumny: the former was imprisoned, then released, accused of having formerly had suspicious relations with the Tsarist police; while the latter, accused of being a German agent, hid with Lenin.

Then began for both men the 'October episode', over which their authorised lives throw a cloak of allusion. From mid-September Lenin demanded that the Central Committee should move towards insurrection. Zinoviev and Kamenev opposed him; they were the only ones to vote on 10 October against the resolution which 'put an armed uprising on the agenda'; they repeated their views on the 16th, and on the 18th published in Gorky's newspaper *Novaya Zhizn* a letter condemning the insurrection as an 'act of despair'.

Lenin demanded the expulsion of these 'strike-breakers', but Stalin took up their defence. Kamenev resigned from the Central Committee. The outbreak of the Revolution put a stop to the conflict—but only

---

[1] In his biography Kamenev omits to mention the struggle that took place for support for the Provisional government, and then against Lenin's April theses. He claims that he only went onto *Pravda* in April—a respectful lie.

for a short time. Indeed, a few days later Zinoviev and Kamenev (who had been elected meanwhile to the Presidency of the Soviet TsIK) led a new right-wing or 'conciliatory' opposition, demanding a coalition government drawn from all the socialist parties—while at that time the Mensheviks and SRs were participating in the Committees of Public Safety that had been set up to fight the Revolution. Resignation from the Central Committee (though Zinoviev was soon back on it) and withdrawal from responsibility. . . .

Once again these disagreements were swept aside by another revolutionary crisis. Obviously in the minority within the Party on the question of the 'infamous peace', Lenin needed all the support he could get. Zinoviev was on his side from the start. Kamenev, who was a member of the delegation at Brest-Litovsk, agreed with Trotsky at Brest, with Lenin in Petrograd. . . . The Civil War soon obliterated the new provisional borderlines and sealed the shared fate of Kamenev and Zinoviev. Neither of them played much of a role in the war. Kamenev, in charge of supplies to the Southern Front in 1915, had a bit more to do with it than Zinoviev, who none the less presents himself in this biography as the 'organiser of the defence of Petrograd'. In May and June 1919, it was Stalin who came to the rescue against Yudenich's first attack, and against the second more serious onslaught in October 1919 it was Trotsky who organised the defence of the former capital. Trotsky described Zinoviev at that time in a state of exhaustion and despair, stretched out on a settee:

Zinoviev was the very centre of the general confusion. [. . .] In good times, when, as Lenin put it, 'We had nothing to fear', Zinoviev went into the seventh heaven at the drop of a hat. But when things were bad, Zinoviev lay down on a divan – literally – and sighed. [. . .] This time I found him on a settee'.

The complementary destinies of Zinoviev and Kamenev were fitted together haphazardly under Lenin's leadership. Zinoviev became President of IKKI and of the Petrograd Soviet, while Kamenev became President of the Moscow Soviet and prepared Lenin's works for publication. When, from the end of 1922, Lenin's illness posed the problem of the succession, they both supported Stalin and formed the *Troika* which set out to oppose Trotsky's prestige—all the more dangerous as Lenin had just asked for his alliance against the Party secretariat on the problems of the foreign trade monopoly and the 'Georgian affair'. They played different roles: Zinoviev used the big stick to run the Petrograd organisation and considered himself to be the head of the *Troika*; it was he who read the political report at the twelfth and thirteenth

Congresses (1922 and 1923). Kamenev ran the Moscow organisation with more flexibility (he was very nearly beaten by the opposition in December 1923 in the discussion of the 'New Course'), and became the theoretician of the group. Both of them thought they were using Stalin and his staff as useful but politically lightweight adjuncts. Accustomed to Lenin's party in which the leader was strong enough to counterbalance the 'machine', they failed to notice that the 'machine' itself was tending more and more to come under the domination of a Party that was no longer what it had been in 1917.

In anxiety over the Party's pro-Kulak direction and the implications of the very new theory of 'socialism in one country', and after Stalin had dropped them, these two lieutenants turned against the man they still saw as their adjutant. In so doing they failed to measure the changes that had occurred since 1917. Kamenev lost the Moscow organisation, and after the fifteenth Congress the Leningrad organisation was wrested from Zinoviev. But when they joined forces with Trotsky, Kamenev declared to him: 'You only need to get onto the same platform as Zinoviev, and the Party will find its true Central Committee'; and Zinoviev stated that if he had ever committed a worse historical error than that of 1917, it was to have invented and denounced 'Trotskyism' in 1923-4. Serge portrays him as calm and optimistic: 'We shall recommence the Zimmerwald movement. . . .'

However, Bukharin took his place at the head of the International, after he had been expelled from the Politburo (1926). On 23 October 1927, together with Trotsky, he was expelled from the Central Committee, and, after the opposition demonstrations in Leningrad, Moscow and Kiev, from the Party. Ten years after the October Revolution, the fifteenth Congress (December 1927) marked the end of the political careers of Zinoviev and Kamenev. Zinoviev said then to Trotsky:'Lev Davidovich, the time has come to have the courage to capitulate.' He received the reply: 'If that sort of courage were enough, the revolution would have engulfed the whole world by now.' Kamenev stated that Trotsky, though he might be useful in an attempt to gain control of the Party, was no more than a stone about the necks of those who only wanted to re-enter it. They capitulated, and in a letter published in *Pravda* on 27 January 1928, denounced the Trotskyites. Whatever judgement one may make of their submission to Stalin, this act of denunciation made them no more than shadows. The Party machine meant them to feel it, too: consideration of their request for membership was postponed for six months.

They did not realise what had happened. In December 1928, they described their tactics thus: 'We must hang on to the rudder. Only by supporting Stalin can we do so. Let us thus not hesitate to pay him his price.' Zinoviev continued to write for *Pravda*, while Kamenev drafted a book on Lenin. In 1932, Stalin expelled them from the Party. After a thorough self-criticism they were readmitted in 1933 in time to sing Stalin's praises at the seventeenth Congress in January 1934—no doubt to expiate the statement they were reputed at that time to have made, that 'our greatest historical error was to have broken with Trotsky in 1927'. The assassination of Kirov sealed their fate. In January 1935 the court judged them morally responsible for the assassination and sentenced Zinoviev to ten years' imprisonment, and Kamenev to five. The following July, at a trial where his own brother was the main prosecution witness, Kamenev received an additional five-year sentence. They were the two inseparable 'stars' of the first Moscow trial—the Trial of the Sixteen (August 1936), which sentenced to death the 'mad dogs' accused of having constituted a terrorist group allied to the Gestapo. Before going to his death, Zinoviev declared that 'Stalin combines both the strength and the firmness of the leadership'; and Kamenev, who wanted to save his wife and three children begged his sons 'to spend their lives defending the great Stalin'.

Krivitsky had seen Zinoviev in one of the Lyubyanka's corridors in 1935. 'He had been a vigorous man. But now he looked pale and exhausted, dragging his feet in the corridor.' Thus the Spartan Zinoviev, with his flowing locks (who had been represented by the bourgeois press as an insatiable snatcher of the daughters of the nobility—a compliment repeated in Lev Granier's semi-official biography of Stalin in 1946— and his sybarite Kamenev, with his red goatee and Latin gesticulations, were thus the first in the long line of victims of what General Gorbatov today refers to as the 'black year'. It was logical for Stalin to begin with them, since they had been for a long time Lenin's closest lieutenants— so close that they tried to imitate him in everything, even down to his handwriting. . . .

'Zinoviev is a disaster,' said Sverdlov. Paul Levi called him a 'donkey with a European reputation'. E. H. Carr drew a cruel portrait of the man:

He had no grasp of political or economic issues, and preferred speech to action [. . .]. He understood nothing [. . .] of the management of men [. . .]. His ambition to assume the mantle of Lenin was so naively displayed as to make his vanity ridiculous. [. . .] Nor had he any gifts as an organiser [. . .]. He acquired an unenviable reputation for shiftiness and lack of scruple.

Angelica Balabanova described him as the 'most despicable person I have known after Mussolini'. Oskar Blum was less harsh, but said nevertheless that he 'was rather a dreamer, even a sleepwalker. That was because he, more than anyone else, lived in the realm of pure literature.'

Zinoviev, then, a self-taught man satisfied with the words and poses of grandeur, was assessed fairly brutally, and this could hardly arouse sympathy for the affable, discreet Kamenev. The former president of the Comintern (which he led through adventure and compromise) got himself a first-class burial, and dragged his blind associate down with him. But this analysis is too simple.

E. H. Carr was less near the truth, in our opinion, than Trotsky, who wrote:

> Certainly, they lacked character. But one must not oversimplify this observation. The resistance of matter is measured by the force of the destructive agents [. . .] Zinoviev and Kamenev had enough character for a dozen men in times of peace. But the period of the greatest social and political upheavals known required these men, assured by their talents of a leading role in the Revolution, to have an absolutely extraordinary firmness. The disproportion between their abilities and their willpower had tragic results.

They were of course not entirely responsible for the disproportion between their enormous historical role and their abilities. And in this, yet again, it is Trotsky who suggested the key to their fate: 'Lenin needed, in practice, submissive collaborators.' Too much the collaborators of Lenin to be themselves, Zinoviev and Kamenev yielded fairly quickly to their leader every time they came up against him. Each time, no doubt, Lenin was right, and this is precisely what Kamenev said to Sukhanov in 1918: 'The more it goes on, the more I am becoming convinced that Ilyich is never mistaken. In the end he's always right . . .' No doubt. But that was hardly likely to forge the character of a leader.

J.-J. M.

Part II

MEN OF OCTOBER

I

Early Bolsheviks

ANDREY ANDREYEVICH ANDREYEV
(autobiography)

I was born in 1895 into a peasant family in Smolensk province. At first my father worked in a Moscow textile factory and then as a caretaker. After attending the village school for two years, I left to earn my living in Moscow where, at the age of thirteen, I found a job in a tavern—washing dishes and cleaning samovars. At fifteen or sixteen, I first came across Party comrades in Moscow, mainly printers. It was also at this time that I began to take a serious interest in underground and legal Marxist writings, as well as broadening my knowledge through self-education. In 1911 I moved to the Caucasus and the south of Russia where I wandered from town to town in search of work. In 1914 I arrived in St Petersburg, worked in an artillery depot making cartridge cases, and then in the insurance-fund offices of the Putilov and Skorokhod factories.

It was with my arrival in the capital that my underground activity really began. I joined the Party and carried out clandestine work right up to the February Revolution. At the end of 1915 and in 1916, I became representative for the Narva district on the Petrograd Bolshevik Committee and I worked with Zalezhsky, Moskvin, Tolmachev and others on its 'Executive'. At the height of the February Revolution, I was active in the districts held by the Party, and also in the new Petrograd Committee. At the same time, I helped to organise the Union of Petrograd Metal-Workers, in which I held the post of district union secretary and was a member of the central administration.

After the October Revolution, I was sent by the provisional Bureau of the All-Russian Union of Metal-Workers to organise a union in the Urals. Until 1919 I worked there in trade union and Party organisations. In 1919 I was transferred to the Ukraine where I became a member both of the Central Committee of the Union of Metal-Workers and the

Presidium of the VTsSPS. In 1920 I was transferred to Moscow as Secretary of the VTsSPS there, and then I was elected President of the Central Committee of the Railwaymen's Union, which position I hold to this day.

I am a member of the TsIK of the USSR, and I was elected a member of the RKP (b) Central Committee at the eleventh Congress in 1920, being re-elected at the twelfth and thirteenth Congresses. At the present time I am also a Party Secretary.

For a long time Andreyev remained an important member of Stalin's entourage: from 1926, he was an alternate member of the Politburo, and he was a full member from 1932. In 1930–1, he was President of the TsKK. From 1931 to 1935 he was Commissar for Communications; then Secretary of the Central Committee from 1935 to 1946, president of the Party Control Commission between 1939 and 1952, Commissar for Agriculture from 1943 to 1946, and Vice-president of the Council of Ministers from 1946 until 1953. He was implicated by a campaign waged in *Pravda* in 1950 against the '*zveno*' ['link'], a work-force unit considered too small in contrast to the 'brigade'. He was removed *de facto* from the Politburo at that time, and the nineteenth Congress confirmed this move by giving him the rank of a plain member of the Central Committee. Khrushchev, who had in fact participated in Andreyev's removal, told the twentieth Congress that 'by a unilateral decision, Stalin had excluded A. A. Andreyev from the work of the Politburo. That was one of his most inexplicable caprices'.

Andreyev began his career with a blunder. First elected on to the Central Committee in 1920, he sided with Trotsky on the union question in 1920–1 and lost his position in 1921. He changed sides, and was re-elected to the Central Committee in 1922, and to the Orgburo, where he remained until 1927. He was also a member of the secretariat in 1924–5. He had leanings towards the right, but did not commit himself to that side in its subdued struggle of 1928–9. 'Andreyev is with us: he's being brought back from the Urals'—to be taken in hand, Kamenev was told by Bukharin. The manoeuvre was successful. In 1937 he was sent by Stalin to purge Uzbekistan. His career remained smooth until it was overturned by the 'zveno', which was loaded with all the problems of the agricultural crisis. Since 1953, Andreyev has been a member of the Presidium of the Supreme Soviet, and no longer plays any part in political life in the USSR. In 1965, the review *Zvezda* began publishing his memoirs of October 1917; but only the first instalment ever appeared. . . .

J.-J. M.

ANDREY SERGEYEVICH BUBNOV
(autobiography)

I was born on 23 March 1883 in Ivanovo-Voznesensk. I was educated at the local secondary school,[1] which I left in 1903. Then I went to the Moscow Agricultural Institute (Timiryazev Academy) but did not graduate.

I joined the RSDRP(b) in 1903, having been a member of revolutionary student circles since 1900–1. I became a convinced Bolshevik from the moment I joined the Party. I worked as an organiser and propagandist mainly in the provinces of the central industrial region and in Moscow. In the course of my work, I was arrested thirteen times and spent over four years in prison, including a period in a fortress.

On my first release from prison, I was delegated by the Ivanovo-Voznesensk organisation to attend the Stockholm Congress of 1906 and the London Congress of 1907. I had been a member of the local Party committee since the summer of 1905, and then of the Ivanovo-Voznesensk RSDRP(b) Union, which united a number of local organisations. In 1907 I was transferred by the Central Committee to Moscow, and from the end of 1907 I was a member of the Party Committee there.

During the harsh Tsarist repressions of 1907–10 I continued my Party work despite repeated arrests. In 1908 I was elected a member of the area bureau of the central industrial region and a delegate to the All-Russian Party Conference. However, I was arrested before I could attend. On my release from prison in 1909, I was made an agent of the Central Committee. In May 1910 I was co-opted onto the staff of the Bolshevik 'centre' in Russia, but at the end of the year I was prosecuted by the Moscow Chamber of Justice under Article 102 (the Trial of the Thirty-four). From 1910 onwards, there was a noticeable upsurge of enthusiasm in the labour movement. In 1911 I was released and became an activist in Nizhny Novgorod and Sormovo. Then I was informed that I had been co-opted onto the Organisation Committee entrusted with the summoning of the All-Russian Party Conference. I attempted to travel abroad, but was again arrested. Elected a candidate member of the CC, I joined Pozern in producing the Bolshevik paper *Povolzhskaya Byl* (six numbers of which appeared). In 1912–13, I was a contributor to *Pravda* in St Petersburg. I was also a member of the Duma 'fraction' and the St Petersburg Party Committee's *ispolkom*.

The World War found me in Kharkov, whither I had been exiled after my arrest in the capital. From the very beginning of the war, I

---

[1] The Russian expression *real'noye uchilishche* is a translation of the German *Realschule*. The nearest English equivalent is the secondary modern school.

maintained a consistent internationalist position. In early August 1914, after the Kharkov Bolsheviks' anti-war proclamation, I was arrested, imprisoned and exiled to Poltava. From there I travelled to Samara and joined the Organisational Bureau created to summon a conference of Bolshevik organisations along the Lower Volga. After its collapse, I was arrested in October 1916, and in February 1917 exiled to the Turukhansk region of Siberia. During this period I did some work on statistics and published a series of research pamphlets on economic problems.

News of the February Revolution reached me in a transit hut in the village of Bobrovka (on the Krasnoyarsk – Yeniseysk highway). I returned to Moscow and joined the Party Bureau for the Central Industrial Region. The sixth Party Congress elected me to the CC. At this time I was also a member of the Moscow Soviet Executive Committee. In August, I was transferred by the CC to Petrograd, where I held seats both on the CC and the Petrograd Soviet Executive Committee, in addition to joining the editorial board of the Party's military newspaper as CC representative. On 10 November I was elected to the Politburo, and on 16 November to the Military Revolutionary Committee charged with directing the rising. In November I was ordered to the south as Commissar for Railways and took part in the struggle against Kaledin (in Rostov-on-Don). After the seventh Party Congress, I travelled to the Ukraine where I was appointed People's Secretary of the Workers' and Peasants' government, and took part in the fight against the Germans. With the defeat of the Ukrainian government, I joined the Insurrectionary Committee. As a member of the Ukrainian Party CC and the All-Ukrainian Military-Revolutionary Committee, I worked in the 'neutral zone' (Chernigov–Kursk region) from August to October, training detachments of the partisan army for the liberation of the Ukraine.

After the second All-Ukrainian Party Conference (in October 1918), I was sent on a secret mission to Kiev. As an experienced conspirator, I was made a member of the clandestine Kiev regional Party Bureau and Chairman of the underground Kiev Soviet. After the overthrow of Petlyura, I joined the new government of the Ukraine. At the eighth Party Congress I was elected a candidate member of the CC, a member of the Commission drafting the Party programme, and a full member of the Ukrainian CC. I was also Chairman of the Kiev Soviet.

In 1919 I was designated a member of the RVS of the Ukrainian Front, and then a member of the fourteenth army RVS. In October of the same year, I was appointed to the RVS of the Kozlov Shock Group. After economic work in Moscow in 1920, I joined the RVS for the North Caucasus Military District. At that time I held seats simultaneously on the Moscow Party Committee, the Don Regional Bureau in Rostov, and the South-East Area Party Committee. During the tenth Party Congress, I was awarded the Order of the Red Banner for my part in the suppression of the Kronstadt mutiny. In 1922-3 I was put in charge of the Agitprop Department of the CC. At the twelfth Party Congress, I was elected a candidate member and at the thirteenth a full member of the Central Committee. In early 1924, I was appointed head of the Political Directorate of the Red Army and a member of the RVS of the USSR. At the same time I held seats on the CC Orgburo and the TsIK of the USSR.

For many years I have undertaken literary tasks on behalf of the Party—my pseudonyms were 'A. Glotov', 'S. Yaglov', and 'A.B.'. I have long been interested in the history of the revolutionary movement and the history of our Party. I wrote the pamphlet *Turning-Points in the Development of the Communist Party in Russia*, which has several times been re-published by many regional Party committees. Amongst my economic works, the most noteworthy is the pamphlet *The Shipment of Grain by River*, published in 1915, and also a series of articles and surveys on general agronomical questions featured in the journal *Zemsky Agronom* (Samara) and in agricultural journals in Kharkov and Poltava.

In October 1917, Bubnov was one of the leaders of the Bolshevik Party: a member of the Central Committee, as well as the Politburo, which, although formed on 10 October, never actually met. He was also on the RVS. Brest-Litovsk was a turning-point: an activist with no theoretical strength, Bubnov was also an extreme left-wing communist. He voted against the peace right up to the end, and resigned all posts of responsibility. He had scarcely returned to the Central Committee in 1919 before he was expelled again the following year, no doubt because he was one of the organisers of the so-called 'Democratic Centralism' opposition, which reproached the leadership for its excessive 'Bureaucratic Centralism'.

In October 1923 he was a signatory of the 'Declaration of the 46'. It was his last act of opposition. Historians agree that his complete about-turn was a function of his appointment in January 1924 as Head of the Political Control of the Red Army and as a member of the RRVS. From then on he allied himself unhesitatingly with the majority and pursued a rapidly rising career. In May 1924 he was elected to the Central Committee and the Orgburo, in December 1925 he became an alternate member of the secretariat. In 1929 he was appointed People's Commissar for Education. He was not a member of the Stalinist nucleus and the General Secretary put him out of action: in 1934 he disappeared from the Orgburo. In 1937 he was arrested and deported to a camp where he met his death in 1940. With Kossarev he shares the bizarre privilege of having been 'seen' in Moscow after his rehabilitation in 1956 by truly perspicacious 'observers'.

J.-J. M.

VLAS YAKOVLEVICH CHUBAR
(autobiography)

I was born in February 1891 in the village of Fyodorovka, Aleksandrovsk district, Ekaterinoslav province. My parents owned a small plot of land and were both illiterate. I entered school in 1897. In the period preceding 1905, when the activity of revolutionary circles was greatly expanding in the village (one was organised by 'Artem'), I participated in them, reading and explaining pamphlets to the illiterate. In 1904 when the circles were crushed, I was detained for the first time and interrogated (with humiliating beatings) by gendarmes who had come to the village to investigate 'sedition'. Under the influence of teachers in the two-class school, I read Darwin's *Origin of the Species* to the circle—it also destroyed my belief in God and led me to search for the meaning of my life.

Whilst living with my parents, I worked both on their land and, as a day labourer, on that of the more prosperous farmers. Seeing that it was not worth looking to farming for a career now that there were eight children in the family, I left school in 1904 and went to Aleksandrovsk to study at the Mechanical and Technical School. In 1905, after a pogrom in which my room was ransacked, I returned to the village and took part in the peasant movement. During my studies, I joined revolutionary circles and brought illegal literature to the village.

In 1907, with the return of some comrades from exile, I joined the Bolshevik Party and made contact with workers. During the summer vacations I worked in railway workshops. In term-time I earned money through lessons, in addition to my *zemstvo* scholarship and the assistance of a *zemstvo* official. In summer 1909 I was detained on a train for having illegal literature but I escaped.

After finishing school in 1911, I worked in factories until spring 1915, the only interruptions being for unemployment and one spell of six months in prison. I worked in a depot, and I was a plater, metal worker, fitter and apprentice at the factories in Kramatorsk and Nikopol-Mariupol, as well as at the Bari Brothers' boiler-making plant in Moscow. During this time I participated in strikes, the insurance campaign, co-operatives and circles. I also undertook agitation and propaganda besides continuing to educate myself.

After May Day 1915 I was mobilised into the army, but after a few months was assigned to the ordnance factory in Petrograd as a lathe operator. I was still there when the February Revolution broke out, and I immediately abandoned work to organise a factory workers' militia and a factory committee in accordance with the Party line. At the first

Conference of Factory Committees of Petrograd, I was elected to the Council.

I devoted myself to this organisation throughout the period up to October, as well as participating in various economic bodies (for example the Factory Conference). At the Congress of Ordnance Factory Workers, I was voted onto the All-Russian Committee (the organ of workers' control), and at the All-Russian Congress of Factory Committees I was elected to the Council. After October I was elected to the Council of Workers' Control and then the VSNKh. During the October days I was Commissar of the Artillery Directorate. Since the third Congress of Soviets I have been a member of the VTsIK, and since the creation of the USSR, a member of the TsIK of the Union and its Presidium.

My work in VSNKh from its creation until 1922 included transport, metallurgy, finance and economics. In 1918–19 I was Chairman of the Directorate for State Factories (Sormovo-Kolomna). In 1919 I was head of the VSNKh Commission charged with the reconstruction of industry in the Urals. In early 1920 I was dispatched to the Ukraine where I headed the VSNKh Industrial Bureau, and then the VSNKh itself. Whilst working in Petrograd, Moscow and Kharkov, I was a member of the Union of Metal-Workers and the CC. I have held seats on the All-Ukrainian Revolutionary Committee, then the All-Ukrainian TsIK (from 1920 until the present), and the Sovnarkom, where I was Deputy Chairman.

In 1922 I was appointed head of the Donbass coal industry, from where I was transferred to Kharkov in July 1923 in connection with my election as Chairman of Ukrainian Sovnarkom.

The fourth Ukrainian Party Conference elected me to its CC in 1920, and since 1921 I have been a candidate and then a full member of the CC of the RKP(b).

A prototype of the Western idea of the 'commissar' in the 1920s, Chubar was an enterprising, hard and energetic organiser. During the difficult years of the Civil War, he was entrusted with the delicate task of restoring the economy. In July 1919, Lenin gave him full powers to implement, by any means and by any representative of Soviet power, whatever measures he deemed necessary in the Urals. From 1920, he was given the Ukrainian economy to restore, and the Ukraine was to remain his field of action. Enjoying Stalin's confidence, he took over from Rakovsky in 1923 as head of the Ukrainian government. For eleven years he filled this politically important and weighty post, supporting Stalin to the hilt in his struggle against the opposition, both in the Ukraine and within the Central Committee. He became one of the pillars of Stalin's teams, first in the field of the economy, and rose to the summit of the Party's hierarchy: from 1922 he was on the Central Committee; in 1926 he became an alternate member and in 1935 a full member of the Politburo of the CPSU. He left the Ukraine in 1934 after being appointed first deputy to the President of the Council of People's Commissars, and in 1937 added to this post that of Minister of Finance. An intimate associate of Stalin and his policies, he was also their victim: in 1938 he was dismissed from his government posts and expelled from the Politburo. He was executed a year later. He was rehabilitated in 1956. (See T. H. Koliak, *Kommunist Vlas Chubar*, Kiev, 1963; and Drobzher and Dukhova, *V. Y. Chubar*, Moscow, 1963.)

G.II.

YAKOV NAUMOVICH DROBNIS
(autobiography)

I was born on 6 March 1890 in the town of Glukhov, Chernigov province. I came from a shoemaking family, and after leaving primary school I too became an apprentice shoemaker. We were a large family and poverty was always present at home. This brutalised my father and he made life stiflingly oppressive for us. Work among the shoemakers, who were noted for their ignorance, drunkenness and debauchery, also had a strong effect on me, and all this combined to drive me away in search of something new.

I left home at the age of thirteen and reached Astrakhan, but as a Jew lacking permission to reside there, I was sent back home. On the way I came across a few political prisoners, and they were my first spur to revolutionary activity. In Glukhov I met a shoemaker called Boris Rogachevsky who had been banished from Baku for propaganda, and he introduced me to other revolutionaries. In addition, I was greatly influenced by the agrarian disorders of 1904–5 which became widespread in the Glukhov area on the many landowners' estates. In 1905 I began to perform various technical services for the local RSDRP organisation, for example hectographing and distributing proclamations, and storing weapons.

In 1906 I officially joined the Glukhov RSDRP organisation. In March 1907 I was imprisoned for taking part in a strike, being released one and a half months later. In January 1908 I was arrested in Glukhov for belonging to the RSDRP. After ten months of detention without trial, I appeared before a Kiev circuit court and was given a sentence of five years' imprisonment, which took into account the fact that I was still a minor. On completion of my sentence I went to Vilno, but was then exiled to Poltava in January 1915 on suspicion of anti-war propaganda. There I worked in an underground RSDRP(b) circle until the outbreak of the Revolution, during which I occupied various Party and Soviet positions.

In 1918 I was one of the founder members of the Ukrainian Bolshevik Communist Party, and was re-elected a member of its Central Committee on five occasions. In the same year, during a mission on which I had been sent to organise Ukrainian partisan detachments to fight against the Petlyura regime, I was arrested and sentenced to be shot. I escaped from the firing squad, but was wounded and forced to hide until the arrival of the Red Army.

In 1919–20 I was sent to the front to fight against Denikin's forces. During the Civil War, I came close to being shot four times. The first occasion was in 1917 when troops of the Central Rada, in particular the Bogdan Khmelnitsky Regiment, smashed the Poltava Soviet. I was arrested with a group of comrades and humiliatingly ill-treated. We were all threatened with death, but as a member of the Poltava Duma, I was released on the latter's insistence. The second occasion is described above. The third occurred during the Denikin invasion of the Ukraine, when I was Military Commissar of the Second Composite Division. When I arrived, during the last days of Soviet power in the Ukraine, the situation was extremely grave. Our headquarters were at the Kruty station in Chernigov province. Our task was to halt Denikin's advance until the evacuation of the town of Nezhin was completed. But this was difficult as the enemy was pressing us hard and our troops were demoralised. A small group and I attempted to beat off a Cossack detachment, but we were surrounded and I was captured, although I escaped in spite of being wounded in the leg. The fourth occasion came when I was Chairman of the Poltava Executive Committee, and I was seized by bandits at Kovyaga station in Kharkov province. I was brutally beaten and thrown into a cellar as a hostage. It was only through the energetic intervention of Berzin, a member of the Southern Front RVS, that I was saved.

In 1922 I was appointed to the Small Council of People's Commissars of the RSFSR, and in 1923 to the Administrative and Financial Commission of the Sovnarkom of the USSR, which positions I still hold today.

As soon as it was founded in the spring of 1919 Drobnis belonged to the opposition group Democratic Centralism, whose most eminent members were Sapronov, Osinsky and Vladimir Smirnov—all former left-wing communists at the time of the debates on the Brest-Litovsk peace treaty. Drobnis's autobiography was written too late to inform us of his own precise position either in the discussion of the Brest-Litovsk terms, or within the Democratic Centralism group (often referred to, after its initials, as the 'Detsist' group), which protested against the bureaucratisation of the Party's life.

In 1923, Drobnis was a signatory of the 'Declaration of the 46' and belonged to the left-wing opposition. In 1925 he was involved in the 'Pililenko affair', as were other 'Detsist' leaders who had joined the left-wing opposition; the affair took its name from a militant who attempted to win new Party members over to the opposition by organising mass demonstrations, beginning in the provinces.

Although he received a stern warning that time, Drobnis joined the United Opposition in 1926, and the fifteenth Congress (December 1927) expelled him from the Party on the list of the seventy-five Trotskyites and not on the list of the twenty-five 'supporters of Sapronov'. In January 1929, he was arrested by the GPU and sent to Siberia. In November 1936, at the Novosibirsk 'sabotage and terrorism' trial, it was claimed that nine of the accused 'Trotskyites' were agents of Pyatakov. The accusations were based on evidence given by Drobnis against Pyatakov. Both men, of course, were among the accused at the second Moscow trial (January 1937), and they were both sentenced to death and shot. Drobnis, who played only a minor role during the trial, begged for a pardon in his final statement:

> If you can find the slightest possibility of allowing me to die otherwise than in disgrace, and to permit me, after the great sufferings of my life, to rejoin the ranks of the class to which I was born, then I should consider it my sacred duty to earn this gift of the working masses and to serve them until my death.

Converted to the majority and robbed of all political power, Drobnis, like Pyatakov and so many others, had thrown himself heart and soul into the mundane task of industrial construction. This pathetic appeal was of no avail.

J.-J. M.

PAVEL EFIMOVICH DYBENKO
(autobiography)

I was born on 16 February 1889 in the village of Lyudkov, Novozybkov district, Chernigov (now Gomel) province. I come from a peasant family, and my relatives – mother, father, brother and sister – still live in Lyudkov and work the land. The peasants of our village and district owned only small plots of land. [. . .]

Our family was no exception, with three *desyatiny*[1] of land, one horse and one cow to support nine people. My parents were constantly engaged in day labour on the large estates, since they were the only members of the family capable of working. The others were six children (the eldest sister being thirteen years old in 1899), and grandfather, who was 102. Poverty, the eternal companion of our family, compelled the young children to find summer jobs in the fields so as to earn some kopecks. By the age of seven, I was already working with my father, helping him to harrow and to spread manure, whilst in my spare time I grazed cattle for small landowners. Mother's burden of numerous children, housework in the early morning and every evening, and work in the fields during the day, led her to hate the landowners. She cursed them for living at the peasants' expense and undervaluing their labour. Hatred for the tyrannical landlords was instilled in all the family from an early age.

Despite these extremely trying conditions, at the age of six, I was sent as the eldest son, to the priest's daughter for lessons which she gave to me and four other children in the cold kitchen, where calves and lambs were also housed. Her methods of education were rather primitive, for example she almost daily boxed our ears and beat us with a ruler. In spite of my desire for learning at whatever cost, this treatment drove me away after four months, and it was only in the following year that I entered primary school. Being a good pupil there, I was well liked by the headmistress, M. K. Davydovich, who was at that time a member of the SD Party.

When I left school, my 'parents refused to let me continue my studies despite my entreaties. It was only thanks to the headmistress's insistence that their resistance was overcome, and in autumn 1899 I entered the three-year municipal school. My parents could not give me any assistance, and so during the holidays I had to work for small gentry landowners to earn money for textbooks and the school uniform. During my four years at this school, I did not lose touch with my former teacher, who had a certain influence on my education. Being still at school in

[1] Roughly eight acres.

1905, and although not properly understanding what was happening, I took part in the strike campaigns at the technical, municipal and 'modern' schools, for which I was brought to trial before the Starodub area court in 1906, after the suppression of the peasant rebellion in Novozybkov district by Dubasov. I was, however, acquitted.

At the age of fourteen, I left the municipal school, after which my parents categorically refused to allow me to study further, pleading their poverty and demanding that I should find a job to help feed the other children. By this time my brother Fyodor (who was a divisional commander in the Civil War and was killed in 1919 during the taking of Debaltsevo station) had also entered the municipal school and demanded that he should be allowed to continue. I had to give way and go to work in the treasurer's office in Novoaleksandrovsk, where the treasurer was a relative of ours. After working for one and a half years, I was dismissed on the insistence of the local police chief for belonging to an illegal organisation. By now seventeen, I went to Riga, where I was employed for two years as a stevedore. This work was seasonal, so that I was idle in winter. During the summer, however, I managed to save a small amount of money which enabled me to take electrical and technical courses in winter.

In 1910 I went to work at the Riga cold store. There I came into contact with a group of Lett Bolsheviks and became involved in their activities, although not to the extent of joining the Party. I was dismissed for participating in a strike. In July 1910 I worked on a building site, where a strike also broke out in August, during which I left for Libau, as I was already being sought by the police. I lived in hiding there till the spring of 1911, when I returned to Riga and was re-employed as a stevedore. In November 1911 I was arrested for failure to report to a recuitment office for my call-up, and I was sent under escort back to Novozybkov.

On arrival there, I was conscripted into the Baltic Fleet as an ordinary seaman. It was whilst I was in the Fleet that, in 1912, I officially joined the Bolshevik Party and collaborated with Sladkov (who died in Kronstadt in 1922). On graduating from the Gunnery and Mining School in 1913, I was posted to the battleship *Emperor Paul I*, which after the Revolution was renamed the *Republic*. On board this vessel, which was nicknamed the 'prison ship' by the sailors, I engaged in militant illegal activity and was one of the instigators of the mutiny in 1915 on the Dreadnought *Petropavlovsk*. In 1916 I was one of a battalion of sailors sent to the Riga Front, to the area of the Ikskile fortified positions. Before it could attack, the battalion had been so stirred by revolutionary propaganda that it refused to obey orders, and it also won over the

Forty-fifth Siberian Infantry Regiment. For this mutiny, the sailors' battalion was immediately withdrawn to Riga where it was disbanded and sent back to Helsinki under escort. On the way, many sailors were arrested. I feigned illness and remained in hospital in Riga for two months, after which I returned and was sentenced to two months' detention.

In 1917, after the February Revolution, I was elected President of the Baltic Fleet Central Committee (*Tsentrobalt*), and although being in the minority (only six members of the Committee were Bolsheviks, and another five were sympathisers), I nevertheless managed to carry through statutes which unambiguously recognised the Provisional government, but which also maintained that all the latter's orders could only be executed with the agreement of the Committee. In July, I was arrested for mutiny, beaten by Kadets, and imprisoned in the Kresty until 4 September. On my release, I returned to Helsinki and resumed work on behalf of the Baltic Fleet Committee which had been dissolved after the July events by Kerensky's Commissar, Onipko. At the beginning of October 1917, during the large-scale German incursion into the Baltic, I took part in the struggle for the islands of Dago and Ezel.

In the October rising, I commanded troops at Tsarskoye Selo and Gatchina, and after crushing the Kerensky 'adventure', I personally arrested Krasnov and took him to the Smolny Palace. In October, I was elected People's Commissar for the Navy, holding the post till April 1918. In May, I was tried for surrendering Narva to the Germans, but was acquitted. After this, I was sent to carry out underground activity in the Ukraine and the Crimea. In August 1918, I was arrested in Sebastopol by the government of General Sulkevich and was imprisoned till the end of September. After attempting to escape from Sebastopol prison, I was put in handcuffs and irons, and transferred to the one at Simferopol. I was released following negotiations for an exchange of prisoners between the Sovnarkom and the Germans. In October, I arrived in the neutral zone near the town of Rylsk in Kursk province, where I was first of all military commissar of a regiment and then commander of a battalion. Later, I commanded troops during the drive to Ekaterinoslav, which included the capture of Kharkov.

In February 1919, I was made Commander of the division beyond the Dnieper which, after gaining control in the Crimea, was re-formed as the Crimean Army and which I led until July 1919, being at the same time the Crimean Republic's Commissar for the Army and Navy. In September 1919, I entered the RKKA Academy, but then these orders were countermanded and I was sent to the South-Eastern Front to lead the Thirty-seventh Infantry Division. On 28 November we took part in the defeat of General Toporkov's White Army Corps at Kachalin and in the capture of Tsaritsyn. In February 1920 I was appointed Commander of the First Caucasian Cossack Division, and after the rout of Denikin's forces, I led a cavalry group in the advance towards Maikop. In July 1920 I commanded the Second Cavalry Division on the Southern Front. In 1921, whilst a student on the preparatory course at the Military Academy, I was sent to help crush the Kronstadt mutiny. When I arrived in Oranienbaum, I took command of a mixed division which was involved in the fighting at Kronstadt, and after the mutiny was over, I was appointed Commandant of the fortress there. Within a few days I was recalled to take part in the fight against Antonov's brigands. After consideration by the RKKA General Staff, I was appointed Commander of the Western Black Sea coast and, in June, Commander of the Fifty-first Perekop Division.

In addition to all this, I was an external student of the Military Academy for eighteen months, from 1 June 1921 until 1 September 1922, when I completed the higher and supplementary courses. In July 1921 I was appointed Commander of the Sixth Infantry Corps. After graduating from the Academy, I was promoted Commander and Commissar of the Fifth Infantry Corps, and then in April 1924 I was made Commander of the Tenth Infantry Corps. On 6 May 1925 I was put in charge of the RKKA artillery forces, and at the third Congress of Soviets I was elected a member of the TsIK.

The military honours I have received are: three Orders of the Red Banner, a gold watch from the VTsIK, a silver watch from the Leningrad Soviet, and a horse.

This 'bearded giant with a placid face' (John Reed), justifiably called by the left-wing SR Steinberg 'the hero of October, the leader of the Baltic seamen . . . with fiery eyes but a calm temper', was a man of enthusiasm and impulsive action. Appointed a member of the War Commissariat on 26 October 1917, he led the counter-offensive against Krasnov's Cossack troops, and signed with him an armistice stipulating the delivery of Kerensky and the removal of Lenin and Trotsky from the government. . . . At the end of January 1918, he left for the Ukraine, in charge of detachments of Red troops. Hostile to the Brest-Litovsk treaty, he decided to throw his troops against the Germans after the signature of the peace, and for this he was arrested, tried for high treason, and acquitted. (It was not for the loss of Narva, as he claimed.) According to Steinberg, 'after his acquittal . . . he nurtured the idea of overthrowing the government by force'. He was expelled from the Party, then readmitted a few months later, and in January found himself entrusted, alongside Voroshilov, with the command of the First Ukrainian Army. He distinguished himself by his great courage in battle and his administrative ineptitude. Lenin reproached him and Voroshilov with wasting all their supplies. In March 1921, the former President of *Tsentrobalt* was at the head of the Soviet detachments that attacked the Kronstadt mutineers over the ice.

Thenceforth Dybenko pursued an ordinary military career: in 1922 he completed his studies at the Military Academy, and then became successively Commander of the Red Army Artillery, head of Supply Services, Commander of the Central Asian Armies, of the Volga Army, and finally Commander for the Leningrad Military District. He was one of the nine judges on the military tribunal that sentenced Tukhachevsky to death for treason. . . . He was himself arrested a few months later. Stalin had him tried *in camera* early in 1938 and, according to *Krasnaya Zvezda*, came to his trial in person. Stalin promised to appoint him to a post in the Urals if he confessed. Dybenko confessed. Stalin sent him to take over the wood industries in the Urals, and had him shot as he got off the train. Since then General Dybenko has been rehabilitated, like all the other generals.

J.-J. M.

ABEL SAFRONOVICH ENUKIDZE

(autobiography)

(Party pseudonyms: 'Goldfish', 'Abdul', 'Abel')

I was born on 7 May 1977 in the village of Tskadisi, Rachi district, Kutaisi province. Until the age of twelve, I grew up in the very beautiful mountain region of Rachi and went to the village school. From 1889 to 1892, I studied at the Mingrelia district school, and then in 1893 moved to Tiflis for further studies, completing my secondary technical education in 1897.

From early 1894, underground student circles began to be formed in Tiflis under the influence of the political strike at the religious seminary (then the centre for revolutionary students), and in other educational establishments. The circle I joined in 1894 had at first a semi-nationalist, semi-Marxist programme. From spring 1896 I was a member of a mixed worker and student circle, and it was then that my Marxist education began. We eagerly devoured all illegal writings of that time, as well as articles from *Sovremmenik*, the new *Mir Bozhy*, *Samarsky Vestnik*, and then *Novoye Slovo*. In the summer of 1897, not having the money to continue my studies, I found a job on the railways and worked in the assembly shop of the main depot of the Transcaucasian railway. There I became for the first time a propagandist and organiser in workers' circles. By this time, the Tiflis organisation had noticeably widened its scope so as to include other factories in the city. We already had links with the St Petersburg 'Union of Struggle for the Emancipation of the Working Class', and after the first RSDRP Congress new ones were forged with other organisations in Russia. In September 1898 I was transferred to the Baku depot as an engine driver's mate. There I soon made contacts not only with railway workers, but also with workers from factories and the oilfields. At that time no SD organisation existed in Baku, apart from a small group of workers who had been exiled from Moscow by the notorious Zubatov. With their help I managed to organise workers' circles in three districts of Baku. Thus the Baku SD organisation can be said to have come into existence in early 1899.

It was with the arrival of the late Vladimir Ketskhoveli, who had been expelled from Tiflis as the organiser of a tram strike, that the activity of the Baku organisation was put on a sound and correct footing. During the years 1899, 1900 and 1901, we managed to form a Baku RSDRP Committee, enlarge our work in the surrounding districts, and create a small, underground printing-press. In spring 1901, the Party suggested that I should devote myself to full-time revolutionary work, and Ketskhoveli and I went underground. In autumn 1901 an *Iskra* group was formed in Baku and from then onwards we were in regular communication with the paper's editorial board. During this time we set up a large printing-press on which we reprinted amongst other things numbers 7 and 11 of *Iskra* and numbers 5 to 8 of *Yuzhny Rabochy*, and we arranged for foreign literature to be smuggled into the country through Batum.

In April 1902 I was arrested for organising a May Day demonstration. On my release in May, I continued my activities until 2 September, when Ketskhoveli and I were arrested and transferred to the Metekhi prison in Tiflis, where we were held until summer 1903. That summer I voted in the elections to choose a delegate for the second RSDRP Congress. In autumn 1903 I was rearrested and exiled to eastern Siberia, but escaped on the way and finally went underground. Following a decision of the Party in 1903, I worked on the large underground CC printing-press until its transfer to St Petersburg in 1906, in which year I joined the organisation in the capital. Upon the dissolution of the State Duma, I was dispatched to work in the Caucasus.

After the All-Caucasian Congress in autumn 1906, I returned to the Baku organisation as a member of its committee, but was arrested on 5 May 1907 at the Baku Bolshevik Conference. In the autumn, I was exiled to Voronezh, but escaped from my escort on the way and returned to Baku, where I remained until the full conference of the Bolshevik Party in Tammerfors. En route to Finland, I was arrested in St Petersburg on 9 November 1907 and incarcerated in the Kresty prison. In May 1908 I was exiled to Archangel province, but escaped back to St Petersburg in September. I rejected a proposal that I should emigrate and after wandering about St Petersburg and Finland for three months, I returned to exile in the Onega area. I completed my sentence in July 1910 and in the autumn returned to the Baku Committee. In September 1911 I was arrested with Shaumyan, Kasparov, Chernomazov and others when preparations for the All-Russian Conference of Bolsheviks were at their height. I remained in prison until July 1912, when I was banished from the Caucasus. From October to December 1912 I worked in Rostov-on-Don. In December I travelled to Moscow, where I was given twenty-four hours to leave, and so went to St Petersburg. On 4 July I was arrested there, and in December exiled to Yenisey province.

At the end of 1916, I was recalled from exile to do my military service. I served as a private in the Thirteenth Company of the Fourteenth Siberian Regiment, and on 22 February 1917 I was sent to join the army at the front via Petrograd. I arrived in Petrograd on 27 February, that is the first day of the Revolution, and from 28 February to 3 March I joined troops in street demonstrations. Until the Congress of Soviets was summoned in April, I was a member of the Petrograd garrison. In April I was voted on to the VTsIK, and at the first Congress of Soviets I was elected a Bolshevik member of the VTsIK, later also becoming a member of the Petrograd Soviet and Executive Committee. In the days preceding the October events, I was elected one of the 'Fifteen'—the Bureau of the Workers' Section of the Petrograd Soviet. I took a very active part both in organising the second Congress of Soviets and in the October Revolution. Since then I have been returned at every election for the VTsIK. At first I directed its Military Department, and then from autumn 1918 until the end of 1922 I was a Presidium member and secretary. Since 30 December 1922 I have been a Presidium member of the VTsIK, and a Presidium member and secretary of the TsIK of the USSR.

One day in 1926, Enukidze confided to Serebryakov: 'We are not afraid of Stalin. As soon as he wants to take on grand airs, we shall eliminate him.' A few years later he wearily confided to the same man: 'What does he want now? I do everything that is demanded of me, but for him it's not enough. What's more, he wants me to consider him a genius.' Enukidze, who had known Koba-Stalin from the early years of militant activity in Georgia and who had been on the Baku Committee with him (1907-8), found it difficult to regard Stalin as a genius at the time when, even for an old friend, it was imperative to do so.

Thus Enukidze became the first major Stalinist to be publicly humiliated and made a victim of the purges. On 1 December 1934, on the evening of Kirov's assassination, Stalin made him sign, in his capacity as Secretary of the Presidium of the VTsIK, the directive which ordered the acceleration of the trials of real or potential 'terrorists' and supressed the right of pardon. On 16 January 1935, *Pravda* published a long self-criticism by Enukidze, in which he revised the historical origins of the Caucasian workers' movement: 'I must correct the errors that slipped into the Granat Encyclopedia and the *Great Soviet Encyclopedia*. The story of my life is told there as if I had founded the Social Democratic organisation in Baku. That is contrary to the truth [. . .] All I did was to help Ketskhoveli.' Enukidze, whom present-day historians have restored to the place he occupied in the celebrated clandestine 'Nina' printing-press, still refused to put Stalin in the front rank. A few weeks later Stalin relieved him of his functions as Secretary of the VTsIK, and appointed him President of the Transcaucasian *Ispolkom*.

He had scarcely taken up his new position when Beria gave a lecture 'On the History of Bolshevik Organisations in Transcaucasia', in which Enukidze was denounced as a falsificator:

Aveli Enukidze, deliberately and with deliberately hostile intentions, has falsified the history of the Bolshevik organisations in Transcaucasia [. . .] Cynically and impudently, he has deformed well-known historical facts, attributing to himself an incorrect role in the creation of the first illegal printing-press in Baku.

There is no doubt that Enukidze was a talkative and rather boastful man; but one can subscribe to the view of him expressed by Bertram Wolfe:

Enukidze was one of the best of that corps of second-string leaders recruited from the working class, which made up the most dependable strength of Lenin's party. Unlike the intellectuals who followed him, these professional revolutionaries from the working class essayed little independent thinking, vacillated less, more seldom questioned or broke with him. They found the meaning of their lives in carrying out the orders of the machine.

Despite this – or rather because of it – Enukidze was expelled from the Party in June 1935 as 'corrupt' and 'politically degenerate'. His political degeneracy stemmed, perhaps, from the fact that this rather easy-going man sent packets to his nephew, Lado Enukidze, who had been deported several years before. . . . It was said in top Party circles that Enukidze was involved in Kirov's assassination. Nevertheless, he did not appear at any of the Moscow trials. He was shot after a secret trial on 20 December 1937. The list of charges states that although Enukidze had been expelled from the Party, he had not been completely unmasked, that he was plotting acts of terror, and had committed treason in close collaboration with the 'General Staff of a Fascist State'.

Enukidze had no political ambitions; he was always prepared to adapt himself to new situations and leaders. He was satisfied at having been an exemplary Bolshevik militant and remained naively attached to the traditions of the revolutionary movement. As Secretary of the VTsIK, he was in charge of supplies to the Kremlin during the Civil War. He involved himself only half-heartedly and reluctantly in the struggle against the left opposition and remained a personal friend of one of its leaders, Serebryakov. He paid for this in 1935 when he was accused of having maintained relationship with 'enemies of the people'. By accusing of corruption the former supplier of the Kremlin, the man who had organised the very banquets at which Stalin and his group had planned their campaign tactics, the General Secretary denounced what Enukize could have become had his personal simplicity and honesty not prevented it.

J.-J. M.

MIKHAIL VASILIEVICH FRUNZE

Mikhail Vasilievich Frunze was born in 1885 in the town of Pishpek, Dzhetysu (formerly Semireche) province (Turkestan). His father, a russified Moldavian peasant from the Tiraspol district of Kherson province, had done his military service in Turkestan and remained there on its completion as assistant to the town's doctor. His mother – a peasant girl from Voronezh province – had moved to Semireche in the 1870s. Frunze was educated in the town school, and then in the Gymnasium at Verny (now Alma-Ata). His childhood was spent in difficult circumstances as he lost his father at an early age and he had to earn his own living. He first became acquainted with revolutionary ideas at the Gymnasium, where he took part in self-development circles. On graduating from the Gymnasium in 1904, Frunze entered the Polytechnical Institute in St Petersburg. Here he participated in student and worker revolutionary circles and joined the SD Party, siding with the Bolsheviks after the split. In November 1904 he was arrested for being involved in a demonstration and banished from the capital.

At first he worked in Moscow, then Ivanovo-Voznesensk, where he was one of the leaders of the famous textile-workers' strike in 1905 which for one and a half months paralysed all industry in the region. Then he took part in the Moscow rising of December 1905, manning barricades in the Presnya district of the city held by the revolutionaries. Frunze was the founder of the Ivanovo-Voznesensk area organisation and then the Ivanovo-Voznesensk RSDRP Union, which included both the town and surrounding districts. He was a delegate to the third Party Congress in London in 1905, and to the fourth in Stockholm in 1906. His subsequent arrest in 1907 in Shuya led to a long break in his revolutionary activity. He was sentenced to four years' hard labour for membership of the SD(b) Party, and to another six years for armed resistance to the police (this case was tried five times, and he was twice condemned to be hanged). He served his sentence in the Vladimir (five and a half years), Nikolaev (two years) and Alexandrov (Siberia) central hard labour prisons.

At the end of 1914, he was allowed to reside in the Verkholensk district of Irkutsk province. In summer 1915 he was arrested for forming an organisation among the exiles. He succeeded in escaping to Chita, where he lived under the name of Vasilenko and helped to edit the Bolshevik daily *Vostochnoye Obozreniye*. After this, when his hiding-place became known to the police, he made his way back to Russia. Under the name of Mikhailov, he joined the All-Russian Union of Zemstvos and worked on the Western Front.

At the outbreak of the February Revolution, he was already at the head of a huge underground revolutionary organisation with its centre in Minsk and sections in the Tenth and Third Armies. He was one of the leaders of the revolutionary movement in Minsk, Byelorussia and the Western Front, and he personally became head of the Minsk citizens' militia. Then he was voted on to the Minsk Soviet of Peasants' and Soldiers' Deputies, to the Army Committee for the Western Front, and he was finally elected President of the Byelorussian Soviet. After the Kornilov rebellion, during which he was the elected chief of staff for the Minsk region, he returned to the place of his former revolutionary activity, Ivanovo-Voznesensk, and in Shuya was elected President of the Zemstvo Board, the town duma, and the local soviet. He represented Shuya at the Democratic Congress in Petrograd. In October, he arrived in Moscow with a force of 2,000 men and took an active part in the battle.

After the October Revolution, he became Chairman of the Voznesensk province *Ispolkom* and RKP Committee as well as Military Commissar for the province. At the Constituent Assembly, he represented the Bolsheviks of Vladimir province. After the Yaroslav rebellion, he was appointed Commissar for the Yaroslav Military District. From there he was transferred to the Urals Front and under his command the Southern Army Group of the Eastern Front inflicted a decisive defeat on Kolchak's troops. Following this, he was put in charge of the whole Eastern Front and directed the operations to sweep the Whites out of Turkestan. During the revolution in Bukhara in August which overthrew the Emir, Frunze secured the revolutionaries' control by driving the Emir's forces out of the Bukharan Republic with detachments of the Red Army. In September 1920, he ordered an offensive against Wrangel on the Southern Front. After the seizure of the Crimea and the elimination of Wrangel's forces, he became commander of all troops in the Crimea and the Ukraine, and representative of the Revolutionary Military Council there. Under his leadership the Perlyura and Makhno rebellions were crushed. He was elected a member of the Ukrainian Bolshevik CC and the Ukrainian TsIK. In 1924 he was appointed Deputy Chairman of the Military Revolutionary Council, at the same time being a Presidium member (since the third Congress of Soviets) of the TsIK of the USSR. On 26 January 1925 he was promoted Chairman of the Revolutionary Military Council and People's Commissar for the Army and Navy. On 31 October 1925 he died after a prolonged illness and an operation.

In 1924, the *Troika* attempted to weaken Trotsky's positions, and replaced his deputy in the War Commissariat, Sklyansky, by Frunze; and when in January 1925 Zinoviev and Kamenev tried to have Trotsky expelled from the Party, the majority in the Central Committee decided to remove him from the War Commissariat and to appoint Frunze in his place. Trotsky rendered homage to his qualities, which in the circumstances can only appear all the more convincing:

> Frunze was a man of serious disposition; as a result of his prison years, he had more authority in the Party than the fresh young Sklyansky. Moreover, during the war Frunze demonstrated undeniable qualities as a war captain. As a military administrator, he was incomparably weaker than Sklyansky. He allowed himself to get carried away by abstract schemes.

Later, Trotsky stated simply that Frunze was 'a highly talented military chief'.

This man, with his square face, cropped hair and clear eyes, seemed predestined to a career as a military chief. He began, all the same, as an 'exemplary' clandestine militant, one of the model convicts of the Bolshevik Party. He was arrested by the police: he was sentenced to four years' hard labour, and sent to Vladimir prison. In 1909 he was accused of organising the attempted murder of a gendarme, and sentenced to death, but the sentence was commuted. In February 1910, he was sentenced to four years' hard labour for his Bolshevik militance at Ivanovo-Voznesensk, and then in September he was again condemned to death for the same attempted murder of the same gendarme. The sentence was commuted to six years' hard labour. He spent four years in the prisons of Vladimir and Nikolaev (not seven and a half, as is stated above in the biography). Banished to Eastern Siberia, he escaped and agitated in the army.

In the February Revolution Frunze's role was as important in the practical sense as it was minor in the political sense. He was one of the leaders of the February Revolution in Byelorussia, but then aligned himself with the position of the Mensheviks and the SRs: critical support for the Provisional government, merger with the Mensheviks.

The Civil War brought out his real qualities: he commanded the Fourth Army on the Eastern Front; then he was at the head of the Southern Army Group during its victorious counter-attack against Kolchak from March to July 1917. From September to November 1919 he led the Soviet Republic's final struggle against Wrangel.

It was then that with Tukhachevsky and Gusev he elaborated the 'Doctrine of Proletarian War', which proclaimed as the pinnacle of achievement the revolutionary initiative embodied in 'manoeuvre' and 'offensive'; both of which were hampered by excessive centralisation, denounced by this group. . . . The group also advocated the replacement of the heavy regular army by mobile militia detachments. At the tenth Congress in 1921, Frunze was elected to the Central Committee. It was no doubt then that he allied himself with Zinoviev, whose faithful supporter he remained to the end of his life. Zinoviev imposed him in Sklyansky's place, and then in Trotsky's, in January 1925, as Commissar for War. The collapse of the *Troika* made Frunze's presence in this position extremely awkward for Stalin. Frunze had formerly suffered from stomach ulcers. The Central Committee doctors, on orders from Stalin, insisted that he should be operated on; Frunze's doctors were opposed to it, for they were certain that his heart would not stand up to the chloroform. The Central Committee doctors had their way, and Frunze died on the operating table on 31 October 1925. . . . Three months later, the novelist Boris Pilnyak published a short story entitled 'The Tale of the Unextinguished Moon' in the January 1926 issue of the review *Krasnaya Nov*. In this story, an army commander called Gavrilov is liquidated by the leader of a powerful *troika*, by 'the man with a straight back'. That issue of the review was seized. A few weeks earlier, Voroshilov had replaced the late Frunze.

At his funeral, Voronsky declared that 'Frunze had a mind that was straight and open. . . . He was spiritually too rich to advance by tortuous or obscure paths'. This battlefield tactician was clearly an 'idealist'. He had to be removed because he appeared inconvertible. By opposing the interference of the GPU in army affairs from the moment he was appointed, Frunze showed, in effect, that he was as stubborn as a People's Commissar as he had been as an army chief. He too had a straight back. . . .

J.-J.M.

MIKHAIL IVANOVICH KALININ
(authorised biography)

Mikhail Ivanovich Kalinin, President of the TsIK of the USSR and RSFSR, was born on 7 November 1875 in the village of Verkhnyaya Troika, Korchev district, Tver province. His parents were poor peasants. Until the age of thirteen, he helped his father on the land. Kalinin learnt to read and write at the age of ten from a semi-literate army veteran, and at eleven started going to the *zemstvo* primary school run by a neighbouring landowner, Mme Mordukhay-Boltovsky, whose children were his playfellows. Leaving the school as one of its top pupils, he entered the service of the Mordukhay-Boltovsky family, who lived at that time in St Petersburg. In his own words, he was sloppy and careless in performing his duties of footman. However, his service did allow him to read many books in the family library. At the age of sixteen, the mistress of the house sent him as an apprentice to the cartridge factory in St Petersburg, where he also attended the factory school in the evenings. After two years there, Kalinin began work at the Putilov factory as a lathe operator. Here he made his first political acquaintances and joined a political circle which soon, however, collapsed. Nevertheless, he continued to be drawn into political activity, meeting an elderly worker called Parshukov and a group of workers who were in touch with underground militants.

In 1898 Kalinin joined the Social Democratic Party, continuing to work at the Putilov factory where there were by this time a number of political circles. In the same year, his first articles appeared in *Rabochaya Mysl*. The following year he was arrested for the first time on the grounds of belonging to the 'St Petersburg Union of Struggle for the Emancipation of the Working Class', one of whose founders was Lenin. After ten months' imprisonment he was exiled to the Caucasus. Calling to see his relatives in the village on the way, he reached Tiflis, where he found a job as a metal craftsman on the railways and conducted clandestine activity amongst the Tiflis workers. Dismissed for striking, he moved to a private factory, but was soon deprived of his right to reside in the Caucasus and went to Revel. There he found work at the Volt factory, and after a year transferred to the railways.

In 1903 Kalinin was again arrested and sent to the prison in St Petersburg where he spent six months in custody. Recalling this time, he wrote: 'In 1903 new ideas were in the air. The prison was crammed with shouting, jostling political prisoners. I cannot remember why the protest started, but the peaceful prison turned into a mad-house.' The prison governor took even more repressive measures, and in reply the prisoners went on hunger strike. Kalinin was transferred to the Kresty prison where he and forty-one other inmates were harshly ill-treated, one of them dying from his injuries. Kalinin was released one and a half months later, was again forced to travel to Revel, and again found a job at the Volt factory.

Early in 1904, he was rearrested and due to be exiled in Siberia. However, in view of the declaration of war on Japan, Siberia was replaced by Olonets province, where he remained until his release in 1905. After a short stay in the country, he returned to the Putilov works in St Petersburg, joining a district committee and the command staff. Dismissed as the result of a strike, he again returned to the country for a few months, only to come back to the cartridge factory in St Petersburg. But he did not succeed in settling anywhere for long; from the cartridge factory he moved to the Reikhel optical works. He was arrested, returned to the country, then went to Moscow, finding work at a tramway station. After two years, he reappeared in St Petersburg, this time at an armaments factory. Finally, after another arrest, he was banished to the countryside, where he remained for a whole year working in agriculture. Throughout all this time he never interrupted his revolutionary activity.

In 1906 he took the side of the Bolsheviks, was on the staff of the Central Union of Metal-Workers, joined district committees, helped to publish a workers' newspaper, and was a delegate to the Stockholm Party Congress. During his time in the country his room was thoroughly searched, but he was left at liberty thanks to the favourable testimony of neighbouring peasants, who kept silent about his political activity.

During the first years of the war, Kalinin worked at the Aivaz factory, one of the most technically advanced and militantly revolutionary factories in Petrograd. In November 1916 he was again arrested and was due to be exiled to Siberia, but the outbreak of revolution in February 1917 freed him to take an active part in the preparations for the October Revolution. At elections for the Petrograd Duma, he was voted mayor. In 1919 he became a member of the Central Committee of the RKP, after the death of Sverdlov became President of the VTsIK, and in 1923 President of the TsIK of the USSR.

Supporting his candidature in 1919, Lenin said:

> The transition to socialist agriculture we consider possible only by means of a series of agreements with the middle peasants. But we know that the comrades who were most active before the Revolution did not always know how to approach the peasants. The question of the middle peasants is more acute for us than for our comrades in Europe, and we ought to ensure that at the head of the Soviet

government there is a man who can show that our attitude towards them will be put into practice 'exactly as the Party Congress laid down. We know that if we can find a comrade who combines broad experience and an acquaintance with the life of the middle peasant, we shall solve this problem, and I think that the candidate announced in the newspaper this morning satisfies all these conditions. It is Kalinin.

Seeing the main task of his appointment as the strengthening of links between workers and peasants, Kalinin has made frequent tours of the provinces. In 1919 he demanded the removal of local rationing restrictions on the grounds of the hostility towards them of the peasantry, who had difficulty in understanding 'the usefulness of such decisions made by higher organs with the aim of fulfilling separate directives'.

Two 'anecdotes' can be used to draw the curve of the career of 'the old fox' (as Panait Istrati called him), who, from March 1919 until his death in 1946, was President of the VTsIK, that is President of the Soviet Republic. In January 1929, as a member of the Politburo but hostile to the accelerated collectivisation policy, he said to Zinoviev: '[Stalin] natters on about left-wing measures, but very soon he'll have to apply my policy in treble quantities. That's why I'm supporting him.' In 1945, when Kalinin, old and half blind, had to visit his wife in prison, Djilas met him at an official reception in the Kremlin. Kalinin asked Tito for a Yugoslav cigarette. 'Don't smoke it,' said Stalin, 'it's a capitalist cigarette.' And Kalinin, in confusion, dropped the cigarette from his trembling fingers, while Stalin laughed and an expression of sadistic pleasure spread across his face.

Although he was still a member of the Politburo, Kalinin had long been nothing more than a dummy figure, whose sly peasant face was a symbol of the Soviet State. The defeat of the right-wing opposition in 1929 had robbed his voice of any real importance.

In fact, Kalinin had a natural tendency to avoid political fights and to let himself float with the tide of events and slogans. In March 1917, he agreed with critical support for the Provisional government and merging with the Mensheviks. Lenin's *April Theses* offended him so much that on 14 April he declared to the Petrograd Conference that he belonged 'to the old Bolshevik-Leninists, and I consider that old-style Leninism has in no way shown itself to be inapplicable to the present moment, strange though it may be, and I am amazed that Lenin should state that the Old Bolsheviks have today become an embarrassment'. He was not opposed to the October insurrection, but adopted a dilatory attitude and proposed that it should be postponed.

He distinguished himself in the political battles of Lenin's era only by his unconditional fidelity to the latter. It was this fidelity, together with his value as a symbol, that earned Kalinin his candidate membership of the Politburo in 1919. In December 1925, he became a full member, at the fifteenth Congress: this was the reward for his fidelity to Stalin, less profound than his attachment to Lenin, but of a permanence that surprised Bukharin in 1928 when Kalinin, who agreed with him, voted with Stalin against him.

Their solidarity had roots in the distant past. In June 1900, when Koba-Stalin came on to the Tiflis Committee of the RSDRP, Kalinin, a metal-craftsman in the Tiflis railway depot, was one of the social democrats leaders of the strike which gained the support of the great majority of the 5,000 railway workers in Tiflis. In 1912, they were both members of the Russian Bureau of the Central Committee. In 1925, Kalinin said of Stalin: 'This horse will one day land our waggon in the ditch.' If he remained loyal, however, it was not just because Stalin went so far as to have a caricature published which showed 'M. K.' in an embarrassing pose. (Kalinin was a bit too fond of pretty actresses at a time when official puritanism was being established and when a militant's private life began to count in his 'career'.) This (effective) blackmail does not account for everything: Kalinin was only capable of following a leader, whose policies, moreover, were close to his own. To follow Stalin no doubt meant breaking with a past to which Kalinin remained sentimentally attached. And Trotsky suggested just that when he wrote that 'Gradually, reluctantly and unwillingly, Kalinin turned first against me, then against Zinoviev, and finally, but completely unwillingly, against Rykov, Bukharin and Tomsky, to whom he was closely related by common political conceptions'. But Kalinin did not have in any way the character of an oppositionist. He thus served to emphasise the permanence, at the head of the State, of a revolutionary tradition in which his entire youth had been cloaked. Is it a pure coincidence that it was in the year of Kalinin's death that Stalin changed the name of the Council of People's Commissars to that of Council of Ministers?

J.-J.M.

SEMYON ARSHAKOVICH
TER-PETROSYAN
(Party name Kamo)

Kamo was born into the family of a prosperous contractor in 1882 in the town of Gori, Tiflis province. His father, a petty tyrant and despot, liked eating well and receiving 'distinguished' guests, but was a miser towards his family. His mother, a young and beautiful woman (when Kamo was born she was still not sixteen) gave birth to nearly a dozen children, of whom five survived, and she doted on her eldest son. At seven, Kamo went to the Armenian school where he was taught in Armenian, even though it is a very difficult language for a child and his parents spoke Georgian at home. At eleven, he transferred to the municipal school where he was forced to learn another completely alien language—Russian. Whilst still a child, he befriended poor people, which provoked his father's displeasure. Witnessing the latter's coarse and insulting behaviour towards the mother he adored, Kamo took her part and defended her energetically when he was older. In 1898 he was expelled from school for misconduct (free-thinking). He decided to volunteer for the army, and with this end in view went to live with his aunt in Tiflis.

He took lessons from Stalin and Vardayants, who both came from his native town of Gori and were actively involved in the revolutionary movement. They brought him into contact with other comrades and taught him the rudiments of revolutionary Marxism. But his mother fell incurably ill and Kamo returned home. His father had by now run into debt, the family was reduced to poverty and there was not enough money for medicines. After his mother's death, Kamo returned to Tiflis with his sisters to live with his aunt. In 1901 he joined the SD Party, for two years carried out various technical assignments and received his pseudonym (a mispronunciation of the Russian word *Komú*). In 1903 he became a member of the RSDRP Caucasian Union Committee, organised its printing-press and energetically helped to send delegates to the second Party Congress. His resourcefulness in distributing illegal literature was inexhaustible.

In November 1903 Kamo was arrested, but he escaped from prison nine months later. In 1904 he joined the Bolshevik Party and, going underground, continued to work in the Caucasian Union Committee. In December 1905 a revolt broke out in Tiflis and during a battle with Cossacks Kamo was wounded, beaten up and arrested. He spent two and a half months in prison and then, after exchanging names with a Georgian, managed to hide. Later he arranged for a shipment of arms and created the opportunity for 32 comrades to escape from the Metekhi fortress. In 1906, aware of the gaps in his knowledge, he considered going to St Petersburg, but the Party gave him a responsible task, that of purchasing arms abroad. The attempt was a failure, as the vessel with the arms on board sank on her way from Bulgaria. In 1907, under the name of Prince Dadiani, he travelled to Finland, stayed with Lenin, and returned to Tiflis with arms and explosives. Here he carried out an extremely daring bank raid and in August 1907 left for Berlin.

In September he was arrested by the German police for being in possession of weapons and a suitcase full of explosives. He was accused of being a terrorist and an anarchist, and threatened with deportation to Russia. Kamo feigned violent insanity and successfully kept this up for four years. In 1908 he was transferred to the Buch mental asylum near Berlin and was put in a ward with ten violent lunatics. In 1909 he was considered cured and transferred to a wing of the Alt-Moabit prison for examination, but here he simulated amnesia. After long and painful tests, the doctors diagnosed insanity and handed him over to Russia. He was escorted by gendarmes to Tiflis and incarcerated in the Metekhi fortress. He was saved from the gallows by the intervention of the German SD press which roundly condemned the German government for extraditing a known sick man to the reactionary Russians as a political criminal. His lawyer, O. Kohn, sent to Tiflis a certificate of mental illness signed by well-known Berlin psychiatrists.

In the courtroom in Tiflis, crowded with people wanting to catch a glimpse of the famous hero, Kamo again feigned insanity. The military court directed that he should be subjected to new tests in the psychiatric hospital in the Metekhi fortress, where for sixteen months he underwent the same tests as in Buch. Here, too, the doctors finally declared him insane and transferred him to the Mikhailov mental hospital, from where he escaped, hiding at first in the flat of a former comrade's mother, and then in the secluded house of a government official for a month. The authorities took all measures to recapture the celebrated revolutionary, the city was cordoned off, and all exit points strictly watched. Kamo, however, managed to escape on a bicycle, disguised as a schoolboy, and he reached first Mtskhet and then Batum.

The comrades in Batum concealed him amongst barrels and boxes in the hold of a ship which took him to Paris. There he met Lenin, who provided him with money, and then went on to Constantinople and Bulgaria. From Burgas, he went via Constantinople to Trebizond. In Constantinople, while attempting to stow away on board a ship going to Batum, he was arrested by the Turkish authorities. Kamo gave his name as Ivan Zoidze, who was known to the Turkish police as a man conducting anti-Russian propaganda in the Caucasus. So they released him and suggested that he went to Athens. Kamo again managed to make his way back to the Caucasus. Here he reassembled his band of irregulars and in 1912 they attempted the 'expropriation' of a mail coach on the Kadjori highway. The raid failed, four men were killed, and Kamo himself was wounded, arrested and again imprisoned in the Metekhi fortress. After a short space of time, he was tried on four charges and on each was sentenced to death. The execution was due to be carried out one month later, but the procurator Golitsinsky was fascinated by Kamo's character and he postponed sending the sentence for confirmation in expectation of an amnesty on the occasion of the tercentenary of the Romanov dynasty. This subterfuge earned him a reprimand and cost him his career, but under the terms of the amnesty Kamo's death sentence was replaced by twenty years' hard labour. In 1915 he was transferred to Kharkov prison where he was put in a cell with common criminals.

He was freed by the February Revolution, went to Moscow and then Petrograd. Lenin sent him to the Caucasus to restore his health, and after resting for a while in a mountain spa, Kamo made his way to Baku where he worked in the Soviet and the Cheka, before going to Moscow. Here the Party CC entrusted him with the organisation of a group operating in Denikin's rear. After recruiting a detachment and testing its mettle in an original way,[1] they set off for the south, but the capture of Rostov upset his calculations. Kamo made for Tiflis, was arrested by the Menshevik government and again found himself in the Metekhi fortress. After his release, he went to Baku, and here he conducted underground activity right up to the entry of the Red Army on 27 April 1920.

At this point his military career ended. He decided to complete his education and Lenin suggested that he should prepare himself for the General Staff Academy. Kamo constantly turned down the responsible posts that were offered to him, considering himself unqualified for them.

On 14 July 1922 he was killed in an accident when a car collided with his bicycle.[2]

There is scarcely anything to add to this biography of one of the legendary figures of the Bolshevik movement. For once, the legend is not

[1] The author is here no doubt alluding to the incident which, according to Svetlana Stalin, affected the sanity of her uncle Fyodor Alleluyev who had joined Kamo's men: 'One day Kamo simulated a White Guard raid: the huts were razed to the ground, and all the Red Guards captured and tied up. On the ground lay the bloodstained body of a commander, and by his side was his heart, like a blood-red ball. Kamo waited: how were his captured soldiers going to react?'

[2] See S. F. Medvedeva, *A Hero of the Revolution—Comrade Kamo* (1925).

false. This Bolshevik Robin Hood was also a keen militant and profoundly upset by schisms. Krupskaya said of him:

> This intrepid Bolshevik of unparalleled temerity and unshakable willpower was at the same time an extremely ingenuous person, a rather naïve and tender comrade. He was passionately attached to Lenin, to Krasin and Bogdanov. . . . He befriended my mother, talked to her about her aunt and sisters. Kamo often came to Petersburg from Finland. He always took his arms with him and at each visit my mother tied his revolver to his back with particular care.

He owed his name to Stalin who was for a time his tutor in 1899, when the young Semyon Ter-Petrosyan was expelled from school for insulting the faith. With his bad Russian accent Ter-Petrosyan once asked Koba-Stalin, 'Kamo [instead of *Komú*, "to whom"] should I take this?' Koba replied with a laugh: 'Ah! that's you, Kamo, Kamo!'

An expert with guns and dynamite, Kamo was a man of sensitivity. In 1907, at the time of the Tiflis 'expropriation', he carefully moved passers-by out of the way. In 1911, he was talking to Lenin of his trials and his latest escape: '. . . and he was taken with pity for this man of limitless daring, but naïve as a child, with an ardent heart and ready for great exploits, but not knowing what work to put himself to now that he had escaped.' The Revolution brought him back from exile and threw him into an adventureless world that bored him: 'The October Revolution threw Kamo out of the life he had made for himself. He was like a great fish out of water.' The irony of history had this daredevil run over by a car while he was riding a bicycle in the streets of Tiflis. Stalin had one of his sisters deported in 1937.

J.–J. M.

SERGEY MIRONOVICH KIROV
(autobiography)

I was born in 1886 in the small country town of Urzhum in Vyatka province. I lost my parents at a very early age and was left with two sisters to be cared for by our grandmother, who received a monthly pension of three roubles as her late husband had been a soldier under Nicholas I. At the age of seven I was placed in an orphanage since she could not afford to feed three grandchildren. A year later I entered primary school and then the municipal school. I was a good pupil and when I finished there, I was awarded a *zemstvo* scholarship to go to the Kazan technical school. Here I led a more or less independent life, though hampered by my limited grant (ninety-six roubles per year). Whilst still in Urzhum, I had met political exiles and I soon came under their influence. Later, during my holidays there, these acquaintanceships became closer and had fairly positive results—I read illegal literature in detail and had discussions with the exiles, etc. This elementary political grounding gave me the opportunity for making contacts among revolutionary students in Kazan, and on graduating from the technical school I became a convinced revolutionary, with a leaning towards social democracy.

After completing my studies with distinction at the technical school, I was keen to continue my education. In autumn 1904 I set off for Tomsk in Siberia with the intention of entering the Technological Institute. There I took courses in general education, and also joined with comrades working in the local SD organisation (including Smirnov). I carried out simple preparatory tasks and helped to organise an armed demonstration in protest against the January events in St Petersburg. On 2 February 1905 I was arrested with forty comrades at an underground Party meeting. I spent two or three months in administrative custody and was then freed. From that moment my real revolutionary career began. I was mainly occupied with the distribution of illegal literature and propaganda. I organised small circles and went to workers' meetings. I joined the small group of Bolsheviks at a time when the majority of the organisation supported the Mensheviks. Then I was introduced to the Tomsk RSDRP Committee (under the pseudonyms 'Sergey', 'Serge' and 'Kostrikov'), and directed the underground printing-press. During the 1905 Revolution I was active partly in Tomsk but mainly at the Raiga station, where I led an extremely successful strike of railway workers with Pisarev, who was killed the same year.

At the very beginning of 1906, the Party ordered me to Moscow and St Petersburg to acquire a good printing machine (the normal hand press could not cope with our demands), but on the day of my departure

I was arrested in the flat of the organisation's treasurer, Tsarevsky. I spent nearly a year in Tomsk prison accused under Article 126 of the Criminal Code, and was then released on bail before the trial.

Next I helped M. A. Popov, G. Shpilev and Reshetov to organise an excellent underground printing-press. It was to be located on the out-skirts of the town in the house of Doctor Gratsianov, later a member of the Kolchak government. We worked indefatigably and the installation was almost completed. Unfortunately we were all caught red-handed one morning. However, the place where the press was installed was not dis-covered in spite of a thorough search (between the ceiling of the hiding-place and the floor of the house, which was not yet laid, there was a layer of earth about two feet deep, and the entrance to the hiding-place from the cellar was carefully camouflaged). We were detained for a long time during the investigation, but the gendarmes could find no evidence. The others were released, but I, under the name of Kostrikov, had to remain in prison after forfeiting my bail once. The trial dealing with the earlier case took place soon afterwards and six comrades were in the dock—myself, Moiseyev, Baron and others. The rest were all sentenced to exile, but because I was still a juvenile, I was given three years in a fortress.

Such a precisely determined period of unavoidable imprisonment gave me full opportunity for self-education. The prison library was quite satisfactory, and in addition one was able to receive all the legal writings of the time. The only hindrances to study were the savage sentences of courts as a result of which tens of people were hanged. On many a night the solitary block of the Tomsk country prison echoed with condemned men shouting heart-rending farewells to life and their comrades as they were led away to execution. But in general, it was immeasurably easier to study in prison than as an underground militant at liberty. The authorities apparently even encouraged such a way of life amongst the prisoners—it made life easier, there were fewer prison 'concerts' and hunger strikes, etc.

After serving my sentence I moved to Irkutsk. The organisations had been smashed. It soon became known that in the house of Doctor Gratsianov in Tomsk, where the underground printing-press had been installed, and above which some police officials now lived, as fate would have it, the stove had collapsed. The gendarmes remembered past con-nections with this house, excavated the hiding-place and all was revealed. I had to escape to the Caucasus since Siberia had proved insecure. Popov and others were arrested in various places, but I reached Vladikavkaz. Here there was no organisation, only individual comrades. Whilst living in secret, I collaborated on the local legal newspaper. In

1915 I was again arrested and escorted to Tomsk for questioning on the printing-press affair. I spent a year in prison, was tried, and acquitted 'for lack of evidence'. In fact, it was not a question of the lack of evidence. A new era was beginning, the Revolution was knocking at the door, and the judges could not fail to hear it.

According to a directive issued by the gendarmerie, I was due to be sent to the Narym region, but this too was not fated to be implemented. I again departed for the Caucasus, where a sort of organisation had begun to be formed by this time. Here I stayed until the 1917 Revolution. I took a direct part in it as a committee member of the Vladikavkaz SD organisation, in which both Bolsheviks and Mensheviks worked. Soon after October, on my return from the Congress of Soviets in Petrograd, the Civil War broke out in the northern Caucasus. I was dispatched by the organisation to Moscow to procure arms and supplies. I was on my way back to the Caucasus via Tsaritsyn in 1918 with a large shipment of arms and military equipment when I met the defeated, retreating Eleventh Army, and was unable to get through. So I was sent to Astrakhan and here collected the remnants of that army. As a member of its RVS, I worked on the defence of Astrakhan and the lower Volga. With the defeat of Denikin, I advanced with the Eleventh Army to the northern Caucasus and then Baku. At the tenth Party Congress I was elected a candidate member, and at the eleventh Congress a full member of the CC of the RKP. After the sovietisation of Azerbaijan, I was appointed the RSFSR emissary in Georgia, and, after some time, a member of the Riga delegation which had talks with Poland. On the conclusion of peace with the Poles, I was sent on Party work to the northern Caucasus where I was CC secretary of the Azerbaijan Communist Party, and a member of the Transcaucasian Area Committee.

Now I am a member of both the CC of the RKP and the TsIK of the USSR.

With the revolver shot that killed Kirov on 1 December 1934, Nikolaev created a myth. When he was assassinated, Kirov did not appear (except in Leningrad and in Party *cadres*) as distinct from the cohort of Stalin's immediate underlings. His death itself became a myth: all the major political trials after December 1934 (with the exception of Tukhachevsky's) gave rise to new 'assassins of Kirov', and it was supposedly to avenge this abominable act that Stalin struck. The Putilov factory, symbol of the October Revolution, was renamed after him. An entire Soviet generation, whose political awareness dates from the Stalinist era, projected onto Kirov its own features, its own fears, its own conformism and dissatisfaction.

The man who was thought of, especially after his assassination, as Stalin's heir apparent, was a perfect example of the young Stalinist *cadres* whose rise coincided with the removal of the great figures of the Revolution and the Civil War. He studied for three years in a small seminary (1895 to 1897), and never came into contact with European workers' movements. Only twice did he ever leave Russia: from May 1920 to February 1921 as ambassador to Menshevik Georgia; and in the course of this posting he went to Riga, between 4 and 12 October 1920, as a member of the Soviet delegation to the Polish-Soviet Peace Conference.

Up to 1917, he was a militant of no particular importance; the articles he published in the newspaper *Terek* between 1914 and 1917 do not appear to have any marked political tendency.

After the February Revolution he became a leader of the joint Menshevik-Bolshevik organisation in Terek (northern Caucasia), where the Mensheviks predominated. The president of the United Regional Committee of the RSDRP for the Terek area was a Menshevik, Skrypnikov: and Kirov was the vice-president. His activities during this period remain obscure, and his Soviet biographers (Krasnikov and Sinelnikov) have observed a discreet silence on the matter.

At the end of September 1917, he was elected to the *Ispolkom* of the Vladicaucasian Soviet, of which the presidency was occupied by a close friend of Stalin, Mamia Orakhelashvili. Kirov went to Petrograd as a delegate to the second Congress of Soviets, and then returned to Terek. He then made the acquaintance of Ordzhonikidze, who was at the time Extraordinary Commissar for southern Russia. In February 1919, Kirov was appointed to the RVS of the disintegrating Eleventh Army, which came under the leadership of Shlyapnikov at that time as part of the Caspian and Caucasus Front; upon the dissolution of which it became part of the Southern Group of the Eastern Front armies, under the group leadership of Frunze, Kuibyshev and Elyava. Kirov was entrusted with the defence of Astrakhan, an SR stronghold, and he spent fourteen months there. Two strange things happened to him during that period: first, Shlyapnikov threatened to sue him for embezzling five million roubles; and a little later, a squad of Cheka came to arrest him on the charge of 'leading the life of a lord'. These were probably either provocations or misunderstandings but, as Isaac Babel used to say, 'Stalin doesn't like spotless lives'.

In April 1920, Kirov was appointed to the Caucasian Bureau of the Central Committee, and at the end of May became Soviet Ambassador to Menshevik Georgia. He used his position to aid the invasion of the country in February 1921, an invasion prepared by Stalin and Ordzhonikidze.

Up to that time Kirov had only participated in the workings of the Party from a distance, except in Astrakhan in 1919 and 1920 when he ran one of the first organised and systematic purges of the Bolshevik Party. He attended a Party Congress (the tenth, 8–16 March) *for the first time* in 1921. The first congress in which he actively participated, and which marked the start of his rise to power, was the one that resolved to prohibit splinter groups. At this congress, Kirov was elected a candidate member of the Central Committee; on 2 May he was appointed to the Presidium of the Central Committee's Caucasian Bureau, soon to become the Transcaucasian Regional Committee (*Zakkraikom*) under the presidency of Ordzhonikidze; and in July he was made First Secretary of the Central Committee of the Azerbaijan Communist Party, a key position for Stalin's group in the coming struggle against the restless Georgian communists. Kirov was personally connected with the group that gradually coalesced around Stalin: Orakhelashvili, Kuibyshev, Ordzhonikidze, Mikoyan. . . .

For five years Kirov was the boss of Baku and of the little Azerbaijan party which he had purged twice since his arrival (in August and in October 1921). In December 1922, he was appointed to the VTsIK, then at the twelfth Congress (in April 1923) he became a full member of the Central Committee. In 1924, Stalin presented him with a copy of his book on Lenin with the following inscription: 'To my cherished brother. With the author's compliments.'

In December 1925, at the fourteenth Congress, the New Opposition was crushed. Stalin needed a shock brigade to purge the Zinovievist Leningrad machine. He entrusted Kirov with this confidential mission and sent him to the Venice of the north together with Petrovsky and Kalinin. On 5 January, Kirov wrote to his wife: 'The stiuation here is very difficult.' He asked for reinforcements: Voroshilov was sent. He went through the factories one by one. A few days later he wrote to Ordzhonikidze: 'Yesterday, I was at the Treugolnik works. 2,200 Party members. The row was incredible; it even ended in a punch-up.' The Putilov workers supported the opposition. Kirov asked for reinforcements again, and on 20 January, nine Central Committee members (including five members of the Politburo—Tomsky, Kalinin, Molotov, Voroshilov and Petrovsky) helped him wrest a meagre victory. In the end, he was sent Dzerzhinsky.

In February, the twenty-third Extraordinary Conference of the Leningrad area elected him First Secretary of the Gubkom. Only in January 1927 – after having personally organised 180 anti-opposition meetings – was he able to declare to the Party at its fourteenth Conference that 'the Leningrad road is blocked for the opposition, definitively blocked'. It was in this rough battle that Kirov earned his stripes, and on 25 July Stalin had him appointed alternate member of the Politburo. He was to become a full member at the sixteenth Congress in 1930.

There then began the most obscure period – the 'political' period – in the life of this *apparatchik* who, like Postyshev in the Ukraine, stood out from the others by his apparent simplicity and approachableness. It seems that this unconditional supporter of Stalin tried to emancipate himself; but in fact very little is known. In September 1932 he was opposed to Stalin's demand for Ryutin's execution. (In a secret document, the right-winger had compared the General Secretary to Azev, the *agent provocateur*.) At the twelfth Congress in January 1934, the anxious delegates greeted Kirov with a massive ovation. He was elected as one of the four secretaries of the Central Committee (the others were Stalin, Kaganovich and Zhdanov). Kirov's Soviet biographer, Krasnikov, wrote that 'numerous delegates at this Congress, and especially those who knew of Lenin's *Testament*, thought the time had come to remove Stalin from his position as General Secretary and to give him different tasks, because he had become convinced of his own infallibility, had begun to ignore the principle of collegiality and was sinking once again into crudity'. Kirov, who at this Congress referred to Stalin as 'the greatest man of all times and all peoples', was doubtless one of, if not the spokesman of, these 'numerous delegates'. On 1 December, at Smolny, he was shot dead by a young communist named Nikolaev. This assassination, according to Khrushchev, was the start of an era of 'massive repression', first of all against the Leningrad militants and Party machine. On 25 September 1936, Stalin and Zhdanov sent the Politburo a telegram in which they demanded the appointment of Yezhov as NKVD Commissar in place of Yagoda, who was, they said, 'incapable of unmasking the Zinovievist-Trotskyite bloc. *The GPU is four years late in this matter*'. Four years: that went back to the Politburo meeting at which Kirov had cornered Stalin. . . .

It is certain that in the period 1931–4 there did exist in the Party a substantial anti-Stalin group. But the correspondents of the *Byulleten Oppozitsii* who mentioned it always named Molotov as its leader in the Politburo. The first Moscow trial, incidentally, showed up the relative and temporary disgrace of Molotov, who was consistently omitted from the lists of potential assassination victims. It is thus possible that a number of currents of opposition have coalesced around Kirov's name, which found their actual expression in Molotov, Ordzhonikidze, Kuibyshev, Voroshilov and of course in Kirov himself. The basis for the various hypotheses summed up in the so-called *Letter from an Old Bolshevik* (written in 1937 by the Menshevik B. Nikolaevsky, from the 'confessions' of Bukharin and other Bolsheviks) is the following: considering that the battle for collectivisation and industrialisation was as good as won, 'Kirov desired the abolition of the terror both in general and inside the Party', and thus the liberation of the Party from the grip of the police. Kirov appeared, in that light, as the defender of the security of the 'victors' against the personal arbitrariness of Stalin: the 'victors' being the small, middling and great *apparatchiki* whom Stalin was to exterminate between 1936 and 1939. The *Letter* claims that *'Stalin's general staff was utterly opposed to any change in the internal policies of the Party* for they realised [. . .] that they could not rely on any mercy if the internal Party regime were to change. . . .' One of Kirov's Soviet biographers, Krasnikov, claims today that his hero 'vigorously condemned the repressive measures' against the peasants.

Did Kirov defend these ideas which corresponded to the interests of a Party machine threatened by what the Tatar Stalinist Sagidulin was to call a little later 'the 18th Brumaire'? After the enormous effort he put into winning over the people of Leningrad, including the working classes, did he in fact come to reflect in some way the reactions of the working class of the city that had made both February and October 1917? In any case, Spiridonov remarked at the twenty-second Congress that 'after Kirov's death, a continuous wave of repressive measures was hurled for four years against innocent men in Leningrad'. Did Kirov, moreover, express the revulsion felt by old militants turned bureaucrats, whose past lives made it difficult to accept the total submission that Stalin required, and which he only got by a thorough renewal of the Party and by training his *own* new men?

These hypotheses are but the various facets of an analysis that leads one to suspect that Kirov was killed because he was threatening Stalin in the name of those very interests for which Stalin had himself fought but which he wished, thenceforth, to subject to his own absolute rule. In this case, as Giuseppe Boffa put it, 'Kirov's assassination resembles the beginning of a *coup d'état*'.

J.-J. M.

STANISLAV VINKENTIEVICH KOSSIOR
(autobiography)

I was born in 1889, the son of a Polish worker, and I studied at the elementary school attached to the Sulin engineering works (in the former province of the Don). At the age of thirteen I became an apprentice metal-worker at the same place, but the Sulin works were closed following a strike in 1905 and I was forced to move to the Yuriev factory near Lugansk. This strike made such an impression on me that with the co-operation of my brother who was a member of the RSDRP, I began to carry out technical tasks for the Party and in 1907 was officially received into membership. Within a short time I was arrested, sent into administrative exile, dismissed from the factory and blacklisted. Then I became apprenticed to a shoemaker. This did not interrupt my Party activities, but one year later the police pounced upon the local Party group and I was obliged to leave the area

In 1909, thanks to old acquaintances, I succeeded in pulling a few strings and was re-engaged at the Sulin works as a clerk. Soon, however, I was arrested and held for six months in the Novocherkassk regional prison, after which I was deported to the Pavlovsk mine in the Donbass where I was due to spend two years under police supervision. Here I made contact with the Yuriev organisation and took part in the pre-election campaign to the third Duma. After four months there, I was banished from Ekaterinoslav province to Kharkov. There I initially engaged in work in the trade unions, and then I came into contact with Party members in the town. Our activity was intensified in spring 1914 in preparation for the May Day strike. An *agent provocateur* called Rudov, however, betrayed us. We were arrested and deported from Kharkov to Poltava. After the declaration of war in 1914, I moved to Kiev, where I met individual Party members and we set up jointly a temporary Bolshevik committee. In 1915 a wave of arrests compelled me to leave for Moscow. There I joined the 'Central Union', a group of Moscow Bolsheviks. I tried to gather together the remnants of the shattered Moscow organisation and I attempted to summon a city conference. This was frustrated by fresh arrests. I myself was taken into custody and deported to Irkutsk province for three years.

After the February Revolution, I returned to Petrograd where I at first undertook Party work in the Narva-Peterhof district, and then was elected to the Petrograd Committee and its Executive Commission, remaining there until the transfer of the government to Moscow in 1918. In the same year I left for the Ukraine and clandestinely carried out the functions of Party Committee Secretary on the right bank of the Don.

In 1919 I was posted to the Uman sector of the front and in December was elected to the Ukrainian CC. In 1922 I moved to Siberia, where I remained until the fourteenth Party Congress, at which I was elected a CC Secretary of the VKP(b).

The life of this working-class revolutionary who rose to the summit of the Soviet hierarchy is to a certain extent an image of the history of the Bolshevik Party before the Revolution and between the two wars. His part in the 1917 Revolution was much greater than he modestly admits it to have been in this autobiography. At the core of the Revolution in Petrograd, he was an active *cadre* in the Bolshevik organisation and held posts at various levels of responsibility in the apparatus. He was a delegate at the celebrated seventh April Conference and at the sixth Congress in July 1917. An active participant in the armed uprising of October, he was a commissar of the Petrograd RVS, and in March 1918 he became a member of the bureau of the Revolutionary Defence Committee.

Kossior, who was then at the head of the committee of the Petrograd Bolshevik Party, represented this organisation at the Central Committee meeting on 11 [NS 24] January 1918, where the question of peace negotiations with Germany was discussed. He protested, with all his strength as a left-wing communist and in the name of the Petrograd organisation, against Lenin's point of view, and called for a revolutionary war. In March 1918 this important member of the left-wing communist group was sent by the Central Committee to the Ukraine, where, with his brother Vladimir, he became one of the leaders of the local Communist Party and an organiser of the struggle against the German occupation.

It was in the Ukraine that he took part in the Civil War, and held various posts in the Party, and the army, as well as carrying out frequent missions, sometimes extremely dangerous ones. For example, he was sent on a secret mission into occupied Ukraine, where he became Secretary of the illegal Bolshevik committee of the Kiev region. A supporter of Pyatakov, Kossior was elected to the Central Committee of the Ukrainian Communist Party at its first meeting. He left the opposition and became a central figure in that group of leaders (which also included Rakovsky, Manuilsky, etc.) who remained faithful to the line taken by Lenin and the Moscow Central Committee. For a short period in December 1919 he was Secretary of the Central Committee of the Ukrainian Communist Party. At its congress in the spring of 1920, however, the opposition regained control of the Central Committee, and it was dissolved shortly afterwards on Lenin's orders. Kossior was a member of the new team then imposed by the Central Committee of the Russian Communist Party and actively participated in the struggle against the opposition. It is from this time that his collaboration with Stalin can be dated, and he did not go unnoticed by the future General Secretary. His rise was thenceforth closely tied to Stalin's politics. Kossior became part of the 'Party machine group' with an evergrowing influence, on which Stalin relied heavily in his struggle for power. In 1922, Kossior gained a new post: Yaroslavsky had become Secretary to the Central Committee, and he took his place as Secretary of the Central Committee's Siberian Bureau.

Elected as a candidate to the Central Committee at the twelfth Congress, and then made a member at the thirteenth, Kossior left his Siberian post in 1925 and was promoted by Stalin to the secretaryship of the Central Committee of the Russian Communist Party. He was elected to the Orgburo by the fourteenth Congress. Thenceforth he belonged to the new team of leaders and in December 1927, at the fifteenth Congress, he reached the pinnacle of the hierarchy: first a candidate member, and then from 1930 to 1939 a full member of the Politburo of the Communist Party. He belonged to the 'moderate Stalinist' wing, supporting the General Secretary in his fight against the united opposition and its former allies 'of the right', but opposing, in 1932, with Kirov's group in the Politburo, Stalin's terror within the Party. Moreover his brother Vladimir, an old Bolshevik from the days of clandestinity who had got Stanislav into the movement and who had been one of the active and indomitable figures in the Trotskyite opposition as well as a CC member, was deported shortly afterwards and died in 1937 in a concentration camp.

Throughout the 1930s, Kossior was the leading figure in the USSR's second republic, the Ukraine. In July 1928 he replaced Kaganovich as the first secretary of the Central Committee of the Ukrainian Communist Party. He applied Stalin's directives with rigour, both in the struggle against nationalism and in the drive towards collectivisation. In January 1938 he was accused of insufficient vigilance, was transferred to Moscow and given the high rank of Vice-president of the Sovnarkom, and President of the State Control Commission. He was arrested on 26 February 1939, accused by Stalin of being a Polish agent, and was shot without trial. Kossior was rehabilitated at the twentieth Congress, where Khrushchev cited him, in his celebrated report, as one of the most striking victims of the 'personality cult'.[1]

G.H.

[1] See A. Melchin, *Stanislav Kossior* (Moscow, 1964).

NIKOLAY NIKOLAYEVICH KRESTINSKY
(autobiography)

I was born on 13 October 1883 in the town of Mogilyov on the Dnieper. My father was a Gymnasium teacher. My parents were Ukrainian, from Chernigov province. Whilst at school, my father had been influenced by the nihilist ideas prevalent in intellectual circles at the time. My mother had been close to the Populists in her youth. Family cares, however, soon compelled my parents to turn their backs on the radical movement: my father became a teacher and government official, my mother a *petit-bourgeois* intellectual. As a result, my family did not develop any revolutionary feelings in me, but did inculcate the need to be guided by more than personal interests in my behaviour. I went to school at the Vilno Gymnasium, from which I graduated in 1901. Then I entered the Law Faculty of St Petersburg University, taking my degree in 1907, after which I worked as a barrister's assistant and as a barrister until 1917.

I first became acquainted with the revolutionary movement and its literature during my last years at the Gymnasium through the influence of schoolmates who had personal contacts with Russian and Polish members of the workers' movement. But I was particularly strongly influenced in this respect by the gymnastics teacher—officer I. O. Klopov, a social democrat.

From the end of 1901, I began to take an active part in the revolutionary movement among students and soldiers. I became a social democrat in 1903 and joined the recently formed Vilno RSDRP organisation, which had not at that time divided into Bolshevik and Menshevik factions. In 1905 I became acquainted with Bolshevik literature from abroad and took the Bolshevik side. From 1903 to 1906 inclusive, I worked in the north-west area in the Vilno, Vitebsk and Kovno organisations, with temporary visits to St Petersburg. Beginning in 1907, I worked in the capital in the Vasilyevsky Ostrov district, then transferred to the trade union movement, worked with the Duma 'fraction' and contributed to the Bolshevik press. At the elections to the fourth Duma, I stood as a Bolshevik candidate.

The first time I was arrested was in Vilno, in autumn 1904, when I was released pending trial. The second time was in St Petersburg in February 1905 during the elections to the Shidlovsky Commission.[1] I was again released pending trial and expelled from St Petersburg. Then

---

[1] This was a mixed commission set up at the end of January to examine workers' grievances. It consisted of officials, employers, and delegates elected by the workers.

followed two administrative arrests in Vilno in the summer and autumn of 1905, but I was released as a result of the 1905 strike and both cases were dropped under the amnesty. I was rearrested in Vitebsk in January 1906, released in April of the same year and expelled from the province. I was again arrested administratively at Vilno in August and October 1906, after which I left for St Petersburg. There I was taken prisoner in a trap on the day of the dissolution of the second Duma, being released after a search in my flat. In 1912, I was accused under Article 102 of belonging to a party connected with *Pravda* and the social insurance movement, as well as the pre-electoral campaign. In 1914, after the declaration of war, I was arrested and deported under an administrative order to the Urals, at first to Ekaterinburg and then to Kungur.

During the first year of the Revolution until December 1917, I remained in the Urals as Chairman of the Ekaterinburg and Urals RSDRP(b) Province Committee. At the sixth Party Congress in July 1917, I was elected in my absence a member of the CC, which I remained until the tenth Party Congress in March 1921. From December 1919 until March 1921, I was also a CC Secretary.

Whilst working in the Urals, I took only a small direct part in the activities of the soviets. I was merely a member of the Ekaterinburg Executive Committee, attended all the regional and area congresses, and was Chairman at the last area congress before October, when the Bolsheviks gained a majority. I was also Chairman of the Ekaterinburg Revolutionary Committee, a temporary organisation with minority SR participation, which preceded the complete transfer of power there to the Bolshevik Soviet. And I was elected to represent Perm province at the Constituent Assembly.

In Petrograd, I joined the Collegium of the People's Commissariat for Finance as Deputy Chief Commisar for the Narodny Bank. When the Soviet government moved to Moscow, I remained in Petrograd, and was simultaneously Deputy Chairman of the Bank and Commissar for Justice in the Petrograd Workers' Commune and the Union of Communes of the Northern Region. In August 1918 I was appointed People's Commissar for Finance and remained in this post effectively until October 1921 and nominally until the end of 1922. From October 1921 I was Soviet plenipotentiary in Germany. I have participated in Party Congresses since the seventh, and in congresses of soviets since the third. Apart from this, I attended the first All-Russian Conference of Soviets in March 1917, and was the delegate from the Ekaterinburg Soviet at the Democratic Conference. I have been a member of the TsIK since its second convocation.

On 27 October 1963, *Izvestia* published a long article by Maisky entitled 'A Diplomat of the Leninist School'. The diplomat in question was Nikolay Krestinsky, who had been shot after the third Moscow trial as a Gestapo agent. . . .

Krestinsky began his 'career' not as a diplomat, but as a rather undisciplined Bolshevik militant. At the March 1917 Conference, he criticised the majority Party line of support for the Provisional government, and then, once elected to the Central Committee (August 1917), wrote for the left-wing Menshevik journal *Novaya Zhizn*. He was a leading member of the Urals Committee; and, like all his co-members, he took the side of the left communists and opposed the Brest-Litovsk settlement. In the end he abstained on the question, like Ioffe and Dzerzhinsky, and like them also he refused to resign from his posts of responsibility. He was re-elected to the Central Committee in 1918, then appointed People's Commissar for Finance (August 1918 to October 1921). In 1919, he found himself at the centre of the machine, having been elected to one of the five seats on the first real Politburo, to the sole secretaryship of the Central Committee (Serebryakov and Preobrazhensky joined him in 1920), and to membership of the Orgburo. . . . In 1920 he neglected the secretariat somewhat and in 1921 found himself eliminated from all his positions for having associated himself with Trotsky's trade union platform.

Then began his career as a diplomat. In October 1921, he was appointed Soviet Minister Plenipotentiary in Berlin. Krestinsky sympathised with the left opposition, then with the United Opposition, though never really becoming involved with their activities, which he repudiated in 1928. He was next appointed People's Vice-Commissar for Foreign Affairs, a position he held until Potyomkin replaced him in 1935. He was expelled from the Party in 1937, and appeared among the defendants at the third Moscow trial (March 1938). He provoked a momentary stir when, on 12 March, he declared to Vyshinsky:

> I do not recognise that I am guilty. I am not a Trotskyite. I was never a member of the 'right-winger and Trotskyite bloc', which I did not know to exist. Nor have I committed a single one of the crimes imputed to me, personally; and in particular I am not guilty of having maintained relations with the German Secret Service.

The next day, Krestinsky withdrew his fleeting resistance:

> Yesterday, a passing but sharp impulse of false shame, created by these surroundings and by the fact that I am on trial, and also by the harsh impression made by the list of charges and by my state of

health, prevented me from telling the truth, from saying that I was guilty. And instead of saying 'Yes, I am guilty', I replied, almost by reflex, 'No, I am not guilty.'

Order was restored; Krestinsky was sentenced to death and shot.

J.-J. M.

NADEZHDA KONSTANTINOVNA KRUPSKAYA
(autobiography)

I was born in 1869 in St Petersburg. My parents, who came from the gentry, were both orphaned at an early age and educated at public expense—my mother in an institute, my father in a military school. On leaving the institute, my mother became a governess; my father graduated from the Military Academy and did his military service. They owned no personal property of any description. Both were soon inflamed with revolutionary ideas, and I saw revolutionaries at home from my earliest years. My father put his revolutionary ideas into practice and for this he was tried, though later acquitted. All their lives my parents had to move from town to town, wherever my father was posted. He died when I was fourteen and after that mother and I lived on various irregular sources of income—copying, lessons, renting out rooms. I went to school in the Obolensky Gymnasium and was awarded a gold medal when I left. For a short time afterwards I became a Tolstoyan.

From 1891 to 1896 I worked in a Sunday school and gave evening classes to workers beyond the Nevskaya Zastava. It was at that time that I became a Marxist, carried out propaganda among workers and helped to found the 'Union of Struggle for the Emancipation of the Working Class'. During the strikes of 1896 I was arrested, imprisoned for six months and then exiled for three years to the village of Shushenskoye in the Minusinsk region. There I married Vladimir Ilyich Ulyanov with whom I had worked earlier in the 'Union of Struggle' in St Petersburg.

I spent the last year of exile in Ufa where I also performed clandestine revolutionary tasks. In 1901 I was issued with a passport to go abroad. Arriving in Munich in spring 1901, I became secretary of *Iskra*, then a member of the 'League of Russian Social Democrats Abroad', then, after the third Party Congress, secretary of the foreign section of the Central Committee and the central organ. At the end of 1905 I returned to Russia where I spent all my time working as secretary to the CC. At the very beginning of 1908, I again travelled abroad. In my absence I was tried on three charges under Article 102. Whilst an *émigrée*, I continued to work as Secretary to the Bolshevik organisation, at the same time studying foreign schools and literature on the theory of education. I contributed articles to *Svobodnoye Vospitaniye* from abroad and worked on a book entitled *Popular Education and Workers' Democracy*.

On my return to Russia, I worked first of all in the CC Secretariat, but was soon elected to the Vyborg district Duma in Petrograd, where I joined the department dealing with popular education and took part in the revolutionary movement. After the October Revolution I became a Collegium member of the People's Commissariat for Education, where I was first of all concerned with extra-mural education, and was then president of the political science section of GUS. Simultaneously I helped to organise the women's section, the Komsomol and the Pioneers, as well as writing for newspapers and journals. All my life since 1894 I have devoted to helping Vladimir Ilyich Lenin as best I could.[1]

Krupskaya was not only Lenin's wife but also his collaborator in every circumstance; and, especially during the years of exile, was herself an active militant. An efficient but retiring woman, she was above all the *confidante* of the founder of Bolshevism. One needs only to read her book *My Life with Lenin* to realise this. But, allowing for the circumstances in which this book was written, it still can be said to give only a relative and incomplete picture of Lenin's concerns. In particular, the dramatic years of 1921–3 are passed over without a word on Lenin's fears for the future of the Revolution, or his assessment of his collaborators. Krupskaya, however, was better informed than anyone else on the last wishes of the founder of the Soviet State. She tried, but failed, to carry out the heavy task of executrix. She wanted to read out Lenin's celebrated *Testament* at the thirteenth Party Congress, but the Central Committee rejected the proposal by thirty votes to ten. She bowed to this decision out of discipline. She had in fact been routed by her former friends Zinoviev and Kamenev, whose subtle alliance with her enemy Stalin she failed to grasp.

Although Krupskaya was a militant even before she met the young Ulyanov, her political activity only took on its full meaning through him. Her devotion to the revolutionary cause had crystallised in her admiration for her husband, and their many years of collaboration robbed her of any independence. It is therefore comprehensible that she was disoriented by Lenin's death, despite the authority she enjoyed. Stalin, who was afraid of her at first, certainly went on to threaten and intimidate her; but he also managed to appeal to her feelings, and particularly to her sense of responsibility, of which he displaced the centre of gravity.

After supporting the opposition led by Zinoviev in 1925–6, Krupskaya yielded to her fear of seeing Lenin's work crumble, of seeing the Party torn asunder by internal strife, and, out of that sense of discipline

[1] Krupskaya wrote numerous works on education which are listed in two bibliographies: E. P. Andreyeva, *N. K. Krupskaya, Bibliografichesky Ukazatyel* (Moscow, 1959); N. I. Monakhov and others, 'Pedagogicheskoye Naslediye N. K. Krupskoy, Ukazatyel', in *Narodnoye Obrazovaniye* no. 2 (1964).

with which she was imbued, capitulated to Stalin. She was then relegated to the thankless and symbolic role of Lenin's widow, and was given honorary and minor positions. At the fifteenth Congress in December 1927 she was elected to membership of the Central Committee and re-elected at both the sixteenth and seventeenth Congresses. In 1929, she was appointed Assistant Commissar for Public Education of the RSFSR. She devoted herself to pedagogic research, in which she had always been passionately interested, to her book on Lenin and to publishing Lenin's work. But there is still much that is unsaid on the drama of her life, on the humiliation she underwent. She had complained to Lenin, earlier on, about Stalin's brutality, and she knew her fears were shared; and yet Stalin managed to obtain her moral authority, witnessed by the declarations she made in his favour. She was a powerless witness of the liquidation of the entire Bolshevik Old Guard—her friends from the difficult times of the foundation of Bolshevism and from the years of exile.

She died on 19 February 1939.

G.H.

MAKSIM MAKSIMOVICH LITVINOV
(autobiography)

(Party pseudonyms: 'Papasha', 'Louvinić', 'Felix', 'Nits', 'Maksimovich', 'Kuznetsov')

I was born in 1876 into a middle-class family and received my education in a 'modern' school. At the age of seventeen I enlisted in the army, and during my service I began to study the social sciences and economics. I became acquainted with Marxism and the history of socialism, and immediately I was discharged in 1898 I embarked upon propaganda in workers' circles, first of all in the workers' settlement at Klintsy in Chernigov province. I had to work alone as there was no organisation there. I founded several circles in which, besides giving workers and craftsmen a general education, I taught them about Marxism and political economy. To escape police shadowing, in 1900 I moved to Kiev, where, after spending some time on peripheral work, I was accepted as a member of the Kiev RSDRP Committee. In 1901 I was arrested with the whole committee, and following the revelations of one of the committee members I was in danger of being exiled to eastern Siberia for five years. Whilst in prison, I joined the *Iskra* organisation, and after eighteen months in custody awaiting trial, I was one of eleven to escape from jail.

I made my way to Switzerland where I helped to edit *Iskra*, and at the congress of the League of Russian Social Democrats Abroad I was elected with Krupskaya and L. Deich to the administrative board of the League, which at that time was considered the effective centre of *Iskra*. After the split at the second Congress in London, I joined the Bolsheviks, in whose ranks I have worked ever since. Early in 1903, I returned secretly to Russia where I worked until the 1905 Revolution, at first as the fully authorised agent of the CC for the north-west area, having my headquarters in Riga and being responsible for the frontier.

At the same time, I joined the Riga RSDRP Committee and as its delegate attended the third Party Congress in London. After the split in the Party became official, I was elected a member of the Bolshevik centre in Russia, which then existed under the name of the 'Bureau of the Committee of the Majority'. I participated in the conference of the northern committees at Kolpino (together with Rykov, Zemlyachka, Vladimirsky, Rumyantsev and others). In summer 1905, on instructions from the CC, I prepared a landing-place on the island of Nargen, near Revel, for a shipment of arms ordered in England by Gapon and due to arrive aboard the *John Grafton*, which subsequently foundered on the Finnish coast. In autumn 1905 I was summoned by the CC to St

Petersburg, where with Krasin I set up the first legal social democratic newspaper *Novaya Zhizn*. With the onslaught of Stolypin's repression, in 1906, I was obliged to escape abroad, where I carried out a number of important assignments for the CC, including the purchase and dispatch of a boatload of arms for the Caucasus. (But the boat sank). In 1907 I again returned to Russia and was almost trapped by the police in Bonch-Bruevich's bookshop in St Petersburg. In the same year I was dispatched by the CC along the Volga to the Urals to organise a regional Party conference. After coming under observation by the police, I was obliged to travel abroad and remained an *émigré* (in London) for nearly ten years.

In 1907 I was a delegate and secretary to the Russian delegation at the International Congress in Stuttgart. I held the post of secretary in the London Bolshevik group and attended the Berne conference of *émigré* organisations in 1912. I was also a delegate in the Bolshevik section of the International Socialist Bureau, taking part in its first and second London Conferences.[1] At the second conference I delivered a protest against the participation of socialists in bourgeois governments and their support for the war, after which I walked out. I have been arrested in almost all the countries of Europe.

After the October Revolution I was appointed the first ambassador to England. Ten months later I was arrested as a hostage for Lockhart and we were later exchanged. In the RSFSR I was a Collegium member of Narkomindel and Rabkrin, plenipotentiary and trade representative in Estonia, where I was empowered by the Sovnarkom to deal in foreign currency, and was then appointed Deputy People's Commissar at Narkomindel. I travelled to Sweden and Denmark for negotiations with the bourgeois governments and concluded a series of agreements on the exchange of prisoners of war. I achieved the removal of the British blockade, made the first trade deals in Europe and dispatched the first cargoes after the blockade had been lifted. I was a member of the RSFSR delegation in Genoa and Chairman of the delegation to the Hague. I presided over the Moscow Disarmament Conference in 1923 and signed trade agreements with Germany and Norway.

Litvinov's autobiography resembles its author: brief, concise, without embellishment—and almost, one might add, too discreet.

He was an excellent organiser, and had been a member of the exiled intelligentsia which, full of initiative and imagination, of foresight and skill, had had the difficult task of managing the Party's secret funds during and after the 1905 Revolution.

[1] In 1913 and 1915.

From 1902, the time of his first exile in London, he became a close collaborator of Lenin, and gained the reputation of being one of the Party's best technicians. In particular, Litvinov was entrusted, in 1906, with the administration of funds accruing from the 'expropriations'. Money deposited with the secretary of the ISB was used in part to buy arms which Litvinov had to get smuggled into Russia. He was also closely involved in operating the exchange of the 500-rouble notes that were acquired at the 'expropriation' in Erevan Square, Tiflis, on 25 July 1907. These funds provoked much discord among Russian socialist exiles, and the whole affair had many stormy vicissitudes which put Litvinov at the centre of attack and controversy. He refused to show to his Menshevik opponents the 'confidential' documents concerning this affair, which had been deposited with the secretary of the ISB. On this occasion he proved himself to be not only a reliable conspirator and technician but also a clever diplomat. He managed to establish excellent relations with the secretary of the ISB.[1]

Litvinov lived in London under the name of Harrison from 1907 on, and was entrusted on several occasions with missions to social democratic parties and the ISB. In June 1914 he took over from Lenin as the RSDRP(b) representative to the ISB. During the First World War he used this position to maintain contacts that he attempted to exploit after the October Revolution.

From that date, his career was mapped out for him: as early as 1918, in Revel, he tried to break the economic blockade of Soviet Russia; after being entrusted with difficult diplomatic missions, he was called in 1921 to preside, at Chicherin's side, over the fate of Soviet foreign policy. The two men had nothing in common, and relations between them were difficult. Their differences were both personal and political. They were opposed both in character and in method. As Mikoyan has emphasised, Litvinov was cold, calculating, and flexible if not opportunist: '. . . he was no dogmatist. He found it easy to make Western politicians listen to him. [. . .] Stalin and the Central Committee held Litvinov in high esteem. It is no coincidence that he took over from Chicherin. He was unpretentious and had a complete mastery of manoeuvre.'[2]

With his lively, methodical and well-informed mind, Litvinov soon gained an international reputation and became the central figure in international conferences at the head of the Soviet delegation. It was he who represented the Soviet government at Geneva, at the meetings of

[1] See G. Haupt, 'Lénine, les Bolchéviques et la IIe Internationale', in *Cahiers du Monde Russe et Soviétique* no. 3 (1966), p. 388.

[2] Z. S. Sheynis, 'V Genne Gaage', in *Novaya i Noveyshaya Istorya* no. 3 (1968), p. 55.

the preparatory commission for the Disarmament Conference (1927–30), where he put forward a plan for general disarmament. In 1930 he succeeded Chicherin at the head of the People's Commissariat for Foreign Affairs.

This was not just a change of face, but a change of policy and staff. From the start Litvinov supported *rapprochement* with Western democracies and entry into the League of Nations. From 1932, he sought to elaborate a foreign policy which would first and foremost secure allies for the USSR against the rise of Fascism. In order to achieve this he had to overcome strong resistance at the top of the Soviet political hierarchy. At Lausanne, in 1932, a delegation of European socialists told him of their fears, and of the necessity of a common front against Germany. Litvinov replied that he was in disagreement with his government's attitude but that he did not dispose of sufficient leverage to change it.

Hitler's *coup* confirmed his position. Whereas Molotov, at the Sovnarkom session on 28 December 1933, only timidly attacked Germany's imperialist policy of annexation, Litvinov was far more virulent and threatened that Russia would enter into an anti-German alliance.

Litvinov's major objective, for which the League of Nations provided him with an audience between 1934 and 1938, while he was the Soviet representative, was to organise a defence system and to block the path of the aggressors, the Fascist states. But he was aware of the obstacles in the way of his anti-Nazi policies. When Léon Blum asked him, shortly before Munich, if France could count on the Soviet Union if the Czech affair deteriorated, Litvinov replied: 'If I remain People's Commissar, yes; if I don't, no.'

When Stalin drew up the policy that was to lead to the signing of the German–Soviet Pact, Litvinov, who was a Jew and Hitler's *bête noire*, was succeeded by Molotov on 4 May 1939. Recent Soviet encyclopedias have discreetly given it to be understood that it was not just a change of Commissar, but of a whole policy that could have been fatal to its author. In May 1939, 'in the condition of the Stalinist personality cult', he was relieved of his duties as Commissar for Foreign Affairs, and in February 1941, at the Party's eighteenth Conference, he was 'arbitrarily expelled from the Central Committee on the grounds that he had not fulfilled his duties as a member of the Central Committee of the Communist Party'.[1] He had in fact been elected to the Central Committee at the seventeenth Congress and re-elected at the subsequent one.

After Germany's aggression against the USSR, Stalin brought Litvinov out of the obscurity to which he had been relegated, in order to reassure his new allies, the USA in particular. It was, as it happened,

[1] *Sovietskaya Istoricheskaya Entsiklopediya*, vol. 8, p. 704.

Litvinov who had conducted the 1933 Washington talks with President Roosevelt which were concluded by the establishment of diplomatic relations with the USA.

In 1941 Litvinov became Deputy Commissar for Foreign Affairs, and Ambassador to Washington, where he spent the next two years. The role he was to play in the allied camp was revealed by his presence at the conference of the Foreign Ministers of the Soviet Union, the United Kingdom and the United States, held in Moscow in October 1943. He remained Deputy Commissar until 1946, but had no longer much weight in decisions on Soviet foreign policy. He had lost his quiet confidence, his dynamism and initiative; and according to Ehrenburg's *Memoirs*, he always had on him a loaded revolver to shoot himself if he were arrested.

Demoted to a subordinate position in the Foreign Ministry, he died on 31 December 1951.

Much ink has been spilled on Litvinov: among other things, on his apocryphal *Memoirs*, so accurate in its dates as to fool a famous historian into writing a preface. Litvinov's name still lives, however: his grandson Pavel has recently been sentenced to five years' 'exile' in Siberia for leading a demonstration against the Bukovsky trial, and another in Red Square against the Soviet invasion of Czechoslovakia.

G.H.

VYACHESLAV MIKHAILOVICH MOLOTOV
(authorised biography)

Vyacheslav Mikhailovich Molotov was born in February 1890 in the village of Kukarki, Nolinsk district, Vyatka province. His real name was Skryabin. He was the third son of a member of the Nolinsk *petite bourgeoisie*, Mikhail Skryabin. His parents devoted much time and effort to providing an education for their children. The latter were sent to the provincial capital to go to school. The brothers were all educated in Kazan, and Vyacheslav went to the 'modern' school there. It must be said that the Skryabin family were all very artistic. Vyacheslav played the violin quite well, with great feeling and expressiveness.

All the brothers, living amiably in a small room together, were drawn towards the most radical students. Kazan, particularly at that time, was literally overflowing with leftist intellectuals. When they went home to Nolinsk, the brothers found there either the same type of revolutionary-minded *déclassé* intellectuals, or political exiles. Coming themselves from a working-class background, the brothers naturally became imbued with the ideas and attitudes rife in this environment. Normally in secondary schools, revolutionary ideas found adherents among two categories of students, and correspondingly were assimilated and understood in two different ways. Firstly there were those elements who sneered at authority; they consisted mainly of the 'Kamchatka clan', that is those who sat in the back-row desks and fired peas at the teachers etc. They were mainly good types, free and easy, but not greatly attracted to learning, and they seized upon revolutionary ideas as something that freed them from the need to submit to teachers and other school 'minions', and justified their disregard for study. In the second category belonged the studious types, those who were among the best students but not the so-called 'swats': they studied out of a thirst for the knowledge that could be acquired at school, albeit in modest quantities. With them, revolutionary ideas provoked deep reflection. Far from distracting them from their school studies, it deepened their interest in theoretical work and made them think for themselves. Thanks to this, although doing schoolwork only in fits and starts while most of the time learning about scientific disciplines which were not taught in schools, a student could still achieve notable success in the 'official' curriculum. Vyacheslav belonged to this category.

Revolutionary ideas first reached him in Nolinsk in 1905. It is sufficient to recall that date for it to be clear that the first revolutionary impression on the soul of the 15-year-old boy occurred when it had been made soft, receptive and expectant by events. More eloquently than all conversations and speeches, the students were affected by the bare news of the railway and then of the general strike, the activity of the St Petersburg Soviet of Workers' Deputies, the blazing landowners' estates in Samara, Saratov, Tambov and Penza provinces, etc. Just at this time the brother of the well-known artist Vasnetsov was living in exile in Nolinsk. In Molotov's own words, Vasnetsov was the first man from whom he not only heard commentaries on everything that was happening, but also received a few practical revolutionary tasks. It was Vasnetsov who first asked the young Molotov whom he thought more suitable: the Mensheviks or the Bolsheviks. However, the same question was posed by the whole of life around him. As for the SR party, which was very active and vocal at that time, the question of joining it never arose for Molotov—possibly because he happened to move in an SD environment. Also the fact that Molotov went to a 'modern' school was important. At that time and later, it was apparent that Gymnasium students, who had a so-called 'classical' education, were drawn to the SR party, whilst 'modern' school pupils, budding engineers and industrial managers, mainly joined the SDs. The category of students to which Molotov belonged in his conception of the revolution was again divided into two groups. As they were thoughtful, and attentive to ideas and theory, some of them – and by no means a small proportion – interpreted revolutionary ideas in an abstract, bookish way. Marx was appreciated as a scholar, not a revolutionary. *Das Kapital* was read only as a theoretical work, not as a call to direct action. For such 'revolutionaries', conspiratorial circles were mainly organisations for self-education.

Molotov was one of those who, whilst striving for a scientific understanding of social problems, did not appreciate revolutionary ideas for their scientific, cognitive value alone. They sensed in them a call to action. Moreover, they were overtaken by events, so that besides theoretical learning one had as well to do practical work. That same Vasnetsov in Nolinsk organised a group of irregulars to manufacture explosives,[1] with Molotov as a member. So for him, self-education circles were both a school in revolution, a school in conspiracy, which would long remain useful, and a detachment of armed irregulars for which one had to learn about street fighting. In revolutionary circles at that time, particularly in the provinces, there were quite a few immature dogmatists who questioned everyone on the party to which they belonged and why, on the fraction to which they belonged inside the party and why, on what they thought of Martov's last attack on Lenin or Plekhanov's on Martynov, etc. Such questioning bewildered very many people and rushed them into a decision as to which group to join.

[1] The so-called 'chemical' group.

But Molotov was not confused by such immature insistence. Throughout all the storms of 1905, he would unfailingly answer: 'I haven't yet made out which SD fraction I belong to.' It was only towards the end of 1906 that his sympathies finally began to lean towards the Bolsheviks. Men of older generations were turning their backs in disappointment, but in their place came 'fresh workers in battle order, ready to do and die'. And as their revolutionary convictions were formed under Dubasov, Trepov, Stolypin and Durnovo, they were few in number, but by their moral fervour, by their fortitude in the ensuing struggle, they proved to be far stronger than many who had joined the Revolution during its romantic period in 1904–5 when its star was rising rather than waning.

From autumn 1906 Molotov worked in the local revolutionary organisation in secondary and higher schools, which disdained all party affiliations. In this organisation, practically the only real, that is convinced, Bolshevik was V. A. Tikhomirnov.[1] He and Molotov formed a tight and vigorous bloc which turned the so-called non-party revolutionary organisations into an arena for the contest of ideas between, on the one hand, Tikhomirnov and Molotov, and on the other, many members of the organisation including the leaders of the SRs. The ideological discussions were a good method of developing and strengthening a point of view and of instilling a long-lasting ideological discipline. Those discussions led by the end of 1907 to the defection of many SR members of the organisation, even some of the leaders, to the Marxist camp.

It was in this organisation that Molotov taught himself the craft of a propagandist. The other side of his work was purely practical. Under these conditions conspiratorial technique was essential, that is it was esssential to have a flat for meetings, methods of communication between various circles, a hidden cash-box with its necessary concomitant—a small accounts room. In addition there was a clandestine library. Molotov took the most active part in all this conspiratorial activity, and it was also necessary to increase the numbers in the organisation. He established contact with the Yelabuga group through Bazhanov[2] and the Penza group. The idea of founding an All-Russian Revolutionary Union of Secondary Schools and Institutes was mooted, which would of course involve the summoning of an illegal congress. Simultaneously a 'printer's' was set up and the first May Day proclamation was published. It was written by Molotov, and should be considered his first written

[1] This in many ways remarkable comrade was a Collegium member of Narkomindel from 1917 to 1919, when he died suddenly in Kazan.
[2] Now a Presidium member of the RSFSR Gosplan.

political statement. But he also put a lot of work into compiling the rules of the Revolutionary Union. He was the main inspiration behind our organisation's encouragement of the fresh student riots of 1909 in the name of the 1905 slogans of school freedom.

Of course, there was no lack of *agents provocateurs*. Just at the moment when the SD part of the organisation which had formed around Tikhomirnov and Molotov began its real propagandistic and ideological activity, that is between 1907 and 1909, two *provocateurs* infiltrated themselves into it. In March, Tikhomirnov was the first to be arrested, followed by Molotov and many other members a few days later.

Kazan prison, in which conditions were the same as those of the St Petersburg prisons in 1905, in other words extremely free and easy, was a real university for all the young people held there. Molotov devoted himself to study, and not merely the study of the social sciences. Besides further work on political economy and the history of the revolutionary movement, his attention was drawn by natural history.

In autumn he was deported with other comrades to Vologda province for two years. They were all pupils at secondary schools with the exception of Kitain, a professional Party worker, and Tikhomirnov, who had already graduated from a 'modern' school. Molotov, like other exiled 'modern' school students, was imprisoned almost the day before his final examinations, when he was in the top (seventh) form. He was confined to the town of Totma by the Vologda governor, Khvostov. There one of his preoccupations was to obtain the minister's permission to take his exams. No sooner, however, had he obtained permission to sit them in the Vologda 'modern' school and had been transferred there from Totma, than he re-established contact with local Party circles and above all with local workers. Consequently, the examinations were in a way pushed into the background. However, he did pass them, and thanks to the forgetfulness of the police authorities, he remained in Vologda. Here he plunged into energetic activity among the railwaymen. He had made contact with them through exiles linked with the Mytishchi workers, who had been expelled from Moscow province and had settled in Vologda, where they were mainly employed on the railway.

Under the eyes of the police in this small town, Molotov still managed, together with other comrades, for example Maltsev, to run an organised Party group, to arrange a few open air mass demonstrations beyond the town limits, and finally to issue a May Day proclamation in 1911, which he composed with other comrades, and which a few of them pasted on walls all over the town the night before without being caught. Soon afterwards, on 16 June 1911, Molotov completed his period of exile. So, too, by this time, had Tikhomirnov, who was allowed to replace part of his exile with emigration. Abroad he met Lenin, and as he had sufficient private means, they discussed the publication of a legal Bolshevik newspaper in Russia. On Lenin's initiative, Tikhomirnov devoted his resources, his energy and his knowledge to its creation. Of course, Tikhomirnov turned first of all to Molotov and his comrades. In 1911, a conference was held near Saratov to discuss the organisation of the paper. This was just after the end of Molotov's exile.

Molotov then went to St Petersburg and entered the Economics Department of the Polytechnical Institute. After joining the ranks of the active Bolsheviks there, he became most directly involved in *Zvezda*, which was then being created and later *Pravda*. Whilst working in the capital, he did not lose touch with his former comrades and used all possible means to attract the maximum number of them either morally or materially to support the great undertaking that had been launched.

Molotov soon became editorial secretary of *Pravda*. At the same time he carried on illegal work both as a member of the St Petersburg Committee and as a propagandist. Finally he took an active part in the work of the Duma 'fraction'. He naturally participated in the discussion of all vital questions of the day, and he was in personal communication with the *émigré* centre and Vladimir Ilyich.

These functions forced him to pay closer attention to purely governmental questions. It was thanks to the energy, resourcefulness and theoretical training of many *Pravda* activists, including Molotov, that there existed the closest contact between the paper, the Duma 'fraction', the *émigré* centre, and the mass of the proletariat of St Petersburg, Moscow, Vladimir, Ivanovo-Voznesensk, in fact of the whole of Russia.

It was at this time that Molotov's first writings appeared in print. His first article was published in *Pravda* under the signature 'Akim P-ta', that is 'Akim Prostota' ('Akim the simple')—one of Molotov's Party pseudonyms. He signed his next articles in *Pravda* with the name 'V. Mikhailov'. The first publication to which he put his own name was a pamphlet that appeared in Petrograd in 1919: *How the Workers Learn to Build Their Economy*.

In 1913 the police came to arrest Molotov at the editorial offices, but he jumped out of the window and escaped. He went underground, though without interrupting his revolutionary activity among the St Petersburg workers.

When it became difficult to continue to live in secret in the capital, he moved to Moscow. Moscow, as is only too well known now, was a city of *agents provocateurs* (at that time we only suspected it). So it was not surprising that Molotov's days of freedom were ended here through betrayal by an *agent provocateur*, and he was again imprisoned. This was to mark a change in his inner development from practical to theoretical studies, although a rapidly issued directive on his deportation to Irkutsk province interrupted his reading. The journey took place under the most unfavourable conditions and on arrival in Siberia he was directed to the village of Manzurka. During his exile he met new comrades—Latsis, Pylyaev and others. They all discussed the question of launching an illegal Bolshevik organ inside Russia itself. To implement this idea and continue the revolutionary struggle, Molotov escaped from Manzurka and reached Kazan. There he found shelter just outside the town in a suburb called Chukashovka, in a dacha belonging to the very same V. A. Tikhomirnov. There, too, he discussed with other comrades the re-establishment of the shattered Bolshevik organisation and the creation of an illegal newspaper.

In autumn 1915, Molotov and Tikhomirnov set off for Petrograd where they founded the '1915 Bolshevik Group'. It included Boky, Bazhanov, Arosev and other comrades. Its main concern was the formation of a permanent organisational nucleus free from *agents provocateurs*. Consequently new members could only be admitted on the unanimous agreement of all existing ones. It was this group that took measures towards the setting up of an illegal paper. In the face of greatly intensified government repression, however, the group disintegrated. Molotov began to rebuild it. He managed to trace almost everybody and obtain an assurance of help with the paper. Pylyaev and Comrade Emma, who had escaped from exile, were preparing to install themselves in an underground press and begin printing the paper. At the end of 1916, Shlyapnikov arrived from abroad as an agent of the CC. In Petrograd a CC bureau was established, of which Molotov was a member. He was also extremely active in the Petrograd organisation, which increasingly expanded its activities.

The 1917 Revolution found Molotov and many other comrades in a state of readiness. In October, he became a member of the Petrograd Military Revolutionary Committee.

After the establishment of Soviet power, he became Chairman of the Economic Council for the Petrograd district. In 1919 he was dispatched by the CC to Nizhny Novgorod where he became Chairman of the province *Ispolkom*. From there, he moved to the Donbass as Secretary of the province's Committee. Then at the All-Ukrainian Party Conference in 1920 he was elected a Secretary of the Ukrainian CP. In 1921 he was a delegate to the All-Russian Party Congress and there, on Lenin's nomination, he was elected a member and a Secretary of the CC of the RKP.

A. Arosev.

Molotov was a Bolshevik militant as early as 1906, and subsequently rose with great speed to the highest responsibilities: by 1912, he was the editorial secretary of *Pravda*. With Stalin and Raskolnikov, he was a 'conciliator' and fought against Lenin's line; but the leader lost his temper with the 'milksops who are ruining the cause' and had Molotov replaced by Sverdlov. By the end of 1916, Molotov was on the reconstituted Central Committee's Russian Bureau, and in this post ran *Pravda* together with Shlyapnikov for a week before being appointed to the Presidium of VTsIK. Feeling too inexperienced for this position, however, he requested to be relieved of his duties. At that time he was on the Party's left wing and opposed to Stalin and Kamenev.

In the following period he played a secondary role. Molotov (whom his less friendly comrades called 'Iron arse') was basically an *apparatchik*—an office man and administrator. As the Civil War subsided and buffers replaced cannon, he went to the Central Committee, as an alternate member in 1920, and as a full member in 1921. At this date he also became one of the three Central Committee secretaries to replace the 'Trotskyites' Serebryakov, Krestinsky and Preobrazhensky, as well as becoming a member of the Orgburo and an alternate member of the Politburo.

Like his old friend Stalin (whom he had known since 1912, and whom he was one of the first to support), Molotov thus found himself at the heart of the machine. He was appointed to full membership of the Politburo in December 1925, and entrusted with the arrangements for the sixth Congress of the International (July 1928), at the head of which he succeeded Bukharin in 1929. On 18 December 1930 he was appointed in Rykov's place to the presidency of the Council of People's Commissars, and appeared to be Stalin's number two. He supported the leader for all he was worth in 1929 to make the Politburo accept increased rates of collectivisation, but it was often rumoured in Moscow in 1930–2, according to the *Byulleten Oppozitsii*'s correspondents, that he was the leader of an anti-Stalin group within the Politburo; and, at the same time, that Stalin was throwing the blame on him for the catastrophes of the so-called 'third period' policies which made social democracy the main enemy. In any case Molotov's name did not appear on the list of potential assassination victims at the first Moscow trial in 1936. Whatever disagreements there may have been were then overcome, since Molotov was on the lists of 'assassination victims' at the two subsequent Moscow trials; and at the end of 1937, it was he who directed the massive purge of the top *cadres* of the Ukrainian CP of old members of Stalin's splinter, such as Kossior and Chubar. . . .

When Stalin decided on the *rapprochement* with Hitler, he replaced

Litvinow with Molotov at the People's Commissariat for Foreign Affairs on 4 May 1939, where the latter stayed until March 1949. In May 1940, Stalin took over from him as president of the Council of People's Commissars. From May 1939 on, he was Stalin's itinerant diplomat, the man of treaties and conferences where his stubbornness was a subject of wonderment. Appointed First Vice-President of the Council of Ministers in March 1946, Molotov seemed destined, towards the end of Stalin's life, to fall by the hand of his former comrade. He was not on the new Secretariat which was to replace the Politburo; and in 1949, Stalin deported Molotov's wife, a Jewish artist, and decimated the ranks of his former collaborators in the Foreign Ministry. At the twentieth Congress, Khrushchev claimed that had Stalin not died so fortunately, Molotov and Mikoyan would probably have been liquidated.

By this time, however, Molotov was already in a bad position. In September 1955 his colleagues on the Presidium forced him to publish a self-criticism in the review *Kommunist* because he had claimed in a speech the preceding February that the USSR had built 'the bases of socialism'. He had to admit that socialism was already fully built in the USSR. In June 1957, he was one of the leaders of the offensive against Khrushchev inside the Politburo, and, once beaten, was eliminated as a member of the 'anti-party group'. At the twenty-second Congress (December 1961), a much more serious offensive was launched against him: he was accused of direct involvement in the murders and provocations that had taken place under Stalin's rule. The following year he was expelled from the Party, with Kaganovich and Malenkov. He was recalled from the minor diplomatic post he held in Vienna, since when he has spent his time tending his garden and writing his memoirs: and every day, the man whom unimaginative journalists dubbed 'Mr Nyet' goes off to the Lenin Library to work on the books he needs for this task.

Molotov was born to play second fiddle. He was certainly Stalin's ideal 'number two' and complemented him. Molotov had no other ambition than to be the leader's executive, and the very signs of his liquidation in 1952–3 cannot be taken to show him as a potential rival.

J.-J. M.

NIKOLAY IVANOVICH MURALOV
(autobiography)

I was born in 1877 on a farm called 'The Companies' near Taganrog. My father was a farmer, and from my earliest childhood until the age of seventeen I helped him on the farm (ploughing, harrowing, scything and threshing). In winter I learned to read and write—my father, Ivan Anastasevich, had started teaching me when I was six. He was a cultured man. He had spent six years in a classical Gymnasium, had volunteered for the army during the Crimean War, had fought at Balaklava, had been awarded the Order of St George, fourth class, for bravery in battle, shortly before being taken prisoner by the British and spending two years in Plymouth. He had made the acquaintance of Herzen, had become one of his admirers and on his return to Russia had received *Kolokol*. He was a very widely read man. When he lost his sight, he made people recite to him literature of all types—*belles-lettres*, history, philosophy, science, natural science, etc.

When I was seventeen, I went away to study, passed the examination for the second year of agricultural school, from which I graduated three years later, and returned to my father. He died soon afterwards. I began my practical work on the estate of a landowner called Plokhovo in the village of Znamenka, Tambov district, but after one season he accused me of familiarity with the workers, we had an argument, and I was engaged as manager of the Meien estate in the village of Nazarov in Moscow province. I attempted to do my military service in Moscow in the Grenadier Regiment. I was accepted as a volunteer, but the all-powerful Trepov would not give me a certificate of political reliability. I had to leave the regiment and return to Taganrog for service there. At call-up time, there was a surplus of recruits, so I was given an exemption and put instead on the first reserve list. After this (in autumn 1899) I went to the town of Maikop in the Caucasus where I became manager first of a distillery and then of a creamery. There I joined a Marxist circle (reading *Das Kapital* and *Iskra*), a workers' circle and a Sunday school.

At the beginning of 1902 I went on holiday to Moscow, when I was arrested and jailed for three months. In the autumn of the same year, I became a member of the Marxist circle in Serpukhov, and I studied *zemstvo* statistics and *zemstvo* insurance. In early 1903 I became assistant *zemstvo* agronomist in the town of Podolsk (Moscow province). It was then and there that I joined the RSDRP(b) Party.

In November 1905 I fought my way out of a Black Hundred[1] pogrom

[1] Black Hundreds were bands of semi-organised, usually anti-semitic, right-wing extremists.

with a gun in my hand, rushed to Moscow, and there took part in the December rising. After its suppression (in January 1906), I escaped to farms on the Don. I worked in the Don organisation and in the Taganrog group (a mixed, almost unnatural organisation of Bolsheviks and Mensheviks), where I was responsible for agrarian affairs. I was searched twice, then arrested, held in custody in Taganrog and later Novonikolaev prison. After my release I went to Moscow, then to Tula province, and in 1907 found a job as manager of an estate. In the village of Podmoklovoye, a group of comrades and myself opened a popular tearoom under the flag of the 'Temperance Society', where we printed proclamations for the Serpukhov organisation, distributed illegal literature, and read lectures on agronomy and the labour movement.

During the Imperialist War, I was called up into the 215th Infantry Regiment, and was then transferred to a transport regiment, where I remained until the February Revolution. With other comrades, I organised the soldiers' section of the Moscow Soviet, and in October I was a member of the Moscow RVS and the revolutionary headquarters staff. After the victory over the cadets, I was appointed Commander of the Moscow Military District. On 19 March 1919 I became a member of the Third Army's RVS. In June I was appointed to the Council for the whole front, in August to the Council of the Twelfth Army, in August 1920 a Collegium member of the People's Commissariat for Agriculture, on 1 March 1921 Commander of the Moscow Military District, and in May 1924 Commander of the North Caucasus Military District. In February 1925 I was detached for 'particularly important' assignments on behalf of the RVS of the USSR.

Muralov was one of the very few personal friends Trotsky had, one of the two or three comrades-in-arms – others were Rakovsky and Ivan Smirnov – of whom he spoke with feeling. In Trotsky's own words, they had been tied since 1917 'by an indissoluble fighting and political friendship'. Muralov, an intrepid and benign giant of a man, was an agronomist who, unlike most other Bolsheviks, did not write very much; by the force of circumstance he became a 'fighter' and subsequently one of the pillars of the Red Army. He was certainly benign: as a member of the Moscow Soviet's RVS in 1917, he agreed to negotiate with the Provisional government in order to avoid bloodshed. When the defeated party demanded the dissolution of the Red Guard and the arrest of the RVS, he became angry and suspended the negotiations; but since the Whites' chauffeur had left, Muralov took them off in his own car so that they would not be lynched by the soldiers.

When on 27 February 1917 the Revolution broke out in Moscow,

Muralov was a soldier in a motorised company. He led a detachment which overran the radio station, and went on to open the prisons. He was on the Presidium of the Soldiers' Section of the Moscow Soviet from its inception. A man of simple manners, he retained friendly, man-to-man relations with the Moscow Cossack troops, his 'countrymen': and in the October battles, the Moscow Cossacks remained neutral. When the military organisation of the Bolshevik Party's Moscow Committee decided, at the end of September, to make practical preparations for an insurrection without making even the sketchiest of plans, Muralov modestly tried to gather information. He kept a cool head just as he had done during the July days, but he did admit that a cool head could not, in the Moscow insurrection, make up for 'our small aptitude at leading the fighting masses [. . .] and our total ignorance of street fighting', made all the worse in his case by an obvious repugnance for bloodshed.

The Civil War brought this professional agronomist to the highest responsibilities. To quote Trotsky again: 'Straightforward and unpretentious, Muralov carried on a tireless propaganda effort throughout the campaign by making himself useful to everybody: in his leisure hours he gave advice to farmers, harvested the wheat, looked after people and livestock.'

After the Civil War, and as General Inspector of the Red Army, he gave his signature to the so-called 'Declaration of the 46' of October 1923, which began the left-wing opposition struggle against the machine. He remained one of the pillars of the opposition until the fifteenth Congress, where he gave a measured but cutting speech which roused the audience to fury. He was constantly interrupted by shouts of 'Liar! Get him off the platform! Go work in the fields! Down with Muralov! Why doesn't he respect the Congress? You're Mensheviks, traitors of the working class! Stop making fun of Congress! Down with the platform!' He ended his speech thus: 'If I criticise, then I am criticising my own Party and my own actions—in the interest of the cause and not to toady to anyone.'

Straight after the Congress he was expelled and sent to work in the country, in Siberia. He was one of the four signatories to the letter sent to the fifteenth Congress in April 1930 by the leaders of the opposition, which demanded free expression for all oppositions which advocated the 'principle of a *single* party and the methods of *reform*'.

While many opposition leaders, under the pressure of the Terror, became demoralised and capitulated, Moralov stood firm. Stalin brought him to Moscow, and then let him out of prison in 1934. Muralov worked in Siberia, far from any political activity, but refused to sign the denunciation of Trotsky. After the capitulation of Sosnovsky and Rakovsky in

1934, he was the last 'big' name of the left-wing opposition not to have publicly denounced his past.

In 1936 he was arrested by the police, who then announced the forth-coming second Moscow trial, with Pyatakov, Radek, Screbyakov and Sokolnikov as star defendants. A second announcement added that Muralov would also be a defendant. At the trial, Radek gave a sarcastic emphasis to the importance of this fact:

> When Nikolay Ivanovich Muralov, the man who was nearest to Trotsky, and who I thought was prepared to die in prison rather than talk, when such a man has made his declaration and justified it by saying that he did not want to die with the idea that his name would become a rallying-point for the counter-revolutionary scum, well then that's the most profound outcome of this trial.

Muralov himself underlined the importance of the service he was ren-dering to Stalin: 'If I had stuck to my guns, I would in a sense have become a rallying-point for the counter-revolutionary elements which unfortunately still exist in the Soviet Republic. I did not wish to be the seed that would grow not into beneficent wheat, but chaff.' Renouncing his whole past life at one go, he said at the end of his final statement: 'For more than ten years I was a faithful soldier of Trotsky, the evil-doer of the working class, the Fascist agent worthy of all our contempt, that enemy of the working class and of the Soviet Union.' This last service rendered, the old revolutionary was no more use: he was sen-tenced to death and shot. Trotsky was hit so hard by this that he hardly mentions Muralov in his account of this second trial.

Muralov was the second Trotskyite to be rehabilitated (after Voron-sky). In 1966, *Sovietskaya Rossiya* hailed him as a 'courageous and stal-wart Leninist, an illustrious statesman and a solid Bolshevik'. It is not known why this official homage should, today, be paid to this obstinate, calm Bolshevik, who had remained unruffled in the harshest difficulties, and who resisted the trials of defeat and terror for seven long years.

J.-J. M.

GRIGORY (SERGO) KONSTANTINOVICH ORDZHONIKIDZE
(authorised biography)

Grigory Konstantinovich Ordzhonikidze was born in 1886 into the family of a minor nobleman in the village of Goresha, Shoropansk district, western Georgia. He received his initial education in the Kharagaul two-year school, after which he went to the Mikhailov Hospital Medical School in Tiflis, graduating in 1905. In 1903 he joined the RSDRP and was a member of the Bolshevik faction until the Party's name was changed. After leaving school, he worked for some time in western Georgia as a propagandist and agitator. In autumn 1905 he took a very active part in Party and revolutionary activity in the town of Gudauta in Abkhazia.

On 24 December 1905 Ordzhonikidze was arrested with other comrades not far from Gudauta in the village of Bombary, whilst they were conveying arms from Gagra. He remained in prison at Sukhum until the end of April when he was charged under Article 126, part 2, and released on bail. After this he went to Germany for a short while. He returned in 1907 to Baku and engaged in Party activity, at the same time working as a doctor's assistant at the Shamsi Asadullayev oilfields in Romany.

On May Day 1907 he was arrested at a demonstration on Mt 'Stenka Razin' and was held for twenty-six days in Baku prison under the name of Kuchkishvili. On his release, he continued his activities. Working with him were Stalin, S. Shaumyan, A. Dzhaparidze, Spandarian, Mdivani and others. In October of the same year he was again arrested and under Article 102 sentenced to deportation for membership of the RSDRP(b), after which he was brought back to Sukhum to stand trial for the 1905 affair and was sentenced to eighteen months in a fortress.

In spring 1909 he was deported to the village of Pataskuya, Pinchuk district, Yenisey province. After two months' exile he made his way to Persia via Baku. At this time the Persian revolution was still in progress and Ordzhonikidze took part in it. Whilst there, he maintained permanent contact with the Bolshevik group in Paris, received through Krupskaya our *émigré* publications and formed groups to advance our cause in Enzeli and Resht. At the end of 1910 he left for Paris.

There he began to work with the Leninist Bolsheviks. In summer 1911 he spent some time at the Party school near Paris which Lenin had organised. After the split in the Foreign Bureau and the creation of an *émigré* commission to organise the summoning of a Party Conference, he was dispatched to Russia with Rykov, Shwartz and Breslav to organise a similar commission inside Russia.

After visiting a number of towns in the north, the south and the Caucasus, he managed to form this commission. Its first meeting took place in Baku, attended by representatives from the Urals (in the person of S. Schwartz), Kiev and Ekaterinoslav. The Moscow and St Petersburg delegates were arrested on their way there. After this first session, and the collapse of the Baku organisation, the commission moved to Tiflis where it completed it work. Elections for the conference were held, and then Ordzhonikidze left for Paris, later going on to Prague where the conference was to meet. When it was over, he immediately returned to Russia to organise the CC Russian Bureau, and went to Vologda to see Stalin who was in exile there. Stalin had been elected to the CC by the Paris Conference and was a member of the Russian Bureau. He and Ordzhonikidze left for the Caucasus.

They returned together to St Petersburg, where Ordzhonikidze was arrested in April 1912, giving the name of Guseinov. The secret police, however, soon discovered his identity, and he was charged with escaping from exile. After six months in custody, he was sentenced to three years' hard labour which he served in the Schlüsselberg fortress.

In autumn 1915 he was deported to the Aleksandrov transit jail in Siberia and in spring 1916 he was sent to Yakutsk. Until the February Revolution he lived in the village of Pokrovsky near Yakutsk, and worked as medical assistant in the clinic there. Together with Gubelman (Yaroslavsky), Kirsanova, G. I. Petrovsky and other comrades, he continued his Party activity. After the February Revolution, he and the above-named comrades, as well as some others, worked for the establishment of Soviet power in Yakutsk, and he was a member of the local Executive Committee. In May he left on the first boat from Yakutsk and in June arrived in Petrograd.

Here, on Lenin's suggestion, he was included in the Petrograd Committee and its Executive Committee. He worked there with Stalin and others until the beginning of autumn when he went to the Caucasus for a brief period, returning to Petrograd on 24 October. After the October Revolution, he and Manuilsky were dispatched to the units fighting against Kerensky near the village of Pulkovo. Then he was appointed emergency Commissar for the Ukraine, southern Russia and the northern Caucasus.

He was at the front throughout the Civil War—first of all at Tsaritsyn and then in the northern Caucasus. After the crushing defeat of our army there and its retreat to Astrakhan, Ordzhonikidze, with A. Nazaretyan, F. Makharadze and a group of hill tribesmen led by B. Kalmykov and

Artskanov, withdrew into the mountains of Ingushetiya. In spring 1919 Ordzhonikidze made his way secretly across the Caucasus mountains into Menshevik Georgia, and thence to Baku. There he, Kamo, Varo Dzhaparidze and others took a Turkmen fishing boat and after drifting for thirteen days, reached Astrakhan. After that he went to Moscow.

Next he was sent to see Stalin, at that time a member of the RVS of the Western Front. Ordzhonikidze was appointed a member of the Twelfth Army's RVS, where he stayed until Mamontov broke through the Southern Front. He was transferred with a Lettish division to that front and made a member of the Fourteenth Army's RVS. After the capture of Kharkov, he was moved to the Caucasian Front as a member of its RVS and Chairman of the Caucasian Revolutionary Committee. Here he worked with Kirov, Mdivani, Stopani, Tukhachevsky and others. He and Kirov were among those who entered Baku at dawn on May Day, and then in 1920 and 1921 he was actively engaged in the establishment of Soviet power in Armenia and Georgia.

At the present time, Ordzhonikidze is Chairman of the TsKK, People's Commissar for Rabkrin, Deputy Chairman of the Sovnarkom of the USSR and Deputy Chairman of the Labour and Defence Council. Since the tenth Party Congress he has been a CC member of the VKP(b); he is Chief Secretary of the Transcaucasian Area Committee, a member of the RVS of the USSR and the Red Army Committee, a member of Transcaucasian TsIK, the Georgian TsIK, and a whole series of Soviet and trade union organisations.

Bombin

Ordzhonikidze was an old friend of Lenin, and an even older friend of Stalin—and for a short while, in 1922–3, he was torn between the two 'faiths'. He chose his countryman, Stalin. True, Lenin was by then bed-ridden and semi-paralysed. 'Sergo' was impetuous, brutal, disorganised and effervescent, quick with his laugh as with his temper. He was half pragmatist, half daredevil—a pragmatist whose political courage was undoubtedly not up to the daredevil's temerity.

After Kirov, he is the second member of the Bolshevik Party's Stalinist splinter to have grown into a myth. As a mustachioed agitator, he was one of Stalin's first companions – they met at Tiflis in 1906, as editors of the newspaper *Dro* – as well as being one of Lenin's first 'pupils'. He was educated in 1911 at the school at Longjumeau, and then elected in 1912 to the officially proclaimed Bolshevik Party's Central Committee and the Russian Bureau of the Central Committee. His death, though less sensational than Kirov's, was none the less suspicious; but since it was of no particular use to the ruling clique, Sergo slowly sank into silence, whence he emerged after Stalin's death: he then appeared to the survivors as a witness of the good old days of 'communism'.

Like Stalin, Ordzhonikidze was both a Georgian and a member of the Baku Committee; and he rose through the Party machine at about the same time as Stalin. Both came into the Party leadership for the first time in 1912. Like Stalin and all his group, Sergo did not appreciate intellectual dispute, and Voznesensky, no doubt unconsciously, reflects this in his poem *Longjumeau* when he shows Sergo asleep. . . .

On the other hand, Sergo was no mere 'internal revolutionary': he was in Berlin from August 1906 until January 1907; in October 1910 he left for Iran, and in November he went on to Paris. Lenin sent him to Russia, and he was back in Paris the following October. He took part in the Prague Conference, but after it went back to Russia, which he never left again.

The February Revolution found him in Yakutia, whither he had been deported in 1915. He remained in this desolate region as a member of the Yakut TsIK until the end of May, and with Petrovsky and Yaroslavsky brought out a newspaper, *Sotsial-Demokrat*, which defended the union with the Mensheviks and a policy of critical support for the Provisional government. On his return to Petrograd he played only a minor role in the Revolution and Civil War. He held various posts on the Southern Front and in the northern Caucasus (Extraordinary Provisional Commissar for the Ukraine Region, then for the Southern District). Having presided over the dislocation of the Eleventh Army, out of hostility for 'specialists' and centralisation, he bombarded Trotsky with attacks in his letters and cables to Lenin: 'All we do is to feed the army with the promises of Trotsky and Shlyapnikov—but that won't beat Denikin.' 'Where is Trotsky's order, discipline and regular army? How can he have let things degenerate this far? [. . .] Where did anyone get the idea that Sokolnikov could command an army? [. . .] It's an insult to the country. Do we have to humour Sokolnikov's pride so far as to let him play around with a whole army?'

This attitude could not but strengthen Sergo's links with Stalin. It was with Stalin that he plotted the invasion of Georgia, which took most of the Politburo by surprise in February 1921. Sergo was the military head of the invasion. As Secretary of the Party's Caucasian (later Transcaucasian) Bureau, and the representative in Georgia of the Russian Republic, he was Stalin's instrument in the country for his russification policy. Many Georgian communists rebelled against this policy and against the draft Constitution in which it was embodied. Unused to discussion and offended at being put in a minority in his homeland, Ordzhonikidze lost his temper, called meetings, dismissed men, moved about, threatened—in short, behaved like a proconsul in a conquered territory. One day, he slapped Kabanidze, a Georgian communist. Lenin was informed of Sergo's conduct and of the methods used to apply a nationalistic policy he himself disliked, and from his sick-bed exclaimed in anger: 'If things went so far as to make Ordzhonikidze so lose his temper as to use physical violence, as comrade Dzerzhinsky tells me, then one can imagine what a morass we have got ourselves into.' Lenin stigmatised Ordzhonikidze's 'exploits' in the use of force, and demanded that he should 'be punished in exemplary fashion (and I say this with regret, all the more since I belong to his circle of friends, and since I worked with him abroad in the emigration)'. Lenin wanted Ordzhonikidze expelled from the Party, but illness prevented him from letting off the 'Georgian bombshell' at the twelfth Congress.

Stalin had his own way of replying to this: three years later, in November 1926, he appointed Ordzhonikidze to the presidency of the Central Control Commission, and entrusted him thereby with the expulsion of the opposition. He carried this out hesitatingly, seeking to slow the rate of expulsions and to reach a compromise, then fell ill when Stalin, a lot less sure of things than he appeared to be, impatiently demanded that the abscess should be lanced before the fifteenth Congress. Ordzhonikidze was even less happy about waging the infinitely less harsh struggle against the right wing. From then on, it seems, he played some kind of double game, no doubt inspired by fear at the rise of Stalin, to whom he nevertheless remained faithful in all public utterances. Zinoviev gave this evidence to the Central Control Commission, presided over by Sergo: 'In 1925, Ordzhonikidze told me to "Write against Stalin".' Three years later, Bukharin told Kamenev that 'Sergo was disloyal. He came to my place, insulted Stalin in the worst possible way, and at the critical moment betrayed him.'

The 'treason' paid off: Sergo was appointed an alternate member of the Politburo in 1926, and a full member in 1930. In 1932, he became Commissar for Heavy Industry. His deputy, Pyatakov, organised the work of this key commissariat during the Five Year Plans, while the disorganised Sergo took all the credit for it.

His position was then threatened: an unseen conflict brought him up against a pure product of Stalinism, Beria. In 1931, Kartvelishvili, First Secretary of the Transcaucasian Bureau and one of Sergo's underlings, tried to stop Beria's rise. He was deported for his pains and succeeded by Beria himself. In November 1936, Sergo's deputy, Pyatakov, was denounced during the Novosibirsk trial, and found himself one of the accused at the second Moscow trial, where he was sentenced to death.

Sergo tried to save him, but, according to Sergo's Soviet biographer, Dubinsky-Mukhadze, Stalin made a cruelly ironical reply: 'Sergo is making his last attempt to explain to his old friend Stalin that the darkest forces are now abusing his traditional and pathological suspicion, and that the Party is losing its best militants'. The net was tightening inexorably around Sergo. Papulya, his elder brother, was shot after torture. Alyosha Svanidze was sentenced to death—Alyosha Svanidze, with whom he had often shared his last crust of bread. Alyosha's sister was Stalin's wife, the mother of his son. . . . Shortly before that, a search had been made of Ordzhonikidze's flat. Offended, and disenchanted, he telephoned Stalin all night long. In the small hours Stalin answered: 'The NKVD is a body that can come and search even my flat. Perfectly in order.'

On the morning of the 17th he had a talk with Stalin, a few hours of face-to-face conversation. Then a second talk on the telephone after Sergo had returned home. It was a very heated exchange, with insults flying in both directions, in Russian and in Georgian.

Sergo died. In the words of Dubinsky-Mukhadze: '. . . shortly afterwards, the Commissar for Health, Kaminsky, was arrested and shot. He had been a Baku militant and a friend of Sergo; and it was with extreme reluctance that he signed the official death "certificate".'

If this means anything, it must mean that Kaminsky found Sergo's death suspicious. It is said that during the furious conversation with Stalin alluded to by Dubinsky-Mukhadze, Sergo had threatened to denounce the General Secretary before the Central Committee Plenum in February and March 1937. And according to Krivitsky, the NKVD encouraged Ordzhonikidze's 'suicide', for he had become, in all evidence, an embarrassing witness for the man whom he had helped gain absolute power.

J.-J. M.

GEORGY LEONIDOVICH PYATAKOV
(autobiography)

I was born on 6 August 1890 at the Maryinsky sugar refinery in Cherkassk district, Kiev province. My father, Leonid Timofeyevich Pyatakov, was an engineer and the director of the refinery. In 1902 I entered the third form of the St Catherine 'modern' school in Kiev. In 1904 I joined a revolutionary student circle of a vaguely social democratic nature. In 1905 I instigated a student 'disturbance', was a member of the student liaison committee, and participated in street demonstrations and meetings. I was expelled from school for leading the 'school revolution', and took the sixth-form examinations externally.

At the same time, I began to associate with anarchists and in summer 1906 spread their propaganda among young peasants and workers. I was the leader of a group of fifty which banded together with another group, headed by Iustin Zhuk, to form an 'expropriation' party led by him. After carrying out the 'expropriations', the groups dissolved. In 1906–7 I re-entered the school but was again expelled for an insolent argument' with the school chaplain. In 1907 I sat the school-leaving examination as an external student. [. . .] In the autumn I joined a completely autonomous terrorist group which aimed at assassinating the Kiev military governor, Sukhomlinov. At this time, however, I began to undergo a serious, inner crisis. Anarchist practices sickened me, and anarchist ideology (I belonged to the Kropotkin type of anarchistic communists) no longer satisfied me. I engaged in a wide and careful study of revolutionary literature. I was particularly impressed by Plekhanov's *The Development of a Monistic View of History* (even before this I had been a materialist and a Darwinist), and Lenin's *The Development of Capitalism* and *What Is To Be Done?*. After that I broke completely with anarchism and took my place as a Marxist.

It was at this time that, after passing the Latin examination as an external student, I entered St Petersburg University. The years 1907–10 I devoted to purely theoretical work, in particular the study of Marx and Marxist literature, the classics of political economy (Quesnay, Adam Smith, Ricardo), contemporary economic literature, the Russian economy, statistics (particularly mathematical statistics), and philosophy (Spinoza, Kant, Fichte, Hegel and contemporary movements). By 1910 I had developed as a fully convinced, orthodox Marxist. I became linked with the university social democrats and joined the Party. At the end of 1910 disturbances took place in the university (the 'Tolstoy' and 'Sazonov' days). I was arrested for participating in them and kept under strict surveillance for three months, after which I was expelled from the university by the Minister of Education, Kasso, and banished from St Petersburg to Kiev.

The SD organisation there had collapsed, and on my arrival I made contact with E. B. Bosch, Ya. Shilgan and other comrades. We formed a group to explore the possibilities of resurrecting the underground organisation. We traced the remnants of the Kiev RSDRP Committee and together summoned a city conference which officially set up the organisation, elected a committee (which included E. B. Bosch, D. Schwartz, V. Averkin and Pigosyants), and delegated D. Schwartz to attend the All-Russian Bolshevik Conference in January 1912, at which the RSDRP CC was re-elected.

Our illegal work was accompanied by a furious struggle with the 'liquidators'. The Lena tragedy gave us the opportunity of making ourselves known publicly with a strike and meetings, which led to the downfall of the Committee and the organisation. A few of us remained at liberty and we had to recommence all our work; at one and the same time I personally had to be Secretary of the Committee, store illegal literature, manage the underground printing-press, write proclamations and print them, re-establish contacts and lead study groups; in a word, do too many things for conditions of secrecy. In June 1912 I was arrested with some other Committee members, and in November 1913 came my trial. I was accused under article 102 and condemned with five comrades to deportation. In April 1914 I arrived at my place of exile in Irkutsk province, but in October escaped abroad via Japan. I did so because I wished to make up my own mind about the international outlook following the collapse of the second International, for from the first days of the war I had adopted a firmly internationalist and anti-war position.

I reached Switzerland just in time for the Berne Bolshevik Conference, whose decisions I wholeheartedly approved. Then Lenin, Zinoviev, Bukharin, Bosch and I combined to publish the journal *Kommunist*, producing the first two editions. In late 1915 a conflict arose between Lenin on the one side, and myself, Bukharin and Bosch on the other, about the nationalities question and the future direction of *Kommunist*. We all followed an incorrect line and the journal closed. The three of us moved to Stockholm where we played some part in the preparations for the Congress of the Swedish left, after which the Swedes were arrested. The same fate befell Bukharin, and later myself, Surits and Gordon.

After our arrest we were all sent to Oslo, which is where the February Revolution found me. Immediately Bosch and I left for Russia, but at the border I was arrested for being in possession of a forged passport, detained in Torneo jail for three days, and then sent under escort to

Petrograd. From there I went to Kiev and without more ado joined the Bolshevik organisation, becoming Chairman of the Kiev Committee and a member of the city Soviet *Ispolkom*. In September I was elected Chairman of the latter, and in October became Chairman of the Revolutionary Committee. I was arrested by cadets and Cossacks, but was released by the rising of workers and soldiers. Then I was summoned to Petrograd by Lenin to take over control of Gosbank, which I did with Osinsky. Until the Brest-Litovsk treaty, I was Assistant Chief Commissar and then Chief Commissar of Gosbank. I disagreed with the CC over the treaty, however, and left for the Ukraine to fight against the advancing German and nationalist forces.

I joined Primakov's detachment in which I performed various functions: I carried out political work, published a news-sheet with Lebedev called *K Oruzhiyu !*, administered justice and inflicted punishment, was a scout and a machine-gunner. By April 1918 we had been driven back to the line Taganrog-Rostov. Here a group of comrades was formed to summon a conference of the Ukrainian CP(b), and the TsIK of the Ukraine formed an underground Government of Workers and Peasants. I was included in both organisations and until the end of 1918 I participated actively in illegal Party and insurrectionary activity in the Ukraine. In summer 1918 I helped suppress the left-wing SR rebellion, and in December, after the German revolution and the start of the Ukraine rising, I became President of the Provisional Workers' and Peasants' Government of the Ukraine.

During the Denikin attack I was appointed to the RVS of the Third Army, and later became Commissar of the Forty-second Division in the same army. When the tide began to turn against Denikin, I was recalled to Moscow where I was briefly Commissar of the General Staff Academy, and then Trotsky and I departed for the Urals with the First Labour Army. But the Polish war broke out and in May 1920 I was posted to the Polish Front as a member of the RVS of the Sixth Army, where I remained until autumn 1920. After the conclusion of peace with Poland I was transferred to the Wrangel Front as a member of the RVS of the Sixth Army. Following Wrangel's defeat I was appointed Chairman of the Central Board for the Coal Industry in the Donbass, since when I have been permanently engaged in economic work, for example as head of the Main Fuel Directorate, Deputy Chairman of Gosplan, Chairman of Glavkontseskom, and, since the summer of 1923, Deputy Chairman of VSNKh.

Pyatakov was a brilliant and gifted man, possessing not only a solid education as an economist and a broad Marxist culture, but also, thanks to his social background, a considerable training in music. Despite their frequent political divergences, Lenin thought of him as one of the younger generation's bright hopes. He saw him as a leader of the top administrators of socialist industry. But Lenin knew Pyatakov well, and although he mentioned him in his *Testament* as one of his six 'heirs', he was aware of the younger man's limitations, and in particular of his lack of political stature.

With his strong personality and volatile temperament, Pyatakov distinguished himself by his great revolutionary zeal and energy, and remained for a long time on the Party's extreme left wing. This explains the positions he took up and which later made him for many years one of the pillars of the opposition. Trotsky, not entirely without malice, said that Pyatakov usually joined every opposition, only to wind up as a government official.[1] In fact, he was consistent: he was always in the left-wing opposition, and always argued as a technocrat. He was marked just as much by the contradictions of his family origins – the upper bourgeoisie with a passion for industry (his father was a sugar manufacturer) – as by his youth, spent among non-conformist, extremist libertarian Russian anarchists. Pyatakov bowed to no authority, not even Lenin's.

As early as 1915, and with his inseparable Eugénie Bosch and his friend Bukharin, Pyatakov formed the 'left communist' group. He was an extreme internationalist, and described Lenin's position as a 'pacifist illusion'. Taking Bukharin's neo-Marxist theory of imperialism as a basis, he was opposed to Lenin's principle of self-determination, and came out in favour of a socialist United States of Europe, to be forged by the international revolutionary proletariat.[2] During the revolution and the years following it, Pyatakov waged a forceful campaign to put over his principles.

In the 1917 Revolution, Pyatakov was the leader of the Ukrainian communists. For a young theorist, he proved himself to be a considerable man of action. After the October victory, Lenin brought him to Moscow to help sort out the mess of the economy. During the differences over Brest-Litovsk, at the beginning of 1918, Pyatakov was President of the State Bank and one of the main inspirers of the left-wing communists who supported a revolutionary war. He considered peace negotiations with Germany to represent a capitulation to German imperialism. When, on 22 February 1918, the terms of the peace with Germany became known, Pyatakov, with other left-wing communists, resigned from all official positions. He considered Lenin's point of view

[1] L. Trotsky, *My Life* (New York, 1960), p. 439.
[2] He published articles under the pseudonym of P. Kievsky.

to be a reflection of populist peasant ideology, and accused him of diverting Bolshevism onto the path of the lower bourgeoisie. When in March 1918 the left communists and SRs accused Lenin of betraying the revolution and decided to unseat him, it was Pyatakov who was designated as his successor at the head of the government.

He was consequently removed from Moscow, and sent to his native Ukraine, where the situation was extremely critical: the Germans were in virtual occupation and had set up a puppet government with Skoropadsky as president. Pyatakov showed himself to be efficient and enterprising. With Eugénie Bosch, he founded the first Soviet government and the Communist Party of the Ukraine, of which he became the leader. He acquired great authority, and the Ukraine, of which he was for a short time President, became to all intents his fief and the bastion of left-wing communism. He virtually eliminated Skrypnik and his supporters. The Central Committee of the Ukrainian CP, elected in March 1919, was made up of Pyatakov's followers who shared the opinions he had been propagating since 1915: the watchword of self-determination was qualified in the Ukraine as 'counter-revolutionary', and, putting the proletariat before the nation, Pyatakov demanded that the workers' movements of all the nations of Russia should be subordinated to the central control of the Communist International.[1]

His views were the subject of a major debate at the eighth Congress of the Russian CP. He was violently attacked by Lenin, who accused him of taking a chauvinistic Great-Russian position. But even criticisms from a man of such great authority failed to shake Pyatakov's influence in the Ukraine.

In 1920, the Central Committee of the Ukrainian CP was regained by Pyatakov's supporters, elected by the Congress. Lenin cancelled the elections, dissolved the Central Committee by decree, and replaced its members with supporters of Skrypnik. Despite his differences with Pyatakov, Lenin bore him no grudge—unlike Stalin, whose task it then was to take over the Ukrainian CP and to rid it of Pyatakov's influence.

At the time of the Civil War, Pyatakov was one of the group of Red Army Commissars who followed Trotsky's line. In May 1919 he was appointed President of the Military Tribunal, and then to membership of the various Revolutionary Councils for the army, as he mentions in his autobiography. At the start, he belonged to the 'Military Opposition', opposed to the use of specialists, that is former officers of the Tsarist army, and in favour of the principle of electing leaders and abolishing military hierarchy and discipline, and so on. But Trotsky was able to

[1] See Yuriy Borys, *The Russian Communist Party and the Sovietisation of the Ukraine* (Stockholm, 1960), pp. 128ff.

soften him up rapidly by giving him responsibilities that 'obliged him to go from words to deeds'. He distinguished himself in particular in the Crimean expedition, which he led, according to Clara Zetkin, in a manner 'as brilliant as it was brave'.

After the Civil War, Lenin put him to work in a vitally important sector where his talents could be used to the full: in the economy. He rapidly gained a reputation as a clever, though sometimes over-zealous, economist and administrator. At the tenth Congress, in 1921, he was elected for the first time to candidate membership of the Central Committee, and he was re-elected at the twelfth, thirteenth and fourteenth Congresses. He was entrusted with various difficult tasks: in 1922, he was appointed President of the Supreme Tribunal, and it was he therefore who was in charge of the trial of the SRs in July of that year; and in the autumn of 1923 the Communist International sent Pyatakov and Radek to Germany to prepare an insurrection with the top leadership of the German CP.

Despite his panache, Pyatakov was an eternal second-in-command. In 1923, he was appointed Vice-President of the Supreme Sovnarkhoz, and he continued in this post even after Dzerzhinsky was appointed President over his head. Despite their political differences, Dzerzhinsky was glad to have such a valuable deputy. Pyatakov belonged to the left opposition and was a signatory, in October 1923, of the 'declaration of the 46'. He was violently opposed to the economic policies of the 'rightist bloc'. He was wholeheartedly for industrialisation, but considered the NEP a temporary necessity; like Preobrazhensky, he thought it was indispensable to put pressure on the peasantry in order to accelerate industrialisation. He defended his views in the great debates on industrialisation between 1924 and 1927. As one of the leaders and chief spokesmen of the Trotskyite opposition, and subsequently of the United Opposition, he signed and helped draw up all the programme documents and declarations of these oppositions. When they were dismantled by Stalin in 1927, Pyatakov was expelled from the Party (at the fifteenth Congress) and sent away to Paris as head of the Soviet Trade Legation. He went through a serious crisis, at that time, as a convinced communist, and declared to Valentinov, 'For me there is no life outside the Party, and in disagreement with the Party.' His quarrel with Stalin over the NEP was not so much a political issue as a question of economic policy. Indeed, 'Pyatakov was more concerned with the proper economic policy than with the conditions of Party democracy'.[1]

When Stalin broke his alliance with the right in 1928 and launched

[1] R. V. Daniels, *The Conscience of Revolution. Communist Opposition in Soviet Russia* (Harvard, 1960), p. 371.

into industrialisation and collectivisation, Pyatakov left the opposition and requested readmission to the Party. He became, first, President of the Soviet State Bank, then in 1930 Ordzhonikidze's deputy at the Commissariat for Heavy Industry, which was responsible for the implementation of the Five-Year Plan. It was Pyatakov who actually ran the Plan, and his contribution to the first two Five-Year plans of super-industrialisation was very great indeed: he turned away from politics and put all his passion and abilities at the service of the Plans. At the seventeenth Congress in 1934 he was re-elected on to the Central Committee. Remaining faithful to the Party line, he wrote an article for *Pravda* on 21 August 1936, in which he approved the execution of Kamenev and Zinoviev, and described their views, as well as Trotsky's, as anti-Leninist; and he paid public hommage to 'our great Stalin, upholder of the general line mapped out by Lenin, and creator of its new development'. A few days later he was arrested by the same NKVD he had glorified in *Pravda* for having 'annihilated the carcasses' of Kamenev and Zinoviev. He was the main defendant in the second great trial, known as the 'trial of the Trotskyite anti-Soviet centre', which took place in Moscow in January 1937. Convicted of counter-revolutionary activities, of sabotage and espionage, he was sentenced to death and executed.

G.H.

NIKOLAY ILYICH PODVOYSKY

The absence of Podvoysky's life from the Granat Encyclopedia is as amazing as it is inexplicable. It is easy to explain why it is amazing: Podvoysky was a member of the Petrograd Committee from March 1917, then President of the Party's Military Organisation, set up in April 1917, then a member of the Bureau of the Petrograd Soviet RVS, of which he was appointed President on 27 October. He was one of the three entrusted with the organisation of the storming of the Winter Palace (the other two were Antonov-Ovseyenko and Chudnovsky), then on the 28th he replaced Antonov-Ovseyenko as Chief of Staff of the RVS, and was put in charge of the defence of Petrograd. Finally, in November 1917, he was made People's Commissar for War. The man John Reed referred to as 'this thin and bearded civilian who was the strategist of the uprising' played a determining role in the October days, in their preparation and in their consolidation. His absence from the Granat is inexplicable because Podvoysky was, at the time of publication, a member of the Central Control Commission and a solid supporter of the majority against the 'Trotskyites'. He did then cease, it is true, to have any political importance; but this ubiquitous figure of the October Revolution, who had already told his life story in numerous memoirs of some value, could hardly have been forgotten.

Nikolay Ilyich Podvoysky was born on 16 February 1880, in the village of Kunochevsk in Chernigov Province. His father had been a teacher originally, but had become a priest. The young Podvoysky had three brothers and three sisters. He began his studies at the small seminary at Nezhin, and then at the Chernigov Seminary, from which he was expelled for revolutionary activity in spring 1901. He enrolled in the Law Faculty at Yaroslavl, and in the same year joined the RSDRP. Under the assumed name of 'Mironich' he soon became one of the leaders of the Yaroslavl circle. He was arrested in 1904, but was soon released. At that time his collaborators in the Yaroslavl circle included Yaroslavsky, Nevsky, Menzhinsky and Kedrov. . . . He was arrested in 1905 for his involvement in the strike of the city's railway workers, but was again soon released. He was wounded in a demonstration, and sought treatment in Germany and Switzerland; on his return in 1906, he campaigned with the St Petersburg organisation. He was arrested in 1908, then released in 1910 in order to go into hospital.

He left St Petersburg to militate in Kostroma and then Baku, where he stayed from January to June 1911, spreading propaganda among the oil-workers. Upon his next return to St Petersburg, he helped set up *Pravda*; and early in 1913 he settled down in Pargovo, near St Petersburg, to organise the smuggling of clandestine Bolshevik literature into Russia; he seemed for a while to be leaving the life of a militant. From February 1915, he was editor of the only legal Bolshevik newspaper, *Voprosi Strakhovaniya*. He was arrested in November 1916, but saved by the February Revolution. He was co-opted on to the Petrograd Committee, and elected on to its Executive Commission, where he represented the left wing and opposed support for the Provisional government. He was appointed to the Military Commission of the Petrograd Committee, and made President of the Party's Military Organisation, which was created on 31 March 1917. He then ran *Soldatskaya Pravda*, the first issue of which appeared on 15 April, and which was banned after the July days.

Podvoysky's role shrank considerably after the October uprising. He seems to have been an excellent insurrectional strategist, but not to have had any real military talent. In the Ukraine he put himself in a bad light, according to a letter of Lenin, by conniving in acts of 'abusive and illegal confiscation, and corruption', and for his incessant and arbitrary interference in the life of the Republic. After 1919 he was mainly occupied with general military instruction and with writing his memoirs. After the struggle against the left opposition he was retired for health reasons in 1934, and died in bed in 1948.

Trotsky, who had no reason to flatter Podvoysky, drew a portrait which appears to be very accurate, particularly if one remembers that, apart from his activity on the Petrograd Committee, Podvoysky never had any real political office and was never a member, either candidate or alternate, of the Central Committee:

> Podvoysky was a brilliant and strange figure in the ranks of Bolshevism, with his traits of the old-style Russian revolutionary, educated in a seminary; a man of great stature, though of undisciplined energy, gifted with a creative imagination which, it must be said, often meandered into fantasy. 'That's a Podvoyskyism,' Lenin used to say with circumspect irony and good nature. But the weaker sides of this effervescent character were to come out especially after the conquest of power, when the multiplicity of possibilities and means gave too much scope to Podvoysky's unrestrained energy and to his passion for decorative enterprises. In the conditions of the revolutionary struggle for power, his optimistic resoluteness, his abnegation and untiringness made him an irreplaceable leader of the awakened mass of soldiers.

J.-J. M

EVGENY ALEKSEYEVICH PREOBRAZHENSKY
(autobiography)

I was born in 1886 into a priest's family in the town of Bolkhov, Oryol province. I learnt to read at a very early age and when only four, I read the tales in Tolstoy's *Alphabet*. As a child, I was very religious. [. . .] I went to the Oryol Gymnasium [. . .] and at the age of fourteen I came to the conclusion that God does not exist. From that moment I began my stubborn struggle inside our family against going to church and other religious ceremonies. This aversion for religion was reinforced by the fact that I could observe all the religious quackery with my own eyes from the wings. [. . .]

It was when I was in the fifth form at the Gymnasium that illegal literature initially came into my hands. Of these first works, I remember Amfiteatrov's hectographed serial *The Obmanov Family* which had previously been printed in the newspaper *Rossiya*, the proclamation of the revolutionary students of the Ekaterinoslav Mining Institute, descriptions of Cossacks beating students, and a few revolutionary poems such as the 'Marseillaise', 'Dubinushka', 'Firm, Boys, Stand Firm', etc. [. . .] In Bolkhovo that summer, the only revolutionary 'cell' consisted of myself and a childhood friend, the son of the local merchant, Ivan Anisimov, who later became a Menshevik and who, I think, emigrated with the Whites. The two of us would set off for the most solitary places outside town and there we expressed our protest against the autocracy by singing the 'Marseillaise', but in such a way that no one could hear us. Whenever we passed the Bolkhovo town jail, a pitiful, old-fashioned, tumble-down building which usually housed a couple of dozen petty thieves and horse-stealers, our thoughts went out to the Kresty and Butyrki, where the heroic enemies of the autocratic regime were languishing.

Returning to the Gymnasium after the holidays, I decided to devote the minimum of time to school work necessary to avoid being given a mark of less than 3.[1] At night I concentrated eagerly on reading foreign works printed on cigarette paper, whilst during the day I read books on the history of culture, on both general history and the history of the revolution, and also on the rudiments of political economy. In addition, Ivan Anisimov and I began to spread our propaganda among the students: we started a couple of circles, and came into contact with some people living under police supervision in Oryol. During this period, I developed a mystical passion for multiplying illegal literature. I had

[1] In Russia, school marks go from 0 to 5.

already abandoned as politically useless the hand-written journal *School Leisure*, which I had founded and run with Aleksandr Tinyakov, the poet who later went mad. Hectographing a few small things did not satisfy me either, although from one master sheet we could obtain a hundred copies. I dreamt of a printing-press. [. . .]

When I moved up into the seventh class, I could no longer remain a vague, wishy-washy revolutionary. I had to choose between the socialist revolutionaries and the social democrats. I was decisively influenced by two works: *The Communist Manifesto*, and *The Development of Scientific Socialism* by Engels. After long meditation over them, I decided that the Populist outlook was untenable and unscientific, and that only Marxism could show me the correct path. This watershed in my beliefs produced certain practical consequences. Previously I had distributed to students not only SD literature which reached us from the Oryol SD Committee through Valeryan Schmidt and Pyotr Semyonovich Bobrovsky (both later Mensheviks,) but also SR literature which was provided by the SR Nikkeleva, although she lived under supervision in Oryol. I recall with what sombre resolution I announced to her that I could no longer help her distribute SR literature because I had become a social democrat.

Of the comrades who at this time were engaged in our revolutionary student organisation, I can remember particularly distinctly Aleksandr and Evgraf Litkens who were both tragically killed (although Evgraf was to become Deputy People's Commissar for Education), D. Kuzovkov, N. Mikheyev, Ledovsky and E. M. Kotina. Among seminarists, I remember Romanov and M. Fenomenov. [. . .] In the autumn of the same year, 1903, we stepped up our activity in educational establishments and constituted ourselves as an SD Party cell.

I consider I have really been a member of the SD Party since the end of 1903, although Litkens, Anisimov and myself were only officially received into the Party two or three months later.

In early 1904, when the Russo-Japanese War began, the Oryol Party Committee issued a proclamation against the war and instructed the three of us to distribute it in large quantities at the Gymnasium. We accomplished this in the following fashion. During one lesson the three of us simultaneously left our respective classes, went to the changing-room where all the students' coats were hung, and, picking the right moment, stuffed 150 or 200 proclamations into the coat pockets of the older pupils. The operation was a great success, and when the pupils were putting on their coats to go home, they were all astonished to find these circulars from the Oryol Committee. A huge scandal followed, the administration frantically hunted for the perpetrators and the gendarmes made an investigation, but nothing came to light. After this, our organisational début, the Oryol Committee agreed to admit us formally to its group of propagandists, which was done after an undemanding interview in 1904.

In spring of that year I was entrusted with a small circle of two workers from the Khrushchev engineering works. I explained the Party programme to them at some length, but not very convincingly. In summer, when I moved up into the eighth class in the Gymnasium and after consultations with the Party, I gave lessons at the Dyadkovo factory in the Maltsev industrial centre, Bryansk district, to the son of the local police chief. I converted my pupil, Nikolay Mikhailovich Zolotov, who now lives in France, to the SD faith. Whilst officially I was teaching him Latin, we devoted our main effort to distributing propaganda among workers at the Dyadkovo, Ivot and other Maltsev factories. It was here that I first met Fokin, who subsequently played a major part in the building of our organisations of Soviet power in the Bryansk district. My pupil's father, the police chief, made great efforts to catch the Dyadkovo cell which distributed proclamations and mimeographed literature. We stored the mimeograph machine and illegal literature in a rather original way. My pupil complained to his father that he had nowhere to keep his books and exercise books, and asked him for a drawer in his father's desk which could be locked. His father readily agreed and we kept our material there, whilst father Zolotov conducted searches through Dyadkovo. Similarly, whenever we needed to organise mass meetings in the forests at individual factories, we asked the police chief for his pair of horses, saying we wanted to go hunting. Without suspecting a thing, he willingly gave them to us and we rode round the organisations in our area. All this only came to light a year later.

In April and May 1905, our group led a general strike in educational establishments in Oryol. Yet despite this and the fact that we had spoken in public at student meetings, I was not arrested and I even received my school-leaving certificate. In summer 1905 I left for Bryansk and there directed the activity of the local committee with two other comrades. With no bed in my room, I slept on newspapers on the floor, lived on smoked sausage and bread, spending no more than twenty kopecks per day, and every evening I walked eighteen versty[1] to Bezhitsa and back to attend workers' circles at the Bryansk locomotive plant. In October 1905, on the suggestion of Olimpy Kvitkin, I was co-opted onto the Oryol Committee, which at the time was a 'conciliatory' organisation. After Kvitkin had departed, its leader, Ponomaryov, would laugh and say to the other Committee members: 'We have two solid Bolsheviks, Mikhail Ekaterinoslavsky who is twenty, and Evgeny Preobrazhensky

[1] Roughly eleven miles.

who is nineteen.' Despite these sallies, I stuck to my guns and defended the position adopted at the third Party Congress. Before this a curious thing had happened in the Oryol organisation. It sent Olimpy Kvitkin as its representative to the third Congress. He left as a Menshevik but returned a convinced Bolshevik and did everything to support Mikhail Ekaterinoslavsky and myself in our Bolshevik views.

In October, after the publication of our famous manifesto, I was involved in a struggle with the pogrom thugs in Oryol and then I was sent to the Bryansk plant. I remained there until the middle of November, when on the suggestion of N. M. Mikheyev, who was working in Moscow, and with the agreement of the Moscow Committee, I moved to Moscow where I was made propagandist for the Presnya district. I worked here permanently until the rising and during it attended District Committee meetings, which directed the Presnya insurrection and gave command of our forces to Sedoy. My functions consisted mainly of organising meetings of strikers at their factories even when under artillery fire from the Vagankovsky cemetery. When Presnya was ablaze and surrounded by the Semyonovsky Regiment, I hid my Browning in the water-closet of my room, slipped through the soldiers' cordon at night, went to Oryol for a few days and then returned to Moscow to put myself at the disposition of its Central Committee, which was led at that time by Rykov.

A. I. Rykov offered me the choice between the two organisations which had suffered the greatest losses—Kostroma, or Perm in the Urals. I chose the Urals, and within five days I had reached there and been introduced to the Perm Committee. One of the permanent workers on its staff was Klavdiya Timofeyevna Novgorodtseva, and we were also visited from time to time by Yakov Mikhailovich Sverdlov who was patching up the whole Urals Party organisation after the January defeat. After working in Perm for two and a half months, I was denounced by an *agent provocateur* called Votinov and on 18 March was arrested with other comrades. This was the first time I had been in prison. After five months and a four-day hunger strike, I was released for lack of evidence with Bina Lobova, Liza Kin and others, but we were kept under police supervision. When I came out of prison and set off through the town with a little bundle of things under my arm, I was met by Aleksandr Minkin, who brought me up to date with Party affairs and suggested that I resume work. The very next day I took part in discussions with SRs on the other bank of the Kama, and the usual routine of underground work was under way again.

In view of the collapse of the regional organisation, I set out for Ekaterinburg, Chelyabinsk and Ufa to re-establish contacts, and arranged a regional conference for the autumn in Vyatka. I myself was not able to attend. Having been sent to St Petersburg by the Perm Committee to buy Brownings to arm detachments of workers, I was betrayed by the *agent provocateur* Foma Lebedev (whom I recognised by chance in Oryol in 1919 and who was later executed in Perm). I was arrested at the Kazan station and sent back to Perm. For the second time I was put in prison there, and then I spent eight months in the notorious penal battalions. When, however, the case concerning our group was transferred to the Kazan Court of Justice, I was again released for lack of evidence.

I went to the southern Urals where I worked mainly in Ufa at the Sima plant and in Zlatoust. We succeeded in re-forming the Urals regional organization, one of whose most prominent activists was Nikolay Nikandrovich Nakoryakov (pseudonym 'Nazar'). At the excellent clandestine printing-press in Ufa, we renewed publication of our local paper *Uralsky Rabochy*, and in addition brought out the *Krestyanskaya Gazeta* and the *Soldatskaya Gazeta*. In 1907 I represented the Urals at the All-Russian Party Conference in Finland, where I first met Lenin. My activity in the Urals continued until March 1908 in ever worsening conditions, amidst growing arrests and intensified repression. In March I was arrested at the Chelyabinsk town conference, swallowed the agenda and coded addresses, and escaped the same night from the police station. I was now a marked man in the Urals, but I could not tear myself away from the area and I escaped from Chelyabinsk to Ufa dressed as a student. I had to summon a regional conference which was due to meet in Zlatoust, but I delayed in Ufa a little while and did not reach the conference. I was arrested in the street at the end of April and immediately identified. [. . .]

I was held for a short time in Ufa prison and then sent to Chelyabinsk where I was tried in autumn 1909. During the trial, as I expected a sentence of hard labour, I made a vain attempt to escape from my escort, who savagely beat me. In fact my sentence turned out to be very light— we were all merely deported. After this I was tried for a second time under Article 102 in Perm and again sentenced to exile.

I reached the Aleksandrov transit centre near Irkutsk, and remained there till summer when I was settled in the area of Karapchanka, Kirensk district. The deportees there lived like a happy family in a commune and included the late Artem Sergeyev, Pyotr Kovalenko and Anatoly Galkin. Apart from daily work with peasants, my main occupation was hunting. In winter 1911 the Ekaterinburg Party Committee made the suggestion that I should escape from exile and represent them at the Party Conference arranged for the following year in Prague. I joyfully accepted their offer, especially as I was corresponding with Krupskaya and had received a brief coded letter from Vladimir Ilyich. Shortly before my escape, the police department made arrangements for me to be searched, and sent Captain Tereshchenkov, later notorious for his massacre of the Lena workers. As the Angara was closed by ice, however, he could not cross the river and returned empty-handed to Kirensk. Then on Christmas Day, the Nizhny-Ilimsk district police officer, who was responsible for us, received a telegram ordering my immediate arrest, as the Ekaterinburg organization had already been uncovered and my links with it had come to light. Since it was Christmas Day, the police officer was blind drunk and it was his secretary who opened the telegram, later blabbing about it to exiles in the town. They immediately dispatched a messenger who galloped over fifty miles through the night to warn me, and less than thirty minutes after his arrival I was sitting on a peasant's cart racing to the railway station at Tulun. When the police officer woke up, read the telegram and set off to arrest me, I had already passed through Nizhny-Ilimsk and was near Tulun.

From there I made my way to Novonikolaevsk where I contributed to the legal Marxist paper *Obskaya Zhizn*, writing several articles defending the Bolshevik position on fundamental questions of the day. In addition I exchanged letters with Zinoviev, asked him to contribute to the paper and received an article which appeared with the signature 'G.Z.'. Vladimir Ilyich also promised to contribute but did not manage to send anything. In autumn 1912 the whole of the Novonikolaevsk organisation was denounced. Pyotr Kovalenko, one of its activists, had been arrested even earlier. I was captured the day before my departure abroad, where I had been invited by Krupskaya to take part in a conference. From Novonikolaevsk I was transferred to Ekaterinburg prison and en route met L. Serebryakov, Zelensky, Kuzmenko and others who were being deported.

In Ekaterinburg, I was tried with Semyon Schwartz, E. Bosch, A. N. Trubina, A. Paramonov and others. As a result of the stupidity of the procurator who confused me in his opening speech with another Evgeny, our defence lawyers, who included N. D. Sokolov, A. F. Kerensky and N. M. Mikheyev, gained my acquittal, to the astonishment of all.

From Ekaterinburg I was sent back to exile after six months in jail for my escape. I remained there for only a short while and in 1915 I was allowed to move to Irkutsk. I joined the local Party organisation, which soon collapsed. After that, to avoid further betrayals, we organised a group of the most 'reliable' comrades, that is Zavadsky, Rom, Dzyarsky,

Krut, Samsonov and myself, equipped a printing-press and planned to begin publication with an anti-war proclamation which I had written. It soon became apparent that there was still an *agent provocateur* in our midst, so we dissolved the group, and it was only after the February Revolution that on the basis of the archives of the Irkutsk Department of Gendarmes we were able to establish who had betrayed us. It was David Krut, who was brought to trial for this in Moscow in 1926. During my stay in Irkutsk, I contributed two articles against the war to the SD paper *Zabaikalskoye Obozreniye*. After Irkutsk I went to Chita, and whilst I was there, the February Revolution began. In April I left Chita as a delegate to the forthcoming first Congress of Soviets, stopping on the way in the Urals to work with old friends there. After the Congress, I was elected to the Urals Regional Committee and was a Urals delegate to the sixth Party Congress, where I was chosen a candidate CC member.

In Zlatoust, where I had returned to work, our Party was in the minority amongst the workers, even during the October Days. The majority supported the SRs. In October I took part in an armed demonstration by the Party under the slogan 'All power to the Soviets', and urged workers so vehemently at the Zlatoust works to support us that I lost my voice. Yet we were only partially successful. In the Sima district, however, where I arrived on 26 October, we managed to take control everywhere and to nationalise all the mines in the area. After the October Days, all the remaining comrades, myself included, concentrated on establishing Soviet power in the Urals and on strengthening our Party organisations.

From spring 1918 we in the Urals had to endure the Czechoslovak onslaught and then create a front against Kolchak. In summer 1918, in my capacity as delegate from the Urals to the Fourth Congress of Soviets, I took part in the suppression of the left-wing SR rising, was slightly wounded in the left temple during the storming of the central telegraph office which was occupied by the SRs, and was then dispatched by the RVS to the Kursk area for a few days to maintain discipline among troops on the Ukrainian border. From Moscow I set off back to the Urals, where Ekaterinburg had already been taken by Kolchak and our forces were retreating northwards. At this time I was Chairman of the Urals Regional Committee, which had taken upon itself the functions of political section of the Third Army. When Kolchak's troops advanced on Perm and bombarded the town, our Revolutionary Committee was evacuated together with the last detachments of Mrachkovsky's division and we then fell back in strength towards Glazov and Vyatka. Afterwards, when the Urals Regional Union had in fact lost almost all its territory, it was dissolved on the orders of the CC, and I was recalled to Moscow to work on *Pravda*. I was a delegate to the eighth Party Congress and a member of the Commission charged with drawing up the Party programme. Then I was sent by VTsIK to deal with trouble in Oryol province.

On returning to Moscow, I was present at the bomb explosion on Leontiev street. After the liberation of the Urals, I was again dispatched for Party and Soviet work in Ufa. I was selected by the Ufa Party organisation to attend the ninth Party Congress where I was elected to the CC, and the CC elected me one of its three secretaries. After the tenth Party Congress I was appointed Chairman of the Financial Committee of the CC and Sovnarkom and directed its work on the adaptation of money circulation and financial control to the conditions of NEP. I then presided over the Main Directorate for Professional Training, was one of the editors of *Pravda*, and performed a number of other functions which it would be tiresome to enumerate.

Of my literary work, apart from small pamphlets and many articles in *Pravda* and journals, I will name: *Anarchism and Communism, The ABC of Communism* written with Bukharin, *Paper Money during the Dictatorship of the Proletariat, The Causes of the Decline of Our Rouble, From NEP to Socialism, On Morals and Class Norms, V. I. Lenin, The Economy and Finances of Contemporary France, On the Economic Crises under NEP*, and finally the first volume of the still unfinished work *The New Economics*.

With his harsh face and goatee beard, Preobrazhensky looked like an academic. Indeed, the first version of his *New Economics* appeared in 1924 in the journal of the Communist Academy, but that is where the resemblance ceases. Preobrazhensky could no doubt have had a first-class 'academic career', but he was a militant: when the revolutionary in him was broken, he was nothing.

In the days that followed the February Revolution, Preobrazhensky was one of the few 'Old Bolshevik' *cadres* who did not adopt the policy of critical support for Prince Lvov's Provisional government, and was therefore one of the first to accept the *April Theses*. The region for which he was responsible, the Urals, quickly became a left-wing stronghold (in 1917–18, the Urals Committee was led by Preobrazhensky, Krestinsky, Beloborodov, Spunde and Sosnovsky). At the sixth Congress of the Bolshevik Party, at which he was elected to alternate membership of the Central Committee, Preobrazhensky came into conflict with Stalin in a prophetic manner: Stalin read a report on the political situation which contained a resolution declaring the task of the Russian people to be 'the seizure of power and, in alliance with the revolutionary proletariat of the

advanced countries, its direction towards peace and the socialist reconstruction of society'. Preobrazhensky objected to this formulation
and proposed the following version: '. . . its direction towards peace,
and, in the event of a proletarian revolution in the West, towards
socialism.' Stalin refused this version, saying that one 'cannot rule out
the possibility of its being precisely Russia that will open the path to
socialism'.

A man whose feelings always appeared subordinated to analysis,
Preobrazhensky sided with the hardest left-wing communists from the
very start of the Brest-Litovsk negotiations. On 28 December, he asked
in *Pravda* whether one can 'wage a revolutionary war', and replied with
arguments almost entirely in the future and conditional tenses. Ten days
later he changed tack, and set against each other 'peace' and 'socialist
war', in which the volunteers' enthusiasm and the low morale of the
German soldiers was enough to offset the disintegration of the old
Russian army, the disorganisation of transport and the invincible problem of supplies.

That was not the only originality of this rigorous economist. The
future (short-lived) secretary of the Party, the future 'inventor' of
'primitive socialist accumulation' (which the soft Bukharin thought a
ferocious theory), always cared deeply for democracy. When in 1918
workers' control over the railways was abolished and replaced by the
dictatorial powers of the Commissariat for Communications, Preobrazhensky protested: 'The Party will soon have this problem on its plate—
how far should the dictatorship of individuals spread from the railways
and other branches of the economy to the Russian CP?' In 1920, as one
of the three secretaries of the Party and a member of the Orgburo, he
drew up a paper on bureaucracy which was circulated, with amendments,
as a Central Committee circular. In January 1922 he claimed that 'the
possibility of extending the freedom to criticise is one of the revolution's
victories'. When Zinoviev, in November 1923, celebrated the anniversary of the Revolution by opening a rather demagogic campaign on
Party problems, Preobrazhensky waged a struggle for democratisation
(the 'New Course') on behalf of the left opposition, and fired his first
broadside in *Pravda* on 28 November 1923.

It was strange, but indicative of the nature of the Bolshevik Party after
the Civil War, that Preobrazhensky was elected one of the three secretaries of the Central Committee, to membership of the Orgburo and to
the Central Control Commission. In this last task he was soon replaced
by one of Stalin's friends, Solts, who was much more at ease than
Preobrazhensky in dealing with purges.

Preobrazhensky was a victim of the Party's sickness. As Serebryakov and Krestinsky were ill for almost the whole of 1920, Preobrazhensky ran the secretariat and the Orgburo almost single-handed—that is to say, set up the Party machine which up to then had grown in bits and pieces, by chance of circumstance. Zinoviev chose this occasion to renew his image by launching a major campaign for internal Party 'democracy' (except in the Petrograd organisation controlled by . . . Zinoviev); the butt of this campaign was the secretariat, above all the Orgburo, and therefore Preobrazhensky. In November 1920, he had a majority of only four against the 'supporters of democracy'—Stalin, Zinoviev, Rudzutak, Kalinin, Tomsky and Petrovsky!

In the union conflict which began at that time as well, Preobrazhensky, with the other two secretaries, Serebryakov and Krestinsky, supported Trotsky's line. The Party machine juggled the votes somewhat, but not in aid of its secretaries' positions. Since the Congress that brought in the ban on splinter groups elected its Central Committee on the basis of attitudes towards the union question, Preobrazhensky disappeared from the Central Committee, never to return.

He was one of the signatories of the 'Declaration of the 46'. In *Pravda*, on 28 November, he denounced the internal regime of which the result had been to reduce the Party to a mere executive function for decisions taken at the top. Stalin replied: 'Preobrazhensky is recommending a return to the past.' It was he who led the left opposition's struggle in the Moscow organisation (December 1923) and at the thirteenth Conference (January 1924). Defeat moved him away from active struggle. and he then devoted himself to *The New Economics*, in which he developed the ideas he had sketched in articles on the need for industrialisation, collectivisation, and planning. A sharp polemic sprang up between Preobrazhensky and Bukharin, whose new slogan for the peasantry was at that time 'Get rich!' Bukharin considered the policies put forward by Preobrazhensky certain to antagonise the peasantry against the regime. In July 1928, when Stalin moved timidly towards collectivisation, Bukharin declared in fright to Kamenev, 'It's the same thing as Preobrazhensky'.

In 1926, Preobrazhensky was one of the main figures in the United Opposition, of which the three fundamental demands (for planning, industrialisation and collectivisation) were the three pillars of his *New Economics*. He was expelled from the Party in October 1927, then deported to Siberia after the fifteenth Congress in December. Agreeing with Bukharin's phrase quoted above, he was one of the first of the opposition leaders to reconcile himself with Stalin. On 12 July 1929, he signed a declaration of realignment with Smilga and Radek. The first Five-Year Plan and collectivisation signified, in Preobrazhensky's view, a turn to the left which granted the main body of the opposition's demands.

Thenceforth Preobrazhensky was only a shadow. He was readmitted to the Party, when expelled again in 1931, readmitted the following year. . . . He had an obscure office job. He was allowed to write a short study on the decline of capitalism, but at the seventeenth Congress in January 1934 he was obliged to make a painful self-criticism: 'My theoretical works, including *The New Economics*, have served as weapons against the Party [. . .] Events have completely invalidated my claims [. . .] Had I foreseen collectivisation? I had not foreseen it.' A joke went around the former opposition circles in Moscow at that time: 'What is Preobrazhensky doing? He's drinking jam tea and playing the guitar.'

All this did not prevent him from being expelled from the Party in 1935, arrested and imprisoned. He was released and in August 1936 served as prosecution witness at the Moscow trial, launching into Zinoviev and once again renouncing his past. A few months later he was arrested again. He was to be among the defendants at the second Moscow trial, but did not appear. The hunched ghost whom Serge had briefly seen two years before and who had told him, 'They are not allowing me to breathe. I expect the worst', had no doubt refused to play the last act of the farce. Preobrazhensky died—somewhere, some time. Official Soviet biographies state that he died in 1937 after being 'convicted'. It is unlikely that Stalin set up a trial *in camera* for him. He was no doubt killed for obstinacy. His family was purged.

J.-J. M.

FYODOR FYODOROVICH RASKOLNIKOV
(autobiography)

I was born on 28 January 1892 in Bolshaya Okhta on the outskirts of St Petersburg. Until 1900 I was brought up by my mother, but in the autumn of that year I was sent to the Prince of Oldenburg's Orphanage which had the status of a 'modern' school. It was a ghastly institution with the customs of an old-fashioned seminary; pupils were made to kneel in front of the whole class for bad marks, and the chaplain, Lisitsyn, boxed boys' ears in public. I was obliged to spend eight years there as a boarder, leaving in 1908. By this time I was sixteen. In the seventh form, I had become an atheist, and in the same year became acquainted with the works of Maksim Gorky, Leonid Andreyev and others, which further strengthened my atheism. In 1909 I entered the Economics Department of the St Petersburg Polytechnical Institute.

At this point, I must briefly describe the formation of my political views. As early as 1905–6, in the fifth and sixth forms, I had twice participated in strikes, and moreover had once been elected to a student delegation which went to see the headmaster with a demand for improvements in living conditions. For this I was nearly expelled. My interest in politics and my sympathy for the revolutionary movement were first aroused by the 1905 Revolution, but as I was then only thirteen I could understand nothing in the disagreements between separate parties.

I called myself quite simply a socialist. My sympathy for the oppressed and exploited was maintained by reading the works of Sheller-Mikhailov, amongst which the novel *An Omelette Needs Broken Eggs* made a particular impression. In this way my political experiences in 1905 and an acute awareness of social injustice led me instinctively to socialism. This inclination found an all the more ready, heartfelt response, as the material conditions of our family were very difficult.

In 1907 my father died, and mother was left with two sons. Her pension of sixty roubles per month only covered day-to-day expenses, whilst an education had to be found for myself and my younger brother Aleksandr (who now works in the Party under the name of Ilin-Zhenevsky). For lack of resources, the latter had to be transferred from the 'modern' school, where he was a boarder, to the Vvedensky Gymnasium. By running into debt, however, mother managed to let me finish secondary school and also, for a while, to pay for me at the Polytechnical Institute. During subsequent terms, in view of our difficult financial position, the board of professors sometimes exempted me from tuition fees.

During my first year there I had occasion to read Plekhanov's works, which made me a Marxist. In summer 1910 I made a thorough study of *Das Kapital*, and in December of the same year I joined the Party. After publication of the first edition of the legal Bolshevik paper *Zvezda*, I went to its offices, declared my full agreement with the paper's line, and offered my services to the editorial staff. The godfather of my literary work for the Party was K. S. Eremeyev. From this moment, I became a very close collaborator on *Zvezda* and *Pravda*. After beginning with the diary of events, I graduated to articles, the first of which was printed in spring 1911. During this period I also worked with V. M. Molotov in the Bolshevik group of the Polytechnical Institute and maintained contact on its behalf with the St Petersburg Committee.

When *Pravda* appeared on 22 April 1912, I became editorial secretary. But I only lasted one month in this post since on the night of 21/22 May I was arrested and taken into custody. I was accused under Article 102 of membership of the RSDRP. After solitary confinement lasting four and a half months, I was condemned to three years' exile in Archangel province, but this was replaced by an exit visa. On 9 October I reached Germany, but not far from the border, at Insterburg where I had stopped to rest for twenty-four hours, I was arrested by the German police and accused of espionage on behalf of Russia. The main evidence was a sketch of the *émigré* quarters in Paris which Eremeyev had drawn for me before my departure. After a few days I was released and made my way back to Russia with a view to working underground, but at Verzhbolov, on the frontier, I was arrested and deported to Archangel. At Mariampol, however, I fell ill and was confined to bed. By this time, the nervous shock of imprisonment was making itself felt and I was soon given permission for treatment in a sanatorium near St Petersburg.

On 21 February 1913 I benefited as a student from the amnesty and so reacquired the right to reside in St Petersburg. Naturally, I immediately resumed my collaboration on *Pravda*, which for censorship reasons was appearing under various, frequently changed names. With the arrival of L. B. Kamenev from abroad in spring 1914, my participation increased. By then long articles which I wrote to order for the editorial board were appearing as commentaries. I visited *Pravda* almost daily, and from time to time the offices of *Prosveshcheniye*, which also printed articles of mine. With the outbreak of war, *Pravda* was suppressed. I escaped arrest only by chance since on that day I had finished my work earlier than normal and gone home just before the police arrived.

From the first days of the imperialist war I adopted an internationalist, Leninist position. I helped compose the collective reply to Vandervelde.

The war turned me, like other contemporaries, into a military man. Having long been attracted by the elemental life at sea, I joined the navy, and despite the lack of a certificate of political reliability, I enrolled for individual classes for naval cadets. During these years I managed to sail on two cruises to the Far East, visiting Japan, Korea and distant Kamchatka. The February Revolution found me sitting my final cadet-ship examinations.

I immediately made contact with the Petrograd Committee and with the newly reappeared *Pravda*, which had arisen like a phoenix from the ashes. In it I wrote a series of articles until, at the end of March, I was sent by the editors of *Pravda* to Kronstadt to take charge of the local Party organ *Golos Pravdy*. In 'red' Kronstadt I could not limit myself merely to editing the paper, and I threw myself into the thick of Party and Soviet activity. We formed a friendly, tightly knit group which included S. G. Roshal, Kirill (Orlov), P. I. Smirnov and myself, and a little later on were joined by Smilga, Deshevoy, Bregman and Flerovsky.

I was soon elected Vice-Chairman of the Kronstadt Soviet (the Chairman was a non-Party man, Lamanov, who during the subsequent Kronstadt rebellion in 1921 revealed his White Guard views). After the July demonstration, in which I and other people from Kronstadt took an active part, I was arrested, imprisoned in the Kresty and accused of being involved in 'the case of the Bolsheviks'. On 13 October I was released and a few days alter was ordered by the Party to Novgorod and Luga to prepared the October Revolution.

During it I was directly involved in the Pulkovo battles. After the defeat of Kerensky's and Krasnov's bands, I was sent as leader of a detachment of sailors to the aid of the revolutionaries in Moscow. I was soon summoned from there and appointed Commissar of the Naval General Staff, then member of the Collegium of the Naval Commissariat and, in 1918, Deputy People's Commissar for Naval Affairs. In June 1918, I carried out a secret mission in Novorossiysk for the Sovnarkom, scuttling the Black Sea Fleet to prevent it from falling into the hands of the imperialist powers. In July 1918 I was directed to the Czechoslovak Front as a member of the RVS of the Eastern Front, and on 22 August I was appointed Commander of the Volga Naval Flotilla, which actively assisted in the capture of Kazan on 10 September, and then pursued the White Guard flotilla with daily engagements up the Kama river, finally driving them into the Belaya river and obliging them to take refuge in Ufa.

We succeeded in clearing the Kama of White Guard bands beyond Sarapul as far as Galyan. Then ice started forming and our flotilla was forced immediately to make for Nizhny Novgorod to winter there. I returned to Moscow where, as a member of the RVS, I took part in all its sessions and directed the Naval Commissariat together with the late Vasily Mikhailovich Altvater.

In late December 1918 I set off on a reconnaissance trip to Revel on board the destroyer *Spartak*. We came across a greatly superior British squadron of five light cruisers with six-inch guns. Whilst beating a retreat back to Kronstadt, our vessel suddenly ran aground, smashing the propeller. So, after being captured by the British, I was taken to London and put in Brixton jail. After five months' captivity I was exchanged for nineteen British officers imprisoned in Russia. The exchange took place at Beloostrov on 27 May 1919. Immediately on my return from England, I was appointed Commander of the Caspian Flotilla. Soon it was joined by the Volga Flotilla which had returned from the Kama, and the combined river and sea-going forces were called the Volga-Caspian Naval Flotilla. Our vessels had to operate in separate units over a huge area from Saratov on the Volga to Lagan and Ganyushkin on the Caspian. The most bitterly fought battles were near Tsaritsyn and Chornoye Yaro. In both cases our ships were subjected to almost daily aerial attacks. However, the combined actions of the Red Army and the Red Flotilla saved Astrakhan which had been encircled by White Guards, holding out only thanks to the one railway line linking it with Saratov. Finally, in 1920, the capture of the Aleksandrov fort and the remnants of the White Guard Ural Cossacks, as well as the expulsion of the British from Enzeli, completed the flotilla's campaign.

During the Civil War I was twice awarded the Order of the Red Banner. In June 1920 I was appointed Commander of the Baltic Fleet. In view of our advance on Warsaw, Kronstadt was put on a state of alert to receive British 'guests'. But to our great disappointment Lloyd George did not send a single British ship into Kronstadt waters.

In March 1921, with the end of the Civil War and the transition to peaceful construction, I demobilized myself and was appointed Ambassador to Afghanistan. In December 1923 I returned to Moscow, becoming editor-in-chief of *Molodaya Gvardiya*, *Krasnaya Nov* and the publishing house *Moskovsky Rabochy*. In spring 1926 I returned to Afghanistan as head of our delegation in a combined Soviet-Afghan Commission.

Raskolnikov was a deeply contradictory character. He was a man of action, convinced of the efficacity of his own will, and a fighting, flailing man with a passionate taste for literature and 'proletarian' culture and writing; he also wrote some lively memoirs and a mediocre play entitled *Robespierre*. He was married to the 'Revolutionary Pallas', Larissa

Reisner, and they made a spectacular couple. Raskolnikov, finally, was so totally alien to theoretical problems that he openly displayed his boredom during the long, general discussions of which the Bolsheviks were so fond until Stalin invented his sharp-edged tool of 'criticism and self-criticism'.

This lack of interest, not so much for political *ideas* as for any general conception going beyond the immediate struggle, often led Raskolnikov into error: in 1912–13, for example, he was the first secretary of the editorial board of *Pravda*—the editorial board of which Lenin had said, 'They're a bunch of milksops, ruining the cause. . . . They must be got rid of.' In March 1917, Sukhanov thought him 'an agreeable man, upright and well thought of. A convinced socialist and extreme Bolshevik, he is, unlike many others, completing his socialist education' —this no doubt because he paid attention to Sukhanov's volubility. But the smell of gunpowder excited him: he was Vice-President of the Kronstadt Sailors' Soviet, which, thanks to his courage, verve and eloquence, he managed to dominate; during the July days, he was given the task of securing the defence of the Bolshevik Party's headquarters in the Kseshinskaya Palace, but he took such glaringly military measures that they appeared to justify the idea that the Bolsheviks were preparing an insurrection. That, and his leading role in the 'Kronstadt Republic', as his opponents called it, led him to Kerensky's prisons.

After the October Revolution he played an important role in the Red Army. As Vice-Commissar for the Navy, he commanded the Volga-Caspian fleet, then the Baltic fleet, and in May 1920 led the attack on Enzeli which enabled the Red Navy to recapture the ships Denikin had abandoned in his retreat. On the other hand, Raskolnikov did not become a *political* figure and held no important post in this field.

In 1920–1 he supported Trotsky on the union question, but it seems this was not really out of any conviction, but more out of sympathy for the man whom he had seconded during the entire Civil War. Thenceforth, moreover, he followed the leadership's line faithfully, and in 1921 left as Ambassador to Afghanistan. In Kabul he waged a vigorously anti-British policy; he was recalled in 1923 when it appeared to be appropriate to tone down anti-British policies. He was appointed under the name of Petrov to the directorship of the Comintern's Eastern Section. He was bored in this post and seemed content to sign his subordinates' reports and circulars.

An Asian communist leader who met him at that time recalls him thus: 'A handsome man, with blue eyes and hair close-cropped more like an English student than a Russian Bolshevik [. . .] He was a natural man of action, quick, direct, incisive [. . .] He had no interest in theoretical problems [. . .] His theoretical talents had never commanded much respect [. . .] Nevertheless, he had a sharp, active mind, though at that time he was more interested in literature than politics.' He was, moreover, at that time a member of the College of the Commissariat for Public Education (headed by Lunacharsky), for a short while president of the Glavrepertkom, chief editor of the publishing house *Moskovsky Rabochy*, editor of the review *Molodaya Gvardia*, and head of Glaviskusstvo. All these activities could only serve to diminish Raskolnikov's authority over the new-style Comintern *cadres*, to whom art and literature were not serious matters. At the end of 1926 he was relieved of his responsibilities in the Comintern.

It was then that he wrote his *Robespierre*, and adapted Tolstoy's *Resurrection* for the cinema. In 1934 he became a member of the Writers' Union. In 1930, he had resumed his diplomatic career, and was ambassador to Estonia, then to Denmark and finally Bulgaria. In 1937, on tour in Sofia, he noticed on a list of forbidden books to be burned his own memoirs on *Kronstadt and Petersburg in 1917*. He was recalled to Moscow in 1938; dismissed before crossing the border, he decided to seek exile in France. From Paris, on 17 August 1939, he wrote Stalin a violent 'Open Letter'. The man who had vehemently denounced Trotsky and Trotskyism from 1924 on suddenly declared: 'You have destroyed Lenin's party, and on its corpse you have built a new "Leninist-Stalinist party" which acts as a cover for your personal power. . . . On the eve of war, you are annihilating the conquests of October. . . . "Father of the people", you have betrayed the Spanish revolutionaries.' This declaration appeared in *Dni*, Kerensky's newspaper. On 12 September 1939, Raskolnikov died in Nice in suspicious circumstances.

In 1963 a volume appeared in Moscow devoted to the *Heroes of the Civil War*. A certain Tikhomirov contributed a long article to it on Raskolnikov, and concluded in the following terms: 'Fyodor Fyodorovich remained to the end of his days a true Leninist, a Soviet patriot and a fearless fighter for the Bolshevik Party.' The author of an article on Raskolnikov in *Voprosy Istorii KPSS* (issue 12 of 1963) mentioned the existence of the 'Open Letter', and wrote that it 'unmasked Stalin's arbitrariness, the discredit which he cast on Soviet democracy and on socialism. Raskolnikov accused Stalin of massive repression of innocent people [. . .] He accused Stalin's *Handbook of the History of the CPSU* of robbing those the General Secretary himself had killed and calumnied, and of ascribing their achievements to himself.'

This radical rehabilitation of Raskolnikov is surprising. Although the old figurehead reminds us that 'I've fought all oppositions on the

ideological front', he none the less ended his letter with a stroke that
went beyond Stalin:

> Feverishly seeking support, you spend yourself in hypocritical com-
> pliments to 'Bolsheviks without a Party', you are creating, one after
> the other, groups of privileged persons, you heap favours on them,
> you feed them on alms, but you cannot guarantee these new 'one-
> hour sultans' not just their privileges, but even their right to live.

J.-J. M.

LEONID PETROVICH SEREBRYAKOV
(autobiography)

I was born in 1890 in Samara. Our family consisted of father (an engineering worker), mother, and six sons. Father had to wander from one town to another in search of work. At the age of nine, I was with our family in Ufa where we lived in difficult material conditions as a result of father's absence, and I was forced to take a job at the Vedenev brewery, earning one rouble twenty kopecks per week. Father soon found a vacancy at the Harriman locomotive plant in Lugansk, where the family joined him. Here my elder brothers worked by his side, and as I now had the opportunity of not working, I entered the town primary school. But school studies do not last long, and when I left, I continued my self-education. In 1904, when I was fourteen, father found a new job in Baku, but my brothers and myself remained in Lugansk. Now I had to think about work on my own account. I was too young to become a worker at an engineering works, but the date of birth entered in my papers was 1887, and thanks to this I was allowed to work at a lathe. At the same time, I became acquainted with the illegal literature which my brothers carefully hid in lofts and sheds. When they noticed that their younger brother was interested in the labour movement, they and their comrades began to entrust me with the distribution of literature, and within a year, by 1905, I was a member of the Lugansk RSDRP(b) Committee.

In 1905 one could not work for the Party with impunity. I was arrested, but the period of 'freedoms' arrived and I was released. In 1906 and 1907 I was subjected to frequent searches and arrests, as well as dismissal from work. In 1908 came a two-year exile to Vologda province. I lived in Ust-Sysolsk with a number of comrades (including Dogadov, Kameron, Kaganovich). I existed on State charity – six roubles twenty kopecks per month – and continued my Marxist education. On completion of my exile, in late 1910 and early 1911, I was ordered by the Party to travel throughout Russia and spread propaganda whilst earning the money for it by factory work.

Without staying for long in any one place, I spent a longer period in Nikolaev, preparing for the Prague Conference with a group of comrades (including Sergo Ordzhonikidze and Semyon Schwartz). On returning from the Conference, I was entrusted with a mission in the Volga region. In 1912 the Samara organisation collapsed and I was sentenced to three years' exile in Narym with Zelensky, Kuchmenko and others. In 1913 I escaped from there to St Petersburg and here I was instructed by the CC Bureau to organise a strike in Baku. After one and a half months there I was obliged to leave, following intensified shadowing and an attempted arrest. I travelled first to Tiflis, then to Sukhum, Nikolaev and finally Odessa, where I was arrested immediately on disembarking and sent back to Narym. In 1914 I again escaped, helped to organise the May Day demonstration in Moscow, was swiftly arrested and again exiled in Narym. In mid-1915 I made another attempt at escape, but in 1916, on completion of my sentence, I settled in Tomsk where I carried on Party work in a military organisation. In late 1916 I moved to Petrograd, participated in the demonstration of 9 January, and at the end of that month, I went to Rybinsk to put my papers in order. There I was called up for military service and ordered to report to the 88th Reserve Infantry Regiment in Kostroma. I continued my Party activity within the ranks and on 1 March led a mutiny. Then with Danilov, Yazykov, Kaganovich and others I organized the Kostroma Soviet of Workers' and Soldiers' Deputies where I worked until mid-1917. At that point I moved to Moscow as a member of the regional Party Committee, attending congresses and conferences in preparation for October.

From October, I was a Presidium member of the Moscow Soviet and Secretary of the regional Party Committee. I was then elected a Presidium member and Secretary of VTsIK. In 1919–20 I was CC Secretary of the RKP(b), Head of the Southern Bureau of the Central Trade Union Council, a member of the RVS of the Southern Front, chief of its political directorate, and then in late 1921 became Commissar for Transport. Since May 1922 I have been Deputy People's Commissar for Transport, carrying out the duties of Commissar, and at the present time am a Collegium member of the same Commissariat.

Serebryakov was a quiet, withdrawn man who scarcely attracted the attention of the writers of memoirs and historical portraits. He was elected to the Central Committee in 1919, and in the following year went on to the Secretariat and the Orgburo. He was ill for much of this time, but distinguished himself in these positions for his desire to smooth over rather than to exacerbate internal conflicts. The 'tact and subtlety' which he manifested at that time did not prevent him from being dismissed in 1921 for having supported Trotsky's platform on the union question. He was never again elected to the Central Committee.

In 1923 he signed the 'Declaration of the 46', and in 1926 played a decisive part in the *rapprochement* between the Zinovievites and the Trotskyites, and subsequently in the internal cohesiveness of the United Opposition. Meanwhile, Stalin sent him, like almost all the other opposition leaders, on diplomatic postings abroad, as a Minister Plenipotentiary to Vienna, where Victor Serge met him in 1924 and described him as 'fair and fat, in good humour'. In August 1927 he was expelled from the

Bolshevik Party with Mrachovsky, Preobrazhensky and the rest of the group that had run the opposition's clandestine printing-press. He was exiled to Siberia and according to Trotsky 'he capitulated to the ruling clique in a more honourable way, it is true, than some, but no less decisively'. In 1930 he was readmitted to the Party and appointed to a high official position in the Commissariat for Communications, then sent on a mission to the United States. As an old friend of Abel Enukidze, he escaped the vicissitudes undergone by most of the former opposition at that time, who were successively expelled and readmitted. In August 1936, however, the defendants at the first Moscow Trial implicated Serebryakov in the 'terrorist' activities, and he was expelled from the Party immediately after the trial. He was among the defendants at the second Moscow Trial in January 1937, where he confessed to amazing acts of sabotage. He was sentenced to death and shot.

Serebryakov was a good-humoured man of action, and wrote very little; his friends had little influence in the Party, and his articles were infrequent. Thus historians have accorded him little importance. Neither a *littérateur* nor an orator, Serebryakov will have to wait until the Soviet archives are opened before he can regain his rightful place in the history of the Russian Revolution.

J.-J. M.

ALEKSANDR GAVRILOVICH SHLYAPNIKOV
(autobiography)

I was born in Murom in Vladimir province. My father came from the lower middle class and had practised many trades: he had been a miller, a labourer, a carpenter and a clerk. My mother was the daughter of an engineering worker at the Dostchatoye plant. My father was drowned when I was only two, leaving my mother with four small children, the youngest of whom was only a few months old.

It was a hard life to be a widow without income or means of support. All the members of the family learnt to do some kind of work from their earliest years so as to be useful and help mother in her struggle to scrape a living. Yet despite all this, she insisted on bringing up her children herself in accordance with traditional customs and the Old Faith. Both my parents' families were Old Believers, belonging to the Pomory sect, which was persecuted by police and clergy. From early childhood I knew what religious persecution meant. My education was greatly influenced by the adults arguing, fighting and brawling on the high street of our remote town.

For all mother's kindness, we were left to our own devices for a large part of our childhood. The harsh struggle to earn even a crust of bread for her children compelled her to seek work wherever she could find it. Some days we did not see her at home from early morning until late at night. There were evenings when, alone in the house without anyone to mind us, we children were particularly worried for her safety. On winter evenings, when she would go and do other people's washing in the Oka, we often hurt ourselves whilst she was away and came home with our feet frozen to our shoes. We would collapse into bed with various ailments for months on end, causing her new worry and expense.

As I came from a family of Old Believers, my date of birth was not registered precisely. In the old town records I have been given three different dates of birth, 1883, 1884 and 1885. This is easy to explain. When I finished primary school, I had to look for work straightaway. This meant increasing my age, and a couple of kopecks slipped to one of the secretaries or clerks in the registry was enough to put one's age up by the desired amount.

At the age of eight, I entered primary school. I left three years later, having learnt to read and write. School was no mother to me, and it was not the teachers who educated me. The divinity teacher, knowing my Old Believer background, persecuted me in all sorts of ways. During these three years, he punished me on the day after each holiday for not having gone to church by making me kneel and do without dinner until five o'clock in the evening. The teachers were young and very rude, and they often meted out justice to their young charges with their fists. Even during these years, life taught me that there is no justice in this world. After reading all manner of religious writings, I was ready to do battle for the truth of the Old Believers' faith in God. As soon as I learned to read, my mother often made me recite *The Lives of the Holy Martyrs* and the Psalms of David, many of which I learnt by heart. The religious bigotry, the persecutions of street and school, the poverty and deprivation in our family—all this turned my childish dreams and inclinations towards struggle and martyrdom.

As soon as I finished school, I immediately began to look for work. At that age there was no job that I thought beneath me. I picked fruit in orchards. I dried sand in foundry shops. I did other manual labouring jobs, earning from fifteen to twenty kopecks for a twelve-hour day. My contact with factory life and artisans of the old school gave me the idea of setting up as an independent artisan myself. I dreamt of being a lathe operator and did my best to become one. In the end, I found a job in the village of Vacha at the engineering works belonging to the heirs of D. D. Kondratov. I began my apprenticeship on a planing machine, and then in 1900 moved to Sormovo where I graduated to a lathe. After a few months there, I went further afield, to St Petersburg. Then followed the long ordeal of looking for work in the capital, but finally I was taken on as an apprentice fitter at the Neva shipbuilding yard. I was not yet eighteen, and despite attempts to change the age on my passport from 15 to 17, I still could not raise it to the one necessary for work on machine tools.

In spring 1901 a large-scale strike broke out in St Petersburg, which was followed by the notorious massacre at the Obukhov factory. Working at the Semyannikov plant, I was very active for my age in the strike, inciting apprentices from all the workshops, shipbuilding as well as joinery, to drive out workers who did not want to join us. We stuffed our pockets with screws and all sorts of scraps of iron, and made for the docks and workshops. Those who went against the general strike decision were pelted with iron fragments, nuts and bolts, and were forced into line. We flocked about the yard of the Semyannikov factory and clustered outside the Obukhov works. Policemen on foot and horseback threatened us with their whips, but this only strengthened our youthful readiness to fight. For such active participation in the strike, I was dismissed from Semyannikov's and blacklisted.

All my attempts to find work at another factory ended in failure. With the help of some workers, I was given a job at the Obukhov works, but was dismissed as a striker after a couple of weeks. Other attempts had the same result. The impossibility of finding a job in a large factory turned me to work in small workshops. The pay there was so paltry that it did not even cover the rent, and I was reduced to spending the night at the town baths which I was supposed to be repairing during the day. After a year of hardship in the capital, I had earned enough money for the fare to Sormovo, and from there I made my way home.

It was during the strike in St Petersburg that I came across revolutionary propaganda in the shape of several pamphlets. I do not remember their titles, but I was not surprised by their contents since they only described what I myself had experienced and realised in these early years. On my way back from St Petersburg to Sormovo, the local social democratic organisation supplied me with a whole series of pamphlets, leaflets, and a few issues of the social democratic newspaper which was coming out at that time in Nizhny Novgorod. With this literature I returned home to Murom. There I soon found work as a stopgap lathe operator cum craftsman. This enabled me to carry out propaganda among workers both at that factory and elsewhere in the area.

In 1903 the Nizhny Novgorod Committee of the RSDRP began to take an interest in our work and to send their own people and literature. A Party Committee was created in Murom to be responsible for the Vyksa and Kulebaki mines, as well as for local textile and other enterprises. But there proved to be *agents provocateurs* in our midst: one was a postal worker called Moshentsev, the other a worker named Moiseyev. Both of them soon aroused suspicion by their behaviour and were expelled. This, however, saved only a part of the organisation, for the nucleus had already been betrayed. At the beginning of 1904 arrests had been carried out in the region. In all, about ten people were detained, among them the writer of these lines. The gendarmes compiled a whole dossier on our organisation, but the case was never brought to court as the *agents provocateurs* had been unmasked by us during the investigation. After being held in custody longer than anyone else – nine months in solitary confinement – I was released under police supervision. This allowed me to find work in a factory again.

In our area the events of January 1905 provoked a wave of strikes and protests in which we were actively involved. In July 1905 we called a mass meeting in memory of the massacre of workers on 'Bloody Sunday'. Intervention by the police turned the meeting into an armed demonstration which set upon policemen and roamed about town for the whole evening. A week later, I was arrested and incarcerated in the Vladimir Central Hard Labour Prison—the Murom jail not being considered strong enough.

The strike of October 1905, which led to an amnesty for political prisoners, also brought about my release. I immediately rejoined the ranks of the revolutionary social democrat workers. On the day of my release, a gang of the Vladimir Black Hundreds beat me up in the street, and I returned home with marks all over my face to prove it. Following the example of the St Petersburg workers, I tried to organise a local soviet of workers' deputies and local trade unionists, whilst the Party organisations turned to legal activity.

It was in the month of October that I became due for military service. My date of birth had been referred to a special commission, which had determined my age by external appearance and had fixed my call-up for 1905. The recruitment campaign of that year took place in an atmosphere of revolutionary fervour among the young. Demonstrations broke out here and there. A significant proportion of the recruits were, as was said at the time, infected with revolutionary propaganda. I personally refused to take the oath of allegiance to Tsar and country, but the authorities did not dare arrest me, since they feared that this would provoke the recruits into riots both at the army offices and in jail.

I did not, however, have to serve in the Tsarist army. Two months after my release from the Vladimir prison, the Governor of the province issued a new order for my arrest. The police made several attempts to take me into custody, but I was saved by the threat of armed resistance. Nevertheless, I was taken by surprise in a barber's shop where I had gone for a shave on Christmas Eve. I was held in prison until the beginning of 1907. In January of that year I was sentenced to a further two years' detention in a fortress, and then released on bail of 300 roubles until my sentence could be served. After this release, I was arrested once more in Moscow during a police drive against SRs at a technical institute. I spent only one month in jail, however, and was still not sent to a fortress.

In 1907 I was active in the Party organisation in the Lefortovo district in Moscow, and then moved to St Petersburg. There I worked as Party organiser for the Peskov (now Rozhdestvensky) district, was a member of the St Petersburg Committee, and participated in various Party conferences until the beginning of 1908. Then I went abroad, where I stayed until 1914, wandering from factory to factory in France, England and Germany.

In April 1914 I returned to Russia with a French passport in the name of Noé. I worked at the Lesner and then the Erikson plant as a lathe operator. I carried out several tasks on behalf of the Duma 'fraction' and the St Petersburg Committee, besides taking part in strikes and mass meetings. At the end of September, the St Petersburg Committee sent me abroad with various messages to liaise with the CC. In 1915 I was in

Sweden, Denmark and Norway, I worked in England, and then returned secretly to the Russian capital in November. There, as I had been instructed, I founded a CC bureau to direct the work of the Party inside Russia. At the beginning of 1916 I again went abroad. During all these years, I remained in the closest possible contact with the *émigré* section of the CC, including Lenin and Zinoviev, and from 1915 I was a co-opted member of the Central Committee myself. In 1916 I went to America to raise funds for Party activity. By this time, too, the CC bureau which I had formed had been partly arrested and partly penetrated by the secret police, so I had to set about the creation of a new one.

During the winter of 1916–17, the work of our Party organisations brought the revolutionary struggle of the masses with Tsarism to a head. In the period preceding the February Revolution, the RSDRP was the only revolutionary party calling the working masses to an armed uprising. As for myself, I was a member of the group which took the initiative of forming the Petrograd Soviet, and on 27 February I was elected to its Executive Committee.

The latter entrusted me with the task of arming the workers, and I equipped the first elements of the Workers' Red Guard with weapons. On the instructions of the Petrograd and Vyborg Party Committees, as well as the Vyborg district Soviet, I drafted the regulations of the Red Guard and the plan of its organisation, as well as improvising the means of procuring its arms. I also helped to organise the return of our *émigrés* from abroad, and the reception for Lenin and the others on 3 April 1917.

During a propaganda drive at the beginning of April, I suffered concussion when my car collided with a tram, and had to spend two weeks in hospital. On my discharge, I returned to Party work, the activities of the Executive Committee, and also the organisation of trade unions in Petrograd. The metal-workers there had elected me their President during April and when, three months later, the All-Russian Union of Metal-Workers was founded, I was voted Chairman of its provisional Central Committee. I took part in the first Congress of Soviets, and in all the events connected with those days. I was also elected a member of the All-Russian TsIK.

It was in the latter capacity that, during the events of 3–5 July,[1] I toured the barracks rescuing Bolshevik comrades from arrest and ill-treatment. As a trade union leader, I was a delegate to various social bodies at that time: I took part in the Moscow Conference and the Petrograd Democratic Conference, and I was elected Vice-President of the conference of factories in the Petrograd industrial district.

As a Party worker and the President of the largest union of metal-

[1] See pp. 222–3.

workers, I participated in various conferences organised by the CC dealing with preparations for the October Revolution. During the Revolution, I mobilised Red Guard detachments and enlisted the active support of trade unions to ensure its success. I attended the second Congress of Soviets, where I was elected a member of the Sovnarkom and People's Commissar for Labour. In this post, I drummed up trade union support for the struggle against organised sabotage and a strike by employees. I directed the work of the People's Commissariat for Trade and Industry until its abolition. I helped to organise the Council for Workers' Control, and took part in the first Trade Union Congress in January 1918. By a decree of the Sovnarkom and the Petrograd Soviet, I was then appointed Chairman of the Commission supervising the evacuation of the capital in view of the German threat.

The summer of 1918 I spent as special envoy with emergency powers to ensure the supply of bread to the industrial areas of Russia. In the process, I became embroiled in the spreading civil war in the Caucasus. I was cut off from Central Russia for several weeks by White Guards, and escaped from their encirclement along secret, hidden paths. In the same year, I was dispatched by a decree of the CC to join the RVS of the Southern Front, and then became President of the Council for the Caspian and Caucasus Front. From 1919 to the beginning of 1920, I was on the Western Front.

These are the outlines of my work up to 1920. To go into greater detail would mean enumerating a considerable number of revolutionary events in which I took part. To enlarge on my activities since 1920 would mean recounting a tiny fragment of the social and political history of our Soviet land, for which I have at present neither time nor opportunity.

Brought up in an atmosphere of religious strictness, Shlyapnikov had a tendency (which some might consider 'naive') to deal with political problems in terms of moral categories: devotion, sacrifice, sincerity . . . to which was added, even more naively, a pride in his horny hands, in his genuine industrial and proletarian origins. Lenin teased him on this during discussion of the trade union question in 1920-1: 'As always, comrade Shlyapnikov harps on his authentically proletarian character'. Shlyapnikov was a somewhat empirical analyst of a particular period, and limited his arguments to the Russian situation during this dispute. He constantly accused Lenin, at this time, of trying to 'terrorise' him, which Lenin described as childish imaginings.

He is one of the best representatives of the hundreds of party *cadres* who had risen from the Russian proletariat and who formed the backbone of the Party, allowing it to survive the collapse of 'social patriotism' in 1914; and to whom the long, clandestine struggle against Tsarism had given a taste for freedom of speech and freedom to criticise.

The deportation of the leading Bolsheviks in Russia (the deputies in the Duma, Kamenev, Sverdlov, Stalin, Spandarian, Ordzhonikidze, Olminsky, etc.), and the dismantling of the Party were the circumstances which put Shlyapnikov at the head of the Russian Bureau of the Central Committee, which had been reorganised at the end of 1916. When war broke out in 1914, Shlyapnikov was at first overcome by the wave of chauvinism which swept the Russian and European workers' movements. According to Krestinsky, he declared in August 1914, 'If I had been in Jules Guesde's shoes, I should have done as he did, and, to speak the truth, if I were now in France I should volunteer for the Foreign Legion.' This patriotic fervour did not last long, and when the February Revolution broke out, Shlyapnikov was Lenin's faithful liaison agent inside Russia. As a leader of the Russian Bureau of the Central Committee, he was, like his colleagues Molotov and Zalutsky, overtaken by events.

Between 1924 and 1928, Shlyapnikov published his memoirs of 1917, in which he presents himself honestly, as he was: an attentive *observer*, following events with only one idea in mind: to oppose the arming of the workers which the leaders of the Vyborg district (Kayurov, Chugurin) were demanding. He himself feared that it would alienate the soldiers from the revolutionary cause.

Shlyapnikov attended the constituent assembly of the Petrograd Soviet on the evening of 27 January. He gave no clearly defined political line, and deserved entirely the assessment which Kayurov made of his actions: 'Comrade Shlyapnikov was incapable of giving directives for the next day.'

Immediately after the Revolution, Shlyapnikov was on the left wing of the Party. He was hostile towards the Provisional government, and favoured the extension of the imperialist war into a civil war, as well as a merger with the anti-defencist *Mezhrayonka*; but from mid-March he was ousted by the Kamenev-Stalin-Muranov bloc. At the Bolshevik Party Conference in March, he took no part in the debates, which saw the emergence of a left wing in opposition to the rightist policies of Kamenev-Stalin, in favour of an alliance with the Mensheviks. He was content to preside at the meeting on 2 April, and to go to greet Lenin at Byeloostrov, on the Finnish frontier, on the evening of the 3rd.

Absent from the April Party Conference because of an accident, Shlyapnikov was not elected to the Central Committee. From then on he moved towards trade union work: he was elected President of the Petrograd Metal-Workers Union in April, and in July he became President of the All-Russian Metal-Workers Union, which he won over to Bolshevism; in June he was delegated with Ryazanov as the Bolshevik representative on the newly elected All-Russian Central Union Council. Faced with the prospect of open insurrection presented by Lenin and Trotsky, Shlyapnikov exhibited both the conservatism of trade unionism in a revolutionary era, and the hesitation of the masses before engaging in an action which put their future at stake. At the enlarged meeting of the Central Committee on 10 October, he declared that 'in the Metal-Workers' Union, Bolshevik influence predominates, but the idea of a Bolshevik uprising is not popular; rumours about it have even created panic'. In the October days he played no role whatsoever. Appointed People's Commissar for Labour, he allied himself to the right wing, which sought a coalition government (Bolsheviks, Mensheviks and SRs). On 4 November the rightists resigned from their positions. Shlyapnikov associated himself with their declaration, but considered it 'inadmissible to renounce responsibilities and duties'. Then he withdrew and remained silent over the Brest-Litovsk crisis.

After that, he was occupied by military missions. In June 1918, he was sent by the Central Committee to the south of Russia together with Stalin, to control supplies. Stalin stopped at Tsaritsyn, while Shlyapnikov went on his way to the Caucasus. In October, he was appointed to the Southern Front RVS, and then in December found himself in command of the newly formed Caspian-Caucasus Front, centred on Astrakhan. The Front covered the Eleventh and Twelfth Armies which soon crumbled. In February 1919 (and not 1920 as he stated) he was called back to Moscow, and replaced in Astrakhan by Mekhonoshin. Elected to candidate membership of the Central Committee at the seventh Congress, he began, in early 1919, to develop the ideas which were to form the Workers' Opposition from September 1920. He was unable to defend these ideas at the eighth Congress since he had been sent by the Sovnarkom on a lengthy mission to Norway. At the same time, he was replaced by Goltsman as President of the Metal-Workers' Union, and he was succeeded by his comrade Medvedev.

In the theses he distributed before the ninth Congress, he stated that the trade unions constituted the only 'responsible organiser of the economy'. The union dispute which broke out at the end of 1920 allowed him to fill out his views, which formed the basis for the Workers' Opposition which he led with the Metal-Workers' Union leaders, Medvedev and Lutovinov, as well as Alexandra Kollontai and the President of the Mine-Workers' Union, Kiselev. The Workers' Opposition united the lower union *cadres* who were hostile to 'specialist' control and to the growing state control of the economy. Shlyapnikov proclaimed:

'Let us finish with state bureaucracy and economic bureaucracy.' The means to this end? 'An All-Russian Congress of producers must elect the economic leadership', or variants on the theme, such as an All-Russian Production Congress, tripartite organisms (Party-soviets-unions) responsible to the unions. In all cases it was the Party's role that was substantially restricted. At the same time he wanted the trade unions to take over the leadership of working-class discontent 'while combatting with all their strength the tendency to foment strikes'. His proposals found an obvious audience in a Party weary of excessive centralism created by the Civil War, while the exhausted, disorganised, fragmented working class was incapable of facing up to the tasks of production.

The Kronstadt revolt and the NEP made the tenth Congress put a provisional ban on splinter groups. Lenin, moreover, had the Workers' Opposition specifically condemned, although two of its leaders, Shlyapnikov and Kutuzov, were elected to the Central Committee. From then on, Shlyapnikov waged a struggle against the subordination of the unions (and in the first instance, of the Metal-Workers' Union) to the central Party machine. This struggle, and the criticisms Shlyapnikov made of Party policy, led Lenin in August 1922 to request his expulsion from the Central Committee; Frunze threatened to convince him 'with a machine-gun'. The Central Committee refused to comply. In February 1922, Shlyapnikov signed the declaration of 'the 22' by which the Workers' Opposition appealed to the International against the sanctions taken against it. Threatened with expulsion, he made a cutting, ironical speech to the eleventh Congress (March 1922), in which he claimed that the Party was as demoralised as it had been in 1907, that it was in full reactionary spate, that the NEP was anti-working class; he stigmatised the pro-peasant direction of the Party and its refusal to engage on a policy of industrialisation. The Congress gave him a stern warning.

From this point the decimated, demoralised Workers' Opposition, overtaken on the left by clandestine groups such as Workers' Truth, the Workers' Group, etc., began to collapse. At the beginning of 1924, at the height of the battle between the left opposition and the Party machine, Shlyapnikov declared that there was no difference between the two sides, for neither gave a fig for the fate of the working classes. He then drew up, with Medvedev, a programme document known as the 'Baku Letter' which at the time remained secret. Then he was sent by the secretariat to Paris as a councillor in the Soviet legation: diplomatic postings were customary at that time for members of the opposition. He remained there during 1924 and 1925, and drafted his memoirs of 1917. On his return to Russia, in the middle of the fight between the United Opposition (which for a time he joined) and the Stalinist leadership,

Pravda published (on 30 July 1926) an article which denounced the 'Baku Letter' (which the GPU had known about for at least a year) as an expression of 'the ultra-rightist views [. . .] of capitulators to international financial plutocracy'. On 29 October 1926, Medvedev and Shlyapnikov sent a letter to the Politburo and to the Presidium of the TsKK in which they stated their withdrawal from opposition and 'condemned any organised expression of opinions contradicting Party decisions'. Shlyapnikov then devoted himself to the third volume of his memoirs of 1917, which was published in 1928. In 1930, the Party secretariat forced him to publish a public confession of his 'political errors'. He was expelled from the Party in 1933 as a 'degenerate'. Imprisoned in 1935, he died in 1937, a forgotten witness of another age.

J.-J. M.

BENYAMIN NIKOLAYEVICH KAYUROV

The fate of Kayurov (forgotten by the Granat Encyclopedia) comple-
ments that of Shlyapnikov. While Shlyapnikov, in February 1917, tried
in vain to rise to the responsibilities imposed upon him by his *de facto*
leadership of the Bolshevik Party, Kayurov, a member of the Vyborg
Committee (which had taken over, effectively, from the Petrograd Committee which had been under arrest since 26 February), with his comrades Chugurin, Khakharev, etc., was in day-to-day control of the
Revolution in the streets. Shlyapnikov belonged to the leadership of the
Bolshevik Party. Kayurov remained in the ranks, and his life is obscure.

Born in a working-class family in 1876, Kayurov joined the RSDRP
in 1900, and allied himself to the Bolshevik faction in 1903. At the
outbreak of the Revolution in February 1917, he was a worker in
the Erikson factory at Vyborg (Petrograd suburb) and a member of the
Vyborg District Committee. After the Revolution, he was elected to the
Executive Committee of the Vyborg District Soviet. In the early summer
of 1918, he was sent on a mission to Siberia. Upon his return, Lenin sent
him to Petrograd with an open letter to the workers of Petrograd, in
which he asked his 'old friend'[1] Kayurov to invite the starving workers
of Petrograd to leave *en masse* for the countryside, to find food and put
down the Kulaks (letter of 12 July 1918). Eight days later, Lenin called
Kayurov to other tasks: the Kazan Front was in a state of collapse. The
regiments of the Fifth Army were fleeing before the Czech legions,
Kazan fell. Trotsky moved back to Sivyazhsk, the stop before Moscow.
To turn around an army reduced to pulp, where mess sergeants and
porters were being armed to hold the front, they needed communists,
Petrograd communists, the sort Lenin referred to in his letter of 12 July
1918—'In all Russia there are no workers more revolutionary than the
workers of Petrograd'. On 20 July 1918, Lenin wrote to Zinoviev,
Lashevich and Stasova: 'We must send down there the *maximum* number
of Petrograd workers: (1) a few dozen "leaders" (like Kayurov); (2) a
few thousand militants "from the ranks".'

A few days later, Kayurov and Chugurin led a detachment of several
thousand Petrograd communist militants to the Kazan Front. It was the
first of the detachments of militants who, after having fought February,
then October, went to perish on one of the eight or nine fronts of the
Civil War. Kayurov and Chugurin were included in the General Staff of

---

[1] After the July days (3rd–5th) and the smear campaign waged against him by
the Plekhanovian and former Bolshevik Aleksinsky (who denounced Lenin and
Zinoviev as German agents), Lenin decided to go into hiding. The first hiding-
place he used, on 6 July, was Kayurov's apartment.

the reconstituted Fifth Army, the Fifth Army of Smirnov and Tukhachevsky which was to shake Kolchak in 1919 and 1920, and enthusiastically win over Siberia to the Soviets. Kayurov was in charge of the
political section of the Fifth Army. He remained in Siberia from 1920 to
1922, in various posts concerned with the economy; in 1921–2 he was
President of the Siberian Regional Committee of the TsKK for the
purging of the Party. He returned to Petrograd in 1923, wrote a few
pages of his memoirs (on the February Revolution, on his meetings with
Lenin). When the struggle between Stalin and the United Opposition
arose after the disintegration of the triumvirate, he supported Zinoviev,
but remained in the background. Already he appeared a man of the past.

In 1932 the right-winger Ryutin drew up a political platform which
denounced Stalin as the 'evil genius of the Russian Revolution', and
compared him to the police *agent provocateur* Azev, who had led the
SRs' terrorist section between 1902 and 1909; he also declared that the
Trotskyites were right about the problems of internal democracy, while
the right-wing was correct on the questions of agricultural policy.
Among Ryutin's contacts was Kayurov, who gave his assent to this
platform. He was expelled from the Party with all Ryutin's supporters.
Stalin requested the execution of Ryutin, who had claimed it was necessary to remove the leader from his post as General Secretary. When in
1936 the wave of terror swept over the Party, stalinised but still an
annoyance to its General Secretary and to the NKVD, Kayurov refused
to confess to the list of crimes he was required to sign. Yagoda's policemen shot him down.

J.-J. M.

NIKOLAY ALEKSEYEVICH SKRYPNIK
(autobiography)[1]

My father was a railway employee—at first a telegraph operator and then an assistant station-master. My parents, simple and uneducated people, had a vaguely hostile attitude towards the existing system of political and economic repression. In the early 1850s my father had been acquainted with Sunday school workers, and he had been educated by them after the emancipation of the serfs, whilst my mother had performed some services for revolutionaries during midwifery courses, which she took in the late 1860s and early 1870s. They both retained from this time a sense of respect for revolutionaries and dissatisfaction with the prevailing conditions, which to some extent they passed on to me.

I was born on 13 January 1872 in the village of Yasinovatoye in Ekaterinoslav province. My early life centred on the railways and stations, my father being transferred from one to another almost every six months, although always in the Ukraine. My first school was the two-year village one at Barbenkovo, Izyum district, Kharkov province, and then I went to the Izyum 'modern' school, from which I was later expelled for propaganda among peasants. I attained revolutionary consciousness without any external influence because in Izyum there was there not a single revolutionary, there was not even one liberal-minded person. The starting-point of my development was a study of Ukrainian history and literature. I was also influenced by family legends about ancestors who had been Cossacks, one of whom had been impaled for his participation in the Zaliznyak and Gonta rebellion against the Poles in the eighteenth century. The poems of Shevchenko led me to read history—Ukrainian history in general, and in particular the history of the period of uprisings, war and destruction. In this way I came across the *Chornaya Rada* (the 'Black Band') and the class rebellions by the oppressed against the Cossack leadership, which strengthened my objections to the rule of the wealthy and stimulated me to read about economic and historical problems. On the other hand, my interest in Ukrainian literature led me to study in succession folklore, linguistics, early history, anthropology, geology and the theory of the evolution of the universe.

Thus I developed along a path very different from that of revolutionaries who originated from the Russian intelligentsia. My beliefs were formed through the painful resolution of many inner contradictions. I tried to obtain books from everywhere, for example from a railway worker and former Polish rebel, and from the library of the old Decem-

[1] Written during the Party purge in 1921.

brist, Rozen. For a long time I did not see a single illegal book, and I extracted information on revolutionary events from reactionary publications, for whose explanations I substituted my own contrary interpretation. With four or five other comrades whose thoughts were developing in the same direction, I spread propaganda among the peasants and craftsmen in Izyum district whilst ostensibly collecting Ukrainian folk-songs. Looking back now, I must say that the information we conveyed was as confused as our own opinions. After a long time, however, I met two peasants who received their revolutionary baptism in my circle. My first contacts were with Ukrainian radicals in Galicia who supplied me with illegal literature. My conversion to Marxism was very difficult. I had to hammer out a definite set of views and renounce indeterminate revolutionism. Although I had read Ziber's book *Ricardo and Marx* and Kautsky's articles in *Severny Vestnik*, it was not until I came across a Polish translation of the *Erfurt Programme* that I became a Marxist, broke with my earlier views, and seriously studied Kautsky and *Das Kapital*. From 1897 I carried out propaganda as a Marxist and social democrat and it is from this time that I considered myself a member of the Party.

My Marxist views were, however, still fairly eclectic. An acquaintance with Russian Marxist-literature, and particularly Plekhanov's *The Development of a Monist View of History*, helped me in 1899, when I was living in Kursk, to purge my opinions of many misconceptions. One may therefore date my adherence to the Party as starting in 1899 or even 1900, when I parted company with a few, to my mind insignificant, influences of the German revisionists. But this constant inner development is still not completed. As for my membership of the Party, it was indeed determined at that time by my acceptance of Marxism and the social democratic programme (which in Russia at that time was the same as the German social democratic Erfurt programme), and by my personal SD underground work. That is why the year of my joining the Party in reality was 1897.

In 1900 I was an external student[1] at Kursk 'modern' school (I had not graduated from the Izyum school as I had been expelled for organising a circle, after which I worked in Ekaterinoslav, Novgorod and Kharkov provinces), and I entered the Technological Institute in St Petersburg. I could not come to terms with the 'Union of Struggle for the Emancipation of the Working Class' in the capital as it was infected with 'economism' at that time, and so I joined the St Petersburg Committee of *Rabocheye Znamya*. On 4 March 1901 I was arrested like many others at the demonstration on Kazan Square and banished to Ekaterino-

[1] An external student takes the examinations without going to classes.

slav. The local committee there also shared the inconsistent, revolutionary, semi-'economist' views of the paper *Yuzhny Rabochy*. Therefore I could not be in full agreement with it and I organised associated, but distinct, workers' circles with another comrade, Kokorin, who had just been exiled to Ekaterinoslav from Simferopol, and a few other revolutionary social democrats (including Kalyaev, still an SD at that time).

I was soon back in St Petersburg. Most contributors to *Rabocheye Znamya* had been arrested, and the remainder were leaning towards those views of *Sotsialist* which most closely corresponded to those of the future SRs (as can be seen merely by recalling some of their names, for example Rutenberg and Savinkov). With the arrival in the capital of the *Iskra* representative, I joined the St Petersburg section of *Iskra* and founded circles in various parts of the city. Arrests in late 1901 severed contact with the central organisation, but with the arrival of a new representative, our section became more secure and we began discussions with the St Petersburg 'Union'.

Early in 1902, however, I was arrested and charged with planning a demonstration. I was soon deported for five years to Yakutsk province. On the way to Krasnoyarsk, the prison doctor, Kheysin (now a Menshevik but then an *Iskra* man), informed me that I was to be tried in the *Iskra* case, and I decided to escape. I succeeded in this only after leaving Irkutsk on the way to the Lena. The comrades closest to me in the Party then were Uritsky, Dzerzhinsky and Lalayants, as well as some Moscow students and future prominent Mensheviks and SRs, including Tseretelli, Budilovich and Khovrin.

By mid-1902 I had reached first Tsaritsyn and then Saratov, where I made contact with the local committee and the *Iskra* representative, E. V. Barmzin. The committee was following a very indeterminate line and still had not fully eliminated the 'economist' influence of *Rabocheye Delo*. I had many arguments on this score at large committee meetings. I carried on propaganda among workers and students, as well as organising circles. Simultaneously I worked for the final split of the SDs from the 'Union of SDs and SRs' which still existed in Saratov. The committee there published scarcely any printed propaganda and I arranged for printing to be done with rubber letters purchased in large, variable assortments. The letters were springy and difficult to keep in place. Nevertheless we managed to progress from hectographed sheets to printed proclamations. Later we managed to obtain print through pedlars and our technical problems were eased. By then I had already devoted myself to propaganda work and had travelled to Volsk for a short time to organise a circle of mill-workers there.

In Saratov I was called 'Ivan Vasilich', and I earned money by giving lessons and doing technical drawings. When the police began to follow me, I left for Samara where the *Iskra* representatives were G. M. Krzhizhanovsky, Z. P. Krzhizhanovskaya and V. P. Artsibushev. After handing over to Krzhizhanovsky 1,000 roubles which I had received in Saratov for revolutionary purposes from a former fellow student of mine at the Technological Institute, Aposov (now serving in the Intelligence Service of the Ukrainian High Command), I went to Kiev for literature which I brought to Kharkov and then went on to Ekaterinburg via Samara.

At that time there was no SD organisation in Ekaterinburg. There was the 'Urals Union of SDs and SRs' from which the SDs had to be disentangled so that they could form an *Iskra* group. It transpired, however, that in the Ekaterinburg branch there were no SDs, only SRs or indeterminate revolutionaries. There were a few people in the town who had been tried in SD cases, but they were apathetic and hostile to the *Iskra* movement. I was obliged to take a job at the power station. Having organised a circle among the electrical workers, I made contact through them with workers from the textile mill, the Yates works and other factories. There was no support from the intelligentsia whatsoever— only later did two comrades arrive from abroad and join the committee together with several workers.

We succeeded in winning over most of the workers' circles from the Ekaterinburg Union, particularly when the majority of the SRs had been arrested. After a visit to Perm, I formalised the split of the social democrats with the SRs, and with that the Union was officially buried. In Nizhny Tagil and other places I managed to form groups and link them together. Then I sent a series of articles and letters to *Iskra* which were signed 'Glasson'.

At that time, the end of summer 1903, Ekaterinburg had become so hazardous for me that once I only evaded the police by slipping through a bawdy-house, so close had the shadowing been. I was even arrested, but I escaped. I was compelled to make a hasty departure from the town.

After interrupting my journey in Kiev to see Krzhizhanovsky who had been elected to the Party Central Committee at the second Congress, I reached Odessa and worked there from autumn 1903 to February 1904. On the Odessa Committee at the time were K. I. Levitsky (a permanent member from 1903 until 1907), Lalayants ('Aristotle'), Max Hochberg (later a Menshevik), Alekseyev (also a future Menshevik—he had controlled SD publications in Odessa during 1905–6), and Dr Bogomolets (who later left the Party and went to Argentina or Brazil). When I took my seat on the committee, its members discussed the split between the

Bolsheviks and Mensheviks, and all definitely sided with the Bolsheviks. Thus when Innokenty Dubrovinsky, a 'conciliator', arrived in late 1903, we refused to allow him to join the committee, particularly as Alekseyev also had by this time declared himself a 'conciliator'. 'Max Hochberg began to lean towards Menshevism, and Bogomolets also began to show faint 'conciliatory' tendencies, although he only broke with Bolshevism much later.

I was organiser for the district of Moldavanka-Kamenolomny-Peresyp, and later for the port as well. The organisation had at first very few contacts but they gradually increased to the point where there was a group in almost every factory. I myself established contacts in Peresyp where I found work as a labourer. Our activity was particularly intense in Kamenolomny, where during the winter I succeeded in organising mass demonstrations of up to several hundred workers. In the port I distributed large quantities of literature among steamship crews in late 1903 so that they could pass them to the soldiers leaving for the Far East, obviously in anticipation of the war with Japan. I left Odessa in January 1904 when the police began to show much greater interest in my movements.

I went to Kiev and arrived in the aftermath of wholesale arrests. Following a meeting with the Krzhizhanovsky's, I noticed that the police were on my heels, and I set off for Ekaterinoslav, arriving on the day when war was declared with Japan. There, too, arrests had decimated the committee before my arrival and our activities were hindered by lack of funds. The liberal bourgeoisie, which until then had contributed material support, now took up the patriotic cause and gave money to the official Red Cross instead of the revolutionary one. But the workers willingly made collections, the organisation was re-established and the publication of anti-war proclamations went on apace. We fought a hectic struggle to prevent the Mensheviks from spreading their propaganda among the workers, but by means of discussions and debates we were able to paralyse their attempts. In view of the fact that Lenin was isolated abroad and had been forced to concede the editorship of *Iskra* to Plekhanov and Martov, we decided to summon a conference of southern Bolshevik committees. I was elected to attend but was arrested on my departure from Ekaterinoslav. Our initiative only bore fruit later when the southern and northern conferences of Bolsheviks formed the BKB (the Bureau of Bolshevik Committees, which summoned the third Party Congress in May 1906).

From Ekaterinoslav I was exiled for five years to the Kem area of Archangel province, since exile to Yakutsk had been temporarily halted by the war. On the way to Kem I again escaped, this time from Snega.

But neither in Yaroslavl nor in Moscow could I communicate with the local organisations as a result of arrests.

I returned to Odessa and found many new faces on the committee. There were also many new Party members who were grossly under-worked, and on the periphery there was strong dissatisfaction with the leadership. In my district I managed to weld all the available members into a single, effective, amicable unit. But soon I was sent by the Odessa Committee as a delegate to the third Party Congress (my pseudonym in the record was 'Shchensky').

After the Congress, I was directed by the CC to the St Petersburg Committee, where I was firstly organiser for the Nevsky district, then Committee Secretary, and finally I was entrusted with the establishment of an organisation of armed workers.

A resolution of the third Congress had ordered 'the preparation of an armed rising' and 'the arming of the workers'. In fact, preparations for an armed struggle remained on an ideological, propagandistic and agita-tional plane. No actual preparations had taken place. Following my report, the St Petersburg Committee recognised the importance of practical steps. The organisation was to consist of detachments of armed workers with as many members from all the factory circles as there were arms—that is the whole organisation was to be put on a military footing. I ensured that each district had its own organiser, its own basic combat unit of eight to ten men and its own cache of weapons, in addition to the central arms dump. A series of lectures was arranged on the techniques and tactics of barricade-building and street-fighting. But our prepara-tions came up against an insurmountable obstacle. Having burst through the dykes of police control, the mass of the workers would only listen to words of revolution and demanded that the Party should respond. Agita-tion was the most vital question of the day, and it drew all our strength. The St Petersburg Committee gave way to their demands and sub-ordinated everything to agitation. I considered that this would wreck our preparations for an armed rising and after many heated arguments announced my resignation from the committee, handing over my work to Bur (the elder Essen).

All this occurred immediately before the Manifesto of October 1905. The CC had just received news from the Riga Committee that a rising was planned in the Ust-Dvinsk fortress with the aim of seizing it. In view of this, the CC directed me to Riga with instructions to verify the state of affairs. On closer examination, the whole idea turned out to be merely the product of revolutionary impatience. At the end of December 1905 I was compelled to leave Riga during the White Terror to avoid the intensive searches being carried out for me after a lecture which Mark had arranged for me to give on the tactics of street-fighting to armed workers. The building where the meeting was being held had been surrounded by troops. Mark and a large number of workers were caught, but I and some others managed to escape by the skin of our teeth. I was later told that I had been sentenced to death in my absence for my part in this.

From Riga I went via St Petersburg to Yaroslavl, where I was arrested quite by accident. The police found on me my resolutions for the planned conference of northern committees and I was exiled for five years to the area of Turukhansk. On the way, after leaving Yeniseysk, I escaped and remained to work in Krasnoyarsk. Here, incidentally, I led an electoral campaign for the second Duma, and after the last meeting, I was arrested in the street. The authorities failed to bring the case to court and I was again exiled to Turukhansk for five years. This time I did not escape until reaching Turukhansk, whence I had to cover nearly 800 miles up the Yenisey by boat and on foot.

Arriving in St Petersburg in October 1907, I found the committee there in a crisis. To all intents and purposes, the split with the Mensheviks had already happened, but in November 1907 there still took place a joint Party Conference in Helsinki, at which I represented the Siberian Union. Already there were indications of the intelligentsia's drift away from the movement, as well as other signs of a new phase. I worked as organiser for the Rozhdestvensky district and, 'to exploit legal opportunities', as a member of the administrative board of the 'Truzhenik' co-operative, I edited trade union journals and attended legal All-Russian Congresses on co-operatives and factory medicine (under the name 'G. G. Ermolaev').

In summer 1908 I was driven abroad by the increased attentions of the police and I spent one and a half months in Geneva. Amongst Bolsheviks there had appeared the tendencies of 'otzovism' and 'ultimatism' which, like 'liquidationism', had to be overcome, and so I was dispatched to Moscow. After a short time as district organiser, I was arrested with the Central Trade Union Bureau, on which I sat as the Moscow Committee's representative, and we were all put under administrative detention for three months. On my release it felt strange to have acquired through my arrest legal validity for my illegal passport.

After this, the struggle with 'otzovism' and 'ultimatism' became more difficult. I worked first as district organiser and then as Committee Secretary. Conditions continued to deteriorate with the hasty desertion of the intelligentsia—not a week went by without an activist or two deserting the cause, moving to another town, returning to study for a diploma, etc. etc. The workers held fast, but provocations thinned their ranks. Every day it became harder to find a room to use as a hideout or as a secret address, now that the 'intelligentsia' to a man was refusing assistance. The printing of appeals became extremely difficult for lack of funds. The students and young people who had stored and distributed material had scattered at the first puff of wind. The organisation was maintained only through the superhuman efforts of remaining militants.

Besides carrying on the struggle for Bolshevism in Moscow and campaigning in the elections for the Bolshevik Conference, I toured the Urals and gave reports. I did not succeed in arranging a Urals conference; nor was there a chance of drawing any local Party workers to the full Conference. I myself, therefore, received a mandate to represent the Urals at the Conference on condition that I should return afterwards to make a report on its proceedings. As is well known, at the Paris Conference of Bolsheviks the *otzovisty* and *ultimatisty* (Bogdanov, Aleksinsky and Volsky) parted company with us. The practice of exploiting both legal and semi-legal opportunities was officially approved. However, I could not pursue those tactics personally: during my tour of the Urals I barely escaped arrest and on arrival in St Petersburg I was soon betrayed by the *agent provocateur* Serova.

I was again administratively exiled, this time to the Vilyuisk area of Yakutsk province, whence I returned only at the end of 1913 to St Petersburg where, at the suggestion of the Party publishing house *Priboy* (Krestinsky, Stuchka, Donskoy, etc.), I accepted the editorship of the insurance journal *Voprosy Strakhovaniya* and the leadership of the 'Workers' Insurance Group'. After the CC Plenum of December 1913 and the removal of Bogdanov from the editorial board of *Pravda*, I took his place, joining Olminsky and K. N. Samoylova. With Kamenev's arrival, the board was reconstituted to consist of Kamenov, Olminsky and myself. From mid-June 1914, after the departure of Olminsky and Kamenev, the editorship fell on me alone during the crucial days of the growing general strike in Petrograd. In early July the strikers took to the barricades. I was arrested in the offices of *Pravda* on, I think, 8 July 1914, when the government smashed all workers' organisations and publications on the eve of war. A court case was planned but the authorities were evidently reluctant to exhibit the absence of 'social peace' at home in wartime (this was before the arrest of our Duma deputies). Therefore the *Pravda* case was settled administratively: I received a sentence of five years (or until the end of the war, I cannot remember exactly) in the Angarsk area, which was changed to exile in Morshansk, Tambov province.

From the very beginning of the imperialist war I adopted a resolutely revolutionary position. For the first months I was housed in a communal cell in the *Spasskaya Chast* in Petrograd with several dozen workers, leading militants and other comrades: amongst them I can now recall I. I. Kiselev and A. S. Enukidze. At our numerous meetings we elaborated our tactics and attitude towards the war. They were expressed in public by the Duma 'fraction' of the Party and were identical with Lenin's own theses which we subsequently received. Hostility towards the war and both warring coalitions, the position of a 'third force' making deals with neither imperialist camp, the goals of a proletarian rising, the overthrow of bourgeois power and a socialist revolution: these were the main points of the resolution which I elaborated and saw adopted by roughly 150 revolutionary activists, who were later scattered throughout the country by the government and obviously served as propagandists for such ideas.

In Morshansk I lived under police supervision throughout the war until the Revolution. With the help of an old comrade from the Odessa Committee, K. I. Levitsky, I managed to find work in a bank, first as a ledger clerk and than as assistant book-keeper. During the war I did not succeed in making contact with the workers, apart from a few individuals, and only in the last months before the Revolution did I organise two small circles on the railways and in a textile factory.

My work after February, like that of every Party member who participated in all the events of the revolutionary struggle, was so closely bound up with the Revolution that if I were to describe it, I would have to write about the Revolution itself. Consequently, I will mention only a few of the tasks that devolved upon me.

In June 1917 I travelled to Petrograd. The CC directed me to work on the Petrograd Central Council of Factory Committees, and I was elected by them to the VTsIK of the first and second convocations, as well as to the 'Pre-Parliament'. At the sixth Party Congress I was one of the delegates of the Petrograd organisation and was elected a candidate CC member.

During the 'Kornilov days', I was a member of the 'Defence Committee' and supervised the distribution of a large number of arms to the workers. At the time of the October Revolution, I had a seat on the Military-Revolutionary Committee and, incidentally, took part in the battle at Pulkovo.

After October I joined the commission entrusted with the organisation of VSNKh and the formulation of its first statutes. I was summoned to the Ukraine by the first All-Ukrainian Congress of Soviets, where I was elected People's Secretary for Labour, and then also Secretary for Trade and Industry. In January 1918 I arranged the first All-Ukrainian Conference of Peasants' Delegates in Kharkov. After the seizure of Kiev by German troops, the Conference of Soviet Representatives in Poltava elected me President of the Government of Workers and Peasants of the Ukraine, and People's Secretary for Foreign Affairs. This was confirmed at the second All-Ukrainian Congress of Soviets in Ekaterinoslav in March 1918. At the last session of the Ukrainian TsIK in Taganrog in April 1918 I was elected to the People's Insurrectionary Secretariat, and at the Party Conference there I was elected a member and Secretary of the KPU Orgburo which was created to summon the first Party Congress. At the latter, I was elected candidate CC member, and in December 1918 I entered the CC as a full member. Also in 1918, the CC directed me to work in the Vecheka where I became a Collegium member and Head of the Department for the Struggle against Counter-Revolution. In January I rejoined the Ukrainian government as People's Commissar for State Control. I was a Ukrainian Party delegate to the first Congress of the Comintern. Then I was given special plenary powers by the Defence Council to deal with the insurrectionary division of the Ataman Zelyony on the right bank of the Dnieper. After the retreat from Kiev I was at first Head of the Political Department of the Gomel fortified district, and then, during Party mobilisation, Head of the Special Section of the South-Eastern (Caucasus) Front.

In April 1920 I returned to the Ukraine and was elected People's Secretary for Rabkrin. Then I became People's Commissar for Ukrainian Internal Affairs, and Presidium member of both the All-Ukrainian and All-Union TsIK. Since the beginning of 1922 I have been People's Commissar for Justice in the Ukraine. At the present time, I am a candidate CC member of the VKP, and a Politburo member of the Ukrainian Party.[1]

As a Ukrainian Communist, Skrypnik was one of the major figures in that group of old Bolsheviks who waged a bitter fight during the 1920s against the tendency towards centralisation and russification. His seniority in Bolshevik ranks and his knowledge of theory gave him great authority in the Party. Having joined the revolutionary movement at a young age, he remained convinced all his life that only communism could bring about the social and national emancipation of his native Ukraine.[2] A professional revoluntionary and a comrade of Lenin from earliest times, he had been arrested fifteen times and sentenced in all to thirty years' prison and seven years' administrative exile.

Skrypnik possessed great intellectual curiosity and acquired by his

[1] In 1927 N. A. Skrypnik was appointed People's Commissar for Education in the Ukraine.

[2] See A. Yaremenko, *Materiali do biografii M. O. Skrypnika* (Kharkov, 1932).

own efforts a considerable knowledge of Marxism. He was a member of the editorial board of *Pravda* in 1914, and after 1917 turned out to be a prolific publicist, propagandist and writer. The bibliography of his works contains some 270 titles of books, brochures, and articles on the most diverse subjects. His complex personality also found expression in political activity. He was sent to Petrograd by the Central Committee and got there early in June 1917. He was on the Bolshevik general staff and played a substantial part in organising the armed insurrection.

At the historic meeting of the Central Committee on 16 [NS 29] October 1917, Skrypnik was an ardent supporter of Lenin's resolution on the immediate seizure of power by the Bolsheviks. He opposed Kamenev in violent terms: 'We are spending too much time talking when action is called for. We are responsible to the masses, they know we are committing a crime if we give them nothing. The preparation of an insurrection and an appeal to the masses are necessary.'[1]

He was an active participant in the uprising, and was a member of the Petrograd RVS. After that he found himself entrusted with extremely diverse tasks, among them the establishment of the repressive machinery of Soviet power, and took an active part in suppressing the left-wing SR insurrection in Moscow in the summer of 1918. He was a political commissar in the Army, the Ukrainian Defence Committee's plenipotentiary during the Civil War, one of the artisans of Soviet power in his homeland, and, up to January 1919, the head of the first Bolshevik government of the Ukraine.

Skrypnik was a founder member of the Ukrainian Communist Party and leader of the faction which demanded that Lenin's principle of self-determination should be applied to ensure the independence of a socialist Ukraine. For several years he was obliged to wage a fierce, often desperate struggle against the left-wing communists, who supported Pyatakov, had a majority in the Central Committee, and were utterly opposed to his position. Skrypnik and his friends, removed from power by the left-wing communists in 1919–20, only gained control of the Ukrainian party after a struggle full of dramatic twists, and thanks to Lenin's support and the intervention of the Moscow Central Committee. During this period Skrypnik, who had to hold his position against the left communists, drew closer to Stalin. From 1921, he sat once again on the Ukrainian Communist Party's Central Committee, and enjoyed an influence well beyond the power of his nominal position. From January 1919, he was People's Commissar at the State Control Commission, then at the Rabkrin, and from July 1921 Commissar for the Interior; from 1922 to 1927 he was both Commissar for Justice and

[1] *Les bolchéviks et la révolution d'octobre* (Paris, 1964), p. 157.

Director of Public Prosecution for the Ukraine. From 1929, he was also on the Ukrainian Politburo. He also took part in the work of the Comintern, of which he could consider himself to be one of the founders. He was a delegate at all its congresses, and was elected in 1928 as a member of IKKI.

Skrypnik was a convinced communist and a ceaseless defender of the Ukraine's national rights. In 1922, during the great debate that preceded the creation of the USSR, he came into open conflict with Stalin. Together with the head of his government, Rakovsky, he rejected Stalin's concept of a centralised State, which he considered alien to communism, and demanded the application of confederate principles.[1] Skrypnik became the leader of the faction opposed to the centralising tendencies, and waged his battle inside the Constitutional Committee, on which he was the Ukrainian representative, and then in the Council of Nationalities of the USSR, where he was a deputy before becoming President in 1927. This battle resulted in a temporary victory, for in 1923 there was in fact a Ukrainianisation of the State machine, of the Party and of cultural institutions. At the start of NEP, Skrypnik collaborated faithfully with the Moscow leadership. In the Party's internal conflicts, he first adopted a neutral position, and then moved to the support of Stalin in the struggle against the left opposition and then the United Opposition.

After the appointment of Kaganovich as secretary of the Ukrainian CP in 1925, the policy of russification recommenced. A whole group of Ukrainian communists, headed by the People's Commissar for Education, Shumsky, were eliminated in 1927: they were accused of nationalism, having fought against the predominance of Russian communists in the Ukrainian party. Kaganovich's policy, inspired by Stalin, gave rise to sharp objections—but Stalin, eager to gain the support of the Ukrainian communists in his struggle against the right-wing allies he wanted to get rid of, had Kaganovich dismissed. According to Bukharin, Stalin managed to 'buy the Ukrainians', including Skrypnik, by this manoeuvre and in October 1927 the latter was appointed People's Commissar for Education of the Ukrainian Soviet Republic. Remaining faithful to his beliefs, Skrypnik made great efforts to develop a national Ukrainian culture: with skill and energy he fought for his policy of Ukrainianisation on two fronts—against russification on the one side, and against the Ukrainian nationalists on the other. He adopted Stalin's line on a culture national in form but proletarian in content. This he considered to be a Leninist and internationalist principle. His policies in the field of

[1] See R. Pipes, *The Formation of the Soviet Union. Communism and Nationalism 1917–1923* (Harvard, 1957).

education resulted in the eradication of illiteracy and a raising of standards at all levels. He carried out his policies with caution and realism. His work gained the approval of the eleventh Congress of the UCP (1930), which none the less demanded, on Stalin's instigation, the strengthening of the struggle against local Ukranian nationalist tendencies. In conditions that became thenceforth extremely difficult, Skrypnik continued in his efforts against the policy of russification.

In February 1933 he was stripped of his post as Commissar for Education and appointed Vice-President of the Council of People's Commissars and President of the Ukrainian Gosplan. This was but the prelude to a vast campaign against him and against his policies. Stalin's suspicions manifested themselves, and Skrypnik was accused of nationalism. He became a kind of scapegoat for the difficulties created in the Ukraine by forced collectivisation. In despair, Skrypnik committed suicide on 7 July 1933. This act wrought havoc within the Party, but gave the press a pretext for launching a massive campaign against Skrypnik. *Pravda* commented on his suicide in very harsh terms, declaring that 'comrade Skrypnik has fallen victim to bourgeois nationalist elements which gained his confidence and exploited his name for their own nationalist and antisemitic ends'. Within a short while, the accusations were even more direct: he was termed a 'degenerate nationalist', and considered the leader of a broad nationalistic deviation.

He was rehabilitated after 1957 and Mykola Skrypnik became once again the 'Party's soldier'.[1]

G.H.

[1] This was the title of a biography of Skrypnik compiled by Yu. Babko and published in Kiev in 1962. See also D. M. Corbett, 'The Rehabilitation of Mykola Skrypnik', *Slavic Review* XXII, no. 1 (March 1963), pp. 304–13.

IVAN TENISOVICH SMILGA
(autobiography)

I was born in 1892 in Livonia into an enlightened family of land-owning farmers. My parents were both highly intellectual. I can remember my father's endless tales from Greek mythology, which he greatly admired. In his political convictions, he can be classed as a democrat.

My revolutionary consciousness was awakened in 1901 by Karpovich's shot at the Minister of Education, Bogolepov. The years 1901–3 were a watershed in my development. However strange it may seem, despite the extremely liberal and free-thinking atmosphere at home, I held strong religious and monarchist views until the age of nine or ten. I remember that after Bogolepov's assassination, it was like a holiday in our family, to which I alone was impervious. The murder of a minister by students seemed to me quite insane. But as I had been an extremely rational being from birth, and was subject to the influence of social democratic students at the time, I soon discarded the beliefs inculcated in me by a few booklets I had read. By 1904–5 I was already a convinced atheist and a supporter of revolution. Events in our area and our family considerably hastened my further evolution. My father moved further to the left at the same time as the rest of society and played an extremely prominent role in the revolutionary events. At the end of 1905, during the abolition of the rural administrative boards, he was elected Chairman of the Revolutionary Administrative Committee for our district. In 1906 he was executed by a punitive expedition of the Tsarist government. In January 1907, whilst a 'modern' school pupil, I joined the Social Democratic Party. It was during my student years (ending in 1909) that my Marxist outlook was finally formed.

My first clash with the police came in 1907 when I was searched and detained for a few hours in connection with the celebration of May Day. I was arrested for the second time in 1910 on Theatre Square in Moscow at a student demonstration against the death penalty on the occasion of the death of Leo Tolstoy. After one month in custody, I was released. In spring 1911 I conducted underground Party work in the Lefortovo district. In July of the same year I was rearrested, and after three months in custody I was deported to Vologda province for three years. Returning from there in 1914, after the outbreak of war, I immediately joined the Petrograd RSDRP(b) Committee and was active until May 1915 when I was again arrested and exiled to the district of Yeniseysk for three years. I returned from there only after the February Revolution.

Almost five years of exile were for me a real university. While in exile, besides studying the history and tactics of our Party, I mainly applied myself to political economy and philosophy. At that time I conceived of my future Party work in terms of propaganda. In fact, things turned out completely differently. At the Party Conference in April 1917 I was elected to the CC, where I remained until 1920. During the October Revolution I was Chairman of the Regional Committee of Russian Soviets in Finland, and in this capacity took the most active part in the overthrow of the Provisional government. In early 1918 I participated in the Finnish revolution.[1] With the outbreak of the Civil War, I was entrusted with military work by the CC.

As a member of the RVS, I commanded armies and fronts in the struggle against the Czechs, Denikin, the Poles and Wrangel. At the end of the Civil War, I moved to economic work. From 1921 to 1923 I was Deputy Chairman of VSNKh and Head of the Main Fuel Directorate. In Autumn 1923 I was appointed Deputy Chairman of the Gosplan of the USSR.

The youngest of the leaders of the 1917 Revolution, Smilga was already an 'Old Bolshevik' at that date, despite his youth. At the age of twenty-five, in April 1917, he was elected to the Central Committee of the Bolshevik Party. He played a big part in preparing the October insurrection: he was President of the Finland soviets, a member of the restricted Central Committee formed in August 1917, the Central Committee's delegate (with Uritsky) on the Petrograd committee, and, most important of all, the Party organiser in the vital Baltic fleet, all the vessels of which came under his control. Within the Central Committee he belonged to the small group of Lenin's men of confidence, who supported the leader in all circumstances and with no reservations. A *confidant* of Lenin one the eve of the insurrection, and convinced of the need for immediate action, Smilga incited Lenin towards it and assured him of the determination of the sailors in the Baltic fleet and of the Finnish army. His Red sailors played a decisive role in the overthrow of the Provisional government.

In 1918 his loyalty to Lenin remained absolute in the debate on Brest-Litovsk. He was a man of action who helped lead the revolution in Finland, and gained distinction in the various posts he held during the Civil War.

At that time he was one of Trotsky's most hostile opponents, and the subjects of disagreement were numerous. In December 1918 there was a violent conflict between Smilga and the Commissar for War. With Lashevich, Smilga carried the accusations of the left-wing communists – that Trotsky had given commands in the Red Army to former Tsarist

[1] See p. 406, note 1.

officers, that he had put communists and commissars before the firing squad – to the Central Committee. A few months later, he supported the appointment of Sergey Kamenev as commander-in-chief—as did Stalin, and against Trotsky's will. In May 1919 he replaced some of Trotsky's friends on the reorganised Revolutionary War Council. As the situation on the Western Front grew more serious, and the conflict between Trotsky and commander-in-chief Kamenev took on larger dimensions, the Politburo supported the latter and sent Smilga and Lashevich to the Ukraine. Smilga drew closer to Stalin for a time, but the Vistula débacle precipitated a fundamental change in their relationship.

During the Polish campaign of 1920, Smilga was on the Council for the Eastern Front, and was political commissar for Tukhachevsky's army—while Stalin fulfilled the same role in the other army under Yegorov. At the end of this disastrous campaign he declared himself openly to be an enemy of Stalin. Seeking to justify his own acts and the fatal delay of the First Cavalry Army, Stalin had tried to make Smilga the culprit of the defeat. At the tenth Congress of the Russian CP Stalin accused Smilga of having deceived the Central Committee by 'promising to take Warsaw on a given date' and by thus falsifying the entire picture. Smilga gave his riposte at the Congress in two printed documents on the situation. Trotsky came to his help, accusing Stalin of being responsible for the defeat by his failure to carry out directives from the commander-in-chief. The Congress did not clear up these questions. Smilga had been demoted to candidate membership of the Central Committee at the ninth Congress, and at the tenth, despite his prominence at the time, he was not re-elected at all.

Banished from the political scene, Smilga devoted himself to a new field, the economy, in which he rapidly won a high reputation. He was re-elected to candidate membership of the Central Committee at the eleventh Congress, then at the fourteenth Congress in 1925 to full membership, occupying positions of high responsibility in the Plan Commission, of which he became Vice-President. He became Secretary to the Supreme Sovnarkhoz, then Rector of the Plekhanov Institute for Economics; he wrote several technical works on economics which were notorious at the time.

Smilga took an active part in the Party's internal struggles. He belonged to Zinoviev's group, then became one of the heads of the United Opposition. On the eve of the fifteenth Congress in 1927 he helped draw up the economic part of the opposition platform, and together with Trotsky, Zinoviev and Kamenev started agitation in the working-class areas of Leningrad and Moscow. Smilga was violently opposed to

Stalin and Bukharin, whom he termed 'political bankrupts'. He wrote a long letter concerning the 'Declaration of the 83' to the Politburo and to *Pravda* refuting the allegations that the Trotskyite opposition was disintegrating and claiming that 'the opposition is a mass movement within the Party'.[1] One week after the opposition demonstration on 7 November, for which he was mainly responsible in Moscow, he was expelled from the Central Committee. This 'fair-haired intellectual . . . with spectacles, goatee, and thinning front hair, ordinary to look at and distinctly the armchair sort',[2] was also a fighter, a first-class agitator and mass leader: he showed these qualities on many occasions. A determined and indomitable opposition leader, he was rightly considered by Stalin to be one of the most dangerous men in the United Opposition. When it was dismantled in December 1927, after the fifteenth Congress, Smilga was removed to Khabarovsk in eastern Siberia, on the right bank of the Amur river. When he was exiled, thousands of oppositionists demonstrated outside the Yaroslav station in protest against this administrative exile: that was 'Smilga's farewell'.

When Stalin broke with the right wing and changed his economic policies, Smilga joined Radek and Preobrazhensky at the head of a conciliation group which repudiated Trotsky and requested readmission to the Party. Returning from Minusinsk, where he had been exiled, Smilga, who had devoted himself entirely to economic issues, was arrested in 1932, refused to confess to anything, was sentenced to five years' prison and disappeared in a concentration camp: according to some sources, he may have died in 1937.

G.H.

[1] *Contre le Courant*, no. 213 (Paris, December 1927), pp. 21–3.
[2] V. Serge, *Memoirs of a Revolutionary* (Oxford, 1963), p. 214.

IVAN NIKITOVICH SMIRNOV

(autobiography)

I was born into a peasant family in Ryazan province. When I was roughly two, our family was ruined by a fire. My father went to work in Moscow and died there a year later. Then my mother went to Moscow to work as a domestic servant. I was eight years old before I was taken to join her there. In Moscow I went to a municipal school and then found work on the railways and in a factory. In 1898 I first became acquainted with SD literature and began to meet a few students who engaged in propaganda, whilst at the factory I came across the two or three workers who remained from the organisation smashed in 1896. We formed a workers' self-education circle with roughly fifteen members, of whom three to my knowledge have remained in the Party.

In 1899 I was arrested for the first time, held for roughly two years and then deported to Irkutsk province for five years. After eight months, however, I escaped. The CC Party Bureau, which at that time was in Pskov, sent me to work in Tver province. The local committee directed me to Vyshny Volochek where there were roughly 10,000 workers with whom it had no contact, and I found a job as a labourer at the Proskuryakov tannery. I worked there for nearly six months. I managed to establish a following in the Prokhorov and Ryabushinsky works, both large factories, but just when the work was beginning to go well, I was denounced by Sladkov, a worker dismissed from the Ryabushinsky factory. I was arrested, and the man sent by the Tver Committee to take my place was also quickly caught. Nevertheless, on May Day 1904, proclamations were distributed in Vyshny Volochek and a small strike took place.

I spent two years in prison. Then I was tried for spreading propaganda (this was already 1905), and, moreover, our case was heard in Moscow two days after the massacre in St Petersburg on 9 January. I was sentenced to one year in a fortress, but the court took into account my preliminary detention and set me free. Since my administrative exile was still not completed, the police made a search for me. At this time I began to work for the Moscow Committee as organiser for the Lefortovo district. In March I was rearrested. It was intended that I should go back to exile in Irkutsk province, but the Trans-Siberian railway was fully occupied with ferrying troops for the Russo-Japanese war, and I was sent instead to Vologda province. On the way I contracted typhus and arrived in exile three months before the strike of October 1905. The amnesty that followed this strike freed me from the rest of my sentence.

I returned to Moscow and resumed my activities. During the armed insurrection I was organiser for the Blagusha sub-district in the Lefortovo district. But as I heavily compromised myself during these days, I had to leave Blagusha once the rising had been crushed, and I moved to the railway district.

I remained in Moscow until 1909 when I was again accused of organising the distribution of banned literature—at this time I was working in the Moscow Committee's bookshop. The charge could not be substantiated with evidence, however, and it was dismissed. In 1909 I was banished from Moscow and went to St Petersburg. I worked for the Committee there as organiser for the Peterburgskaya Storona district. In June 1910 I was betrayed by the *agent provocateur* Bryandinsky and after a short spell in custody I was deported to the area of Narym, where I remained for eighteen months. Then I learnt that I might be moved from Narym to the Turukhansk region. So I escaped with a group of comrades who were all threatened with the same fate. After my escape I worked in Rostov and Kharkov.

In 1913 I managed to unite the two separate groups of Bolsheviks and Mensheviks in Kharkov, and I was active there until July. Then the organisation was penetrated by two skilful *provocateurs* (Sigaev and Rudov), and I was arrested. I was sent to Narym, and moreover was sentenced to six months imprisonment for a trivial matter (a demonstration). After I had served this sentence, I was mistakenly released at the prison gates and I escaped to Krasnoyarsk. When I had received good identity papers, I returned to Moscow.

There, at the beginning of the war, a group of comrades and I attempted to resurrect the local organisation, but after six months I was arrested on information from the *agent provocateur* Poskrebukhin, and deported back to Narym. The case could not be brought to trial for lack of compromising documents.

I remained in Narym until 1916 when I was pressed into the Tsarist army. The exiles who were called up discussed whether they ought to obey the call or escape, although the latter would have been very difficult. They decided to join, but with the aim of agitating against the war. In Narym a committee was chosen for our future military organisation and I was included in it. Immediately on arrival in Tomsk, we contacted the local organisation. With money received from Moscow, we equipped an underground printing-press and set to work. Our military organisation had very great success and, as far as I know, it was the only one existing at that time. It involved up to two hundred soldiers in Tomsk and a large number in Novonikolaevsk. Proclamations were distributed throughout Siberia. A *provacateur*, Tsvetkov, joined the committee and, as was later revealed during the February Revolution, he was awaiting a suitable moment for betrayal, but events forestalled him. The military union lost only one comrade, Nakhanovich, who worked on the printing-press and subsequently perished in Kolchak's jail. Our union played a very important role in the February uprising. During it I was a member of the Executive Committee of Soldiers' Deputies. In August I left for Moscow where, on the suggestion of the local committee and the Bureau of the Central Region, I founded the Party publication *Volna*.

At the outbreak of Civil War, the CC sent me to Kazan. There I was appointed member of the RVS on the Eastern Front. In December 1919 I changed from military work to conspiratorial activity in the enemy's rear, for which I joined the newly formed CC Siberian Bureau. Subsequently, in the aftermath of the defeat of the Fifth Army, I was appointed to its RVS, combining this with my other work. After the defeat of Kolchak, I was made Chairman of the Siberian Revolutionary Committee. In 1921 I was transferred to Party work in Petrograd where I was Secretary of the local committee and the North-Western Regional Bureau of the CC. After six months in these positions, I worked for a year in the VSNKh where I was in charge of the armaments industry. Then I was appointed to the People's Commissariat for Trade and Industry.

In all I spent roughly six years in prison and never completed a sentence of banishment, although I did spend roughly four years in exile.

First and foremost, Ivan Smirnov was the man of the Fifth Army, the army which repulsed Kolchak and the Czech Legion on the Eastern Front, liberated Siberia and managed to absorb an enormous army of peasant partisans. He was a member of the Eastern Front RVS, then a member of the Fifth Army RVS and President of the Siberian Bureau, which operated clandestinely in Siberia under Kolchak's occupation. Subsequently, in 1921 and 1922, Smirnov ran the war industries. Elected to alternate membership of the Central Committee in March 1919, and to full membership in April 1920, he joined Trotsky's platform on the union question, and was only re-elected to alternate membership in March 1921. In 1922, he lost his position on the Central Committee altogether and for good.

Later on, a member of the Marxist-Leninist Institute recalled that at a preparatory meeting before the twelfth Congress, Ivan Smirnov's name was put to Lenin for the secretaryship of the Party. Smirnov had just lost the secretaryship of the Petrograd organisation (replaced by Uglanov) and had been transferred to Siberia. Lenin, according to the story, hesitated before replying, 'Ivan Smirnov is essential in Siberia'.

He was signatory to the 'Declaration of the 46', Commissar for Posts from 1923 to 1927, leader of the United Opposition, and was expelled from the Party in 1927 before being exiled to Siberia. Smirnov was scarcely an 'ideologist', but he was greedy for action. . . . He rallied to Stalin at the end of the summer of 1929: he could not watch 'the building of socialism' without having a part in it, even if he rejected some of its methods. But disillusionment was quick to come. In 1932 he entrusted Leon Sedov with an unsigned article for the *Byulleten Oppozitsii*. A few months later, early in 1933, he was arrested by the police in connection with the Ryutin affair. In August 1936, he was among the defendants at the first Moscow Trial, and 'confessed' to having participated in the assassination of Kirov, even though he was in prison at the time. Sentenced to death like the other fifteen defendants, he refused to sign his appeal for pardon out of anger at having been led to make incriminating confessions. . . .

Larissa Reisner wrote of him thus: 'Outside any rank or right, Smirnov was the incarnation of the revolutionary ethic, he was the highest moral criterion of the communist consciousness at Sviyazhsk. Comrade Smirnov's exceptional purity and probity imposed themselves even on the mass of non-party soldiers and on the communists who had not known him before.' He had a gentle sense of humour which pierces through his few written works, and even more in an anecdote told by Victor Serge. Dismissed from the People's Commissariat for Posts in 1927, Smirnov commented: 'It would do us all good to go back to the ranks for a while'—and being penniless went to the Labour Exchange where he registered as an unemployed precision machinist. On his card under the heading 'Last job held' he wrote 'People's Commissar for Posts'. Serge adds: 'For the younger generation he incarnated the idealism of his Party, without rhetoric or embroidery.' Smirnov's name is still omitted from republications of contemporary texts. He has not yet been allowed back onto the General Staff or the RVS of the Fifth Army, which, without Rosengolts or Smirnov, look rather skeletal. . . .

J.-J. M.

GRIGORY YAKOVLEVICH SOKOLNIKOV
('Brilliant')
(autobiography)

I was born on 15 August 1888 in Romny, a provincial town of Poltava province, where my father worked as a doctor on the Libau-Romny railway. I learnt to read at the age of five. After my family's removal to Moscow, I entered the Fifth Classical Gymnasium there which retained the teaching of Latin and Greek in its curriculum. As a Jew, I was forced to endure persecution from the Gymnasium authorities. 'Classical' studies drove me into self-education circles which were then flourishing like mushrooms, and which spontaneously developed into political circles. In the latter, the youthful supporters of the proletariat were sorted into the categories of sheep and goats by the conditions of the rapidly growing revolutionary movement (1903–5).

After reading Populist and Marxist literature I joined the Moscow Marxist circles (and was particularly close to that of M. Lunts and Narkirier), where the basic legal Marxist books were carefully studied, and illegal journals and pamphlets were read regularly. Foreign literature, delivered to me for safe keeping at home, introduced me to the theoretical and tactical disagreements then being discussed in the SD press abroad. At clandestine parties I had arguments with young SRs and Tolstoyans (S. Durylin and Gusev). Among the first underground activists I knew was Loginov (Anton), through whom I made contact with the Moscow Bolshevik Committee. In 1905 I joined its organisation, directed the SD student movement, and participated in the December insurrection. In connection with the youth movement, I often met M. N. Pokrovsky, N. N. Rozhkov, Mitskevich and Tseytlin. I based my decision to join the Bolsheviks rather than the Mensheviks largely on my assessment of their attitudes towards the role of the proletariat in the democratic revolution and participation in a provisional government.

In spring 1906 I joined the group of propagandists in the Gorodskoy district, being active mainly among printing workers. Then I worked in Sokolniki district, at first as propagandist among the weavers and later as a member of the district committee—as organiser, agitator and propagandist. After this, I worked in the Moscow Committee's 'Military-Technical Bureau', the centre for the detachments of armed Bolshevik workers. My acquaintance with 'Viktor' (Taratut), 'Bur' (Essen), and 'Mark' (Lyubimov) can be dated from this time. I had a particularly close working relationship with 'Vlas' (Likhachov). In the bureau I was linked with 'Semyon Semyonovich' (Kostitsyn) and 'Erot' (P. K.

Shternberg). Street meetings, mass demonstrations in forests, sudden appearances of Bolshevik orators in workers' barracks, proclamations and primitive leaflets written and printed by workers—all this led to a threefold increase in shadowing by the police.

The Sokolniki organisation was crushed during the mass police arrests in Moscow in autumn 1907. After being arrested at a meeting surrounded by police, I spent a few days in the Sokolniki police station and was then transferred to the Butyrki prison, from where I was deported in February 1909. Until my transfer to solitary confinement, I was sent out to work with ordinary criminals and swept Dolgorukov Street, receiving the traditional kopecks from warm-hearted passers-by. Shortly before my departure for Siberia I was thrown into an underground punishment cell, clapped in irons and given convict status for a refusal to doff my hat when the prison governor walked past. I came before the court in autumn 1908, accused of belonging to the Sokolniki district SD(b) Committee (Article 102), and was sentenced to permanent exile. My eighteen months in solitary confinement were a time of systematic reading in economics, history and philosophy. For variety, I also played chess with my neighbours by knocking on the walls. Despite confiscation of the chess set, which was fashioned out of bread, and punishments for knocking, this game flourished. During these years, the regime in 'solitary' in the Butyrki was comparatively tolerable, the deterioration setting in only at the end of 1908. A hand written prison journal was produced by B. Plyusnin, and one of his most active colaborators was N. L. Meshcheryakov, who was awaiting trial with N. Sokolov and Veselov. Heated arguments about empiriomonism and dialectics were conducted in the prison bath-house, amidst thick steam, splashing water and clattering wooden bathtubs. The unsuccessful attempt of a maximalist expropriator to escape from the baths disguised as a warder led, however, to a revision of the charter of liberties allowed in the bath-house and a marked reduction in them.

After four months of wandering from one staging-post or transit jail to another, I was finally delivered to my place of exile, the village of Rybnoye on the Angara (Yeniseysk region). In the Krasnoyarsk transit jail I had met Ordzhonikidze, Erkomashvili and Shklovsky. By the Angara, polemical papers against the SRs and organisational meetings of exiles alternated with excursions into the taiga and the delivery of bark to a local merchant. With Shklovsky I escaped after six weeks in Rybnoye. I made my way via Moscow to Mariampol (near the Prussian border), and with the assistance of Stoklitsky escaped over the frontier. After settling in Paris in autumn 1909, I was entrusted by Lenin with managing the *Proletary* workers' club. *Emigré* meetings took place at that time in the Russian library on the Avenue des Gobelins, where Lenin fulminated against the 'liquidators' and the *otzovisty*. I became acquainted with Nadezhda Konstantinovna Krupskaya in the editorial offices of the central organ *Sotsial-Demokrat*, where she usually collected painstaking information from new arrivals about events in Russia. I first saw Lenin at a meeting of the Paris Bolshevik group: it was the occasion of his report on the two possible paths of agrarian development in Russia. At this time reaction was at its height in Russia, but Lenin radiated invincible firmness and courage. He lived in a tiny flat on the Rue Marie-Rose, spent long hours in the Bibliothèque Nationale, and in the evening chatted with comrades in the small, sparkling kitchen over the simplest of suppers.

It was in Paris that I finished my courses for the Law Faculty and took my doctorate in economic sciences. When the split came after the CC plenum in spring 1910, I sided with the Bolshevik group that included 'Mark' (Lyubimov), 'Lev' (Vladimirov), 'Lozovsky' (Dridzo), and I helped with the group's paper *Za Partiyu*. I met Plekhanov a couple of times while he was rallying around him the Menshevik 'anti-liquidators': the arrogance he showed could not hide the fact that he had already lost the ability to understand Russian affairs. Later, in Switzerland, I organised the Swiss Bureau of *Émigré* Groups and Bolshevik Party Members. After adopting an internationalist position from the first days of the war, I was active in the Swiss Socialist Party, collaborated on the internationalist newspaper *Nashe Slovo*, published in Paris and which Trotsky helped to edit, read reports on imperialism and the prospects for a socialist revolution in a number of Swiss towns and, supporting the Zimmerwald left after the conference there, drew closer to the position of the Bolshevik CC.

After the February Revolution I was among the first group of *émigrés* to leave for Russia—it included Lenin, Zinoviev, Radek, Kharitonov, Inessa Armand, Miringof, Lilin and Usnevich. The journey in the sealed train through Germany was filled with discussions of tactical platforms, but was done on an empty stomach—on principle we had decided to refuse the watery soup to which the German Red Cross was ready to treat us. Two delegates from the CC of the German SD Party who attempted to board the train to greet Lenin were forced to make a hasty retreat when they were presented with an ultimatum— they could either go away or be thrown out. This ultimatum was presented by Lenin without any rhetorical courtesy and had the desired effect. The news of the campaign of slander opened against him and his companions forced us to allow for the possibility that the Provisional government would attempt to arrest us as we crossed the Russian border. As a precaution (on Lenin's suggestion), we agreed how to behave under interrogation.

In Petrograd I entered into discussions about common action with the leaders of the so-called *Mezhrayonka*—a group of internationalists and unifiers, with whom *émigré* Bolshevik groups had been in contact. This organisation, which subsequently was incorporated into the Bolshevik Party, spoke against an immediate merger at that time and this circumstance made an alliance impossible.

After leaving Petrograd for Moscow (in April 1917), I rejoined the Moscow organisation, which soon voted me on to its Committee and Regional Bureau. I was also a member of the Executive Committee of the Moscow Soviet. At this time I worked closely with Bukharin, V. M. Smirnov, Osinsky, Yakovleva, Bubnov, Stukov and Sapronov. Whilst still abroad I had spoken in favour of the seizure of power by the soviets and the first move towards the socialist revolution. Consequently I supported Lenin's *April Theses* against that section of the Bolsheviks who at first opposed them. In the course of an agitational tour of the Moscow region, I was arrested by some officers in Kineshma, but was freed by soldiers from a reserve detachment there. I wrote an article for a collection published in Moscow—my contribution was called 'On the Question of the Revision of the Party Programme' and it advocated a reform of the principal part of the old (SD) programme.

At the fifth Congress[1] I was elected to the CC and the editorial board of the central organ. With Stalin, I helped edit the papers that came out in place of *Pravda* after the 'July days'—*Rabochy i Soldat*, *Put Pravdy*, *Golos Pravdy* (for these papers I wrote a number of editorials and other articles, as well as a review of the other press), and then *Pravda* again from the moment of the October Revolution. After the July defeat, Lenin thought a more or less prolonged period of counter-revolutionary violence against the masses was likely. He demanded the preparation of underground organs of the press and for a while considered the hopes of retaining legal Bolshevik papers to be illusory. The failure of the Kornilov *putsch*, however, changed the situation radically, for it showed that the active proletarian forces would enter battle only under Bolshevik leadership. The 'Kornilov days' were a kind of 'rehearsal' for October. On returning from hiding in Finland, Lenin led the revolutionary forces in a headlong assault. I was a member of the Petrograd Soviet Executive Committee and then of the Soviet TsIK. I belonged to the majority in the CC which voted with Lenin for a rising and carried it out. During the preparations for the insurrection, I was also elected to the newly formed Politburo. After October I was in-

[1] No doubt a misprint for the sixth Congress.

structed to go with the delegation to Brest-Litovsk to open negotiations for a cease-fire. On my return from there, I formulated the outline of a decree for the nationalisation of private banks, was in charge of the nationalisation itself and with a group of bankers (Tumanov, Basias, Kogan) reorganised and merged the banks. I participated in the 'seizure' of the State Bank and in its revolutionary reorganisation. And I was elected to the Constituent Assembly as one of the Bolshevik list of candidates.

In spring 1918 I made a second journey to Brest to head the Soviet delegation in the new negotiations over a cease-fire (after the breakdown of peace negotiations and renewed German attacks). We were authorised by the CC to accept the ultimatum of the German High Command and sign the peace treaty (also in the delegation were Chicherin, Ioffe and Karakhan). During the disagreements inside the CC over the resumption of negotiations and the declaration of our willingness to sign the peace, I supported Lenin's position. There was of course, no certainty that the peace proposals would be accepted by the German government, and when the first words of the German reply agreeing to the resumption of talks appeared on the tape of the Hughes apparatus at dead of night, it was a complete surprise to everyone, particularly as the delay in replying, the continued movement of German troops and their capture of Pskov had made us more convinced with the passing of every hour that our initiative had failed.

The Soviet delegation, unable to reach Pskov by train following the destruction of the railway line, transferred to trolleys and then covered the final stage of the journey on foot. The commander of the advance troops, unaware of the resumption of negotiations, was greatly perplexed and at first did not know what to do with the delegation which had appeared in such a strange and unexpected fashion at dead of night. The German soldiers justified their attack by the alleged need to liberate neighbouring peoples from the Russian yoke. The departure of the delegation from Pskov for Brest attracted a hostile demonstration by a mass of local inhabitants who believed a malicious rumour that the delegation's departure was only a cover for the escape of members of the Soviet government which had been overthrown in Russia. The German government announced that the advance would continue until the signing of the peace treaty. The peace delegation, however, did not have a mandate to hold lengthy discussions: in view of the complete defencelessness of the front, the massive retreat of units of the old army for a hundred miles and more to the rear, and the weakness of organised Red detachments, resistance to the German ultimatum was impossible. Its terms were made even harsher by the inclusion at the last minute of new

Turkish demands. On signing the peace, as head of our delegation (the head of the German delegation was von Rosenberg, subsequently Minister of Foreign Affairs), I made a speech in which, to the great indignation of the German generals present led by General Hoffmann, I gave a biting assessment of the German ultimatum and expressed my certainty that the triumph of imperialism over the land of the Soviets would be short-lived.

On my return from Brest, I moved to Moscow with the rest of the CC and resumed work on *Pravda* which had also been transferred to Moscow. In the pamphlet *On the Question of Nationalising the Banks*, I estimated the significance of their nationalisation and the future role of credit institutions. At the first All-Russian Congress of Sovnarkhozes (Councils of National Economy), I made a report on the bases of financial policy in the transitional period, rejecting a policy of the gradual abolition of money. I defended the same principles in articles in *Narodnoye Khozyaistvo*. In June I was included in the commission dispatched to Berlin to conclude economic and legal agreements arising out of the peace treaty. At the same time Krasin made a trip to Ludendorf's headquarters to discuss the halting of the German troops' advance on Baku. Ludendorf's firm plan for the dismemberment of the Caucasus and Turkestan was frustrated by the landing of American troops in France, which created a new military situation and thwarted the schemes of the extreme right-wing German imperialists.

In Berlin I made reports at meetings of independent socialists and Spartakus circles. With Bukharin I visited Kautsky, but our conversations were rapidly abandoned in view of their obvious futility. After the assassination of Mirbach,[1] negotiations with the German government were interrupted and the committee returned home. Back in Moscow, I reported to Lenin on the growth of the revolutionary movement in Germany, the rapid demoralisation of the army, and the soldiers' mutinies.

Meanwhile the White Guard insurrection beyond the Volga, encouraged by the SR committee in the Constituent Assembly and supported by the Czech legions, began to pose a serious threat—and the epic struggle of the Civil War loomed nearer. As a member of the Second Army's RVS on the Eastern Front, I left for Vyatka (with S. Gusev). The RVS promoted Colonel Shorin, a former Tsarist officer and one of the first 'military specialists' in the Red Army, to be commander of the Second Army. The latter was ordered to crush the rising at the Izhevsk and Votkinsk factories and to prevent the rebels from uniting with the Constituent Assembly's troops. Kulak rebellions were taking place

[1] In July 1917. Mirbach was the German envoy to Russia.

round Vyatka and some of the provisioning detachments sent from Moscow went over to the rebels.

In its first engagements the Second Army suffered a number of reverses. This motley collection of units was originally far from being a single, unified whole. It consisted of worker partisans, sailors and volunteer soldiers who had gone through the school of the imperialist war and been transferred from the German Front. The requisition of supplies, horses, hay and buildings provoked sharp clashes with the peasantry. The mobilisation of local peasants into the ranks of the Red Army met with enormous difficulties: conscripts deserted after receiving their uniforms, or surrendered to the enemy in the first skirmish; there were even cases of outright treason by units large and small. Whilst the main forces of the reorganised Second Army made an advance on Izhevsk, a separate division, which I helped to raise, was ordered to march on the Votkinsk factory. The division could only be slowly built up between battles, which, in the wooded foothills by the Kama, amounted to a frenzied struggle for small Tartar villages, all of which suffered raids by day and night. The front line existed only in name: separate units had difficulty keeping contact and on more than one occasion companies of Reds were in the rear of the Whites in one area, whilst elsewhere Whites found themselves in the rear of the Reds. Sometimes the 'front' moved twenty-five miles forward during the day and forty-five miles back during the night.

The regular element in the division was the Lett regiment under Colonel Tauman who preferred to act cautiously, slowly and surely. The shock role was performed by the partisan sailors' detachment, who could barely be controlled by their Commissar, Baryshnikov (later military commander of the Glazov district), although he was himself a man of boundless courage. The battalions of conscripts were commanded by their Commissar, Malygin (who originally came from among the local peasantry) and the 'specialists'—young officers from the old army including Captain Ginet, who was cut to pieces by the Whites when he tried to hold back the enemy with a few soldiers as the rest fled. The Whites, able to rely on the armaments factories, had more weapons and ammunition, and at dangerous moments mobilised every single worker, driving them into battle with a second line of punitive companies to shoot those who retreated.

After two months' fighting, during which the leadership of the rebellion passed more and more from the SRs and Mensheviks into the hands of monarchist officials and officers who had settled in Izhevsk in particularly large numbers, the Whites retreated over the Kama (subsequently joining Kolchak's army). The shift in the sympathies of the peasants beyond the Volga and the defeat of the Constituent Assembly's army near Kazan decided the fate of the Izhevsk and Votkinsk rebellions.

After the liquidation of the Izhevsk rising, I was transferred to the Southern Front and the RVS of the Ninth Army, whose Commissar was Knyagnitsky (an engineer and old Bolshevik). Other members of the RVS were Dashkevich and Vladimir Baryshnikov (a Moscow Party worker, later captured by General Mamontov and executed after prolonged torture). The basic elements of the Ninth Army were the volunteer partisan divisions of Kikvidze and Sivers, and the mounted Cossack partisan division of Mironov. Kikvidze was one of the best partisan organisers. His units consisted of experienced troops who had marched with him from the Austrian border to the Volga, fighting Germans, Petlyura's men and Cossacks all the way; their numbers were swelled during this long march by reliable volunteers from among local workers. Kikvidze himself was on good terms with the left-wing SRs, but in spite of the urgings of Proshian (who had come to see him after the collapse of the left-wing SR rising in Moscow in summer 1918), he refused to support their movement. Full of mistrust for the Army Command, he jealously defended his 'autonomy' and his division's freedom of manoeuvre. A similar 'line' was drawn in Siver's division, although less zealously.

Things were considerably worse among Mironov's Cossacks, who would have no truck with military commissars, objected to political work and allowed undisguised anti-communist agitation. Until the Party line on the peasant question was changed (the condemnation at the eighth Congress of the forcible introduction of socialism in the villages), the mood of the conscripted peasants was frequently anti-communist. Meanwhile the Cossacks' sector of the front was undermined by fatigue, a struggle between the old men and the young ones, the appearance of monarchist tendencies among the Don High Command, and a longing for work in the fields. At the same time, supplies, equipment and recruitment of the Red troops continually improved. The machinery of a regular, revolutionary army began to fit together and work correctly. In spring 1919, Krasnov's army suffered a series of crushing defeats and disintegrated with astonishing speed. The Cossack regiments threw away their arms and surrendered. Krasnov handed over command of the remnants to Denikin, but the latter's volunteer army, relying on Anglo-French military support and having regiments of regular officers at its disposal, halted the advance of the Soviet armies not far from Novocherkassk.

I crossed the Don steppes with the advancing units before leaving for Moscow, where I participated in the eighth Congress as a member of the Commission for the Revision of the Party Programme. I also spoke

on questions of military organisation and advocated the need for a speedy
transition from partisan 'separatism' to a centralised, 'regular', revolutionary army. After the Congress I was sent by the Southern Front's
RVS to the Thirteenth Army, whose Commissar, Kozhevnikov, embodied all the worst traditions of partisan warfare. Then I helped to
organise the struggle with the Cossack rebellion on the upper Don. This
rising, which took place in villages that had split from Krasnov not long
before, was partly caused by mistakes of Soviet punitive and provisioning organs, and represented an attempt to find a native Cossack political
solution which would reconcile the positions of landowners, workers and
peasants. The social basis for the rising was the antagonism between the
interests of Cossacks and peasants in neighbouring provinces. The prosperous Cossacks, with plenty of land and cattle, had been evolving from
small-holdings and single farmsteads towards capitalist farming and the
export of grain. On the other hand, the peasants, who had earlier been
hired to work for the Cossacks and now owned small plots of land, had
proceeded to divide land and property equally in the aftermath of the
Soviet victory. The rising was to a certain extent a war about iron roofs
and straw ones—as a rule a Cossack's house can be distinguished from a
peasant's by its roof. With the advance of Denikin's army towards
Moscow, the Red Army was forced to abandon the line along the lower
Don, and the rebellious villages of the upper Don merged with the
Denikin Front.

During Mamontov's raid in the rear of the Red armies on the
Southern Front, I was sent to the Eighth Army's RVS in Voronezh. I
participated in the attack by the Eighth and Thirteenth armies against
Kharkov which, after succeeding as a show of force (patrols from the
Eighth Army were ten miles from the town), and drawing the enemy's
forces on itself, put the Eighth Army in an extremely difficult position
and compelled it to retreat. Surrounded on three sides and sometimes
completely cut off, the army withdrew from Volchansk to Voronezh,
maintaining only intermittent contact with the neighbouring Thirteenth
Army and the front's commander by means of radio and aeroplane. The
raids by Mamontov had a disorganising and demoralising effect. It was
at this time that Vladimir Baryshnikov, a member of the Eighth Army's
RVS, was captured by an enemy patrol. The army's staff wandered from
place to place, always in danger of being caught unawares. Some deserted and a few defected to the Whites.

It was under these conditions that I was appointed Commander of
the army, a move intended to strengthen confidence in the leadership.
Denikin's march on Moscow was then at the height of its success. Oryol
had been captured. Tula was threatened. But these successes swallowed

up all his remaining forces. Peasants flocked into the Red Army to swell its reserves, whilst the Whites were beset by an atmosphere of peasant hostility. Powerful units transferred from the Eastern Front, together with the Mounted Army withdrawn from Tsaritsyn, enabled the Red Army to go over to the offensive. Denikin's army began to roll back towards Kuban. The difficult march from Voronezh to Rostov necessitated a breathing-space, and the need to regroup our forces after the capture of Rostov reduced military activity for a while. An attempt by the Whites to recapture Rostov ended in failure. The Kuban Cossacks, antagonised by Denikin's reprisals (for example the hanging of Bych) against the *petit-bourgeois*, democratic wing of the Kuban *Rada*, did not provide the retreating 'Kadets' with sufficient support. Whole units of Cossacks and conscripted peasants came over to the Reds, bringing with them shells, cartridges and equipment. The further the advance went, the more it was carried out by former deserters. By the end of the campaign, many regiments had an overwhelming majority of soldiers, and in a few cases commissars, who had once fought for the Whites.

Denikin was no more successful in holding the Kuban line. The Eighth Army made a swift, outflanking movement along the coast towards Novorossiysk and reduced the Whites to sheer panic. The officers' regiments were hurriedly withdrawn from the front and embarked on ships inside twenty-four hours under cover of British guns and a British landing. The Cossacks surrendered in their thousands. The prize of Novorossiysk, with its extremely rich stocks of equipment, weapons and all types of military stores, fell into the hands of the Red armies. A large number of horses were drowned in the sea by the enemy. But an even larger number swarmed freely about the town and its suburbs, and although local peasants collected as many of them as they could, hundreds starved to death. [. . .]

After reaching Novorossiysk with units of the Eighth Army, I returned to Moscow and, thinking the period of civil war essentially over, went back to work on *Pravda*. I joined the Moscow Committee, directed the School for Propagandists and attended the second Comintern Congress. In August 1920 I was sent to Turkestan as Chairman of the Turkestan Commission of the VTsIK and Commander of the Turkestan Front (other members of the Commission were Safarov, Koganovich and Peters). I directed the consolidation of Soviet power in Bukhara after the overthrow of the Emir. I was closely connected with military operations against the Basmachi in Fergan, which ended in the rout of one of their leaders, Khol-Khadzhi. The latter, a former convict and a bandit of unusual height and strength, escaped with his gang into the mountains, heading for the Chinese frontier, but he perished under an avalanche on the narrow path. Although the Basmachi later spread the story that he had been saved from death by angels flying down to him, his disappearance was none the less final.

However, economic and other measures no less than military ones helped to weaken the Basmachi movement. A monetary reform was carried out, abolishing the special Turkestan coins – *turkbony* – which lost their value even faster than ordinary Soviet ones; they were exchanged for Soviet money, and prices and wages were re-calculated in the new currency. The surplus appropriation system was abolished (at first on a local scale and then generally) and replaced by a tax. General labour conscription was discontinued, and the right of free access and trading was introduced in bazaars. The mullahs were released after affirming their political loyalty. The organs of Soviet administration were transferred from Russian to native towns and quarters. In Semi-reche a start was made on returning land to the Kirghiz, which had been seized from them without warrant by Russian settlers. Measures were taken to re-establish the cotton industry in Fergan and the necessity of support for craftsmen was recognised by the authorities. In addition organisational plans were made for a Union of the Village Poor (*koshchi*). All these measures taken by the Turkestan Commission with the aid of Kirghiz, Uzbek and Turkmen activists who had been enlisted in responsible government work (Rakhimbaev, Turyakulov, Khodzhanov, Atabaev, Biryushev) combined to create a calmer atmosphere in Turkestan and established the preconditions for the consolidation of Soviet power, the development of the economy and the freeing of local administration from the influence of the native bourgeoisie (the *bai*).

In the discussions about trade unions that began at the end of 1920, I supported the 'buffer faction', although I considered that the basic problem to be decided did not concern trade unions, but our relations with the peasantry and the necessary concessions that ought to be made to them. From the beginning of 1921 until the autumn, serious illness prevented me from working. In November 1921 I returned to financial work for the first time since 1918 to deal with changes in the Party's financial policy arising out of NEP. I was appointed a Collegium member of the People's Commissariat for Finance and soon afterwards Deputy Commissar. As a result of the absence of the Commissar, Krestinsky (appointed Plenipotentiary in Germany in autumn 1921), I directed the Commissariat, and in autumn 1922 was appointed Commissar myself, which post I held until January 1926. My main tasks over this period were: the organisation of the Commissariat of Finance, which had been almost completely abolished under War Communism, the creation of a strong, balanced budget and the drafting of the norms of Soviet budgetary law, the abolition of taxation in kind and the organisation of a system of monetary taxes and incomes, the introduction of a stable currency, the formation of a system of banking institutions underneath the State Bank, the organisation of state credit facilities (short-term and long-term loans), the foundation of the State Insurance Organisation and State savings-banks, the differentiation between State and local budgets, the widespread development of the latter, in particular of rural district budgets, and the introduction of financial discipline and accountability. The greatest difficulties were presented by the abolition of taxes in kind and the introduction of a graduated income tax in the countryside, the cessation of the practice of issuing paper money to cover budget requirements, the struggle against unrealistic economic plans which threatened to stimulate inflation, the establishment of the proportions in which national, republic and local interests would be satisfied, and the defence of correct priorities in fulfilling the country's cultural, economic and purely political needs. The most active workers in the Commissariat over this period were Vladimirov, Sheinman, Reinhold, Tumanov, Yurovsky, Shleifer, Bryukhanov, Polyudov, Kuznetsov and R. Levin.

In summer 1922 I went with the Soviet delegation to the Hague Conference and at one of the sessions made a detailed report on the financial state of the Soviet Union, which provoked fierce attacks from all the bourgeois press. In autumn 1923, whilst preparing the monetary reform, I defended a policy of credit restrictions and reduction in industrial prices. In the political discussion I sided with the majority of the CC. In autumn 1925 I defended the necessity for a distinct, class policy in the countryside, as well as the need to ensure rapid growth in agriculture as the basis for a powerful industry, and in the intra-Party disagreements of 1925–6 I supported the minority in the CC. In spring 1926 I was appointed Deputy Chairman of Gosplan. In summer 1926 I went with my wife, G. O. Serebryakova, to the United States for discussions about a financial agreement, but our visit was halted half-way by Kellogg's withdrawal of the entry visa that he had promised.

I made speeches on questions of financial policy at the congresses of Soviets and sessions of the TsIK. At the fifth Party Congress I made a report on behalf of the CC about financial policy and defended the outline resolution which laid down guidelines for the construction of the Soviet financial system.

My writings on financial problems are collected in the books, *The Financial Policy of the Revolution* (two volumes) and *Monetary Reform*. Pamphlets devoted to the economic difficulties at the end of 1926 are entitled *Autumn Hazards and the Problems of Economic Assessment* and *The Path So Far and New Tasks*.

I have attended Comintern Congresses and was a member of the Party CC from 1917 to 1919, and from 1922 to the present.

Sokolnikov was a conciliator in the period 1908–10, associated in the war years with the editorial board of *Nashe Slovo* and, more loosely, with the Mezhrayonka group, but after his election to the Central Committee in August 1917 he became one of Lenin's firm supporters in 1917–18: with Stalin, he was a co-director of *Pravda*, and a member of the shadow Politburo set up on 10 October. He supported the insurrection, the homogeneous Bolshevik government, and the Brest-Litovsk peace terms. In November 1917, he and Bukharin were entrusted with controlling the 'parliamentary' Bolshevik splinter group in the soviets, dominated by right-wingers.

A member, successively, of the RVS for the Second, Ninth, Thirteenth and Eighth Armies, he defended Trotsky's military policy at the eighth Congress, and maintained that the partisans' war was mere 'banditry and pillage'. No doubt because of this attitude and because of the hostility he drew from Stalin's group, Congress did not re-elect him to the Central Committee. Ordzhonikidze, in effect, wrote to Lenin in October 1919: 'Where did the idea come from that Sokolnikov could command an army? [. . .] Is it to protect Sokolnikov's pride that he has to be allowed to play with a whole army?'

In 1920, he organised the Soviet uprising in Bukhara; after supporting the 'buffer group', he rallied to Trotsky's platform on the union question; in 1921 he was appointed People's Vice-Commissar for Finance, and in 1922 Commissar for Finance, in which post he pursued a policy of monetary re-stabilisation. In the same year he regained his seat on the Central Committee. Believing that the development of the Soviet economy would depend for many years more on the enrichment of the peasantry and on trade with the capitalist countries, he opposed the monopoly on foreign trade, and succeeded in making the Central Committee reconsider the matter on 6 October 1922. He was supported by Bukharin and Stalin, who was to denounce Sokolnikov's ideas to the fifteenth Congress as leading to a 'Dawes-isation' of the Soviet Union.

He also believed that Soviet industry needed to develop without state subsidies, by straightforward self-financing, and thus opposed the left opposition with its proposals for industrialisation and planning. He rejoined Zinoviev's group and was elected an alternate member of the Politburo in 1924. He suffered the effects of the rout of the new opposition, and lost his seat on the Politburo as well as his post as People's Commissar for Finance after the fifteenth Congress in 1926; after which he became Vice-President of Gosplan. He then maintained the need of the Soviet regime to tolerate the existence of several parties, and provoked the thunder of the Party machine. He occupied a rather deviant position in the United Opposition, and left it after the declaration of 16 October 1926, in which the United Opposition renounced splinter struggles. This explains the curious – but politically logical – affirmation of Trotsky's, 'Sokolnikov never joined the opposition bloc formed in 1926–7', whilst he *was* one of the six signatories of the declaration of October 1926! Sokolnikov the administrator fitted in badly with the image of a left-wing oppositionist. . . .

Having rallied to the majority before the Opposition struggle on the Chinese question, he was re-elected to the Central Committee by the fifteenth Congress (1927) and subsequently supported the right-wing struggle on behalf of the peasants. In 1929, Stalin sent him to Britain as Soviet Plenipotentiary. He returned to Russia in 1934, and was appointed People's Vice-Commissar for Foreign Affairs. He was eliminated from the Central Committee by the sixteenth Congress in 1930, and in 1936 he was arrested and tried at the second Moscow trial in January 1937. Like Radek, he was sentenced to only ten years' prison. He had asked for indulgence in his final speech, in which he had 'openly made honourable amends'. He died in obscure circumstances in 1939.

J.-J. M.

LEV SEMYONOVICH SOSNOVSKY
(autobiography)

I was born in 1886 in Orienburg. [. . .] My father, a retired soldier who had served for twenty-five years during the reign of Nicholas I, had been still a little boy when he was forcibly taken from his father and draped in a greatcoat at the military school. What military service, and in particular life at such a school, was like, I only discovered when I had grown up, and then not from him. At rare moments during his reminiscences about his past, my father would talk graphically about the way he had been often and harshly beaten. He recounted how they had tried to convert him to Orthodoxy by beatings, humiliation and even torture. He had even been chased into the river and threatened with drowning if he would not cross himself. Many of his contemporaries had embraced Orthodoxy, but for some reason he had remained a Jew. At the bazaar he showed me old stall-holders with genuine Russian names but genuine Jewish noses and beards, and he explained that they had been brought to see the truth of the Orthodox faith with birches and fists. [. . .]

My father spent whole days in the Saratov Inn near the bazaar. That was his reception room, there he practised as a 'lawyer'. He was only semi-literate. How he coped as a lawyer, I do not know. But I do know that when I was nine, he made me write fair copies of the petitions and complaints which he composed for his clients. Even at that age I could write better than he. [. . .]

The barefoot period of my life with games in the street and day-long fun on the bank of the peaceful, shallow Urals soon came to an end. I began classes at a Gymnasium. [. . .] It is difficult to speak well of this period. There was the callousness of the school system, the cowering pupils, the mediocre teachers, the cramming, the boredom. [. . .]

The faster I developed mentally, the more unbearable my time in the Gymnasium became. Above all I was oppressed by the humiliation, the arbitrariness, the constant expectance of boorishness, humiliation or punishment. [. . .] I longed for freedom and left school. [. . .] I found a job as pupil in a chemist's shop in Samara. At first I received no pay, as was the custom. The work was hard and the days were long. I had to work on holidays just as on weekdays, enjoying only occasional free days. And soon I was involved in night duty. [. . .]

One day the chemist, who was German and very strict, struck a pupil, and we went on strike out of solidarity. He did not even notice our strike, however, with so many boys like us eager for work. But I was the richer for a new sensation—the desire to chasten the exploiters and oppressors of the workers.

We prompted a comrade to write an article for the local Samara paper under the title 'The White Slaves', about the life of pharmacy employees. At roughly the same time I was introduced into a social democrat circle. There we were told of the massacre of workers at Zlatoust, there we read *Iskra*. I began to render such services to the Party (of a technical nature) as I could, and from this time (1903) I considered myself a Party member.

After Samara I wandered for a while from one pharmacy to another (Oboyan, Chelyabinsk), arriving in Ekaterinburg in 1904. Here I soon made the acquaintance of Bolsheviks. At first they employed me in a technical capacity. The chemist's shop where I worked was very convenient, both for storing illegal things and as a rendezvous for underground activists. Letters, including some from abroad, arrived in my name. Party workers from elsewhere would present themselves at the chemist's and I would direct them to a secret address. [. . .]

In spring 1905 I met and soon became familiar with the leaders of the Bolshevik organisation in the Urals. Ya. M. Sverdlov appeared and immediately enchanted me as a model revolutionary. I began to visit meetings and mass demonstrations. I duplicated proclamations and carried out various small assignments. Then the events of autumn 1905 came upon us. The organisation had powerful forces at its disposal. Sverdlov, Chutskaev, Syromolotov and many other comrades were experienced, resolute Bolsheviks, from whom we could learn much.

The days of October 1905 had the scent of a real struggle. Our meeting of 19 October was attacked by the Black Hundreds. Several people were injured (including Minkin). But a couple of days later our organisation was ready to withstand any onslaught and threw down a challenge to the Black Hundreds. Under the protection of armed Bolshevik workers, we held public meetings in the municipal theatre, where Sverdlov made exceptionally successful speeches. I remember nights when the group of Bolsheviks was ready to give an armed rebuff to the attack they expected hourly. These were marvellous nights and they forged a genuine iron determination in everyone. [. . .]

In November I was advised to go to Zlatoust where the social revolutionaries were in the ascendancy. I set off there with misgivings, for I felt myself very poorly prepared as a Bolshevik. In Zlatoust my first duty was to look for work at the factory. I had already been accepted as a lathe operator when the management found a cunning method of rejecting me: I was found unfit at the medical examination. So I would walk about the factory, carry on a little propaganda and take part in disputes with SRs, where I was again and again convinced of my insufficient preparation as a propagandist, particularly on the agrarian question.

It was in Zlatoust that I addressed a huge workers' meeting for the first time. It commemorated the first anniversary of a massacre of workers by the Tsarist butchers on the town square. It was freezing hard. Even without that I could hardly breathe. What with the cold and my agitation, I was shivering. In my short speech I displayed such hatred for Tsarism that even my friends were astonished at my eloquence and predicted a career as an orator for me. Soon, however, the punitive expedition of one of the bloodthirsty generals advanced across the Urals and I had to slip away. I reached Samara in an empty goods wagon, half dead from cold. I could find none of the Party workers in the town, so I went on to Odessa, where I had been given a few addresses. I had no more luck there, so I decided to escape over the frontier in the hope of learning about Marxism, seeing for myself the labour movement abroad, and simply breathing free air.

After a series of unsuccessful attempts to leave, I decided to travel like the heroes of novels I had read. I stowed away on board the first ship I saw without even asking where it was bound. When we had passed Constantinople, I climbed out of the hold and was made to scrub decks by the captain. In Algiers I escaped from the ship, as he was threatening to hand me over to the courts in England. I began my life as an *émigré* with three roubles in my pocket. I worked in a tobacco factory and a pharmacy before reaching Paris.

There I lived the life of an *émigré* for roughly a year. Out of work, hungry, often with no home, I eagerly absorbed the impressions of my new surroundings. I attended lectures and debates, studied in libraries, went to trade union meetings and even the French Trade Union Congress at Amiens in 1906. I gained a great deal from Paris, but I began to long for Russia and work. After spending some time in Geneva and Vienna, I took the firm decision to return to Russia. I reached Tashkent where I found a job as type-setter on the local bourgeois newspaper *Turkestansky Kurier*. I organised a Union of Printing Workers. Sometimes I collaborated on the local SD paper which was published by my old comrade, M. V. Morozov. The proprietor of my printing works and the paper's editor, Rabbi Kirsner, hurriedly dismissed me. The Union declared a strike. On the same night we were arrested. The Union continued the strike until we were set free and Kirsner himself had to arrange our release. Soon I was employed as clerk in the Druzhkin company. [. . .]

After leaving Tashkent, I tried to settle in Orienburg. Whilst I was there, the dissolution of the second Duma took place, as well as the beginning of even more savage reprisals by the Tsarist authorities against revolutionary activists and the working class. According to some accounts I heard, the smouldering revolutionary flame was brightest in the Caucasus, and I was drawn there.

I found myself in Baku. I lived then in secret, working at first as a clerk in a restaurant and hotel, where I could observe the debauchery of Baku merchants. Then I found work in a chemist's shop. I soon made contact with the local organisation through Semkov, a friend from my days in Paris. Baku taught me an immense amount. There was large-scale industry; there were many nationalities among the proletariat; and the peculiar position of the oil industry allowed workers and the Party to breathe more freely than in the rest of Russia. There, mass trade unions operated openly and a workers' press appeared. Time and again the proletariat erupted in impressive political and economic action. The capitalists entered into negotiations with the workers' unions over a collective agreement. In a word, the class struggle was at its height and took the most varied forms. The opportunities for propaganda and agitation were immeasurably greater than in other parts of Russia. The combination of legal and underground revolutionary activity enabled us to be active on many fronts. During my stay in Baku, I was in turn district organiser of the (underground) Party organisation and Secretary of the Union of Joiners and Builders, while at the same time participating in the work of clubs and co-operatives. The work was flourishing and absorbing, but my arrest brought it to an end. I managed to escape after a few days, however, and I went to ground in the oil district of Balakhany. [. . .]

There I lived with workers and shared their life. I worked as a labourer on the Rothschild oil fields, but was dismissed. I worked with Samartsev in the pipe-laying artel for unemployed workers. This was onerous, and at times highly dangerous work (for example when a pipe had to be laid over a marsh).

After Baku I made my way to Moscow with a passport given to me by Nikolay Krayushkin, an engineering worker. I began to work as secretary of two trade unions, those of the textile-workers and the leather-workers. Both unions shared a tiny room belonging to a dress-maker in the Zamoskvoreche district. Essentially my function was that of agitator rather than organiser. Workers' meetings took place quite legally in the guise of union meetings, where legal social democratic propaganda and agitation was carried on. [. . .]

I also did some journalism for the Party in Moscow. The Bolsheviks at that time published a political and trade union journal. It was banned, but reappeared under new names (*Rabocheye Delo*, *Vestnik Truda*, etc.). M. I. Frumkin and Skvortsov-Stepanov were among those who contributed to it.

In winter 1909 I was arrested. [. . .] Although finally released, I was compelled to do my military service. This meant prison, travel under escort, army hospitals, medical examinations, and there I was in Ekaterinburg in soldier's uniform, with the rights of a 'defender of Tsar and country' under supervision. After a few months of strict supervision, I began to steal out of the barracks and search for old friends of 1905. To my great delight I did find one or two of them. I began to receive *Zvezda* and a few illegal writings. [. . .]

After two years in the army, I slipped a bribe to the army doctor to declare me unfit for service. I was demobilised and given full legal status. [. . .]

Soon *Pravda* began to appear. After receiving the first ten or twenty numbers, my thoughts began to turn towards St Petersburg. I had no connections in the capital but I took a chance and moved there. At first I endured hardships for several months, but then I found my way into *Pravda* and became an enthusiastic worker on it.

Simultaneously I undertook semi-legal activity in workers' clubs and trade unions—I helped to eradicate Menshevik influence in the Union of Metal-Workers and some clubs. [. . .] In spring 1913 I was arrested, but after a few months' 'preventive', I was released and no further action was taken. Of course, I immediately returned to *Pravda*. Soon several comrades and myself began to organise a workers' journal, *Voprosy Strakhovaniya*, for which I was secretary until my second arrest in autumn 1913. This time, after spending winter in custody, I was banished to Chelyabinsk.

There, I spread the influence of *Pravda* among the working masses as far as I was able, recruited subscribers and correspondents, joined cooperatives and unions, and exploited all possible opportunities for legal and semi-legal activity. With the declaration of war, I was arrested on orders from St Petersburg and held for several months in such strict isolation that it was only on my release that I discovered who was fighting whom. In 1915 I was arrested yet again, but not for long. At this time I managed to make contact with comrades in other towns in the Urals. A small Party conference to discuss our attitude towards the war was held in Ekaterinburg, attended by amongst others Krestinsky, Sevruk (then a Bolshevik) and myself. Still lacking documents from the CC relating to the Party's attitude towards the war and deprived of information, we did, however, instinctively adopt the correct position, and our resolution, subsequently printed in the *émigré* journal *Sotsial-Demokrat*, received the approval of the CC as one of the first reactions from local Party organisations.

With the end of my time in exile, I took up residence in Ekaterinburg. I earned a living with contributions to the local newspaper *Uralskaya Zhizn,* which by that time was relatively radical. Thus for example, during the elections for the military-industrial committees, we succeeded in printing discreet exhortations for a boycott, which corresponded to the Party line. This did not prevent the paper from following a generally 'defencist' policy. Little by little a strong group of Bolshevik activists came together in legal and clandestine work. Not long before the February Revolution a number of them were arrested, and the remainder were searched and carefully shadowed. I escaped to the Satkin factory (southern Urals) where I found work in the office. But hardly had I unpacked my cases when news of the Tsarist collapse forced me to return to Ekaterinburg. There I went directly from the station to a large meeting in the town theatre.

From February to October of that unforgettable year, I was active in Ekaterinburg. I worked most of all as agitator, journalist and editor, but I had to cope with everything. I occupied leading positions in the Soviet from its foundation (Assistant-Chairman and then Chairman of the Urals Regional Soviet, President of the Regional Board of the Urals Trade Union Councils, member of the regional Party committee, etc.) [. . .]

In December 1917 Krestinsky and myself were elected to the Constituent Assembly from the list of Bolshevik candidates and we left for Petrograd. The Assembly was dissolved after one day and I was left behind to work in the capital. The Petrograd Soviet decided to publish a popular newspaper for the working masses and it was entrusted to Volodarsky and myself. Thus *Krasnaya Gazeta* was born. Of the two of us, Volodarsky was more occupied with Party (mainly agitational) activity and would appear in the offices only in the evening to write a rousing leading article on the vital issue of the moment. I, on the other hand, spent whole days in the editorial office, selecting contributors for this new type of paper and looking through all the copy. At the same time I had to make speeches at meetings of workers and soldiers to exhort them to fight against the Mensheviks and SRs.

As a Presidium member (until 1924) of the VTsIK, I moved to Moscow with the rest of the central government. In Moscow I was entrusted with the task of creating a mass peasant newspaper. I was forced to merge the existing Party papers *Derevenskaya Bednota* (Petrograd) and *Derevenskaya Pravda* (Moscow). In spring came the first issue of *Bednota,* of which I remained editor for over six years. Work on *Bednota,* and the flood of letters from peasants and soldiers that I had to read, brought me into intimate contact with peasant affairs for the first time. [. . .]

With the Urals liberated from Kolchak, the CC instructed a group of Party workers to go there. We consisted mainly of former activists from that area. I was appointed Chairman of the Provincial Revolutionary Committee in Ekaterinburg. Following the year-long dictatorship of the White Guards, we had to concentrate on reconstruction.

In the winter of 1919–20 I was ordered to Kharkov, which had only just been liberated from Denikin, but I was only due to work there for three months as head of the Party Committee for the province. On my return to Moscow, I took up a post in the Main Political Transport Directorate (an organisation conducting political work throughout the transport system). I suggested to Trotsky, then Commissar for Transport, that we should publish a mass paper for railway-workers. After receiving his agreement and the approval of the CC, I organised *Gudok* and was its editor during the first months. In 1921 I was appointed head of the CC's Agitprop Department.

In 1922 I was a member of the Soviet delegation to the international conference at Genoa. The trip gave me the opportunity of looking more closely at life in Europe since 1905. Of later periods in my life there remains to be noted only my appointment as Collegium member of the People's Commissariat for Agriculture, although I did very little work there, my main functions being confined to journalism.

This was my basic occupation during the Revolution. From spring 1918 until the present, I have been a permanent contributor to *Pravda*, combining this with many other tasks, but without devoting nearly as much energy to them as to *Pravda*. It fell to me to blaze a trail for Soviet satirists. During the first months of the Revolution, D. Bedny and myself were alone in writing satire. Then appeared V. Knyazev, and others after him. Some of our works were published in two volumes entitled *Things and People*. Apart from this, small books of articles have appeared in various editions: *Soviet Virgin Soil*, *On Music and Other Things*, *Dymovka*, *Painful Questions*, *On Culture and Philistinism*.

From time to time I wrote articles on literary topics, for example about Demyan Bedny, against the Futurists, against decadent literary works à la Esenin, and against the distortion of Soviet reality by Pilnyak. Contributions on agriculture occupied a particular place in my literary output. [. . .] Some of my satirical sketches were translated into German and, I think, other languages, whilst a small illustrated collection appeared in Esperanto.

A passionate and ironical journalist, Sosnovsky became by the end of the Civil War a symbol of two struggles that in his view were complementary: the struggle against bureaucracy and the struggle against the

Kulaks. He waged these campaigns in the columns of *Pravda* and in *Bednota*, which he edited between 1918 and 1924. He was a member of TsIK and one of the spokesmen of its communist fraction; he soon turned his intransigence against the Party and State machines. He wrote of the *'apparatchiki*, neither hot nor cold', who skim through all the circulars, record, note, cover reams of paper, file, seal, label and 'are happy when calm reigns over their organisation'.

He supported Trotsky in the union dispute of 1920-1, and was a signatory of the so-called 'Declaration of the 46'; he belonged to the left opposition, then to the United Opposition. In 1924, he played a decisive role in the celebrated Dymovka affair, where he unmasked the assassins of one of *Bednota's* 'Selkors' (peasant correspondent), which allowed him to launch violent attacks on the Kulaks, whom he accused of having plotted the murder.

At the fifteenth Congress he was expelled as a Trotskyite. Yaroslavsky declared, from the speaker's tribune, that Sosnovsky had told the TsKK that the Party had 'sunk to the level of the Kuomintang'. In 1928 he was deported, and in the summer of the same year wrote three 'letters from exile' to Trotsky from his place of banishment, Barnaul, as well as a fourth letter to the oppositionist Vardin, who had just capitulated. These letters earned him a sentence of six years in the Chelyabinsk 'isolator'. All four were published in issues 3 and 4 of the *Byulleten Oppozitsii*. In Siberia, Sosnovsky studied all the manifestations of the struggle between the *Byednyaki* (poor peasants) and the *Kulaks* (rich peasants), whose existence had just been officially admitted, and recounted the remark of a discontented *byednyak*: 'Meetings for the *byednyaki*, land for the *Kulaki*.' On 30 May 1928 he wrote to Vardin, who had rallied to Stalin by describing the evils of 'former Trotskyism':

> With a philosophy like yours one becomes more easily a *servant* (let us say, even, a *lackey*) than a revolutionary militant [. . .] I have asked Vaganian to tell you about a detail of Jewish funeral rites. As the corpse is about to be carried out of the synagogue and off to the cemetery, a verger leans over the deceased and calling him by his name, says, 'Know that thou art dead.' It is an excellent custom.

Sosnovsky resisted pressures and threats for a long time. One of his guards was shot for having passed on one of his letters. On 27 February 1934, a few days after the eighteenth Congress (the 'Congress of Victors'), he capitulated. Trotsky commented: 'The declarations of capitulation by Sosnovsky and Preobrazhensky show the same frame of mind: they are closing their eyes to the situation of the world proletariat.

Only that can allow them to accept the national perspective of Soviet bureaucracy.'

In 1935, Sosnovsky was readmitted to the Party. In 1936 he was again expelled and was murdered the same year, for having refused to play the farce of improbable confessions.

J.-J. M.

ELENA DMITRIEVNA STASOVA
(autobiography)

I was born on 16 October 1873. I was the fifth child in our family, with two elder brothers and two elder sisters. [. . .] My father, Dmitry Vasilievich, a lawyer by training (he had graduated from the School of Jurisprudence in St Petersburg in 1847 at the age of nineteen), had soon found advancement in the Senate and would probably have achieved high office, judging by the beginning of his career, since he was herald at the coronation of Alexander II. His views and interests, however, developed in an undesirable direction from the government's point of view and in 1861, one month after his marriage, he was arrested during a student demonstration for collecting signatures against the matriculation of students. His career of course was in ruins. He never worked in government service again and became first an attorney, then a lawyer. [. . .]

He was President of the first Council of Lawyers in Russia (St Petersburg). With short interludes he remained in this post right up to his death in 1918, for lawyers considered him the 'conscience' of the profession. His enormous civil practice did not prevent him from appearing in political cases both in the old courts and in the reformed ones (including the trials of the 50, of the 193, and of Karakozov). As a result of this activity, and the endlesss number of defendants for whom he stood bail, he was more than once arrested and searched, and in 1880 he was banished from St Petersburg to Tula, for Alexander II had declared: 'One can't spit without hitting Stasov, he's involved in everything.' Besides his work as a lawyer, he devoted much effort and time to music: he was an excellent piano player and a highly knowledgeable musician. With Anton Rubinstein and Kologrivov, he founded the St Petersburg Conservatoire and the Russian Musical Society, which right up to the Revolution organised symphony concerts in St Petersburg and other major towns, and encouraged the spread of music in Russia. [. . .]

Until the age of thirteen I studied at home, and by that time I could already speak two languages (French and German). In spring 1887 I entered the fifth form of the Tagantsev private Gymnasium for girls. I was a very good pupil, and graduated with a gold medal.

The year 1892–3 was an extremely significant one for my intellectual development. In that year I attended a special course of lectures given by Professor A. S. Lappo-Danilevsky on the history of man's primitive culture. As I now remember, I was enormously impressed by his exposition of man's concept of property. I decided there and then that to understand life, it was essential to read about political economy. [. . .]

Life in a deeply humanitarian family which had retained all the best features of the Russian intelligentsia of the 1860s, and constant contact with the cream of Russian artists and musicians, all this undoubtedly had a strong influence on me. I remember that inside me grew an even stronger feeling of debt to the people, the workers and peasants who had provided us, the intelligentsia, with the opportunity of living as we did. I think that these thoughts of our unpaid debt were also formed partly by my reading. Looking back, I can remember the impression made on me by Ivanyukov's book *The Decline of Serfdom in Russia*. It pointed out a gap in my education and I took to studying Semyovsky's *History of the Peasantry*. It is obvious that all this reflection, plus external events which often involved student incidents, forced me to seek a practical outlet for my energies, such as teaching in the classes given in the evenings and on Sundays for adolescents and adult female workers in Ligovo, and working for a mobile exhibition of educational textbooks. My work amongst tobacco and textile workers brought me into direct contact with the working class, and through my acquaintance with Krupskaya, Yakubova, Nevzorova, Ustrugova and Sibileva, I came across militant political activists.

Gradually I began to work in the political Red Cross. Lectures on its behalf (with an admission fee) were more than once arranged at home, which was a very popular thing to do at that time and was supported by all the humanitarian intelligentsia, including my parents. Simultaneously militant comrades began to ask me and my acquaintances to store literature, Party archives and printed matter. It grew to the stage where, after the arrest of the comrade in charge of storing literature, I was entrusted with all the St Petersburg Committee archives. This was in 1898, and that is why I consider my entry into the Party as having taken place then, although as early as spring 1896 I had been keeping *The Workers' Day*, *Who Lives on What*, and *You Can't Do Anything about Us*. Little by little the work grew, and my province came to include not only the caches of literature but everything connected with the technical side of the St Petersburg Committee, that is finding rooms for meetings, secret addresses and beds for a night, receiving and distributing literature, equipping duplicating machines and printing-presses, as well as maintaining correspondence with abroad.

From the first appearance of *Iskra* and the beginning of the campaign for a tighter-knit Party, I worked a great deal with I. I. Radchenko. He had come from Geneva and had been given my address by Krupskaya. He was the local representative of *Iskra* and he asked me to put him in touch with the 'Union of Struggle'. I introduced him to N. A. Anosov, but maintained personal contact with him as well, and the correspondence between *Iskra* and St Petersburg was conducted by us jointly. We were also greatly helped by Varvara Fyodorovna Kozhevnikova-Shtremer and N. N. Shtremer. This was our compact *Iskra* company, which waged an energetic campaign against the 'economists'—Tokarev, Anosov, etc. The 'Union of Struggle' and *Iskra* did not merge in St Petersburg and were represented separately at the second Congress.

I continued working for the St Petersburg Committee until January 1904 when, as a result of my arrest, due to the blunder of an inexperienced girl who had only just joined the organisation as technical assistant, I was obliged to leave the capital. My departure coincided with a call from G. M. Krzhizhanovsky, a CC member, for me to come to Kiev. I was not able to stay there, however, as a result of arrests on the day before my arrival, and with M. M. Essen ('Zver') I left for Minsk where we were hidden by M. N. Kuznetsov, an engineer. Essen soon went abroad and I was given the task of working with 'Mark' (Lyubimov) on technical matters for the CC. I had to move to Oryol, and from there I went to F. G. Gusarev in Smolensk and Klopov in Vilno on a matter of passports, links with the military organisations and escape routes over the frontier. In early spring I made my way to Moscow where Krasikov, Lengnik, Galperin, Bauman and myself were entrusted with organising the Northern Bureau of the CC. In June Bauman, his wife and Lengnik were arrested, and I had to transfer the Northern Bureau to Nizhny Novgorod. But arrests had taken place simultaneously in Moscow and among the Southern Bureau in Odessa, and 'Mysh' (Kulyabko) had moved to Moscow. It was decided that he should become Secretary of the Northern Bureau, and that I should take over the Southern. Whilst on my way to hand over to him, however, I was arrested in Nizhny Novgorod and within a day was transported to the Taganka in Moscow. I remained there until December 1904 when I was released on bail. From Moscow I went to St Petersburg, where I immediately rejoined the organisation. Zemlyachka passed on all the contacts to me and I again became Secretary of the city committee. Then when A. I. Rykov was arrested on his return from the Congress in the spring, I also performed the function of CC Secretary throughout the summer. In autumn I handed over my technical responsibilities to the engineer V. S. Lavrov and my secretaryship to V. Ksandrov, although I continued in the latter post until August. Then I was ordered to Geneva as CC technical representative.

In January 1906 I returned to St Petersburg as Secretary of the committee there. Then in February I was instructed to go to Finland and take over from German Fyodorovich (N. E. Burenin) all links with abroad (the escape route into Sweden and the shipment of arms, both via the land route Tornio-Haparanda and the sea route Turku-Hanko-Vaasa-Stockholm). Simultaneously I was to prepare a unifying congress in Sweden, making arrangements for delegates both to leave and re-enter Russia clandestinely. When this was completed, I returned to St Petersburg and until my arrest on 7 July 1906 I was joint Committee Secretary with Raisa Arkadevna Karfunkel, a Menshevik—since the Unification Congress, the St Petersburg Committee had been reunified. Together we organised a city conference which met first in the building of the Society of Engineers, 21 Zagorodny Prospekt; then at Terijoki in the hall of the Narodny Dom; and finally in the house of the Society of Technologists on Anglisky Prospekt. This last session did not actually take place as too few people came, and on leaving, Karfunkel, Krasikov and myself were arrested. Karfunkel and I were taken to the Lithuanian Castle, and Krasikov to the Kresty. Since nothing was found at home apart from articles on the organisation intended for our legal paper *Ekho*, I was merely banished from the capital, and in January 1907 I was allowed to return following appeals from my father. I worked in the city committee until March when illness obliged me to move to the Caucasus. I was active in Tiflis as a propagandist in various circles from autumn 1907 until autumn 1910, when Spandarian and Ordzhonikidze drew me into working for the CC, at first on preparations for the Prague Conference, and then in the CC section dealing with literature and technical matters.

In November 1913 I left Tiflis for exile and on 9 January 1914 arrived at the appointed place—the village of Rybinskoye, Kansk district, Yenisey province. I had been sentenced in Tiflis under article 102 at the same time as Vera Schweitzer, Maria Vokhmina, Armenuya Ovvyan, Vaso Khachaturiant, Suren Spandarian and Nerses Nersesyan. We had all been arrested in May and June 1912, but evidence to incriminate me was only found after the arrest of Ovvyan and Vokhmina. [. . .]

Our trial was held on 2 May 1913 and we were all sentenced to deportation. My sentence was confirmed in September, and on 25 November, Ovvyan and I set off for Krasnoyarsk via Baku, Kozlov, Ryazhsk, Samara and Chelyabinsk. In Samara we met quite a number of male comrades (including Serebryakov and V. M. Sverdlov), and we were joined in Chelyabinsk by Semyon Schwartz, Anna Trubina and Marusya Cherepanova, the latter also being destined for Rybinskoye.

In autumn 1916 I received permission to make a visit to Petrograd 'to see my aged parents', for so ran the article under which exiles were strictly entitled to leave Siberia. In Petrograd I made immediate contact with Shlyapnikov, Molotov, Zalutsky, M. I. Ulyanova and others so that I could undertake Party work. I did not return to Siberia as I fell seriously ill, my stay in the capital was extended and then the Revolution broke out. The Tsarist police, however, did not leave me in peace and visited me on the night of 25/26 February 1917. They carried out a fruitless search and took me to the Liteyny police station where I found at first only one political prisoner, though during the night we were joined by another sixteen.

I was released by the popular uprising on the evening of 27 February. The following day I went to the Tauride Palace and was delegated by Shlyapnikov to form the Secretariat of the CC Bureau. From then until the ninth Congress I was a CC Secretary in Petrograd and Moscow. Then I moved back to Petrograd and from May 1920 was organiser for the Party gubkom until it was merged with the city committee. I was sent to Baku by the CC to organise the first Congress of Peoples of the East, and to work in the CC Caucasus Bureau. After the Congress, I was elected a member and Secretary of the Council for Propaganda and Action of the Peoples of the East, whilst simultaneously carrying on my functions in the Caucasian Bureau. From April 1921 until February 1926 I was at the disposal of the Comintern. At the present time, I am working in the CC Secretariat of the VKP(b).

Stasova was for many years a close collaborator of Lenin, and she became one of the last survivors of the Bolshevik Old Guard. Her life was characterised throughout by discipline and unconditional devotion to the Party line. On many essential points in her life, of importance for the history of the Communist Party of the USSR, our knowledge is slim—particularly on her activities between 1917 and 1920, when she was Secretary to the Central Committee of the Russian CP. The fragmentary memoirs published in 1957 under the title *Pages from My Life and Struggle*[1] reveal a little, despite their mediocrity, about her activities after July 1920 as Secretary of the Central Committee's Transcaucasian Bureau, where she worked with Sergo Ordzhonikidze. In May 1921 she carried out underground work in Germany as representative of the Comintern. 'First, I was appointed Secretary at the CC organisation, then President of the Central Committee of the MOPBR.' Her party pseudonym in Germany was Herta. She lived in the Weimar Republic until February 1926, with a passport made out in the name of Lydia Wilhelm which she obtained by formally marrying a certain Ernst Wilhelm. In 1926 Stalin accepted her request for transfer to Moscow, to the information bureau of the Central Committee of the Communist

[1] *Stranitsy zhizni i borbi* (Moscow, 1957), 144 pp.

Party of the USSR. From 1927 to 1938 she was president of MOPBR. At the start of the great purges Stasova was on the various purge commissions. Subsequently she was in fact confined to the role of a figurehead, and took part in numerous international feminist, anti-fascist, etc. congresses. From 1938 to 1946 she edited the French and English edition of *International Literature*. After the twentieth Congress of the Communist Party of the USSR, Stasova regained celebrity as the senior Old Bolshevik, and attracted attention at the twenty-second Congress by a violent diatribe against Stalin's misdeeds. She died at the age of 93 and was buried in the Kremlin wall in January 1967, with all the honours due to a veteran; the Central Committee had set up a special commission under Suslov to organise the funeral.

G. H.

MIKHAIL PAVLOVICH TOMSKY (Efremov)
(authorised biography)

Mikhail Pavlovich Tomsky was born on 31 October 1880 in St Petersburg. His mother, an intelligent, sturdy woman, parted from his father, a St Petersburg factory worker, as she could not 'get used to' the beatings he inflicted on her when he arrived home drunk almost every day. Tomsky never knew his father since he was born after the separation; and as his father would not acknowledge him, Tomsky was registered as 'illegitimate'. This was a cross that caused him great pain in early childhood.

Until he was six, Tomsky, his 25-year-old brother and 11-year-old sister lived with their grandfather, who worked for the Sheremetievs. With his grandfather's death, his mother had to take care of the whole family, living from hand to mouth and barely subsisting on the pittance she earned by sewing. His brother had no profession although he was widely read. Ill with tuberculosis and often unemployed, he dealt savagely with little Misha, turning him into a timid, weak-kneed boy by the time he was eleven.

Tomsky first had classes at the age of five in a private boarding-school where he and his sister were accepted out of kindness as his aunt was a servant there. Tomsky only spent a year there but learnt to read well.

At the age of nine, he was sent to a three-class primary school, where he received free education. On leaving school he worked at the Theodor Kibbel box factory for a wage of five kopecks per day. After injuring a finger, he was dismissed. He found work first at the Laferme tobacco factory, then back at the Theodor Kibbel factory at a wage of five roubles per month, and from there he went to the Bruno Hofmark engineering works. When he was fourteen and working at the small Smirnov factory manufacturing 'Rus' engineering products, he was one of the leaders of a strike, which earned him his dismissal when it collapsed. After a few months of unemployment, he became apprentice to the chromolithographer, V. Nessler. At the age of twenty-one, he completed his apprenticeship and worked in various chromolithographic factories in St Petersburg.

In 1903 he first came across socialist literature, and in 1904 he joined a social democrat circle. Whilst working at the Haimovich tin factory, he became known as a socialist, for which he was dismissed in 1905. After wandering about St Petersburg for several months without work, he went to Revel. There he found a job as a lithographer at the Zvezda factory which manufactured preserve boxes. It was here in Revel in 1905 that Tomsky began his revolutionary career in earnest.

First he was elected spokesman for the factory's workers and joined the Revel Council of Workers' Representatives, whose task was to hold discussions with the managements of various types of factories about the workers' economic and political demands. With his energetic encouragement, the Revel Soviet of Workers' Deputies was formed after the fashion of the St Petersburg one, and he subsequently became a member of its Presidium. He organised a protest strike against the massacre of Revel demonstrators on 16 December 1905.

His first experience of trade union work came at this time with the organisation of the Revel Union of Metal-Workers. In January 1906 he was arrested as a member of the Revel Soviet and was imprisoned in the death cell. After four months in custody, he was deported to Siberia to the village of Parabel in the region of Narym. During discussions in exile he showed himself an advocate of armed rebellion in opposition to those who supported the amnesty. He spent two months in Parabel, escaped to Tomsk with a small group of comrades and for the first time was hidden by the Party; he also acquired his pseudonym of 'Tomsky'.

In August 1906 he made his way secretly to St Petersburg, where he found work at the Haimovich tin works under the name of Artomonov. At first under the pseudonym 'Mikhail Vasileostrovsky', and then 'Mikhail Tomsky', he performed tasks for the Party in the district of Vasilievsky Ostrov. He formed the Union of Engravers and Chromolithographers and was elected their President. With the merger of the lithographers and printers in one union, he was elected to the joint management committee. In early January 1907, he was elected to the St Petersburg RSDRP Committee at the conference of the city organisation and he began to perform Party work in various districts. The committee then elected him to the enlarged editorial staff of the CC organ *Proletary* and the editorial commission of *Vperyod*.

In spring 1907 he was a St Petersburg delegate to the fifth Party Congress in London. There he made a speech on behalf of the Bolsheviks against the idea of an 'All-Russian Workers' Congress', as proposed by Akselrod and supported by Plekhanov. He also attended the All-Russian Party Conference in Helsinki. On his return from the latter, he was arrested at a session of the St Petersburg Committee. After four months' preliminary detention in the Kresty, he was condemned by a court in May 1908 to one year in a fortress for membership of the RSDRP. A few months before the completion of his sentence, he was released on bail following the exertions of Poletaev, then a member of the State Duma. With unquenchable energy he again threw himself into Party work, but not for long.

In November 1908 he was denounced by the *agent provocateur*

Konovalov, arrested and put in solitary confinement until April 1909. In May he went to Paris for the enlarged session of the editorial staff of *Vperyod*. From Paris the CC directed him to Moscow as their representative in the Moscow central industrial region. On arrival, he re-established the smashed Bolshevik organisation there, simultaneously working as a member of the Regional Bureau, the Moscow Committee and the Area Committee. He organised an underground printing-press and took an active part in the reappearance of the regional Party paper *Rabocheye Znamya*, of which he was editor-in-chief. After the arrest of the Moscow Committee and the subsequent discovery of the printing-press, Tomsky succeeded in evading strenuous police searches.

He was arrested in December 1909 at the station in St Petersburg where he had arrived from the Southern Regional Bureau in Odessa. He was transferred from St Petersburg to Moscow, where he was held in connection with the Trial of the 33. In November 1911, after an eleven-day hearing, the Moscow Chamber of Justice brought in its verdict. Tomsky was sentenced to five years' hard labour for membership of the RSDRP, the sentence to be served in the Butyrki prison in Moscow.

During his imprisonment he energetically occupied himself with broadening his knowledge, chiefly of Marxism. On completion of his sentence of hard labour, he was banished for life to the Kirensk district of Irkutsk province in Siberia. In exile he worked at first as an agricultural statistician. The February Revolution and the amnesty found him still in exile, where he helped to organise a Committee of Public Security, and to arrest and disarm the police and gendarmes.

At the end of March, without waiting for the Lena to be freed from ice, he made his way on horseback to Irkutsk and then to Moscow. His long isolation prevented an early return to Party activity. With Lenin's arrival, Tomsky went to Petrograd, where, after a conversation with Lenin, he began work in the Petrograd Committee as a member of its Executive Commission. He represented the Petrograd Committee at the third All-Russian Conference of Trade Unions (June 1917).

After the 'July days' he moved to Moscow where he worked in the Commission supervising elections to the Moscow district dumas. Later he became editor of the journal *Metallist* for the Union of Metal-Workers. They made him their delegate to the Moscow Council of Trade Unions, where he was elected President in December 1917. Simultaneously he was editor of the Central Trade Union Council journal *Professionalny Vestnik*.

At the first Trade Union Congress (January 1918), Tomsky put the Bolshevik case in his closing speech on Zinoviev's report about the tasks of unions.

At the fourth Conference of Trade Unions in 1918, he was elected to the Presidium of their Central Council, and at their second and third Congresses, he was chosen as President. In 1920 he helped to organise the Red International of Trade Unions (Profintern) and became its first General Secretary. In May 1921, with his appointment as Chairman of the Commission for Turkestan Affairs, he temporarily left trade union work.

In January 1922 he returned to the VTsSPS, at first as its Secretary and then, from its fifth Congress, as President. At the eighth Party Congress he was elected to the CC, and at the eleventh to the Politburo. From 1920 until the present day he has been a Presidium member of VTsIK, and since the first Congress of the USSR he has been Presidium member of the TsIK of the USSR.

In 1924 he was included in the Soviet delegation sent to hold negotiations with the British government. Whilst in London, he made contact with representatives of the British trade union movement, who subsequently invited Soviet trade union representatives to their next Congress in Hull in September 1924. There Tomsky made a speech outlining the revolutionary class position of trade unions in the USSR.

Almost all Tomsky's literary works have been devoted to problems of the trade union and labour movement. The main ones are: *Principles for the Organisation of Trade Unions, Trade Unions on New Paths, An Outline of the Trade Union Movement in Russia,* and *The Tasks of Communists in the Trade Union Movement.* They set forth the role, organisational methods and tactics of trade union work. The first three have been translated into Asian languages, the fourth into European ones.

P. Kashin

Tomsky was a working-class militant and belonged to a profession – typography – whose trade union was a citadel of Menshevism. Nevertheless he soon became a Bolshevik without renouncing, for all that, what constituted the basis of his political thought and militant activity: namely, trade unionism, which placed him at all times on his party's right wing. In 1917, he already had ten years' prison and deportation behind him when he emerged in the whirlwind of the Revolution. Unimpressed by Lenin's authority at the Central Committee meeting of May 1917, he first opposed the project to emphasise the propaganda work by creating a larger *Pravda*. A working class supporter, he defended the autonomy of the Petrograd Committee against the theoreticians. The speech he made on that occasion reveals the depth of his hostility towards intellectuals returned from exile: 'You don't write in

Russian, we can't all understand your articles.'[1] And Lénin was put in a minority.

Although he had lost touch a little during the years of deportation, he soon regained a prime position in the Bolshevik Party. He was an excellent civil servant, and his political realism constituted a valuable asset. From 1919 he presided over the trade unions. In 1919 he was elected to the Central Committee, and in 1922 entered the Politburo, where he sat until his expulsion in 1929. He was so typified by his post at the head of the trade unions that according to Trotsky he was a tendency all on his own. As Arthur Rosenberg observed,

> Tomsky represented the views of a minority of skilled and better-paid Russian workmen who had grown weary of revolution and refused to listen any longer to the socialist fables. Their desire was to defend and improve their living conditions with the assistance of the trade unions. If the Soviet State were to take on a semi-middle-class character, that would not cause them any anxiety. Tomsky regarded the Soviet State after the fashion in which a Western European socialist trade union leader looks upon his middle-class capitalist State.[2]

This position cut both ways. After the tenth Congress D. Ryazanov, who had gained a position of responsibility in the trade unions, proposed that union members should be allowed to choose their own leaders. Tomsky did not object to this proposal, was dismissed from his post in the Trade Unions' Central Council and sent to Turkestan. When he had recognised the correctness of the Party line, he was recalled and reappointed to his former post.

Among certain categories of workers, Tomsky enjoyed great popularity which Stalin put to good use in 1925 when the 'right-wing bloc' came to power. Tomsky was one of the pillars of this bloc, both in his political convictions and in his deep animosity towards the left-wing leaders, particularly Trotsky: in 1917, he called him an 'ever-juggling whale', and in 1920, at the time of the union quarrel, he attacked Trotsky by accusing him, at the November meeting of the Central Committee, of wanting to eliminate elected leaders—a criticism to which Lenin paid some attention.

Between 1925 and 1927, he was an ardent supporter of the union of Russian workers and Western trade unions. He was the main architect of the *rapprochement* with the British trade unions, and, in 1925, of the

[1] Quoted in G. Walter, *Lénine* (Verviers), p. 312.
[2] A. Rosenberg, *A History of Bolshevism. From Marx to the First Five Year Plan* (New York, 1967), p. 230.

Anglo-Soviet Trades Union Committee. This earned him attacks from the left wing, all the more so since the British TUC denounced the alliance in 1927.

He was above all a trade unionist, but his administrative sense brought him close to Stalin: 'It is impossible to run the Party without Rykov, Kalinin, Tomsky and Bukharin,' the leader replied to Kamenev's accusation, at the fifteenth Congress, that he wanted to control the machine and run it with his own clique of 'faithfuls'. When this speech was reprinted in his complete works, the names of Rykov, Bukharin and Tomsky were omitted. These two facts give a rapid glimpse of Tomsky's fall between 1925 and 1936.

At the fifteenth Congress Stalin tried to eliminate the opposition, and leant heavily for support on the right-wing bloc, which included Tomsky. But although he supported Stalin's general political line, he was opposed to his methods, and in particular to the expulsion of Trotsky from the USSR.

As soon as Stalin had achieved his aim and the Congress was over, the change of direction in economic policy that he began to consider fostered rumours of the creation of a 'rightist' opposition, and the names of Bukharin, Rykov and Tomsky were mentioned in this connection as early as December 1927. The conflict only came out in the open, however, in 1928, when Stalin turned about and launched the programme of industrialisation and collectivisation. In June, Bukharin, Rykov and Tomsky, in agreement with Uglanov, formed what is known as the 'trio': they wanted to stop Stalin speeding up collectivisation, which, they thought, endangered the results already achieved. Thenceforth and until his death, Tomsky's name was inseparable from those of his two companions.

For Stalin Tomsky became an important target, for he held authority over the enormous trade union machine. Even before the conflict became overt, all preparations had been made for replacing Tomsky. Although he had not actually been accused of *dirigisme*, a decision was made in favour of internal trade union 'democracy' which nevertheless allowed the Party to tighten its control and political leadership without admitting it was doing so. Tomsky offered his resignation in irritation at this in December, but the Politburo refused to accept it.

Early in 1929, the trio attempted their final assault, sharper than their earlier attempts, by submitting their resignations collectively. The game was played according to the usual rules, and they were offered concessions: if on the one hand they withdrew their resignations and held limited independence in their respective branches, the Politburo would promise not to submit to the Central Committee the act of accusation it had drawn up against them. Indignant at this political 'cooking', they rejected the proposal—and Tomsky was expelled from the Politburo. Consequently, all three were condemned by the Central Committee in April 1929, and on 2 June Tomsky was stripped of his position at the head of the trade unions. At the plenary session of the Central Committee in November 1929, Tomsky was given a serious warning and, with Bukharin and Rykov, he signed the required declaration.

At the sixteenth Party Congress in the summer of 1930, Tomsky had to make a self-criticism, but none the less, like Bukharin and Rykov, he was re-elected to the Central Committee. At the following Congress, in early 1934, when he was director of the State Publishing House, he was re-elected as a candidate member.

He was not spared by the purges which began shortly afterwards. The names of Bukharin, Rykov and Tomsky had been mentioned during the first trial, and Vyshinsky announced that an inquiry had been set up. Tomsky feared the worst and committed suicide on 23 August 1936. He had not been mistaken—two years later, Bukharin named him during his trial as the liaison agent between the 'rightist opposition' and 'a group of conspirators' in the Red Army.

G. H.

KLIMENT EFREMOVICH VOROSHILOV
(autobiography)

I was born in 1881 in the village of Verkhneye, Ekaterinoslav province. My father was a level-crossing keeper at the time, my mother a charwoman. My father, who had been a soldier under Nicholas I, was a freethinker with a will of his own. Performing the most onerous tasks on landlords' estates, down mines and on the railways, he was often obliged to change his place of work as a result of arguments with proprietors and the management. Consequently, I became acquainted with the most abject poverty from early childhood. During one period of my father's unemployment, my sister and I had to go begging for bread. At the age of six or seven, I found work sorting pyrites in the coal-mines, for which I received ten kopecks per day. When I was ten, I helped my father graze cattle for a landowner. It was at this time that I first came across the rapacity of the kulaks. During one of the regular lean periods in our family (father had disappeared in search of work), I was 'invited' to stay with an uncle, my father's brother, who lived a wealthy life in the country. Instead of being a guest, I was turned into a farm labourer and subjected to the cruellest exploitation for a whole year. Then I went back to the mines as an apprentice. There I was brutally beaten by peasants hired from a neighbouring village. They seized on a trivial pretext, but it was really because I had been hired in the workshops instead of one of them. This experience – being beaten as a boy by a whole artel of adults – remained a painful memory throughout my life.

I grew up illiterate, which greatly distressed my mother who had set her heart on my becoming sufficiently 'educated' to be able to read the psalter and prayer-book like her father. Her dreams did not extend further than this. Unfortunately, there were no schools in the places where we lived. In 1893 a *zemstvo* school was opened in the village of Vasilyevka, Slavyansk district, and I was accepted there. I remained a pupil for two winters and successfully completed the whole course. In two years, we had three form masters and the last of them, S. M. Ryzhkov, proved to be an excellent teacher and educator. He took a great liking to me and often invited me home, where I was treated as one of the family. Subsequently he became a *trudovik* deputy in the first Duma and its Second Secretary. He was an intelligent, honest, cheerful man with an instinctive, well-developed social conscience. Whilst at school, at the age of fourteen or fifteen, I began reading literary classics and books on the natural sciences under his guidance, and I also began to form clear ideas about religion.

In 1896 I found a job at a factory near the village of Alchevskaya.

Whilst working there, I continued my reading, and contact with my teacher brought swift progress both mentally and culturally. Once, in either 1897 or 1898, a police officer was appointed to the factory. This marked the beginning of my political activity. The police officer, Grekov, arrived to see the postmaster and ordered ten or fifteen adolescents to file in front of him. All greeted the policeman politely except me. Grekov was zealous and stupid. He jumped from the bench where he had been sitting in the company of 'ladies', rushed up to me, threatened me with his fists, and demanded to know why I had not bowed to him. I laughed in his face. He angrily grabbed hold of my shirt and I, in turn, laid my hands on the tie of this brutal satrap. The postmaster and all my comrades disappeared, and I was beaten, albeit not severely, before being thrown into jail. I was released the following day, but then began to be subjected to systematic and determined persecution. At first I was shadowed 'secretly', then agents began walking at my heels. The persecution had its effect: I not only turned conversations with Ryzhkov to openly political topics, but also looked for acquaintances both at the factory and among the teachers.

In 1899 the roller operators in the foundry came out on strike under my leadership. After a little while, I was searched and briefly arrested. Ryzhov was also searched. Then he was summoned to St Petersburg, I think to the Ministry of Education, where he was warned against further contact with me. I was out of work for three years because I was black-listed by all the factories and mines in the Donbass. In 1903 I found work at the Hartmann factory in Lugansk, but after two or three months the police drove me out of the town. During this time I officially joined the Party, became a Bolshevik and took a seat on the Lugansk Committee. In summer 1904, with Ryzhkov's help, I was again given a job at the Hartmann factory. In February and June I led strikes there. I was also elected Chairman of the Works Soviet. In July I was arrested in the course of the strike, beaten half to death and imprisoned until December. Then I was released on bail on the demand of a thousand workers who had come to the jail. Soon I escaped from the surging tide of reaction. In 1906 I travelled to the Stockholm Congress and for the first time met the light of our Party—Ilyich.

On my return, we made strenuous preparations for an armed struggle. I went twice to Finland to fetch large consignments of arms bought from Finnish revolutionaries. The present Chairman of the Comintern Executive Committee, G. E. Zinoviev, also had to deal with these arms. The Lugansk organisation had the best armed detachments and an excellent laboratory manufacturing bombs in unlimited quantities. Whilst remaining President of the deputies' Assembly, I was elected

President of the newly-organised Workers' Union at the Hartmann factory. Management of the works effectively passed to the workers, and the director of the factory retained only nominal control.

In October I and several others were due to be tried at an assize session of the Kharkov Chamber of Justice, but a general strike of Lugansk workers prevented it at that time. In spring 1907 I was tried and acquitted, after which I represented the Lugansk organisation at the London Party Congress. Previously, I had been a delegate to the first All-Russian Conference of Trade Unions in Moscow. In July 1907 I was arrested, and in October of the same year deported to Archangel province for three years.

In December 1907 I escaped from exile and was directed by the CC to Baku. Here I worked with comrades Shaumyan, Dzhaparidze, Stalin, Sosnovsky and others until autumn 1908 when I went to St Petersburg. There I was rearrested in September and sent back to Archangel. Whilst in exile in Kholmogory, I was put in custody in January 1911, imprisoned until November, and then deported to Mezen district. On my release from exile in 1912, I went to work in the workers' co-operative at the Dyumo factory, but after three to four months I was again arrested and deported to the area of Cherdyn. I was released in 1914 and found a job at the Tsaritsyn ordnance factory. There I drew together old Bolsheviks scattered throughout factories and enterprises in the locality, but I soon had to go to Petrograd to escape from the Tsarist army. In the capital I was again subjected to searches and shadowing.

From the first days of the February Revolution I was a member of the Petrograd Soviet and our Party Bureau. In March I was in the Donbass. In April I was a delegate to the Party Conference and then the sixth Party Congress. In Lugansk, where I was active in 1917, I presided over the town Soviet, duma and Party Committee. I was a delegate to the Democratic Conference, and was then elected to the Constituent Assembly on behalf of Ekaterinoslav province.

I began my military activity by commanding the detachment organised in March 1918 to fight against the German occupation troops. I was soon appointed commander of the Fifth Ukrainian Army, and then of the detachments retreating from the Ukraine to Tsaritsyn and the Volga under German pressure. An important battle took place at Likhaya station. Our detachments came up against the bullets of rebellious Cossacks and fled in panic towards the river Belaya.

Tens of thousands of demoralised, exhausted, ragged people and thousands of wagons filled with workers' families and their chattels had to be brought through the rebellious Cossack areas of the Don. For three whole months, surrounded on all sides by Generals Mamontov, Fitskanaurov, Denisov and others, my units tried to break out, re-laying the railway lines which had been torn up and burnt for tens of miles, building new bridges, and raising embankments and dykes. After three months, the Voroshilov army group fought its way through to Tsaritsyn. Here it became the backbone of the newly formed Tenth Red Army, whose command I assumed.

In 1918 I became a member of the Ukrainian government, and then was appointed Commander of the Kharkov Military District. After this I was put in charge of the Fourteenth Army and the internal Ukrainian front. At the end of 1919, I joined the First Mounted Army's RVS and in 1921 the Party CC. I subsequently commanded the Northern Caucausus Military District and was promoted to the RVS of the USSR, becoming a member of its Presidium in 1924. In May 1924 I was appointed Commander of the Moscow Military District. At the present time I am a member of the Party's Moscow Bureau, the Presidium of the Moscow Soviet, President of the Moscow Aviakhim, Deputy-President of the Aviakhim of the RSFSR, and special delegate from the RVS of the USSR to the Council of People's Commissars of the RSFSR.

From the days of the Baku Committee to the Second World War, Voroshilov was one of Stalin's closest political companions—at Tsaritsyn, in the struggle against the left opposition, down to the purge of the marshals and generals in 1937-8. It was to this intimate association that Khrushchev was ironically alluding in his report to the twentieth Congress when he addressed Voroshilov in the following terms: 'May our dear friend Kliment Efremovich find the necessary courage to write the truth about Stalin—for after all, he knows how Stalin "fought". It is a difficult task for comrade Voroshilov to undertake, but it is meet that he should do it.'

This was a cruel taunt to the man who set up Stalin's military legend, from *Stalin and the Red Army* (1929) down to *The Captain of Genius of the Great National War* (1950). Perhaps a prisoner of the blunder he committed in August 1914, when in a fit of patriotic fervour he volunteered for the Tsarist army, Voroshilov always remained in effect a pawn in the hands of Stalin, who used him, from Tsaritsyn (1918) to the liquidation of the marshals (1937), but was never quite sure of him. Krivitsky has recounted how Stalin had all Voroshilov's correspondence photocopied, and Khrushchev has affirmed that Stalin had Voroshilov 'bugged' and did not allow him into Politburo meetings for several years since he feared he was an agent of MI5. . . .

Voroshilov was a good cavalry officer and a good partisan leader, but did not really have the stature of a military chief. In any case, throughout the 1930s he used his memories of the Southern Front to oppose a wing of the high command, which included Tukhachevsky, in their desire to modernise the army, just as in 1918–19 he had opposed the construction of a centralised army, and favoured small, independent and mobile units capable of carrying out isolated *coups*. When war broke out in 1941, Voroshilov was appointed a member of the GKO and Supreme Commander of the Northern Front—which was the quickest to yield to the Germans, and where the mistakes of the command were the most serious (for example, no measures were taken to evacuate civilians from Leningrad before it was too late). Voroshilov had exhorted Soviet troops, in February 1938, to be 'ever ready and capable not only of riposting to any enemy who might attack us, but also of destroying him before he enters Soviet territory'. In December 1941 he was dismissed, and the same misadventure occurred to his other companion from Tsaritsyn, Budyonny, who was just as outdated as he.

In 1918, Voroshilov had stirred up the 'NCO opposition' to centralisation, and in 1925 he took over from Frunze at the War Commissariat. One month later he was elected to the Politburo—a stunning ascent, considering he had only been on the Central Committee since 1922. But in order to run a commissariat that still bore the mark both of Trotsky and of the Zinoviest Frunze, Voroshilov needed a title. In 1928, he supported Bukharin but abandoned him at the last moment: 'Voroshilov and Kalinin betrayed us at the eleventh hour', Bukharin confided to Kamenev.

In 1935 he was appointed Marshal of the USSR. Stalin made him give his approval to the liquidation of the entire General Staff of the Red Army, from Tukhachevsky to Blücher. After the Finnish campaign, Stalin's personal secretary, Mekhlis, tried to throw the blame for the campaign's misadventures on Voroshilov, but the General Staff collectively defended the last but one survivor of the Civil War's military leaders. In May 1940 he left the Defence Commissariat for the vice-presidency of the Council of People's Commissars, where he remained until 1953.

From March 1953 to May 1960 he was President of the Presidium of the Supreme Soviet of the USSR, that is to say, nominal head of state. Since May 1960 he has only been a member of the Presidium of the Central Council (the old and new name for the Politburo). Khrushchev removed him as an accomplice of the 'anti-party group' (Molotov, Malenkov, Kaganovich) which was routed in June 1957, and denounced him at the twenty-second Congress in December 1961 as an accomplice of Stalin. Voroshilov was not re-elected to the Central Committee at that Congress, but was 'rehabilitated' by the twenty-third, which put him back on the Central Committee as an alternate member. For many years now he has been a mere effigy.

J.-J. M.

2

Former Dissidents

ALEKSANDR ALEKSANDROVICH BOGDANOV (MALINOVSKY)
(autobiography)

I was born on 10 August 1873, the second of six children. My father, at first a village primary school teacher, was soon promoted to be teacher and inspector in a municipal school, and thanks to this I had access for six or seven years to the library there, as well as later to its small physics laboratory. I received a scholarship to the Tula Gymnasium, where I lived as a boarder in conditions reminiscent of a barracks or a prison. Experience of the malicious and obtuse authorities there taught me to hate rulers and deny all authority. I was awarded a gold medal on completion of my studies and then entered the Natural Science Faculty at Moscow University. In December 1894 I was arrested for being a member of the Union Council of Regional Societies (*zemlyachestva*)[1] and banished to Tula. There I was persuaded by a gunsmith worker, I. I. Saveliev, to work in circles as a propagandist. Soon I was joined by V. Bazarov and I. Stepanov. It was during this activity in 1896 that I rejected Populist ideas for social democracy, and on the basis of my lectures to the circles I composed a *Short Course in Economics*, which appeared mutilated by censorship at the end of 1897 and was warmly reviewed by Lenin in *Mir Bozhy*, 1898, no. 4.

From autumn 1895 I spent part of my time in Kharkov, studying at the Medical Faculty. I frequented local SD circles – their leader was Cherevanin – but I split with them over the question of morality, to which they attributed absolute importance. In 1898, as an attempt to reply to the demands of our workers for a general world view, I wrote my first philosophical book, *The Basic Elements of a Historical View of Nature*. In autumn 1899 I graduated from the university and was then

[1] *Zemlyachestva* were unofficial organisations linking students from the same region.

arrested for propaganda. There followed six months in custody in Moscow, banishment to Kaluga and three years' exile in Vologda. I studied and wrote a great deal. In 1902 I organised and edited a collection of articles against idealists entitled *Outlines of the Realistic Philosophy of Life*. Then came eighteen months as a physician in a psychiatric hospital. From the end of 1903 I edited the Marxist journal *Pravda* which was published in Moscow.

In autumn 1903 I sided with the Bolsheviks, and soon after serving my term of exile in spring 1904, I left for Switzerland where I joined Lenin. At the meeting of the Twenty-Two, I was elected to the Bureau of Committees of Bolsheviks (BKB), the first Bolshevik 'centre'. It was approximately at the same time that I was first excommunicated from Marxism by the Menshevik *Iskra* (see the article by 'Orthodox' in no. 70, accusing me of philosophical idealism). In autumn I returned to Russia, and from December 1904 I was active in St Petersburg in the BKB and the local committee. It was I who wrote the BKB tactical leaflets about an armed rising and the summoning of a Party congress. In spring 1905, at the third Party Congress in London, I presented a report on organisation and the question of an armed rising, and I was elected to the first Bolshevik CC. I worked in St Petersburg, helped edit the Bolshevik *Novaya Zhizn*, and was CC representative in the Soviet of Workers' Deputies, where I was arrested on 2 December 1905. Released in May on bail, I was nominated by the Bolsheviks to represent them in the new, Menshevik-controlled CC; exiled abroad, I returned clandestinely and lived in Kuokkala with Lenin, working on Bolshevik papers and with the Duma 'fractions' in the first, second and third Dumas. I had advocated a boycott of the third Duma, but after the rejection of this line by the Party conference, I conducted an electoral campaign in the illegal workers' paper *Vperyod*, of which I was editor.

At the end of 1907, I was sent abroad by the comrades to be one of the three editors (with Lenin and Innokenty) of the Bolshevik organ *Proletary*. In summer 1909 L. B. Krasin and I were excluded from the Bolshevik centre as left-wingers, and in January 1910, on the union of Bolsheviks and Mensheviks, from the CC as well. In autumn 1909 I participated in the organisation of the first School for Party Workers in Capri, and in autumn 1910 in the second School at Bologna. In December 1909 I made a speech on behalf of the platform of the 'Group of Bolsheviks', who soon adopted the name '*Vperyod* Literary Group'. This platform – *The Contemporary Situation and Party Tasks* – first formulated the slogan of proletarian culture. In spring 1911, when the *Vperyod* group began to move from cultural and propaganda activity to politics in the Western manner, I abandoned them and politics. From then until the Revolution, I merely wrote propaganda articles for *Pravda* and other workers' papers.

On returning to Russia in 1914, I was sent to the front as a doctor. The Revolution found me in Moscow. There I wrote political and propaganda articles at first—in one of them in January 1918 I presented a diagnosis of War Communism. Then I devoted myself completely to cultural and scientific work—in *Proletkult*, and at the Proletarian University, etc. In autumn 1921 this activity came to an end and I returned to purely scientific work. From 1918 until the present I have been a member of the Communist (formerly Socialist) Academy.

My chief writings are:

(1) On political economy: *A Short Course in Economics*, written from a historical viewpoint (the latest editions have been reworked in collaboration with Sh. M. Dvolaitsky) and translated into English and several other languages; *An Introductory Course in Political Economy*, written in the form of questions and answers; a lengthy *Course in Political Economy* (in collaboration with I. I. Stepanov); an article in the collection *Outlines of the Realistic Philosophy of Life* (1903) entitled 'Exchange and Technology', proving for the first time the theory of labour and value based on the principle of equilibrium.

(2) On historical materialism: *Science of Social Consciousness*, a historical account of the development of ideologies, mainly forms of thinking, with an explanation of their genesis from production relations (this book has been translated into German); *On the Psychology of Society* (a collection of articles, 1902-6); 'The Organisational Principles of Socialist Techniques and Economics' (*Vestnik Sotsialisticheskoy Akademii*, 1923, no. 4)—an explanation of forms of co-operation through technical relations.

(3) On philosophy: *Empiriomonism*, parts 1, 2, 3 (1903-7), a picture of the world from an organisational standpoint, that is as a process of formation, conflict and interaction by complexes and systems of various types and degrees of organisation; *The Philosophy of Living Experience* (1911), a review of the development of realistic systems of philosophy, ending in Empiriomonism; *From Religious to Scientific Monism* (a lecture appended to the third edition of *The Philosophy of Living Experience*—the foundation of the struggle for a scientific monism which dismisses philosophy entirely).

(4) On organisational science: *The General Science of Organisation*: *Tektology*, parts 1, 2, 3 (1913-22), a general study of the forms and laws of the organisation of all elements of nature, practice and thought (part 1

is published in German); 'The Principles of Unified Economic Planning' (*Vestnik Truda*, nos. 4–6, 1921), and 'Labour and the Needs of the Worker' (*Molodaya Gvardiya*, no. 3, 1922)—both are applications of organisational laws to the solution of basic economic tasks; 'The Objective Understanding of the Principle of Relativity' (*Vestnik Kommunisticheskoy Akademii*, no. 8, 1924).

(5) On proletarian culture: *The New World* (1904–6), a popular account of the highest cultural type of life; *The Cultural Tasks of the Working Class* (1911), the basis of the programme for proletarian culture; *Art and the Working Class* (translated into German); *Socialism and Science*, on proletarian science (in part also translated into German); *The Elements of Proletarian Culture in the Development of the Working Class*, a historical analysis; *On Proletarian Culture*, a collection of articles written between 1904 and 1924. To these can also be added two novels: *Red Star* (1907), a picture of Utopia (translated into French, German and several other languages); and *Engineer Menni* (1912), which depicts the clash between proletarian and bourgeois cultures.

In addition I have published several books, several dozen articles, pamphlets and lectures, and even more newspaper articles and leaflets, chiefly of a propagandistic nature.[1]

Bogdanov, whom his biographer called 'the Red Hamlet',[2] was for a short time during the emigration Lenin's main rival for leadership of the Bolshevik splinter group. His political career was over well before the October Revolution. Nevertheless, from the end of the nineteenth century, he was the leader of that brilliant generation of Russian Marxist intellectuals to which his brother-in-law Lunacharsky and Bazarov belonged. Lunacharsky met him for the first time in 1900, and speaks of him thus:

> We became close friends, all the more so since our philosophic ideas were very similar, and for a long time afterwards we found mutual enrichment in each other. In social democrat circles we were considered the closest companions-in-arms. One may say that my literary activity is inseparable from Bogdanov's.[3]

Bogdanov's earliest philosophical researches date from the end of the nineteenth century: his work was principally concerned with epistemology and ethics. After the failure of the 1905 Revolution, his research led him to develop his own theory of knowledge, known as

---

[1] A bibliography of Bogdanov's works has been compiled by A. Yassour and published in *Cahiers du Monde Russe et Soviétique*, x, nos. 3–4, pp.546–84.

[2] D. Grille, *Lenins Rivale. Bogodanov und seine Philosophie* (Cologne, 1966).

[3] V. I. Lunacharsky, *Veliki Povorot* (Moscow, 1922), p. 22.

empiriomonism, on the basis of the critical-empirical concepts of Avenarius, the Swiss psychologist. As a young doctor, Malinovsky, who later used the pen-name Bogdanov, soon showed his vocation as a theoretician. In exile in Vologda at the beginning of the century, he led the great polemic against his fellow exile Berdyaev from a rigorously Marxist position. Berdyaev gave this account of his opponent:

> He was a remarkable man, extremely sincere and utterly devoted to his ideas; but he had a rather narrow mind, and constantly engaged in finicky and sterile sophistry. I was already well known for my tendencies, both avowed and hidden, towards 'idealism', and Bogdanov considered them as symptoms of psychological abnormality.'[1]

It is not known whether Bogdanov was working at the Kushinov hospital at that time, or whether he was undergoing treatment there for a nervous disorder, as Berdyaev seems to imply. It is certain that Vologda became a centre of philosophical discussion, and that news of it reached the RSDRP abroad.

Bogdanov began to publish in 1897, and long before the appearance of his major work, *Empiriomonism*, he had acquired great notoriety. According to the memoirs of Valentinov, he was 'very well known among social democrats, had good literary contacts in Petersburg and Moscow, in particular with Gorky.'[2]

After a stay in Tver, Bogdanov went abroad in the spring of 1904. He met Lenin and brought him out of isolation; he immediately became a leader of the Bolshevik splinter group, brought his friends Skvortsov, Bazarov and Lunacharsky into the Bolshevik group, and endowed it both with his numerous contacts inside Russia and with substantial financial support. With Lenin he launched the publication of their organ, *Vperyod*; he took an active part in the discussions between the Bolsheviks and the Mensheviks, and counter-attacked against Rosa Luxemburg on question of organisation.

Later on, Lenin related the state of their platform of collaboration in a letter to Gorky: 'In autumn 1904, Bogdanov and I reached a definitive agreement as Bolsheviks, and formed a bloc which tacitly left philosophical questions to one side as a neutral terrain. The bloc lasted throughout the period of revolution (1905–6).'[3]

---

[1] N. Berdyaev, *Dream and Reality: An Essay in Autobiography* (New York, 1962), p. 130.

[2] N. Valentinov, *Encounters with Lenin* (London, 1968), p. 235.

[3] V. I. Lenin, M. Gorky, *Pisma, vospominanya, dokumenti* (Moscow, 1958), p. 28.

On his return to Russia, he prepared the ground for the third Congress of the RSDRP which was held in London, and at which he, together with Lenin and Krasin, was elected to the first Bolshevik Central Committee. He returned to St Petersburg at the height of the Revolution, and he, Krasin and Rumyantsev set up the permanent bureau of the Central Committee. As spokesman of the latter organisation, he played an important role in the Petersburg Soviet. It was then that his first disagreements with Lenin took shape; before his return to Russia in November 1905, the leader violently criticised the lack of news and of practical activity on the part of the Bolsheviks and of the CC in Russia, and the Committee, for its part, was rather reticent in carrying out all of Lenin's demands.

During the Revolution Bogdanov began to impose himself as the principal figure in the Bolshevik splinter group, and even to eclipse Lenin. At the RSDRP's reunification congress at Stockholm, in effect, he was elected to the CC and at the following congress, where he launched a violent attack on the Mensheviks, he was elected to alternate membership; whereas Lenin was on neither of the two Central Committees. Their rivalry and latent ideological divergence came out into the open in 1907 after the dissolution of the second Duma, where the Bolshevik splinter had been led by Bogdanov. The majority of the Bolsheviks thought that the situation was ripe for a popular revolt, and grouped around Bogdanov who advocated a boycott of the third Duma. Thus the leadership of the Bolshevik splinter group slipped from Lenin's hands and passed provisionally to the left-wing 'Bolshevik' Bogdanov. This victory was however short-lived. As was often the case in the history of socialism, the political conflict overlay a profound ideological dispute. For Lenin, it was not so much a matter of eliminating a philosophical heresy, as is now widely believed, but rather, the stake in the battle of theory was the direction and leadership of the Bolshevik splinter. In his *Materialism and Empiriocriticism*, Lenin followed Plekhanov, who later also backed him up, in giving a decisive reply to Bogdanov, whom he accused of revisionism. And Lenin, taking advantage of the tactical errors of the 'left-wing Bolsheviks', soon managed to turn the situation to his own advantage.

Attacked on all fronts, including liberals such as Struve and Bulgakov, Bogdanov and his supporters on the paper *Vperiod* found an ally in Maxim Gorky, who described the conflict in the following terms:

The controversy between Lenin and Plekhanov on the one hand, and Bogdanov, Bazarov and co. on the other, has great importance and a profound significance. The first two disagreeing on tactical questions, believe in 'historical' fatalism and preach it, whereas their opponents profess a philosophy of action.

Bogdanov's experiment in running the Party's first school on Capri was approved of by the leadership, but he became weary of the disputes of *émigré* life and denounced what he saw as fossilisation of minds before leaving the RSDRP for good in 1911. He returned to Russia in 1913. He never ceased to regard Lenin, even after 1917, with certain reservations. He worked for the Revolution without actually going under Lenin's flag. He was entrusted with the directorship of the Socialist Academy of Social Sciences, which in 1924 became the Communist Academy. He was also a professor at Moscow University and an instigator of *Proletkult*, as well as a member of the Presidium of the National Economic Council (*Sovnarkhoz*).

After Lenin's death, Bogdanov was asked to join the opposition, in virtue of his earlier political position, but he refused to become involved in the Party's internal struggles and obtained Stalin's protection. He died in 1928 as a result of an experiment which he knew to be dangerous but which he none the less performed on himself. Was this an application of his theory that any being who ceases to produce becomes a 'vampire' and should relieve the earth of his encumbering presence ? Or was it a tragic accident ?

G.H.

ALEKSANDR LOZOVSKY (pseudonym of SOLOMON ABRAMOVICH DRIDZO)
(autobiography)

I was born on 16 March 1878 in the village of Danilovka, Aleksandrovsk district, Ekaterinoslav province. My childhood was spent in Tsaredarovsk and in the settlement adjoining the Lozovaya railway station in the Pavlograd district of the same province. I began work at the age of eight, selling matches, tobacco, lemons, etc. at bazaars and fairs. My father was a poor Jewish teacher (a *melamed*) and my mother had a haberdashery stall at the bazaar. I went to school at a *Kheder*. When I was eleven, I was given the job of errand boy in a butcher's shop, where I spent eighteen months, after which I worked for several months as assistant in a grocer's shop. At the age of fourteen, I was made apprentice in a smithy, and after three years worked as a blacksmith in Lozovaya, Pavlograd and Melitopol. When twenty, I was enabled by financial assistance from my brother to devote myself to full-time study, covering all the material of four classes of Gymnasium.

At the end of 1899 I joined the 236th Laishevsky Reserve Battalion in Kazan as a volunteer. While in the army, I occasionally stored SD literature, although I did not formally belong to the Party and could not go to meetings. I also studied for the school-leaving certificate with the help of a few students, and in May 1901 I passed the examinations in Simbirsk. In late 1901 I moved to Lozovaya where I began to give lessons and organise SD circles, having links with Party groups in Kharkov and Ekaterinoslav.

I also organised circles for railway workers at Panyutino station. In August 1903 I moved to St Petersburg. Here, under the name 'Matvey Grigorievich', I began organisational work, first on Vasilievsky Ostrov, and then beyond the Nevskaya Zastava. To obtain a residence permit, I registered as a chemistry student, but never became one. I was arrested on 30 October 1903 and held in custody until 31 October 1904. No formal charge was laid against me, although the gendarmes produced a few photographs and suspected me of being involved in organisational and propaganda activity.

After my release from jail, I was banished to Kazan, where I immediately joined the local Bolshevik organisation. From May 1905 I was an unofficial member of the Kazan RSDRP(b) Committee. For a speech made to workers going home from the Alafuzov factory in Kazan (in June 1905) I was arrested but was released the same evening by workers threatening to wreck the factory. In summer 1905 I participated in the Volga Conference of Bolsheviks at Samara. After travelling about Russia,

I returned to Kazan in July and resumed my activity among workers and soldiers. To them I was known as 'the worker Aleksey'. During the October days of 1905 I was at the head of demonstrators who disarmed the police stations in Kazan and then distributed outside the university the weapons they had seized. For two and a half days, the Bolsheviks were in control. Then infantry, cadets and artillery surrounded the town duma building and on 21 October arrested all inside. I spent three weeks in prison and was then released after signing a declaration that I would not leave town. In late November 1905 I was delegated by the Kazan organisation to attend the Bolshevik conference which took place in early December in Tammerfors (Finland). Afterwards, I became an SD activist in St Petersburg both on Vasilievsky Ostrov and in the harbour area. In January 1906 I was arrested in the flat of a man called Shitikov, a worker at the Baltic shipyard (where a trap had been set). I was held in custody at the local police station where I gave my name as Karl Karlovich Witke. Three days later, I escaped. The Central Committee then sent me to Kharkov, where I lived under the name of Ivan Aleksandrovich Kuznetsov and conducted propaganda in factories. In March 1906 I was arrested and in early June released on bail as Kuznetsov, but at the end of the month I was rearrested following the receipt of information from Kharkov, and was held in Kharkov and Kholmogory prisons until May 1908. The Kharkov Chamber of Justice sentenced me to exile for belonging to the armed section of the Kharkov RSDRP(b) Committee. In May I was deported, and after three months in the Aleksandrovsk central transit jail (Irkutsk province) I was sent on to Preobrazhenka, Kirensk district. I only went as far as Chechuisk before escaping abroad.

I arrived in Geneva at the end of October 1908, and in early January 1909 I moved to Paris where I joined the RSDRP(b) group. I sometimes wrote articles for *Proletary* and *Sotsial-Demokrat*. I was Secretary of the Parisian Bureau of Labour for Russian *Émigrés*, and for a short time administrator of an electricians' school for adults. For two years I was General Secretary of the French Union of Hatters, for ten months I directed a bakers' co-operative, and for a few months I was director of a garage. Whilst in Paris I learnt to drive and worked in a factory as a smith and metal-worker. Throughout my stay I was a member of the French Socialist Party. From 1912 I became one of the leaders of the group of 'Party Bolsheviks'. After the declaration of war in 1914, I worked for six weeks as a labourer in vineyards near Montpellier, and then I returned to Paris where I became co-editor of *Golos*, as well as of its successors *Nashe Slovo*, *Nachalo*, and *Novaya Epokha*. From 1914 I took an active part in organising internationalist groups in the Party and French trade unions. I was a member of the 'Committee for the Re-establishment of International Links'. I wrote, albeit rarely, for *Sovremennik*, *Letopis* and Gorky's *Novaya Zhizn*.

I arrived in Russia in June 1917 (for nearly two months the French government had refused to allow internationalists to leave the country), and at the third All-Russian Conference of Trade Unions (20–28 July), I was elected Secretary of the VTsSPS. I remained in this post until the first All-Russian Trade Union Congress (3–9 January 1918). On the eve of the congress I was expelled from the Party for opposition. In February 1918 I became Chief Secretary of the Union of Textile Workers, and in July of the same year I was appointed to the equivalent post in the Union of Railwaymen. For a short time I was Chairman of the Moscow province's Trade Union Council. From March 1918 till December 1919, I was Chairman of the CC of the Internationalist RSDRP and editor of its chief organ *Proletary*. In December 1919 this party merged with the RKP.

Since 1917 I have been a Presidium member of the VTsSPS and was for a short time the editor of its main paper. In August 1920 I represented this body abroad. My journey was terminated by my arrest and expulsion from Germany. In 1920 I was one of the founders of the Profintern and since May 1921 I have been its General Secretary. I edit its organ *Krasny Internatsional Profsoyuzov*, as well as an encyclopedia of the international trade union movement. I have made speeches on this subject at international congresses of the Comintern and Profintern. I am a contributor to Soviet newspapers and journals on problems of the international labour movement and international affairs. I am also a Presidium member of the Communist Academy of the USSR, Professor at the Moscow State University, lecturer in Soviet and Party schools, and a member of the VTsIK of the USSR.

Lozovsky took an active part in the dissensions and divergences which rent the émigré Bolshevik Party after the failure of the 1905 Revolution. In 1910 he was one of the instigators and leaders of the small group of 'Bolshevik conciliators', who were opposed to the struggle against the liquidators. They also accused Lenin of sectarianism and intolerance towards Bogdanov and his supporters. According to Alin, Lozovsky was in a particularly fulminating mood in Paris and 'was preparing to unmask the sordid affairs of Lenin's boys'.[1]

Lozovsky was an active militant in the French workers' movement, and from 1912 he was a leader of the small trade union of the Jewish Hatmakers' Employees. He was especially close to the revolutionary trade

[1] Alin *Lénine à Paris, Souvenirs inédits* (Paris, n.d.), p. 53.

unionists, and to Monatte and Rosmer in particular. During the war his relations with the minority Internationalists were strengthened. He worked actively for the 'Committee for the Resumption of International Relations' and in the ranks of the Russian Socialist Internationalists who had gathered round the newspaper *Nashe Slovo*.[1] He was an assiduous collaborator on this paper, and wrote the columns on French politics and trade union affairs, but was in open conflict with Trotsky, who accused him of being an 'organic pacifist' and a 'centrist'.

After his return to Russia he threw himself into the revolutionary whirlwind of 1917 as the leader of the trade unions. He rejoined the Bolshevik Party, which he had left in 1912. Nevertheless he remained very attached to the revolutionary syndicalist ideas which he had absorbed in France. Secretary of the All-Russian Union of Trade Unions, he was in his capacity as the Bolshevik representative an advocate of union autonomy from Party and soviets. Early in November 1917 he joined Kamenev's opposition and the group of Commissars in the first Soviet government who resigned and demanded the formation of a coalition government. Lozovsky published a resounding letter of protest in Gorky's paper *Novaya Zhizn*, violently attacking the Central Committee's tactics which, he said, were leading to the 'isolation of the proletarian *avant-garde* and a civil war within the working class'. He denounced the arbitrary measures and persecutions as so much evidence of the need for socialist coalition government, for 'outside of this solution, there remains only one way to retain a purely Bolshevik government—political terror'.[2]

Since he persisted in opposition on the trade union question, Lozovsky was expelled from the Bolshevik Party early in 1918, on Lenin's proposition. He rejoined the small United Internationalist Social Democratic Party, which had held its founding congress in January 1918, and he became its leader. He was violently opposed to the Brest-Litovsk peace talks, and in his writings accused the Bolsheviks of 'underhand collusion with German imperialism'; but at the same time he declared himself ready to struggle with them, whatever their differences, against imperialism and for the Russian Revolution. On this basis a *rapprochement* took place, and it culminated in December 1919 in Lozovsky's being readmitted to the Bolshevik Party, together with his Internationalist Social Democratic Party.

In 1920 he was President of the Moscow Regional Trade Union

[1] A. Rosmer, *Le Mouvement ouvrier pendant la première guerre mondiale*, vol. 1 (Paris, 1936).
[2] Reprinted in I. M. Lyubimov *Revolyutsiya 1917. Khronika Sobytii*, vol. VI, Moscow–Leningrad, 1930).

Council, and did much work preparatory to the creation of the Profintern (Red International of Trade Unions), of which he was the General Secretary until 1937. His knowledge of Western life and languages was of great use to him in this task. He came to France several times to take part in trade union congresses and to renew contact with his old trade union friends. He was present at all the many trade union demonstrations abroad, and provided the main force behind the congresses of the Profintern. He was an inexhaustible orator and his lectures were printed in various languages and widely distributed throughout Europe. 'He had the air of a slightly fastidious schoolmaster amidst his world-wide assortment of trade union militants', but, says Victor Serge, 'he was quite open-minded, lively and easy-going'.[1]

With his sense for political direction and instinctive flair, he also gained a seat on the controlling bodies of the Comintern: he was a member of IKKI, and an influential member of the Presidium from his election in December 1927 until the seventh Congress in 1935.

During the great purges Lozovsky went into a temporary eclipse. From 1937 to 1939 he was a director of the State Publishing House. But this democratic oppositionist who had become a disciplined civil servant returned to the forefront in 1939, as deputy Commissar in Narkomindel, where he stayed until 1946. He was promoted to full membership of the Central Committee at the eighteenth Congress; he had been an alternate member since the fifteenth.

During the Second World War Lozovsky's anti-Fascist activities earned him the highest Soviet honours and gave him great notoriety on the international scene. He was also at this time second deputy in the Soviet Information Bureau.

Despite his political past, Lozovsky had supported Stalin in his fight against the oppositions and had gained his confidence; and thus he escaped all the purges before the war. In 1949, however, he was arrested and deported, together with the entire Jewish Anti-Fascist Committee which he had run during the Second World War.

He died in 1952 in a concentration camp, and was rehabilitated in 1956. The official explanation: 'In 1949 Lozovsky fell victim to enemy slander.'

G.H.

[1] *Memoirs of a Revolutionary* (Oxford, 1963), p. 146.

LEONID BORISOVICH KRASIN
(authorised biography)

Leonid Borisovich Krasin was born on 15 July 1870 in the small provincial town of Kurgan, Tobolsk province. His father, Boris Ivanovich, was an average member of the intelligentsia with genuinely democratic beliefs and vague, though quite strong, tendencies towards political and social radicalism. Of great significance in this respect was his close acquaintance with some Polish insurrectionists and later with Populists and *narodovoltsy* exiled to Siberia. In addition, Krasin's father had a gift for administration. From him Krasin evidently inherited his skill at, and love for, work. His general spiritual development was strongly influenced by his mother, Antonina Grigorievna, a typical Russian woman of the 1860s, very well educated and with wide spiritual interests.

Social conditions during his childhood and youth were also factors affecting his development. In the 1880s Siberia was one of the few hotbeds of social and political radicalism (another was the Volga region). The constant influx of exiles from Russia had a considerable impact on the spiritual life of the Siberian intelligentsia. Krasin's childhood and youth was marked by the influence of these exiles. He grew up in 'ideal' family surroundings, having a truly happy childhood. It must be added that this was by no means an atmosphere of luxury. On the contrary, his father's family – quite large incidentally – could hardly make ends meet. Long before he entered the business and political arena, Krasin had learnt what a budget was and what it meant to balance income and expenditure.

He received his secondary education in the Tyumen 'modern' school, from where he graduated at the age of seventeen. By this time he had developed a definite preference for the exact sciences. In 1887 he entered the St Petersburg Technological Institute. During his first years there, he began to take a serious interest in Marxism, so that within a short space of time he was considered an expert on the subject among his fellow students.

His political baptism of fire occurred in 1890 when he was banished for a short time from St Petersburg for his participation in student disorders. On his return, he joined a propaganda circle in October of that year. This was one of the first social democratic organisations in Russia and was active among the capital's workers. It had been founded by M. I. Brusnev and B. S. Golubev, and subsequently grew into the Union of Struggle for the Emancipation of the Working Class, whose organiser was Lenin. But Krasin's acquaintance with Lenin and their joint activity dates from a later period. By the time the Union of Struggle was founded, Krasin was no longer in St Petersburg, since he had been banished in connection with a student demonstration during the funeral of the writer Shelgunov. At the same time, he was expelled from the Technological Institute and deprived of the right of readmission.

From this moment, Krasin's biography becomes typical for a Russian revolutionary. After his banishment, he did his military service in Nizhny Novgorod. During this period he also conducted Marxist propaganda in various circles in the town, carrying on a bitter struggle among the intelligentsia against Populism, which was then disintegrating but which had such noted spokesmen in Nizhny Novgorod as N. F. Annensky, Zverev and Karelin. At the same time, Krasin did not break his links with M. I. Brusnev, and he collaborated in the organisation of propaganda in Moscow textile factories. After Brusnev's arrest in 1892, Krasin himself was put into custody and transferred to the Taganka prison, where he was kept in solitary confinement for roughly ten months. When released, he completed his military service in 1893 in Tula, where he was under constant open supervision.

He always recalls his time in the Taganka with great pleasure. After initial interrogations, the gendarmes left him in peace and he devoted his enforced leisure to the most strenuous work: he learnt German and read almost all the works of Schiller and Goethe in the original, he discovered Schopenhauer and Kant, he made a thorough study of Mill's logic and Wundt's psychology, he struggled through a large number of the historical works of Solovyov and Chernyshevsky, in a word he amplified the fairly meagre theoretical learning of a Russian student driven by fate from town to town. The knowledge of German alone gave him a great advantage in his further self-education. He was able to cope with the harsh conditions of solitary confinement thanks to his youth, the good health he had inherited from his parents, and the carefree, joyous view of life he had brought from the unending Siberian plains and dense taiga. In 1894 there followed another banishment—from the Crimea, where he had been spending the summer, on the occasion of the arrival there of Alexander III, Krasin then chose to reside in the village of Kalach, Voronezh province, where he was employed as a labourer and then a foreman on railway construction. Whilst applying all his energies to his immediate work, he nevertheless did not neglect his revolutionary activity and was soon dismissed as politically unreliable. Then in January 1895 he was rearrested, as he had been sentenced in connection with the Brusnev case to three months in prison and deportation to Yarensk district in Vologda province—the latter being replaced by banishment to eastern Siberia for three years. Krasin chose Irkutsk as his place of exile. The three years he spent there, with no opportunity for active political work, were mainly devoted to polemics with Populists, who comprised almost the whole of the Irkutsk colony of exiles. During this time he worked as draughtsman and technician on the Siberian railways, and towards the end was given responsible work as a construction engineer.

After serving his period of exile, Krasin succeeded in entering the Kharkov Technological Institute to complete his higher technical education and receive a diploma in engineering. He only graduated from the Institute in 1900, however, since the normal course of his studies was repeatedly interrupted by temporary banishments from Kharkov and field work as a railway surveyor. On graduation, he was offered a job as an engineer in Baku, where he spent four years working on the construction of large electrical power stations. There were two sides to his activities in these years. On the one hand, he was very energetic in his professional work—these were indeed years of massive expansion in the Baku oil industry, which included the electrification of the oil-wells; on the other hand, with all the fervour of a revolutionary who has languished idly in Siberia, he threw himself into clandestine social democratic activity in Baku and the other most important centres of the Caucasus. His efforts on behalf of the cause developed in two directions. He engaged in intensive propaganda among the Baku proletariat. The city at that time was one of the largest proletarian centres of Russia. The disgraceful working conditions in the oil fields naturally provided sufficient material for rousing, effective propaganda and agitation. The activity of Krasin and other social democrats led to the famous Baku strike of 1903 which in turn was the harbinger, the first symptom of the approaching revolution of 1905.

The other facet of Krasin's revolutionary work was the setting up of the first large-scale, clandestine printing-presses in Russia. They were situated in Baku itself and they played a very important part in the life of the still united SD Party. *Iskra*, which was formed and edited at first in Zurich[1] and then in London, was printed in Baku from matrixes received directly from abroad, which served to make stereotypes. Krasin's work in Baku made his name as an outstanding engineer, an energetic revolutionary and a first-class underground agent. He came to the notice of the central Party organs and after the second Party Congress in 1903 was co-opted on to the CC. In 1904, after catching malaria, he was forced to move to central Russia and he found a new job near Moscow in the large industrial centre at Orekhovo-Zuyevo. This move was connected with an intensification of revolutionary activity, and one of its consequences was the establishment of closer relations between the

[1] In fact *Iskra* was first edited in Munich.

Party and the industrialist Savva Morozov. Krasin's Party work grew at an ever increasing pace and ended with his going underground (after the arrest of the CC in the flat of the writer L. N. Andreyev).

In 1905 Krasin was a delegate to the third Congress of the Party in London, which had been, as is well known, summoned by the Bureau of Committees of the Majority contrary to the wishes of the Mensheviks, and at which the Bolsheviks organised themselves into a separate party. Krasin, who was using the pseudonym of Zimin-Winter, was elected Chairman of the congress and played a large part in it. He made key speeches on a series of organisational and political questions, and in particular he and Lenin secured the congress's approval of the fundamental resolution on the participation of the SD Party in a provisional revolutionary government. The congress re-elected him to the CC. After returning to Russia, he continued his energetic Party work, without for all that abandoning his professional career (by this time, as a result of the rising tide of revolution, he had managed to acquire a legal identity). His work as engineer in charge of the St Petersburg lighting system was perfect cover for a revolutionary.

In 1908 Krasin was finally unmasked and arrested in Finland. Even now, however, the gendarmes and procurator's office could find no incriminating material, and on special instructions from the Vyborg governor he was released. Not wishing to tempt fate by returning to St Petersburg, he became an *émigré*.

Then followed years when practical work in Russia was impossible with the complete triumph of reaction. Not being a literary man and not finding an application for his energies in the *émigré* circles, Krasin made use of this enforced interruption in his revolutionary career to devote himself more fully to work as an engineer. Settling in Berlin, he became engrossed in engineering and by dint of hard work achieved a position of respect even among the highly qualified German experts.

When the Revolution broke out, Krasin responded to the very first appeal of the Bolshevik Party. On the invitation of Lenin and Trotsky, he took an active part in the Brest-Litovsk negotiations, and was one of the authors of the so-called 'August Supplementary Agreement' concluded in Berlin in August 1918. Following his return from there, Krasin headed the Emergency Commission entrusted with supplying the Red Army. At the same time he assumed the responsibilities of Presidium member of the VSNKh and People's Commissar for Trade and Industry. In March 1919 he was also appointed Commissar for Transport. Within a short time, however, Krasin's economic work was replaced by diplomacy. He and Litvinov were representatives of the Soviet Union in its first encounter with the bourgeois world, in the shape of neighbouring Estonia, at a conference in Pskov in September 1919. In December of the same year he was appointed leader of the peace delegation which later signed the Yuriev treaty with Estonia, one of the first breaches in the blockade. The final draft of the treaty, however, was drawn up by Ioffe. In 1920 the Soviet mission in London was being constituted and, on Lenin's instructions, Krasin was made its head. In March 1921 he signed the Anglo-Soviet agreement, the first of a series of similar accords which now link the Soviet Union and the capitalist world.

Afterwards, Krasin remained in London as Plenipotentiary of the Soviet republics. In this capacity he was included in the Soviet delegations to the Genoa and Hague conferences. Then he was appointed Commissar for Foreign Trade and he introduced the State monopoly on foreign trade.

In late 1924 he was appointed USSR Plenipotentiary in Paris, resigning as Commissar for Foreign Trade. At the thirteenth RKP Congress he was elected to the CC.

M. Levidov

In a letter to Maslov in 1925, Stalin enumerated a group of 'former Bolshevik leaders who no longer play more than secondary roles': Lunacharsky, Bogdanov, Pokrovsky and Krasin. There is indeed a striking contrast between the two moments of Krasin's Bolshevik 'career', moments separated by a gulf of ten years spent in a brilliant industrial career. The contrast is all the more striking in that it is difficult not to use the words 'amazing', 'brilliant' or 'exceptional' at every turn of the life of this Protean figure. . . . As Trotsky said, he was 'above all else, an intelligent man'. Krasin was one of the real makers of the social democratic movement in Baku and the Caucasus. He and Ketskhoveli ran 'Nina', the secret Baku press which reprinted *Pravda* and clandestine brochures in thousands of copies. He was a strange double figure, playing as it were the role of militant in the dark, and appearing as an upper bourgeois in the light. He was one of the best engineers in the Russian Empire and as deputy director of a power station he played his game so well that the workers demanded his dismissal.

In 1903 he was a Bolshevik, a member of the Central Committee and leader, shortly afterwards, of the 'conciliatory' tendency which favoured unity with the Mensheviks. Lenin made desperate efforts to win over this intellectual man of action, and gradually succeeded. He left the Caucasus for Petersburg in 1904, and on the outbreak of revolution he headed the Party's technical staff: he was the real boss of the '*boyeviki*', as well as being Kamo's venerated adviser. He ran the Bolshevik arsenal, which he enriched with explosives of his own invention, and also masterminded the 'expropriations' which kept the roubles flowing into the Party's coffers. In all, he was the real technical genius of the insurrection. Few details are known about his activities at that time, which have remained more or less secret. In 1928 Lyadov wrote: 'Suffice to say that the device that blew up Stolypin's villa on Aptekarsky Island and the bombs thrown from Fanarny Street had been made under Nikitich's direction.' Lyadov also indicates that all the 'expropriations' organised by Kamo had been planned by Krasin, who even succeeded in doctoring and distributing some of the 500-rouble notes brought in by the Erevan 'expropriation' in June 1907. From 1907 the Bolshevik Party was in fact run by a triumvirate: Lenin, Krasin and Bogdanov. After the Stockholm Congress Krasin was one of the three Bolsheviks on the Central Committee of the reunited Party; after the London Congress he was only an alternate member, but the Bolsheviks had had unknown young men elected so that they could get back into Russia. The split in the ruling trio took shape in the summer of 1907, moreover. At the conference at Kotke (near Vyborg) in July 1907, Krasin and Bogdanov turned out firmly in favour of boycotting the Duma elections, in which Lenin wanted Bolshevik participation.

A convinced *otzovist* and supporter of the boycott, Krasin joined the *Vperyod* group which left the Bolshevik Party in 1910. Krasin had been living abroad since 1908: he was arrested at Kuokkala in March 1908 and interned in Vyborg prison. He avoided being hanged only thanks to the last vestiges of Finnish independence. In 1910 he settled in Berlin, joined Siemens as an engineer and rose rapidly in the company before returning to Russia in 1912 as director of Siemens' Russian subsidiary. From 1910 he completely abandoned political activity, and when the February Revolution triumphed he was far more favourable to the conciliators than to the Bolsheviks; as indeed he was at the October Revolution, which he thought would bring nothing but disorder and famine.

The Bolsheviks needed men, and Krasin needed action: Siemens shut its doors. From early 1918 he was back at the grindstone, as a member of the financial commission during the Brest-Litovsk talks. In August he entered the Presidium of the Sovnarkhoz, and then directed the work of the commission entrusted with providing supplies for the Red Army. From March 1919 to March 1920 he was People's Commissar for Communications; in March 1920 he led the Soviet delegation to the talks on commercial exchanges with the countries of the *Entente*, and after that date carried out numerous diplomatic missions (commercial negotiations with the United Kingdom, membership of the Soviet delegation to the Genoa Conference, negotiations with Urquhart, etc.). From 1922 to 1924 he was People's Commissar for Foreign Trade, and in autumn 1922 he waged a vigorous campaign in favour of the foreign trade monopoly, which was in danger of being abolished by the Central Committee. But he never acquired any *political* responsibility. Of the Krasin of 1900 only the technician remained, and the diplomat had taken the place of the explosives manufacturer who dreamt of making bombs the size of walnuts. He was Soviet Plenipotentiary to France in 1924, then to Britain in 1925–6. He died in London on 24 November 1926. His wife later wrote a book about him in order to explain that in the last analysis he had always been alien to the vulgar Bolsheviks. . . .

J.-J. M.

ANATOLY VASILIEVICH LUNACHARSKY
(autobiography)

I was born in 1875 in Poltava, the son of an official. As a result of the radical atmosphere prevailing in our family, I was liberated from religious prejudices whilst still a child and imbued with sympathy for the revolutionary movement. I received my education in the First Kiev Gymnasium. At the age of fifteen, I began to study Marxism assiduously under the influence of some Polish comrades and I considered myself a Marxist. I was one of the leaders of a large student organisation which had cells in all secondary education establishments in Kiev. When seventeen, I undertook propaganda among workers and craftsmen in the railway workshops. On graduating from the Gymnasium, I refused to enter a Russian university and went abroad where I could study philosophy and the social sciences more freely. I entered Zurich University and for two years worked on the natural sciences and philosophy, mainly in the circle of the founder of Empiriocriticism, Richard Avenarius, whilst at the same time deepening my knowledge of Marxism under the guidance of Akselrod and also partly Plekhanov.

The serious illness of my elder brother, Platon Vasilievich, compelled me to interrupt my studies. I had to live for a short time in Nice, then in Rheims and finally in Paris. It was at this time that I made the acquaintance of Professor M. M. Kovalevsky, from whose library and advice I profited greatly and with whom I was on very good terms, although we were constantly arguing. In spite of my brother's illness, I succeeded in winning over both him and his wife, Sofia Nikolaevna, now Smidovich, to social democracy, and subsequently both played a prominent part in the labour movement.

In 1899 I returned with them to Moscow. Here, together with A. I. Elizarova (Lenin's sister), Vladimirsky and some others, I revived the Moscow Committee, conducted propaganda in workers' circles, wrote leaflets, and helped to lead strikes. As a result of betrayal by A. E. Serebryakova, who was a member of a peripheral organisation attached to the Moscow Committee, most of the organisation was arrested, myself included. After a short while, however, I was released on my father's surety for lack of serious evidence and allowed to go back to Poltava province. Soon I received permission to move to Kiev. Here I resumed my activities but unfortunately I was arrested with several others at a lecture on Ibsen given to raise money for students. There followed two months in the Lukianovka prison, where incidentally I became a friend of M. S. Uritsky. No sooner had I been released from this prison than I was rearrested in connection with the Moscow affair. I was escorted back there and incarcerated for eight months in the Taganka prison. I used this detention for intensive work on philosophy and history, in particular the history of religion, which I had also studied for two years in Paris at the Musée Guimet. Both solitary confinement and hard work seriously affected my health, but in the end I was released and banished temporarily to Kaluga whilst awaiting a further administrative sentence. In Kaluga a close Marxist circle was formed which included A. A. Bogdanov, I. I. Skvortsov (Stepanov), V. P. Avilov and V. A. Bazarov. This was a time of intense intellectual inquiry, and translations of classic German texts were published with the help of a young, Marxist-inclined manufacturer called D. D. Goncharov. Soon after A. A. Bogdanov's departure, Skvortsov and I embarked upon active agitation at the railway depot and among teachers. My friendship with the Goncharov family continued to grow. I lived at their linen factory, propagandized the workers and wrote my first literary works for the newspaper *Kurier*.

Finally I was sentenced to be deported to Vologda province for three years, but I succeeded in remaining in the town of Vologda which by that time had become a significant centre for exiles. A. A. Bogdanov already lived there and I moved in with him. Here arguments raged with the Idealists, whose leader was Berdyaev. Savinkov, Shchegolev, Zhdanov, A. Remizov and many others also took an active part in them. My stay in Vologda was chiefly remarkable for this struggle against Idealism. The late S. Suvorov also joined the old and still united Kaluga group, and as an attack on the book *Problems of Idealism*, they published jointly *Outlines of the Rationalist View of Life*. This book went into two editions. I wrote many articles on psychological and philosophical problems for *Obrazovaniye* and *Pravda* in an attempt to combat Idealism. Simultaneously, however, the whole group departed from Plekhanov's interpretation of Marxist materialism. Thus by no means all social democrats shared the views of this group which had acquired considerable authority in the Russian intellectual world of the time.

A quarrel with the governor Ladyzhensky, which was accompanied by a multitude of bizarre incidents, landed me in the small town of Totma, where I was then the only exile. Attempts by the local intelligentsia to communicate with me were stopped by a threatening bark from the local police chief, and I lived in almost complete isolation with my wife, A. A. Malinovskaya (A. A. Bogdanov's sister). Here were written all the works which were later included in the collection *Critical and Polemical Studies*. I also wrote here a popularised version of Avenarius' philosophy. I continued my education in the most energetic fashion, surrounding myself with books.

On completion of my exile in 1903, I returned to Kiev and began work on the semi-Marxist legal paper *Kievskiye Otkliki*. Meanwhile a split had occurred in the Party, and the 'conciliatory' Central Committee, headed by Krasin, Karpov and others, approached me with a request to support their policy. Soon, however, under the influence of Bogdanov, I abandoned the 'conciliators' and wholeheartedly joined the Bolsheviks.

Lenin wrote me a letter from Geneva, inviting me to Switzerland immediately to help edit the central Bolshevik paper. My first years in emigration passed in innumerable arguments with the Mensheviks. My work consisted not so much of writing copy for *Vperyod* and *Proletary*, as of travelling round all the *émigré* colonies in Europe and giving lectures about the essence of the split. Besides political speeches, I also spoke on philosophical topics.

At the end of 1904, illness obliged me to move to Florence. It was there that news of the Revolution reached me, and an order from the CC to return immediately to Russia, which I obeyed with the greatest pleasure. On my arrival in Moscow, I joined the editorial board of *Novaya Zhizn* and the legal newspapers that succeeded it, and conducted intensive oral propaganda among workers and students. Even before this, Vladimir Ilyich had entrusted me with a report on the subject of an armed rising at the third Congress. I participated in the Stockholm 'Reunification' Congress on 1 January 1906. I was arrested at a workers' meeting, but was released from the Kresty one month later. A little later, however, extremely serious charges were laid against me, exposing me to the direst punishments. I took the advice of the Party organisation and decided to emigrate, which I did in March 1906 via Finland.

Abroad I joined Bogdanov's group and organised with him the *Vperyod* group, helped to edit its journal and was one of the most active leaders of its Party schools on Capri and in Bologna. At the same time I published my two-volume work *Religion and Socialism*. This provoked fairly strong condemnation from the majority of Party critics, who saw in it a deviation towards some kind of refined religion. The terminological muddle in this book gave sufficient foundation for such accusations. During my stay in Italy I became an intimate friend of Gorky, which was reflected in, among other things, his story *Confession*, also quite harshly condemned by Plekhanov.

In 1911 I moved to Paris. Here the *Vperyod* group took a rather different direction thanks to the departure of Bogdanov. It attempted, vainly, to create a united party. Among those adhering to it at that time were M. N. Pokrovsky, F. Kalinin, Manuilsky and Aleksinsky.

I was included in the Bolshevik delegation to the International Socialist Congress in Stuttgart (1907) and represented them in the section which formulated the well-known resolution on the revolutionary significance of trade unions. In the process, fairly sharp clashes took place between myself and Plekhanov. Roughly the same thing happened at the Copenhagen Congress (1910). I was the delegate there of some members of the *Vperyod* group, but I concurred on all major points with the Bolsheviks, and on Lenin's insistence represented them in the commission on co-operatives. Here too I encountered sharp opposition from Plekhanov, who represented the Mensheviks.

As soon as war broke out, I joined the internationalists, and with Trotsky, Manuilsky and Antonov-Ovseyenko edited the anti-militarist journal *Nashe Slovo* in Paris. Realising the impossibility of observing the war objectively from the French capital, I moved to Switzerland and settled in Saint-Léger, near Vevey. It was then that I became a fairly intimate acquaintance of Romain Rolland, a friend of Auguste Forel, and also of the great Swiss poet K. Spitteler, part of whose works I translated into Russian (not yet published).

After the February Revolution I immediately rejoined Lenin and Zinoviev, declared to them that I was now an unshakable supporter of theirs and offered to put myself at the disposal of the Bolshevik CC. My offer was accepted.

I returned to Russia a few days later than Lenin but by the same route, via Germany. I immediately began the most hectic work in preparation for the Revolution. There were no disagreements between the Bolsheviks and myself, but following a directive from the CC, both Trotsky and I remained in the *Mezhrayonka* group, so as to be able to join the Bolshevik organisation later with the maximum number of supporters. This manoeuvre was successfully executed. The CC directed me to municipal work. I was elected to the city Duma and was leader of the Bolsheviks and *mezhrayontsy* in it. During the July days I took an active part in events, was accused with Lenin and others of treason and spying for the Germans, and was imprisoned. Both before and during imprisonment my life was in danger. On my release, the Bolshevik vote in the new city Duma elections grew considerably and I was elected deputy mayor with responsibility for culture in the capital. Simultaneously, I conducted the most indefatigable and vehement agitation, mainly in the Modern Circus, but also at numerous works and factories.

Immediately after the October Revolution, the Bolshevik CC formed the first Council of People's Commissars and gave me a seat on it as Commissar for Education. On the transfer of the whole government to Moscow, I preferred to remain in Petrograd so as to work with Com-

rades Zinoviev and Uritsky, who were left to occupy dangerous positions. I stayed there for more than a year and the Commissariat was
directed from Moscow by my deputy, M. N. Pokrovsky. During the
Civil War, I constantly had to tear myself away from the Commissariat,
since I visited almost all the fronts of the Civil and Polish wars as an
envoy of the RVS, raising the morale of troops and civilians at or near
the front. I was also appointed RVS representative in the Tula fortified camp during the worst days of the Denikin offensive.

Whilst working as a Party agitator, a member of the Sovnarkom and
People's Commissar for Education, I continued to write, in particular
as a dramatist. I completed a whole series of plays, some of which have
been staged and have run or are running in the capital and many provincial towns.

Lunacharsky belonged to the intellectual élite of Berdyaev's generation,
a generation of wide-ranging brilliance which brought such a sudden
blossoming of Russian thought that scholars have termed the period the
'twentieth-century Russian Renaissance'. In the words of Pierre Pascal,

> this Russian Renaissance recalls the Italian Renaissance in that the
> men who created it had not specialised in any one branch of intel-
> lectual activity, but excelled in several at the same time. . . . All
> shared the ambition of reaching the peaks of culture. All were per-
> meated with the works of the West, both contemporary and classical.[1]

Lunacharsky had a sound philosophical training and a wide culture;
he was perfectly fluent in all the Western languages and had a passionate
interest in all fields of art and literature. With his learning, sense of taste
and originality, he became at a very young age a man who counted in
Russia in the world of thought and letters. His manifold talents as critic,
publicist, writer, dramatist and essayist were recognised by friends and
foes alike. Lenin did not like him particularly, but said enthusiastically
that he was 'an exceptionally gifted man'. Gorky met him in 1907 and
was overwhelmed by this 'brilliant and resourceful man', 'this man with
a future' of 'astonishing cleverness' and 'great talents', 'well placed to
advance revolutionary thought'. He noted all the same one of Lunacharsky's more negative traits: he was 'a bit too much of a bookworm,
and he gives the impression of being perhaps too careless in his relations
with other people'.[2] Berdyaev was his great rival from early youth and
was constantly in open conflict with him, but had to admit his 'numerous

---

[1] 'Les grands courants de la pensée russe contemporaine', *Cahiers du Monde
Russe et Soviétique*, no. 1 (1962), p. 14.

[2] M. Gorky, *Sobraniye Sochineniya*, vol. 29 (Moscow, 1954), pp. 32–4.

talents', his wide culture and literary taste; though he did not fail to omit, and with good reason, that 'Lunacharsky was something of a provincial schoolmaster turned journalist'.[1] Trotsky, on the other hand, considered Lunacharsky's extraordinary gift for writing, his ability to improvise and his unlimited erudition as the expression of a brilliant, exceptionally gifted intellectual and aristocratic dilettante.[2] But he was not only a dilettante by intellect, it was a fundamental trait of the character of this gentle but impulsive man.

He was an anti-orthodox, anti-conformist Marxist, the originator of new heresies and researches, and enjoyed a high reputation from the beginning of the century among both the intelligentsia and Russian social democrat circles. At this time his intellectual masters included Marx and the German philosophers, in particular Nietzsche and Avenarius. His great friend and spiritual brother was Bogdanov; and his enemies included the spiritualists, led by the neo-Kantian Berdyaev, and the narrow orthodox views of Plekhanov who, he claimed, 'based Marxism on the materialism of the French Encyclopedists'. His great ambition, which he shared with his inseparable Bogdanov, was to use Marxism as a basis for a solution to the great problems that beset his generation in the fields of epistemology and aesthetics, and at the same time to contribute to the development of Marxist theory, which was incomplete in these domains. From the beginning of this century, Lunacharsky's work centred on the elaboration of a Marxist theory of values based on aesthetics, and on the application of such a theory to artistic critiscm.

He may have been an intellectual of great stature, but he was insignificant as a politician and militant—which it was his first ambition to be. He was weak, indecisive and unreliable. Proof of this can be found in the history of his relations with Lenin. He was won over by the Bolshevik leader and on Lenin's demand went to Geneva at the end of 1904 to help bring out his newspaper, on which he used the pseudonyms 'Voinov', 'Minonosets', etc. After the failure of the 1905 Revolution, there was an ideological split. Lunacharsky adopted Bogdanov's theory of knowledge, empiriomonism, and started up the theory of the 'new religion'. In his book *Religion and Socialism* he attempted to place socialism in the context of other religious systems, and Gorky developed this idea further, naming it 'the building of God' (*Bogostroitelstvo*). This book and this theory had the effect of a bombshell on the Russian socialist milieu, and it brought down on Lunacharsky the combined fury of Lenin and Plekhanov. Lenin was not sparing in his use of in-

[1] N. Berdyaev, *Dream and Reality*, p. 125.
[2] See L. D. Trotsky, *Literature and Revolution* (Michigan, 1960.)

vective on Lunacharsky's account in his letters and articles. Despite this open hostility, Lunacharsky, who remained one of the central figures in Bogdanov's group, always responded favourably to Lenin whenever he was solicited for support. The two men moved closer together during the First World War. As a consistent internationalist, Lunacharsky launched the idea of a third International as early as 1915. In Switzerland, after the February Revolution but before Lenin's departure for Russia, the two men reached a definite reconciliation.

In 1917 Lunacharsky became immensely popular, for he was, with Trotsky, one of the most eloquent of the revolutionary agitators. He exercised his oratorical talents before full houses in the Modern Circus. His fiery speeches and improvisations made a deep impression on his audiences. The public thought of him as one of the main Bolshevik leaders, whereas he was no more a member of the political leadership than he was in agreement with Lenin's tactics. For him, the Revolution was to have been a triumphal march into a Russia ripe 'for a socialist government'. In early November, when he learnt that the seizure of power in Moscow had followed a bloody struggle resulting in thousands of deaths and the destruction of monuments, he was the first to resign from the Bolshevik government, with much publicity, and accusing the Bolsheviks of mounting a *putsch*. A few days later, however, Lenin managed to persuade him to go back on his decision.

Although without any real political prerogatives, Lunacharsky was in the European public's eye one of the most representative figures of Soviet power. Culture and education remained his fief, and he enjoyed considerable freedom in managing his own policies in these fields. He wanted to put Kautsky's theory into practice, the concept of 'total anarchy of art in the first phase of the Revolution'—that is to say, freedom for diverse schools and tendencies in art and literature to exist and to struggle against each other. The Futurists and the representatives of the other movements found in Lunacharsky a staunch defender, even though all of the Commissar's efforts were aimed at creating and upholding a proletarian culture. He was a brilliant speaker and a master in the art of improvisation. He attended all the intellectual and cultural meetings of the period. He was an ideological inspirer and an instigator, but not really an administrator: his Ministry in fact was run by his deputies. 'His whimsicality,' said Trotsky, 'was equalled only by his administrative incompetence.' To convert the former intelligentsia to the new regime, to protect young artists, help proletarian artists, inspire intellectual activity, cultural and artistic life—such was the role that Lunacharsky assigned himself. At the same time he tried to remain creative himself, and untiringly composed plays, enormous treatises on literature, studies of aesthetics, as well as innumerable articles and speeches touching on literally all periods and fields of art.

After 1924 Lunacharsky was obliged to yield and to conform progressively to the leadership's prescriptions. Only the style of his cultural policies remained, not their content. He retained his post of People's Commissar for Education until 1929. He wisely kept out of all the Party's internal struggles. After being Litvinov's deputy on the Preparatory Commission for the Geneva disarmament conference, he was appointed Ambassador to Spain in 1933, but died at Menton on his way to take up his position. His complete works (minus his philosophical research) were recently published in eight volumes in the Soviet Union, with some cuts in the political texts.

DMITRI ZAKHARIEVICH MANUILSKY
(authorised biography)

Dmitri Zakharievich Manuilsky was born on 21 September 1883 in the village of Svyatets, Kremenets district, Volhynia province. His father came from peasant stock and was a rural scribe. Manuilsky attended the village school and then, on the insistence of the teacher, who said that he showed promise, he was sent to the Gymnasium in Ostrog. From the fourth form onwards, he earned his own living by giving lessons. In the Gymnasium he organised self-education circles, for which he suffered reprisals at the hands of the teaching staff. In 1903 he graduated from there and entered St Petersburg University, where he became linked with revolutionary circles and the local social democratic organisation. He participated in student assemblies, and secretly mimeographed proclamations. On 28 November 1904 he joined the demonstration on the Nevsky Prospekt against the Russo-Japanese War, and was savagely beaten and arrested. The revolutionary year of 1905 found him in the role of Bolshevik agitator, one of the collegium of agitators attached to the St Petersburg Party Committee. In November 1905 he was directed by the Central Committee to Dvinsk, where he worked under the pseudonym of 'Methodius'. In spring 1906 he returned to the capital to help the area organisation in Kronstadt.

Manuilsky represented the Kronstadt organisation on the St Petersburg Committee under the name 'Foma'. He participated in both the preparations and the actual rising on the night of 19/20 July, three days after the insurrection in Sveaborg (Suomenlinna). After the rising had been crushed, he was spirited away from Kronstadt to Oranienbaum by local comrades in a rowing-boat.

But on 24 July he was betrayed in St Petersburg by an *agent provocateur* called Olderman, arrested, held in custody for two weeks and then transferred to the Kronstadt naval prison. In winter 1906 he was banished to Archangel province but his journey was interrupted in Vologda. The Minister of Internal Affairs, Makarov, issued a special decree confining him to Yakutsk province for five years. In addition, news reached the ears of comrades following the outcome of the Kronstadt insurrection that General Adelberg, the Commandant of Kronstadt, had proposed that Manuilsky should be tried by a military court. But in December he succeeded in escaping from prison. [. . .]

After this he went to Kiev, where he became an activist in the military organisation under the pseudonym 'Ionych' and joined the Kiev Committee. During the elections to the third Duma, he advocated a boycott and defended this position at public meetings.

After wholesale arrests among the Kiev military organisation in autumn 1907, Manuilsky made his way abroad. As an *émigré* in Paris, he declared himself an *otzovist* and joined the *Vperyod* group, collaborating on its periodical under the name of 'Ivan the workless'. From the first days of the war he opposed it, defending this line in the paper *Golos* which was founded by Antonov-Ovseyenko and himself, and which was closed by the French government after the 101st edition. He edited *Nashe Slovo* with Trotsky, Antonov-Ovseyenko and others until it too was banned by the French authorities for its anti-war campaign.

Manuilsky returned to Russia in May 1917 via Germany in the sealed train. In Petrograd he joined the *mezhrayontsy*, for whom he undertook propaganda in the district of Vasilievsky Ostrov, and he entered the city Duma as a Bolshevik representative following the merger of the *Mezhrayonka* and the Bolsheviks in August 1917. During the fighting to repulse the Kerensky-Krasnov advance, he was Commissar of Krasnoye Selo. After our victory, he was appointed a Collegium member of the People's Commissariat for Food, in which post he remained until spring 1918. In April of that year he was dispatched with Rakovsky to the Ukraine as a member of the peace delegation for negotiations with the hetman regime.

In January 1919 Manuilsky was sent with Laftyan and the late Inessa Armand on a Red Cross mission, and was interned in Dunkirk. After an exchange of prisoners, he returned to the Ukraine where he held the following posts: member of the All-Ukrainian Revolutionary Committee in early 1920; Commissar for Agriculture, 1920-1; Secretary of the Ukrainian CC in 1921; editor of the newspaper *Kommunist*; member of the Ukrainian CC since 1920; member of the All-Russian CC since the twelfth Party Congress. At present his principal position is Presidium member and Secretary of the Executive Committee of the Comintern. Simultaneously he is a member of the TsIK of the Union and deputy editor of *Pravda*.

S. Sirotinsky

Manuilsky has gone down in history as one of Stalin's close collaborators and advisers: and he was the 'boss' of Comintern for twenty years, until its dissolution. Beneath his jovial air and inexhaustible stock of stories and jokes, he applied Stalin's policies without mercy, and imposed them on the Comintern. Manuilsky was remarkably intelligent and an extremely clever tactician—a mixture of cynicism and disabused bitterness.

He was a lawyer by training, and had completed his studies in exile in Paris, at the Law Faculty of the Sorbonne. After the defeat of the Russian Revolution of 1905, he became one of the pillars of the left-wing opposition led by Bogdanov and centred on the newspaper *Vperyod*.

In the internal struggles of the Russian Social Democratic Party he manifested a virulent animosity towards Lenin. He returned to Russia in 1912, worked secretly in Moscow, and then returned to exile in Paris in 1913. After the outbreak of the First World War he became an internationalist, joined Trotsky's group, wrote for *Nashe Slovo* and became its legal manager, as well as the spokesman for the editorial board's pro-Bolshevik faction.[1] It was as a member of *Mezhrayonka* that he, like Trotsky, adhered to the Bolshevik Party in 1917. He was used principally as a journalist. In August 1917, he was on the editorial committee of the CC's mass propaganda paper, *Vperyod*. Stalin also belonged to the five-man editorial committee, and it was then that the two began their collaboration.

At the time of the uprising in October 1917 Manuilsky was a Political Commissar in Tsarskoye Selo, in the outer suburbs of Petrograd, which became a crisis spot when Krasnov's Cossack troops attempted to retake the city. Manuilsky held various posts, as his biography states, and in 1920 he found himself in the Ukraine in the middle of the struggle against the majority group of left wing communists. As a member of the Ukrainian Revolutionary Council and leader of the Party's regional committee, Manuilsky aligned himself with the delegate from the RKP's Central Committee, namely Stalin, whose job it was to oust the opposition. It was for this that he became for a short time in 1921 Secretary of the Ukrainian CP and a member of its Politburo from 1921 to 1923. As a supporter of Stalin he was elected first to candidate membership of the Central Committee at the eleventh Congress, and in 1923 to full membership which he held without interruption from the twelfth Congress to the nineteenth, in 1952.

During 1922 he began to work for the Comintern, and in September of that year was sent as its delegate to the second Congress of the French CP. He attended the fourth World Congress and played an important part in the next (fifth) Congress of 1924 reporting on the national question. He represented the IKKI on various missions and in 1924 was elected a member of the IKKI and of its Presidium. In 1924-5, as the Comintern's Plenipotentiary, he attempted without great success to interfere in the affairs of the German CP. He suffered a particularly sharp defeat at the German Party's tenth Congress in 1925 when he tried to impose his own men on the Central Committee.[2] After a lengthy struggle involving the expulsion of numerous dissident leaders, he managed to tame the German Party.

[1] See I. Deutscher, *The Prophet Armed* (Oxford, 1954).
[2] See H. Weber, *Die Wandlungen des deutschen Kommunismus. Die Stalinisierung der KPD in der Weimarer Republik*, vol 1 (Frankfurt, 1969), pp. 116–17.

He was likewise in constant touch with the affairs of the French CP, and after Trotsky's eviction he became the Comintern's specialist in 'French affairs'. In 1924 he went to Paris as Zinoviev's emissary in order to isolate Suvarin, who was opposed to the anti-Trotsky campaign. In 1931 he took part in the elimination of the Barbé-Célor splinter group; in 1933–4, despite teasing Thorez at first for his 'blind obedience', he helped him overcome Doriot; and although at first he underestimated German national socialism, he contributed to the drawing up of the French CP's tactics of opposition to the rise of Fascism.

After Bukharin's eviction from the presidency of the Comintern, Manuilsky, a man in whom Stalin had confidence, became a central figure. From 1926 until the dissolution of the Comintern he occupied the key post of Secretary, to which he was appointed at the time when Stalin began to concern himself intensely with the Comintern, namely after its fifth Congress. And in fact, control of the Comintern turned out to be a position of strength for members of the Russian Party's Politburo in their internal struggle. In 1930 Molotov was appointed President of the Soviet government, and Manuilsky became head of the Soviet CP's delegation and in fact directed the Comintern. This situation was not changed after Dimitrov's appointment as General Secretary in 1935, when Manuilsky became in name his deputy. As the *rapporteur* at the Comintern's enlarged Executive Committees and Congresses, Manuilsky's name is indissolubly attached to the vicissitudes of that organisation. He was one of the signatories of the resolution of 22 May 1943 which dissolved the Comintern, and was with Togliatti and Dimitrov a member of the liquidation commission.

During the Second World War, Manuilsky worked in the Central Committee apparatus and in the higher political control of the Red Army. In 1944 he began a new, principally diplomatic career. He was appointed Vice-President of the Ukrainian Council of Ministers and Ukrainian Foreign Minister. He led the Ukrainian delegation to the UN, and was with Vyshinsky one of the Soviet government spokesmen there. He held these posts officially until 1952, but had in fact been ousted already in 1950. He was disgraced and only just escaped the fate of his friend Lozovsky, who was deported. Manuilsky withdrew from political life in 1953 and died in 1959.

G.H.

ALEKSEY IVANOVICH RYKOV

Aleksey Ivanovich Rykov was born on 13 February 1881 in the town of Saratov. His father, a peasant from the hamlet of Kukarka, Yaransk district, Vyatka province, had earlier worked the land and been a trader in Saratov, before finally going in search of work to Merv, where he died of cholera, leaving a family of six children from his two marriages. Rykov was then not eight years old. His childhood was spent in great poverty. His stepmother could only feed her own children. The elder sister, Klavdia Ivanovna, went out to work in the Office of the Ryazan-Uralsk railway and also gave private lessons. She took charge of Aleksey and helped him to enter the Gymnasium. Then, when he was thirteen, Rykov moved into a higher form and started giving lessons himself. His favourite subjects at school were mathematics, physics and the natural sciences. As early as the fourth form he threw his religious beliefs overboard, and stopped going to church and confession, to the great dismay of the well-disposed school authorities, who thought highly of Rykov for his academic brilliance. As the years passed, however, relations between the budding revolutionary and the school authorities became strained to the point where he was more than once in danger of expulsion. He was only saved by success in his studies.

On the eve of his final examinations, the Rykov home was searched, although nothing was found thanks to the ingenuity of Aleksey who had hidden all the illegal literature in time. He was, however, only given a mark of four out of five for conduct, which deprived him of the right to enter the universities of Moscow and St Petersburg, and in 1900 he was obliged to go to Kazan University to complete his education in the law faculty.

Rykov's youth coincided with a massive upsurge in the labour movement in Russia which stirred young people. Saratov at that time was an 'exile town' for 'political' workers and students. Revolutionary circles flourished. In them, people not only read Mikhailovsky, Pisarev and Chernyshevsky, but even Marx. It was there that Rykov became acquainted with the history of the revolutionary movement in Russia and with revolutionary literature, there that he read the works of Marx for the first time and the chief books on the labour question and the trade union movement in Western Europe. He also participated in a clandestine journal produced in Saratov. The circle in which he was an active participant was led by Rakitnikov, who subsequently played a prominent role in the Socialist Revolutionary Party, and Rykov was impelled to study the peasant movement by his acquaintance with V. Balmashev, an old member of *Narodnaya Volya*, with whose son,

Stepan (who assassinated Sipyagin, the Minister of Internal Affairs, in 1902), he was on friendly terms.

Rykov's involvement in the revolutionary organisations of Saratov while still at the Gymnasium decided his future. After entering Kazan University at the age of nineteen, he immediately joined the local SD Party Committee, directing workers' circles, as well as the student committee. He was only able to devote a short period of time to this intensive revolutionary activity, since in March 1901 the police pounced on both the workers' and students' organisations, and Rykov was sent to Kazan prison for nine months' 'rest' before being released under the supervision of the Saratov police to await an administrative sentence.

By 1902, Saratov had become a sort of 'Russian centre', where both SDs and SRs conducted intensive agitation among the working masses. Rykov, as a member of the SD Committee, attempted to create a united revolutionary organisation. But after the official formation of the SR Party, Rykov took the initiative, as a staunch *Iskra* supporter, in disbanding this organisation. At the May Day demonstration of 1902 which was attacked by the Black Hundreds, the police and the gendarmes, Rykov was singled out as one of its organisers. He was set upon and only just managed to run through someone's yard, clamber over the fence, and make good his escape, covered in blood.

Soon the police department issued its verdict on the Kazan affair and Rykov was sentenced to exile in Archangel province. Instead he preferred to go underground, where he remained until 1917, wandering from town to town and from prison to prison, changing his passport with great regularity. Later, in a letter, he described this period of his life in the following way:

> No sooner had I taken my seat on the students' bench than I found myself in clink. Twelve years have passed since then, but roughly five and a half of them were spent inside. In addition, three years of my life were filled by three journeys into exile. During my brief glimpses of 'freedom', villages, towns, people and events flashed before my eyes as in a cinema, and I was constantly on the move, either by coach, horse or boat. In no room did I spend more than two months. I have reached the age of thirty and I still do not know how to obtain a passport. I have no idea of what it means to rent a room permanently.

The Russian Bureau of *Iskra* in Kiev sent word for Rykov to go abroad secretly and he set off for Geneva. Here he made the personal acquaintance of Lenin and the rest of the *Iskra* group. Two months later, armed with addresses, meeting-places and a false passport, he returned to clandestine activity in Russia. He was drawn by the fascinating, fearful routine of underground life. He began to work on the Northern Committee of the SD Party, which covered mainly Yaroslavl and Kostroma provinces. There he gave guidance to local SD organisations in Yaroslavl, Rybinsk, Kineshma and elsewhere. After a police raid and arrests in Yaroslavl, Rykov moved to Nizhny Novgorod. In 1904 he succeeded in leading a large strike at a factory in Sormovo with fairly successful results. Following this, he was transferred to Moscow as an outstanding Party organiser, since the SD organisation there had been crippled by numerous arrests. Rykov quickly rebuilt it and soon under his leadership it became one of the largest organisations in the Party. He collected round the SD Committee a large number of scattered, isolated SD circles and groups, re-established agitation in the working-class areas, and was himself extremely active in the Sokolniki and Lefortovo districts. He developed close links between the Moscow Committee and a group of Marxist writers. The latter, Skvortsov-Stepanov, Pokrovsky, Rozhkov, Friche and others, proceeded to found a Marxist journal. The revitalisation of the labour movement throughout Russia found expression in a whole series of strikes in Moscow, and the massacre of 9 January led to the building of the first barricades in Zamoskvoreche.

In March 1905 Rykov was elected chief organizer and leader of the Moscow Committee at the third Party Congress in London, where he was also elected to the CC. Apart from a brief interlude, he has remained ever since a CC member of the RSDRP(b) and then the VKP(b).

On returning to Russia from London, he was put at the head of the St Petersburg Committee, but on 14 May the whole committee was arrested during one of its sessions. Rykov was sentenced to nine years' exile, but following the Amnesty of 17 October 1905 he was released. He immediately joined the St Petersburg Soviet of Workers' Deputies, and after it had been crushed was obliged to move to Moscow. Here he posed as a doctor's assistant called Mikhail Alekseyevich Sukhoruchenko, and in close collaboration with Lenin, who once came to see him in Moscow, he directed preparations for the fourth 'unifying' Congress in Stockholm. In mid-1906 he travelled to Odessa to combat the Mensheviks and organise Bolshevik cells. He was searched and went into hiding in Moscow. However, he was very soon arrested and banished to Peniga in Archangel province for three years. He escaped from exile back to Moscow, resumed work there, and led the Committee for the Industrial Region. Thanks to his personal and close acquaintance with the revolutionary Schmidt, he was directly involved in the transfer to the Party of the large fortune which Schmidt had inherited from his father, a manufacturer. On 1 May 1907 Rykov was denounced by Putyata, an *agent provocateur*; he was again arrested, and incarcerated for seventeen months in the Taganka prison while his case was being investigated. It was only on 28 June 1908 that, after allowance had been made for time already spent in custody, he was sentenced to two years' exile in Samara.

Lenin summoned Rykov abroad in view of the ripening conflict between the Bolsheviks and the Mensheviks, who proposed the abolition of the underground organisation. Rykov was instructed to enter into negotiations with all currents and groups inside the Party with a view to forming a united bloc against the 'liquidators'. In summer 1909 he returned to Russia, immediately came under observation by the secret police, and on 7 September was arrested in Moscow where he was living under the name of I. Biletsky, supposedly an inhabitant of Kharkov. After being imprisoned for three months for being in possession of false papers, he was deported to Ust-Tsilma on the river Pechora in Archangel province. The police temporarily allowed him to stay in Pinega to recover from an illness and from there he again escaped abroad and was specially summoned by Lenin to the Bolshevik centre in Paris.

In August 1911 he returned to Russia to prepare for the new Party Conference, but on the way from the station in Moscow he was again arrested. He languished for nine months in prison, and then was escorted back to Pinega for the third time in his life to serve his three years of exile. His enforced idleness was filled with reading, and then with work as a reporter for the newspaper *Arkhangelsk*. 'All the time I am reading learned books, journals and newspapers, especially newspapers, since Russian life has begun to smile and gather momentum,' he wrote from Pinega, sharply aware, even from afar, of the rising tide of the labour movement in 1912. But returning to St Petersburg in 1913, he came across a degeneration among many former Party workers who had abandoned active revolutionary work under the impact of reaction and had devoted themselves to their wives and families. 'The new way of life and the goal of personal, private interests,' wrote Rykov, 'made a breach even in the ranks of Bolshevik officials and created completely new feelings and a new mentality. The workers remained untouched by this transformation of our intelligentsia and instinctively, spontaneously opposed them.'

Rykov moved to Moscow where he again directed the Bolshevik Party organisation. But in July 1913 he was rearrested and exiled for four years to the area of Narym, being escorted there from Moscow in mid-November, part of the way in chains. In spite of the strictest super-vision, he escaped from exile in September 1915, making his way along the Ob, Irtysh, Tobol and Tura rivers to Samara. He was not due to remain at liberty for long: in October of the same year he was detained, spent seven months in prison and was sent back to Narym, where he remained until the Revolution.

From the very beginning of the war Rykov adopted a consistently internationalist, 'defeatist' position. Not for a moment did he succumb to the patriotic fervour that gripped even some of the exiles. He organ-ised anti-war circles where he defended the Zimmerwald line, and thanks to his immense energy, he won over many workers who had been de-ported to Narym. The burden of exile became ever heavier, and this led to a wave of suicides there. With his wife, Nina Semyonovna, and close comrades, Rykov tried strenuously to come to grips with this despair. As the head of the local Bolshevik group, he expanded their political activity and improved communication with the Russian and émigré Party centres. Lenin tried to keep him in touch with Party policy. When news came of the February Revolution, a telegram was received from the Tomsk Social Committee, offering to free 700 of the exiles, to be designated by Rykov and two comrades, and to send them home.

Rykov left Narym with the last party of exiles and made for Moscow. The Party detailed him to work in the Moscow Soviet of Workers' Deputies and very soon he was elected to its Presidium. Here he was particularly active in settling clashes between manufacturers and workers (for example the arrest by workers of Vtorov, one of the largest manufacturers, and the conflict at Orekhovo-Zuyevo). On his initiative the Moscow Soviet confiscated the Lykin texitle mill two or three months before the October Revolution and transferred it to workers' manage-ment. In the Soviet, where the majority were Mensheviks or SRs, he followed the Bolshevik line, organising, for example, contrary to the will of the majority, a massive strike of tram workers and a one-day general strike throughout Moscow in protest against the August 'National Con-ference' summoned in Moscow by the Kerensky government. It was his speech on the political situation in Russia which induced the plenum of the Soviet to reject the Menshevik and SR resolution and to accept the Bolshevik platform directed against the Kerensky regime. In October Rykov was one of the organisers and leaders of the armed rising, and he entered the Council of People's Commissars on its creation as Com-missar for Internal Affairs. In view of the grave shortage of food, he was entrusted with responsibility for putting to rights the delivery of pro-visions to Moscow. In February 1918 he made a tour of the grain-producing areas: Tula, Oryol, Tambov, the banks of the Volga, and

Kharkov. He speeded up overdue grain convoys and somewhat improved the regular food supply.

Still in 1918, at height of the upheaval, the government assigned Rykov to the direction of the Supreme Council of the Economy (VSNKh). It was under his guidance that the nationalisation of industry and the creation of a state monopoly in the distribution of manufactured goods were implemented. The outbreak of the Civil War required the planning of supplies for the Red Army as it fought on numerous fronts. In view of the shortage of provisions and clothing for soldiers and workers, a special institution was created to co-ordinate the workings of the VSNKh and economic organs, and to organise uninterrupted supplies for the Red Army. Rykov was put in charge of it as 'emergency representative of the STO for the supply of the Red Army and Navy'. Thanks to his energy, stores and depots were ransacked for everything that could in any way be used to arm the Revolution and supply the army. Under his personal direction the chief armament factories were put back into production, and the army began to receive regular and sufficient deliveries of equipment and cartridges. When the war industry had been put on its feet, Rykov proceeded to revitalize the industries of peace.

In summer 1921, following Lenin's illness, Rykov was appointed his deputy, temporarily abandoning his work in the VSNKh. In 1923 he returned there as its Chairman, simultaneously fulfilling the functions of Deputy Chairman of the Sovnarkom. In addition, he directed the work of commissions dealing with, amongst other things, the creation of a uniform agricultural tax, the improvement of wages, the division of industry into trusts, and the drafting of measures designed to implement a monopoly on foreign trade. One commission over which he presided (the so-called 'scissors' commission), worked out a programme of economic measures to reduce the prices of consumer goods and increase the price of bread and agricultural produce. This programme received Party approval and formed the basis for a swift solution to the market crisis of autumn 1923 and ensured rapid economic growth for 1924-5.

When Lenin died, the Party put forward Rykov's name for the post of Chairman of the Sovnarkom of the USSR and the RSFSR, and he was elected on 2 February. Since 1926 he has also been in direct control of the STO. At congresses and sessions of the TsIK and VTsIK, he has made key speeches on general questions of the internal and external policies and the Party and government.

Most of his speeches have appeared in special printed editions, of which the most important are: the report at the fourteenth Party Conference, *The Countryside, NEP and Co-operation*; the report of the government at the third Congress of Soviets (published with a separate introduction, 'At the Turning-Point'), which described in detail the approaching stage of development of the USSR; and his report at the fifteenth Party Conference, *The Economic Stage of the Country and the Tasks of the Party*. This last work outlines in practical terms the policy of the Party and government for industrialising the country. A complete edition of Rykov's works is in preparation. The first volume, covering the period 1918–21, has already appeared.

As for the Party line, Rykov, being one of the oldest members of the CC and since 1919 a Politburo member, is one of the staunchest, most unshakable defenders of the principles of Leninism. In this respect, his speeches at the fourteenth Congress (published separately under the title *On the New Opposition*) and the fifteenth Congress are particularly significant, for they give a detailed evaluation of the economic programme of the opposition.

Apart from small biographies of Rykov, two full-scale ones have appeared, one by A. Lomov called *A. I. Rykov* (1924), and the other by I. I. Vorobyov, V. V. Miller and A. M. Pankratova entitled *A. I. Rykov—His Life and Work* (1924).

R.S.D.

After Lenin's death, Rykov took his place at the summit of the governmental hierarchy by succeeding the leader as President of the Council of People's Commissars. During Lenin's illness he had been nominated by him as acting President of the Council, and he behaved as the acknowledged heir, and then as the strong man of the right-wing bloc in power. His position on the Party's right wing was not mere chance, and there is a definite continuity to it. Born a peasant, Rykov had played a front-line part ever since the dawn of Bolshevism. In 1905, at the London Congress, he had opposed Lenin with all the fervour and cheekiness of youth; he thus took the leadership of the *Komitetchiki* and in 1910 became the main figure in the conciliatory faction.

Although Rykov gained notoriety abroad, the main field of his political activity was always inside Russia, though his numerous arrests often put a brake on him. One of the principles of his action was to doubt whether agrarian Russia would ever be ready for a socialist revolution. Thus immediately after the October Revolution he supported the idea of an alliance with the Mensheviks and the SRs. It was only with regret that Lenin allowed him into the first Bolshevik government as People's Commissar for the Interior. In March 1918 he and Milyutin were given the Supreme Sovnarkhoz, which they efficiently set themselves to reorganise.

He supported Trotsky in his demands for a peace treaty with Poland, but opposed him bitterly over the union question. This cost him his position on the Supreme Sovnarkhoz, but he recuperated it in 1923. He then crowned this position with that of President of the Council of People's Commissars. Lenin was only half-satisfied with his handling of this latter function, but none the less paid hommage to his qualities as an administrator.

The second factor that governed his political activity was his attachment to Party unity, which for him took precedence over individuals, whose sacrifice to Party unity he thought inevitable. On this basis he struggled against the left opposition and even more fiercely, since he judged it even more dangerous, against the United Opposition. After the elimination of these oppositions, the logic of his convictions brought him into opposition to the politices of super-industrialisation; Rykov's name was the first to be linked to the notion of a right-wing opposition, before being definitively associated with those of Bukharin and Tomsky.

The trial of the counter-revolutionary Donets engineers gave Stalin his first point of attack against the man who as head of government had been the author of the 1927 economic plan. The resignation that Rykov submitted and then withdrew at the same time as Tomsky and Bukharin was part of the battle of concessions and counter-attacks. But even though Rykov was the first man to be labelled a right-winger, he was also the first to attempt to mask the divergences and followed Stalin in denouncing the rightist tendency as a deviation inspired by kulak pressure. In fact, he was not stripped of his government post until much later than Bukharin. At the sixteenth Congress in 1930 he was still at the head of the government, and he defended himself by saying that he had never really been an oppositionist. It was only at the end of 1930 that he had to give up his position on the Politburo and the presidency of the Council of People's Commissars. He was then transferred to a job in the Postal Administration.

Rykov was implicated by statements made at the first Moscow trial, but the inquiry set up to examine his case dismissed all charges. Nevertheless, he was arrested in 1937 with Bukharin. As one of the star defendants at the third Moscow trial in March 1938 he was convicted and executed.

In 1956 he was indirectly rehabilitated when *Pravda* published a letter from Lenin to Rykov.

G.H.

3

Recruits from Other Parties, Other Lands

VLADIMIR ALEKSANDROVICH ANTONOV-OVSEYENKO
(autobiography)

I was born on 9 March 1884 in Chernigov. My father, at that time lieutenant in a reserve infantry regiment and an impoverished landowner, died in 1902 after rising to the rank of captain.

In 1901 I graduated from the Voronezh Military School and entered the Nikolaev Army Engineering College. One month later I was arrested for refusing to take the oath of loyalty to Tsar and country; I was detained for eleven days and then released on my father's surety. This refusal was motivated by an 'organic repugnance for militarism'. In the winter of 1901 I entered a student SD circle in Warsaw (previously I had had no revolutionary acquaintances and had arrived at this aversion for militarism quite independently as a result of the degrading and humiliating atmosphere of the school and college). In spring 1902 I left home, worked as a labourer in the Alexander docks in St Petersburg, and then as a coachman for the Society for the Protection of Animals.

In autumn 1902, in my eagerness for definite revolutionary activity, I entered the St Petersburg Military Academy and carried on propaganda there on behalf of the capital's SD organisation, which supplied me with literature. In 1903 Comrade Stomonyakov (Party pseudonym 'Kuznetsov', and now a Collegium member of Vneshtorg), put me in touch with the Bolsehevik organisation.

In August 1904 I was caught in possession of illegal literature, detained for ten days and then released on direct instructions from Grand Prince Konstantin Konstantinovich, who prided himself on his liberalism.

On graduation from the Academy, where I left behind a strong SD circle, I was posted as an officer to the Fortieth Kolyvan Infantry Regiment stationed in Warsaw. In autumn 1904, on instructions from the St

Petersburg Bolshevik organisation, I travelled to Moscow, Ekaterinoslav, Odessa, Kiev and Vilno to link the Party with newly graduated officers from my circle. In Vilno I made contact with the local military group, and in Warsaw I established relations with the SD, Polish Socialist Party, *Proletariat* and Bund organisations. I founded the Warsaw RSDRP Military Committee (which subsequently included Comrade Surits, our ambassador to Turkey, and Comrade Bogodsky, our representative in Switzerland). In spring 1905 I received an unexpected posting to the Far East, and so I went into hiding, aided by the SD group, and Comrade 'Nikolay' (Hanecki) in particular. I set off for Krakow and Lvov, keeping in touch with the Polish SDs, and I returned to Poland two weeks later to direct the unsuccessful Novo-Aleksandria mutiny of two infantry regiments and an artillery brigade. (A description by me of this mutiny can be found in *Iskra*, no. 100, under the signature 'Shtyk'.)

After this I went to Vienna. I was introduced to the so-called 'Party Council' (Menshevik), which sent me on a mission to St Petersburg where I arrived at the end of May, and I was active in the Menshevik Military Committee and agitational group. At the end of June I was arrested in Kronstadt at a meeting of soldiers and sailors (betrayed by 'Nikolay with the gold glasses', otherwise known as Dobroskok). I was released under an assumed name following the October amnesty. I joined the United Military Committee, which was led by Comrade Nogin ('Makar'). From there I passed to the United St Petersburg Committee and edited the very successful underground paper *Kazarma*.

At the beginning of April 1906, I was arrested with Emelian Yaroslavsky, Zemlyachka and others at a congress of the military organisations. Five days later, Emelian, myself and three other comrades escaped from the Sushchevsky jail by breaking through a wall. Within a month I was in Sebastopol under orders from the CC to prepare an insurrection. It broke out suddenly in June, and I was arrested in the street as I tried to shoot my way through a cordon of police and soldiers surrounding the house where a meeting of representatives from military units was in progress. I was imprisoned for a year without my true identity being revealed – I gave my name as Kabanov – and then I was sentenced to death, which eight days later was commuted to twenty years' hard labour. Within a month, in June 1907, and on the eve of our departure from Sebastopol, I escaped with twenty others during an exercise period by blowing a hole in the wall and firing on the warders and sentry. This break-out was organised by Comrade Konstantin who had come from Moscow. After hiding in the mountains for a week, I set off for Moscow. On the way I had to jump from a train to avoid detectives. After many ordeals I reached Moscow and I sought out the CC Bureau. They directed me to Finland, from where I went to St Petersburg two months later armed with a 'cast-iron' passport.

In the capital I embarked upon propaganda among sailors on the yacht *Shtandart*, but increased police attention obliged me to leave for Moscow. There I progressed from Bolshevik workers' circles in the Suchchevsky-Marinsky district to activity in legal organisations, joining with the 'liquidators'. During the winter of 1908 I organised workers' co-operatives in various districts: the *Zhizn* co-operative in Lefortovo (Blagushe), *Trud* (in Presnya), and *Obyedineniye* (in Sokolniki). Simultaneously I worked for the Union of Printing Workers (whose weekly journal I edited with the Bolshevik Comrade Lyubimov). I assisted in the take-over of the Lefortovo Temperance Society by Bolshevik workers, and founded the 'Club for Sensible Amusements', which promoted widespread revolutionary activity before being quickly closed. In these respects I worked side by side with Bolshevik activities. In spring 1909 I participated in a clandestine conference in Nizhny Novgorod, where underground organisations from Nizhny Novgorod, Sormovo, Moscow and Bogorodsk were represented, and where it was decided that an underground newspaper supporting the Plekhanov line should be published by me in Moscow. Whilst attending the Congress of Factory Doctors in Moscow (this was my new field of activity instead of workers' co-operatives), I was arrested at an SD meeting following betrayal by Malinovsky, but I was released after three days and went to Kiev. As a result of mass arrests there I returned to Moscow, where I was again arrested and held for six months. After my identity had been 'established' in the village of Kreslavka, Dvinsk district (this cost 400 roubles, which were collected by Bolshevik workers' organisations), I was released in February 1910 under the name of Anton Guk.

Arrests in Moscow, the impossibility of finding a reliable passport and uninterrupted shadowing by the police all drove me abroad (in July 1910). I had no sooner crossed the frontier than I was seized by Prussian police officers, but they did not hand me over to the Russian authorities thanks to the intervention of German social democrats. I was in Paris until 1914 as an adherent of the Menshevik group, but simultaneously I worked with Bolsheviks (Vladimirov, Lozovsky, Sokolnikov) both in the circle assisting the SD Duma 'fraction' and in several publishing ventures. I was Secretary of the Paris Labour Bureau, consisting of representatives from Russian cells of workers' syndicates. Beginning in September 1914, I joined with D. Manuilsky (then a member of the *Vperyod* group) in issuing and editing *Golos*. The paper grew rapidly and attracted articles from some of the most prominent internationalists of varying shades of opinion—Martov, Trotsky, Lunacharsky, M. Pokrovsky, 'Volonter' (pseudonym of M. Pavlovich), Lozovsky, Vladimirov, etc. It remained in existence under various names until April 1917. In late 1914 I left the Mensheviks as a result of their readiness to agree with the 'socialist' patriots, remained active in the *Nashe Slovo* group, joined Bolsheviks (Grisha Belensky, etc.) in the SD Internationalist Club and adopted a left-wing editorial policy for *Golos* (*Nashe Slovo*), which coincided on all fundamental points with the Bolshevik line.

In May 1917 I benefited from the amnesty and returned to Russia. On my arrival I presented myself to the Party CC and formally joined the Party, publicly announcing my split with the *mezhrayontsy*. I became an activist in Helsinki, edited *Volna*, and was also an agitator in Petrograd, where I joined the Party Committee and the city Duma. On 15 July I was arrested in Helsinki on instructions from Kerensky and imprisoned in the Kresty for one month. I was a member of the Finnish Regional Commission, represented the Northern Front in the Constituent Assembly, was Secretary of the Committee of Northern Soviets and of the Petrograd Military Revolutionary Committee. On 25 October I directed the seizure of the Winter Palace and the arrest of the Provisional government. Afterwards, I was elected to the Sovnarkom and the Commissariat for Military Affairs, and was also appointed Commander of the Petrograd Military District. On 6 December I left for the Ukraine to lead the struggle against the partisans of Kaledin, Kornilov and the Rada. From March until May 1918 I was Commander-in-Chief of Military Forces for the southern Soviet republics. I also held seats on the RVS of the Republic and the Collegium of the Commissariat of Military Affairs. In September and October I commanded the Second and Third Armies, from 11 November the Kursk group, and from January until June 1919, the Ukrainian Front. In August and September of that year I was given plenary powers by the VTsIK to enforce compulsory food deliveries in Vitebsk province. From November 1919 until April 1920 I performed the same function in Tambov province, as well as being Chairman of the province's Party and Executive Committees.

In April 1920 I became Deputy Chairman of the Chief Labour Committee and Collegium member of the People's Commissariat for Labour. From November until January I was a Collegium member of the Commissariat for Internal Affairs and Deputy Chairman of the Small Sovnarkom. From mid-January until the beginning of February 1921 I was given plenary powers by VTsIK in Perm province (Chairman of the Soviet, Party Committee, and Committee for Political Education). From mid-February until mid-July 1921 I headed the VTsIK special committee charged with eliminating banditry in Tambov province. From October 1921 I was Chairman of the Executive Committee of Samara province where I directed the drive against famine. From autumn 1922 till February 1924 I was head of the Political Directorate of the Republic and member of the RVS. Since then I have been at the disposal of the People's Commissariat for Foreign Affairs.

Antonov-Ovseyenko was the main architect of the armed insurrection in Petrograd on 7 November 1916, and shared with Podvoysky the leadership of the RVS which ran all military operations including the taking of the Winter Palace. He was a member of the first Soviet government as one of the three Commissars for War. No one was better prepared by training and experience for these tasks than Antonov-Ovseyenko. This former officer, who had joined the revolutionary movement in 1901, was one of the military experts in Russian social democracy at the time of the 1905 Revolution, when he gained considerable experience of agitating among the troops and of organising an armed insurrection.

He was arrested several times and sentenced to death after the failure of the Sebastopol uprising, which he had instigated. He enjoyed a great reputation for courage and calmness in social democrat circles. After his escape he went into exile and settled in France in 1910. Although he had till then remained outside all splinter groups, Antonov-Ovseyenko joined the Mensheviks, drew closer to Trotsky and in 1913 joined the August bloc.

Among socialist émigrés in Paris on the eve of the First World War, Antonov-Ovseyenko was a character well known both for his position and for his violent anti-Bolshevik speeches at various meetings. In his memoirs on Lenin in Paris, Alin described him thus: 'Antonov-Ovseyenko, his curls down his back, called down thunder from heaven, and shook his first at the "corrupters", that is to say, Lenin and his supporters.'[1]

After the outbreak of the First World War, Antonov Ovseyenko acquired a role of some importance; it was he who ran the newspapers *Golos* then *Nashe Slovo* in Paris. Around Antonov-Ovseyenko, Trotsky and Martov, all the Russian internationalist tendencies regrouped. His military skills were put to use and an important part was his in the preparation of the October insurrection. He was a member of the 'troika' in charge of operations.

He was asked to intervene at various strategic points: in December 1918 he was appointed Commander-in-Chief on the Ukrainian Front. He was dismissed in June 1919 on Trotsky's urgent demand and following

[1] Alin, *Lénine à Paris. Souvenirs inédits*, p. 53.

his military defeat. He was given new postings. He took part in virtually all the revolutionary campaigns, and in numerous areas where there was trouble in establishing Soviet power—in the struggles against the uprisings, against famine, and so on.

Although a soldier, he none the less remained a political activist. At the eleventh Congress in 1922, he was the spokesman of the dissatisfied Old Guard, and violently attacked Lenin and Trotsky with accusations of capitulating to the kulaks and to foreign capitalism. Despite some differences, he remained close to Trotsky throughout these years, and shared his political ideas. When Trotsky counter-attacked in 1922, he replaced his adversary Gusev at the head of the political leadership of the RVS with Antonov-Ovseyenko. In this crucial post, he was, next to Pyatakov, one of the most resolute and daring leaders of the Trotskyite opposition in 1923. He signed the celebrated 'Declaration of the 46'. When Stalin undertook the dismantling of the opposition he began by stripping Antonov-Ovseyenko of his post. He was dismissed from his post at the head of the army's political administration on the pretext that he had sent out a circular on workers' democracy without referring it to the Central Committee, and thus disobeying its orders. Like the other opposition leaders, he was neutralised by his transfer to the diplomatic service; he was removed from the centre in 1925 when he was appointed Soviet Political Representative (ambassador) to Czechoslovakia, whence he was later transferred to Lithuania. In 1928 he left the United Opposition and moved himself, baggage and all, into Stalin's camp. He made a shattering declaration which absolved Stalin of the accusations that Lenin had set down in his *Testament*. In the same year he was appointed Soviet Political Representative to Poland. In his diplomatic post he devoted himself to drawing up his four volumes of notes and documents on the Civil War, an indigestible but valuable work.

In 1936, he was Consul-General in Barcelona. Practically nothing is known about his activities during the Spanish Civil War. Was he involved in the liquidation of Poum and of the foreign Trotskyites, as some writers have claimed? It is not improbable. Antonov-Ovseyenko's end was tragically ironic. He was recalled to Moscow in August 1937 and saw Stalin in the Kremlin. In 1938, *Pravda* and *Izvestia* published the decree of his appointment as People's Commissar for Justice in the RSFSR. A few weeks later, he was arrested, and was shot without trial in 1939. He was one of the first men to be rehabilitated in 1956, with the group of Civil War army chiefs.

G.H.

GEORGY VASILIEVICH CHICHERIN
(authorised biography)

Georgy Vasilievich Chicherin was born on 12 November 1872 at Karaul on the estate of his uncle Boris Nikolaevich. He came from an aristocratic family imbued with moderately liberal traditions. His grandfather, Nikolay Vasilievich Chicherin, was considered an extremely educated man and a liberal. He lived almost permanently in Karaul on his estate, which he had turned into a noted centre of provincial intellectual life. Boris Nikolaevich, the well-known lawyer, philosopher and publicist, was his eldest son. His second son, Vasily Nikolaevich, Chicherin's father, was a refined, worldly man, who could speak and write excellent French, and had devoted himself to a diplomatic career. He was a secretary at the mission in Piedmont in 1859 during the Italian War and in that year married Baroness Georgina Egorovna Meyendorf, whose family had also provided the Tsarist government with a number of outstanding diplomats. [. . .] Chicherin's father died after a long illness in 1882. The last years cast gloom over the family and Chicherin grew up alone in an atmosphere of pietism, deprived of companions of the same age.

His main childhood memories are of constant prayers, combined singing of hymns, recitation of the Bible, and of a generally ecstatic, highly charged atmosphere. The basic attitude of his childhood was a sort of messianism, the expectation of another reality, the Kingdom of God, in place of the existing one. His family lived on their limited income in Tambov, but they maintained the traditions of aristocratic culture, which set them sharply apart from provincial society. It was as if the solitary child had been walled off from life around. His sensitive and artistic mother educated him in the traditions of refined culture, teaching him to love works of art. From early childhood he adored historical books, being fascinated by the bright, colourful pageantry of historical events, the fluctuations of circumstance, the distinctive style of each succeeding age. His mother's vivid tales and reminiscences about her earlier life evoked the diplomatic milieu. Pietism and fanatical exaltation coexisted in him with a tendency to admire the refined, mocking scepticism of the eighteenth century, which still lives on in Western high society. He loved reading and re-reading diplomatic documents which his mother had kept, for example peace treaties. [. . .]

When he entered the first form of the Tambov Gymnasium, he became painfully aware of the contrast between his home environment and the provincial milieu. He learnt to make a careful distinction between 'official' and 'non-official' reality. He made very few close friends at school. On the one hand he acquired the knack of 'official' behaviour, whilst on the other he was drawn into shunning tell-tales, idealising mischievous pranks and treating teachers as enemies. In a provincial Gymnasium of that time, there were the most heterogeneous elements side by side. Chicherin observed repeated injustices with his own eyes, the victimisation of the poorest students by the school authorities and the tragic scenes of their despair.

All this was interrupted, however, by the family's move to St Petersburg, where he entered the fourth form of the Eighth Gymnasium. Here almost all the students came from the same official background, and their musical and other cultural interests were more highly developed. Chicherin could not at first accommodate himself to the new environment and his first two years there passed in isolation. It was his mother's old milieu, but she returned impoverished and estranged from that way of life. The family only frequented relatives and a very few acquaintances, among them another impoverished lady, Mme Albedinskaya, the former Princess Dolgorukova and a favourite of Alexander II in her youth.

Society life dazzled Chicherin's imagination, but at the same time he was disgusted by its intellectual vacuity. As a result of his family's straitened circumstances, he fell into the frame of mind of *The Humiliated and the Insulted*, a tendency towards moral self-flagellation and self-abasement. His shy reserve reached extreme proportions, yet it was curiously mingled with instinctive high spirits which had been repressed by an unhappy life, just as his exaltation and striving for the all-embracing Idea had been combined with an admiration for the refined scepticism of the eighteenth century or French Stendhalism. His study of ancient Greece filled him with boundless delight and he devoted his leisure to reading the Greek lyric poets. A passionate devotee of history, he particularly liked Kostomarov during his school years for the latter's critical method and evocation of the mind of the popular masses. On the long, wearisome, lonely winter evenings, when the dim lanterns on Vasilievsky Ostrov gave off but a glimmer of light, the Russian countryside would float into his imagination radiant in beauty, and the peasantry, imbued with the harmony of a life of labour, would appear as the bearer of the superior human type. He regularly visited his grandmother Meyendorf, a lively and witty woman, and he delighted in listening to her memories of the old diplomatic life in Metternich's time. He also visited his aunt, Aleksandra Nikolaevna Naryshkina, and her husband, Emmanuel Dmitrievich, but only out of family duty. They lived in luxury and he smarted at being in the acutely humiliating position of a poor, despised relative. This life of poverty in the capital had a tremendous effect on him. Lacking both intellectual guidance and the companionship of friends, he was inwardly torn by ever more acute contradictions.

A turning-point in his life came whilst he was in the sixth form of the Gymnasium—he discovered the later music of Wagner, when *Der Ring des Nibelungen* was performed in St Petersburg. Its pantheism led him to study oriental cultures and engendered a passionate love of the Orient. In Wagner's music he also perceived heroic power and fierce revolutionary energy. He saw in his favourite opera, *Die Walküre*, the dazzling enactment of a tragedy of rebels perishing as a result of their rebellion, but leaving behind a legacy for future generations. It was at this time that he became more friendly with his classmates. Whereas once he had idealised the St Petersburg bureaucratic milieu, he now found in it only trivial love-affairs, interminable games of cards, and a constant rivalry in indecent stories and witticisms. He became very close to some students at the Gymnasium thanks to common musical and other cultural interests, but in general he was more and more overwhelmed by frustration with the emptiness of life and the sense of being a failure.

After enrolling in the History and Philology Faculty, he wrote to his grandmother Meyendorf that history for him was bound up with life and that he would encounter his subject face to face in the street. At university he went to as many and varying lectures as he could. Lacking guidance, he eagerly sampled all possible sciences. The strongest and most lasting impression was made on him by Klyuchevsky's duplicated lecture notes with their economic analysis of the historical process and their sharp, critical approach. Isaev's lectures and his conversations in the corridors first made him aware of the workers' movement, though this was still distorted by a mass of undigested intellectual impressions. The student disorders of 1895 caught his passionate imagination, but were soon over.

By the end of his university course, his dissatisfaction with the futility and emptiness of life, his moral self-flagellation and his lack of positive ideals had reached the point of the most acute inner tragedy. As Caesar says in Julian's *Dialogues of the Dead*, which he assiduously read: 'One must come second in nothing.' Being lower than anyone else in any respect seemed to him grounds for unlimited self-abhorrence. He later developed these attitudes in the abstract to the point where it was impossible to be reconciled with the notion that he was only an individual, limited and transient phenomenon. He found in Schopenhauer a formula to describe the internal contradiction of the human personality, that it is the eye of the world and at the same time a detail in the world. Suicide in his view was no solution to the problem. He decided to punish the unknown forces that had created him against his will by gradually destroying himself and doing everything that might undermine his health. Experiencing the most painful spiritual torments, he threw himself into society life on the spur of the moment, but it disgusted him. He was suddenly overwhelmed by social grief but it led to nothing and evaporated into thin air.

He found echoes of his pessimism in the work of the reactionary writer B. V. Nikolsky, only the least interesting of whose writings were published. In them he found contempt for life, self and every being raised to an absolute. But this very contempt finally dissolved in a vacuum: 'In the heights where contempt sleeps, where delight sleeps, the rooks can fly and eagles can hover, but as for him who sees all, whither can he fly?' Nikolsky's development of his basic idea led to ultimate absurdity and thus helped Chicherin to grope his way towards the opposite path. The initial stage in this process was individual anarchism, which at first seemed to Chicherin the height of revolutionary action. [. . .] But after discovering the futility of a philosophy based upon the notion of the individual personality as the supreme principle, he finally stumbled upon the opposite path, the understanding of oneself as part of a collective.

In the meantime, the moment when he left university was the beginning of the most difficult period in his life. He was in a state of utter depression, aggravated by poor physical health. He pored over Dostoevsky and Nietzsche. In addition to an agonising hatred of life and a cultivation of the superman, he became absorbed by music and mystical pantheism, studying the Gnostics in particular. During his first trip abroad since early childhood, he was captivated by the medieval towns he saw and he longed to sink into the ordered life of bygone ages. Between 1895 and 1897 he was fascinated by 'stylisation' and 'daily life', which were such an important influence on later, pre-war literature. In 1896, despite the indignant protests of his highly placed relatives, he joined the records office of the Ministry of Foreign Affairs, wishing to be as far removed as possible from the real work of the Tsarist State machine.

After two years of almost total despair, a sudden transformation came over Chicherin in 1897 induced by the famine and the official measures to hush up the news. He suddenly heard the voice of real life, the call to practical work and the struggle for social goals. He was seized by an eagerness to fight by the side of suffering humanity. But another seven years of inner ferment and spiritual zigzags were needed before he found the path of revolution. He began to be influenced by the labour movement as it engaged in massive strikes, but was at first put off by the primitive thinking of *Rabochaya Mysl*. The student disturbances of 1899 and Finland's struggle for a constitution confirmed this feeling. Then he was introduced by a close friend, a young neurologist, to some people whom the latter knew and who were members of revolutionary parties. He began to perform technical services for them. The aesthete in him clashed with the revolutionary and did not as yet unite in a synthesis. Kant came into conflict with Marx, of whom he had only a hazy understanding, but he was already groping for positive ideals, and the solution to his prolonged spiritual crisis was in sight. He became a close friend of his immediate superior in the Ministry archives, N. P. Pavlov-Silvansky, and together they prepared a history of the Russian Department of Foreign Affairs for its anniversary. After making a detailed study of Russian foreign policy throughout the nineteenth century, Chicherin undertook a special analysis of it during the reign of Alexander II, reading archive material, historical literature and memoirs. At the same time, the horrors of Russian reality came to appal him and brought home to him the impossibility of further passivity. His acute hatred of the old world, which had brought him so many torments, became unbearable.

At the beginning of 1904 he took the decision to emigrate with the aim of studying revolutionary literature, revolutionary parties and the Western labour movement, drawing practical conclusions, and then returning to Russia for revolutionary work. The technical help he had given to other revolutionaries put him in danger of arrest, but in spring 1904 he went abroad with a legal passport. At first he kept up his close ties with Pavlov-Silvansky, who was himself connected with the left-wing Kadets and SRs and forwarded material to him through the Ministry of Foreign Affairs. But he concealed his true aims from relatives and former acquaintances.

1904 saw the beginning of his new life. He devoured revolutionary literature with boundless enthusiasm, moved in revolutionary circles and associated himself with the German working class. He was most profoundly impressed by the personality of Karl Liebknecht, who rapidly became a close friend. He experienced the rapture of rebirth, the palpable reality of life with a clear goal where group interests predominated over personal ones. He had found the synthesis of ecstatic enthusiasm and cold realism, of the joy of living and of asceticism, of a crowning ideal and of daily, routine work. His earlier mental convulsions were cured by his awareness of being part of a collective. He had been accustomed to think historically since his youth and he now asked himself what was the immediate task of history and what was its prime driving force. He found the answer in Marxism. Immediately after his arrival abroad, he had intended joining the SRs, but their eclecticism, their lack of self-discipline and historical sense, their subjectivism, their reliance on feelings and emotions all quickly repelled him. The Marxist analysis gave him the key to all social phenomena. As the ideological bond uniting the *avant-garde* of the revolutionary class, Marxism linked him with the countless suffering masses. Where he had been suffocating in the world of the philistine and the *petit-bourgeois*, he now discovered the heroic man in the proletarian revolution. Whilst trying to win genuine acceptance among the core of the proletariat, as far as political conditions allowed, he came under the very strong ideological influence of German social democracy which was to weigh heavily on him for a long time. Already, however, he was painfully shocked by the *petit-bourgeois* mentality widespread among social democratic leaders. He only felt complete solidarity with Karl Liebknecht, to whom he became personally very attached.

In 1905 he joined the local Bolshevik organisation, the so-called Berlin section of the Foreign Organisational Committee (KZO). He had been induced to do this by the argument over the seizure of power. The Menshevik thesis of refusal to do this, even if the revolution should evolve to a point where it became feasible, seemed to him to contradict the fundamental requirements of the revolutionary struggle. He prepared to return to Russia illegally, but fell ill and was detained for a long time in Berlin by the after-effects. Meanwhile, the two factions had merged and the KZO ceased to exist. United groups of the RSDRP were formed abroad with a Central Foreign Bureau. In 1907 Chicherin was elected Secretary of the latter and attended the London Congress in this capacity. The huge influence of German social demoracy pushed him towards the Mensheviks, whose tactics he saw as closer to those of the Germans. While staying in the same hotel as Tyszka, he had long discussions with him every evening. The famous Krokhmal was the Menshevik delegate who had the strongest influence on him. Chicherin attempted to prove to Tyszka that the Bolshevik tactics of a permanent coalition with the left-wing SRs was nothing other than Jaurès's plan for a permanent union with the *petite-bourgeoisie*, only in a revolutionary situation. He preferred alliances of circumstance with everyone up to the Kadets, whilst preserving permanent freedom of action for the SDs. This he saw as being closer to the German tactics. All his past evolution had prepared him for a cult of the masses and he was now carried away by the idea of a workers' congress. Consequently, he was particularly hurt by the Bolshevik resolution forbidding agitation among the masses on this topic and he joined the group which soon came to call itself 'Golos SD'.

He was arrested in late 1907, tried by the court at Charlottenburg for being in possession of false papers, fined, and sentenced to be deported from Prussia. N. P. Pavlov-Silvansky wrote to him about the police material which had been received in connection with his case, from which it was apparent that he was the object of particular attention and that it would be impossible for him to return to Russia. Chicherin lived in secret for a while in Leiben, near Dresden, making occasional clandestine visits to Berlin. After the transfer of the editorial board of *Golos SD* to Paris, he lived in the French capital almost as a recluse. Everything paled for him by comparison with the problem of Party unity. As he conceived the proletariat to be the only historical force opposing the old world, he was acutely distressed by all the Party splits. It seemed that the very basis of his ideals was crumbling. But the campaign of the Vienna *Pravda* for unity struck him as superficial and appealing to mere sentiment, without fulfilling the historical necessity of fully overcoming essential disagreements. He sharply condemned the 'liquidators', and sought a counterweight to them in *Golos SD*, deploring the latter's tendency towards amorphism and its readiness to make concessions.

In 1908 he was particularly active in the summoning of the Basel congress of *émigré* groups. He saw the budgetary autonomy of these groups as the only means of preventing them from being split over the question of finance for this or that Party organ. He did his utmost to preserve the groups as Party rather than factional entities, insisted on them allocating 10 per cent of their funds to the Central Committee as laid down by the Party rules, and tried to sponsor papers by members of all factions. He devoted all his time to petty chores for the various groups, saying, 'When opposite sides are brought together, even the most trifling work has its satisfactions'. At the same time he became active in the fourteenth section of the French Socialist Party and made personal acquaintances among the French workers, but he was shocked by the intellectual approach of the former, and he was exasperated by the disdain for organisation among the latter. So he attempted to influence the young workers and gave them a great deal of his time.

In 1912 he welcomed the August bloc as a step towards Party unity, especially in view of its inclusion of the *Vperyod* group, and he put himself at the disposal of the Organisational Committee. Trotsky's resignation from the bloc was a particularly painful blow. Chicherin's hopes were dashed. Meanwhile, the growing middle-class attitudes of leaders of the second International caused him both anxiety and indignation. Pannekoek's pronouncements were too woolly for his liking, but he did welcome the attempt which they represented to resurrect the revolutionary labour movement. Both the opportunism of *Luch*[1] and the

[1] The legal Menshevik daily paper in St Petersburg.

rigidity of the German SD leadership sickened him. All his hopes were pinned on Liebknecht as the standard-bearer of a new era in the labour movement. Having been connected with the socialist youth movement since 1907, Chicherin found in it the embryo of a brighter future for the whole of the working class and did everything he could to encourage it. In 1914, whilst studying the state of the Party in Lille, he uncovered appalling *petit-bourgeois* careerism behind the veil of fine socialist phrases. With Bruno, the local socialist youth leader and a genuine revolutionary, he pleaded for a demonstration to be arranged in Lille against the war.

After the outbreak of hostilities, he left Lille for Brussels where he joined the so-called 'intransigent' *émigré* commission, inveighed against volunteers for military service, and then went to London. The war drove him into a searching reappraisal of his ideas. Both voting for war credits and enlistment in the army were clearly inadmissible. But what next? He could not accept the former anarchist programme of desertion. The Stuttgart and Copenhagen resolutions provided no answer as they left too much unsaid and were full of internal contradictions. He found that Bolsehvik literature supplied an outline of tasks connected with the war: in Russia, the destruction of the autocratic and aristocratic order; in Germany and Austria, the elimination of the last vestiges of monarchical feudalism; and in other countries, the social revolution itself. Thus in Germany, Austria and Russia there were still tasks outstanding for the revolutionary movement to perform within the limits of the bourgeois state. There could be no equation of them with the bourgeois, democratic countries. Confused by these complexities, Chicherin attempted to solve them by distinguishing between the concept of action and the concept of analysis: the SD Party had to direct political action against all governments alike, but in its theoretical assessment of the importance of military events for various states, it could draw distinctions between the latter.

This speculative house of cards, however, did not survive for long. Chicherin was visited in London by the Secretary of the Paris Union of Youth, whom he had known earlier as a brilliant revolutionary activist, and who told him that the war had opened his eyes to the common interests of capital and labour in every country. These words were a blinding revelation for Chicherin of the fact that the slogan of 'defencism' meant capitulation by labour to capital. As time passed, this fact was increasingly illustrated by the 'defencist' press and literature of all countries. He clearly perceived that British capitalists were exploiting this slogan to keep the British working class in their power. The political reality in Britain revealed with dazzling clarity the role of democracy as the most refined form of the domination of capital, and acquainted him with its innumerable ways of acting on the masses. He became once and for all convinced of the absolute necessity for a merciless struggle against all the warring bourgeois governments. He began regular contributions to *Nash Golos*, which was a stepping-stone for him. He considered that the Organisational Committee had become hopelessly entangled in the 'defencist' quagmire and had betrayed the cause of the Revolution. The Gvozdev saga[1] had been monstrous and the Mensheviks' behaviour in this affair had been shameful. He no longer had anything in common with them.

From the very first he had been close to the left wing of the British Labour Party, and with Petrov had been a passionate opponent of Hyndham. So he joyfully welcomed the creation of the British Socialist Party. Collections on behalf of Russian political prisoners were made, accompanied by agitation to counteract patriotic British attempts to whitewash Tsarism which were then at their height. This brought Chicherin into contact with the leftist minorities in the trade unions and he began to write for trade union papers.

The February Revolution shocked him by its crude 'defencist' refrains. The newly arrived representative in London of the so-called 'socialist bloc' was a 'defencist' of the vilest kind. The commission of Rusanov, Erlich, Goldenberg and Smirnov paraded about Europe in what Chicherin was convinced was a vain search for democracy. In London the main practical task was to organise the return of *émigrés*. Chicherin, who was by then secretary of most *émigré* organisations there, was also made secretary of the commission delegated to deal with this problem. The SR representative on it, Dr Gavronsky, a narrow-minded man capable of any mean action, had agreed with the *chargé d'affaires*, Nabokov, to try to delay the return of the Bolsheviks. At the height of the argument, Chicherin was detained without trial in Brixton jail, where he remained until he was exchanged for the British Ambassador, Buchanan, at the start of 1918. He returned to Petrograd in January, and thus began a fresh page in his life.

Chicherin was by birth an aristocrat, related to the Baltic nobility, and he received a solid university education, particularly in history; he began a diplomatic career before breaking irrevocably with his background and involving himself in the revolutionary movement. Amongst his fellow political exiles, however, Chicherin, who used the pseudonym Ornatsky during the emigration, always remained a strange figure: this Red aristocrat and former Tsarist civil servant cut something of a contrast in a

[1] K. A. Gvozdev, with B. O. Bogdanov, led a strong Workers' Group of 'liquidators', elected to the Central War Industry Committee in November 1915.

Bohemian milieu. It was precisely his qualities as a civil servant that were appreciated, however: he was given the important post of secretary of the social democrat organisation in exile. Chicherin was a Menshevik and among Lenin's staunchest opponents. In Paris, where, since he had contacts in the French socialist world, he spent much of his period of exile, he came into frequent and sharp conflict with the Bolshevik leader. A contemporary account of Lenin in Paris speaks of Chicherin thus:

> Chicherin was a picturesque figure among the *émigrés*. Easy, calm, slow and quiet of speech, he never got excited, never spoke with raised voice. He sincerely disliked the Bolsheviks, and considered them to be human monsters; he was persuaded that their existence constituted an abnormal phenomenon. He never lost control of himself or got angry, he did not speak at the big meetings, but he had his audience, with whom he kept up regular relations; he wrote a great number of letters to all the Menshevik orgnisations in existence outside Russia, and also to individual *émigrés* spread around Europe and America.[1]

Chicherin did not struggle against Lenin in *émigré* circles only, but fought him with all his strength on the international scene. After the Prague Congress in 1912, he was one of the first to lay accusations against Lenin before the ISB; on the eve of the First World War, he was utterly opposed to any attempt at a merger of Mensheviks and Bolsheviks. He was all the more dangerous as an opponent since he enjoyed good relations with and exercised some influence over a faction in the European socialist movement with which Lenin was attempting to establish points of contact—namely, the left and the extreme left.

Chicherin's sympathies extended, in fact, to revolutionary tendencies on an international level: he was in close touch with Pannekoek's extremist group in Bremen; he was friendly with Karl Liebknecht and, above all, played a major role in that seedbed of the left wing, the Socialist Youth International. He had solid contacts, likewise, in the French and Belgian socialist movements, and during the war in England, where he was one of the first members of the British Socialist Party.

He was not understood, but he was respected, by both his political friends and his enemies (including Lenin) in the divided and quarrelsome world of political *émigrés*. The war marks a turning-point in Chicherin's relations with the Bolshevik leadership. After a brief and falsely patriotic spell of hesitancy, Chicherin became a resolute inter-

[1] Alin, *Lénine à Paris*, p. 54.

nationalist,[1] and his political stand after 1916 was warmly applauded by Lenin. On returning to Russia in January 1918 after the adventure of his imprisonment in England, Chicherin joined the Bolshevik Party. The Commissar for Foreign Affairs greeted him with great warmth: his name was Trotsky. 'Chicherin arrived in Moscow at the most opportune moment,' he wrote later. Indeed, Chicherin arrived in the middle of controversy and crisis in the leadership over the Brest–Litovsk agreement. Trotsky opposed the agreement and wanted to resign from his post as Commissar for Foreign Affairs. He saw Chicherin as his ideal replacement, particularly since Lenin held Chicherin's diplomatic talents in high esteem. With a sigh of relief, Trotsky confessed, 'I handed the diplomatic helm over to him'.[2] He was immediately appointed Deputy Commissar and on 30 May 1918 became head of the Commissariat for Foreign Affairs. It was he who signed the Brest–Litovsk peace treaty, and he ran Soviet foreign policy with a great deal of skill. His name is closely involved in all Soviet diplomatic initiatives up to 1927. He led the Soviet delegations to Genoa and Lausanne, and he engineered the Rapallo agreement. Even after the Revolution, Chicherin remained faithful to himself and to his simple way of life. He was a tireless worker, an excellent functionary but a hopeless organiser: he tried to do everything himself, down to the last detail, and ended up being overwhelmed. He was a fragile man, easily excited, unsure of himself and of his position; a sensitive but very intelligent man whose opinions and thoughts were highly charged with emotion.

His predecessor had regarded his job in terms of politics and revolution; Chicherin's style was that of diplomat and high functionary. In his memoirs, he does not hide that he supported no particular political line: acting according to Lenin's directives, he was content to be a skilful executant. This did not change under Stalin. Louis Fischer has described his foreign policy line thus: 'In Chicherin's concept, Germany was the pivot of Soviet foreign policy and Asia its special concern . . . In broad terms, Chicherin's policy was isolationist and anti-West. . . .'[3] Chicherin remained outside the internal struggles in the Party leadership, despite the fact that he was a member of the CC after the fourteenth and fifteenth Congresses (1925 and 1927 respectively). Suffering from a serious illness, he spent the year 1928–9 under treatment in Germany and was released from his duties 'on his own request' in 1930. He died in 1936.

G. H.

[1] See R. K. Debo, 'The Making of a Bolshevik: Georgii Chicherin in England, 1914–1918', *Slavic Review* XXV, no. 4 (December 1966), pp. 651–62.

[2] L. Trotsky, *My Life* (New York, 1960), p. 348.

[3] L. Fischer, *The Soviets in World Affairs* (Princeton, 1960), p. 12.

FELIX EDMUNDOVICH DZERZHINSKY
(autobiography)

I was born in 1877, the son of a small landowner. I went to school at the Vilno Gymnasium. In 1894, when I was in the seventh form, I entered an SD self-education circle, joined the Lithuanian SD Party the following year, and was the leader of circles for apprentice workers and craftsmen (who knew me as 'Jacek'), whilst at the same time studying Marxism. I chose to leave school at the end of the eighth class in 1896 so as to be closer to the working masses. During my time at the Gymnasium, I was constantly at loggerheads with the administration, being of a hasty and impulsive nature. Again in 1896, I asked the comrades to send me among the masses and not confine me to militancy in the circles. At that time there was friction between the intelligentsia and the workers' leaders. The latter demanded that the intellectuals should teach them general knowledge and how to read and write, without meddling in things that did not concern them, that is the masses. Despite this, I succeeded in becoming an agitator and reached previously untouched workers by talking to them in their bars in the evenings.

In early 1897 the Party sent me to Kovno, an industrial town where there was as yet no SD organisation and where the local group of the Polish Socialist Party (PPS) had been netted by the police. Here I infiltrated myself among the hard core of the factory workers, coming across appalling poverty and exploitation, particularly of female labour, and it was here that I learnt by practice how to organise strikes. During the second half of the year I was arrested in the street after being betrayed for ten roubles by an apprentice. Not wishing to reveal where I was living, I gave my name as Jebrovski, and in 1898 I was deported to Vyatka province for three years. First I went to Nolinsk, but then I was sent over 300 miles further north to the village of Kaigorodsk as a punishment for obstinate behaviour, a row with the police, and also for having found work at a tobacco factory. In August 1899 I escaped in a boat and returned to Vilno, where I found that the Lithuanian SDs were negotiating a union with the PPS. I was violently hostile to nationalism, and the fact that in 1898, whilst I was in prison, the Lithuanian SDs had not joined the RSDRP, was in my view the worst of crimes. Moreover, I had written a letter to this effect from prison to the leader of the Lithuanian social democrats, Dr Domashevich.

When I reached Vilno, my former comrades were already in exile and students had taken over the leadership of the movement. I was not allowed to make contact with the workers and I was pressed to go abroad, being put in touch with some smugglers who drove me by coach along the Vilkomirsk road to the frontier. In the coach I met a boy who, for ten roubles, managed to obtain a passport for me in a small town. I went to the railway station and took a ticket for Warsaw, where I had the address of a member of the Bund. At that time Warsaw had only PPS and Bund groups, the SD organisation having been decimated. I made contact with the workers and rapidly succeeded in re-establishing our organisation, winning over from the PPS first some shoemakers, and then whole groups of carpenters, bakers, engineering and leather workers. At this point, the clash with the PPS came into the open and inevitably ended in our victory even though we had neither financial support, nor literature, nor the intelligentsia at our disposal. At that time I was active under the names of 'The Astronomer' and 'Franek'. In February 1900 I was arrested at a meeting and held first in the Warsaw citadel, and then in the Siedlce prison. In 1902 I was exiled for five years to eastern Siberia, but at Vekholenko, on the way to Vilyuisk, I escaped with the SR Sladkopevets and made my way abroad with the help of the Bund.

Soon after my arrival, in August of the same year, a conference of the Polish and Lithuanian SD Party was held in Berlin, at which it was decided to publish *Czerwony Sztandar*. I settled in Krakow under the pseudonym 'Jozef' to organise the smuggling of Party materials over the border. Until 1905, I made several visits to Russian Poland, at first for clandestine activity and then as a member of the Main Directorate of the Polish and Lithuanian SD Party. In July 1905 I was arrested and only released under the October amnesty. In 1906 I was a delegate to the 'unifying' Congress of the RSDRP in Stockholm and entered the Central Committee as representative for Poland and Lithuania. In late 1906 I was arrested in Warsaw, and released on bail in June 1907. On 13 April 1908 I was rearrested, tried on two counts, one old and one new, and in late 1909 I was deported to Taseyevka in Siberia. I spent only seven days there before escaping abroad via Warsaw. I settled afresh in Krakow, and visited Russian Poland several times. In 1912 I was arrested in Warsaw, tried for escaping from exile, and condemned to three years' hard labour. In 1914 I was transferred to Oryol, where I served the remainder of my sentence. Then I was sent to Moscow in 1916, tried for my Party activity during the period 1910–12, and a further six years' hard labour were added to my sentence.

The February Revolution freed me from the central Moscow prison. Until August 1917, I worked in Moscow, and then in that month I was one of the Moscow delegates to the RSDRP(b) Congress at which I was elected to the CC. I remained in Petrograd. In the October Revolution, I was a member of the Military Revolutionary Committee, and then I was entrusted with the task of organising the *Vecheka* [Extraordinary Commission for the Struggle against Sabotage and Counter-Revolution]. I was appointed its Chairman, holding at the same time the post of Commissar for Internal Affairs. From 14 April 1921 I was also Commissar for Transport, and then in 1924 became head of the VSNKh of the USSR. I have been a member of the CC of the RKP(b) continuously since 1917. Until then, I was a professional, clandestine revolutionary spending in all eleven years in exile, deportation, hard labour and prison.

In March 1917, the Revolution freed Dzerzhinsky from prison in Moscow, and he then joined the Bolshevik Party for the first time. In this experienced Polish revolutionary, Lenin's Party acquired a first-class recruit. He had behind him twenty years' experience of revolutionary work and eleven years of prison and exile. As well as a fanatic and efficient organiser, Dzerzhinsky was 'a man of strong willpower . . . and explosive passion. His energy was kept under pressure by constant electrical charges, as it were. . . . Despite this nervous tension, Dzerzhinsky did not suffer from periods of depression or apathy. He seemed always to be at full steam. Lenin once compared him to "the fieriest of thoroughbred horses" ' (Trotsky). Lenin had known him since 1906, and held his qualities as a revolutionary in high esteem. In 1906, Dzerzhinsky had been one of Rosa Luxemburg's lieutenants, and he remained attached to her for many years. His pro-Bolshevik sympathies date from this period, and he supported Lenin's Party in its struggle within the Russian Party. After 1911, when the schism in the Polish Party brought out and added to Rosa Luxemburg's hostility to Lenin, Dzerzhinsky was torn between his sympathies and his loyalties: so he supported the Bolsheviks in Russian affairs while continuing to fight against them with Rosa Luxemburg in Polish affairs.

In 1917 his entry into the Bolshevik Party was wholehearted, and he put all his talents and ardour at the service of the October Revolution. In July 1917 he was elected by Congress to the Central Committee, and was called to contribute to the running of the Party as a member of the Secretariat. In the turbulent period that preceded the October Revolution, when the Party's leadership was split, he gave all his support to Lenin, who was in fact in the minority. At the decisive moment of the Extraordinary Central Committee meeting on 16 October, he was one of those who defended Lenin's resolution against Kamenev and Zinoviev, and supported the insurrection and immediate action. He then became a member of the Central Committee's RVS, which became part of the Petrograd Soviet RVS, and he was an energetic and active member. On 24 October he was given the task of watching over the actions and orders of the Provisional government. Then in December 1917 he was entrusted with the thankless and heavy job of organising and running the famous Extraordinary All-Russian Commission for the Struggle against Counter-Revolution (*Vecheka*) which later became the GPU, the political police which Dzerzhinsky continued to run. During the Civil War, this energetic man was called on in cases of extreme difficulty or when exceptional measures were thought necessary—for example, at the time of the Perm catastrophe on the Eastern Front, in 1919, and in the winter of 1920 when he had to face enormous transport problems caused by snowstorms.

He was an important personage in the Central Committee, and played a part in the internal struggles that the Bolshevik Party went through in the years immediately following the Revolution. As a left-wing communist, he opposed peace negotiations with the Germans in January 1918, and stood against Lenin to the extent of demanding his dismissal.

At the CC meeting on 11 [NS 24] January 1918 he delivered a violent diatribe against Lenin, accusing him of 'doing under cover what Kamenev and Zinoviev had done in October'.[1]

Within the CC he moved closer to Trotsky's position and in the end voted for the motion of conciliation. Until 1921 he supported the left-wing tendency in the CC and, according to Trotsky, was particularly attracted towards the leader of the left himself in 1920–1. In 1922 he opposed Lenin's principle of self-determination, and came closer to Stalin on the question of nationalities. In the celebrated Georgian affair, in which the Caucasian CC came up against the integrationist policies of Stalin and Sergo Ordzhonikidze, Dzerzhinsky, who was in charge of the inquiry commission set up by the CC, manoeuvred in favour of the Commissar for Nationalities.[2] There is nothing surprising about this alliance: as regards the question of nationalities, Dzerzhinsky was still faithful to Rosa Luxemburg. Lenin, though bedridden, realised that an attempt was being made to mislead him, and he riposted by making Stalin and Dzerzhinsky carry all responsibility for the policy of Russification. This opprobrium only served to bring Dzerzhinsky closer to Stalin, whom he aided during the struggle against the opposition. In October 1923 he headed the CC's sub-commission which presented a report on the political situation. The clarity of his statements inside the sub-commission on the death of democracy in the Party's internal affairs are in strong contrast to the final report which demanded a strengthening of repressive measures and which led Trotsky to take an even clearer stand. Indeed, for the latter democracy could only exist within the Party.

Stalin did all he could to retain the support of the influential

---

[1] *Les Bolchéviks et la Révolution d'octobre* (Paris, 1964), p. 239.
[2] See M. Lewin, *Lenin's Last Struggle* (New York, 1969).

Dzerzhinsky, who said himself that he 'could only love and hate totally, never by halves', since his heart was 'completely Bolshevik'.

Dzerzhinsky had always dreamt of a position in the management of the economy, and in 1924 Stalin made the dream come true by appointing him President of the Sovnarkhoz. He remained president of the GPU none the less. In his post at the Sovnarkhoz, he was one of the architects of NEP. He sympathised with the right wing under Bukharin's leadership, and maintained his alliance with Stalin. As an alternate member of the Politburo, to which he was elected in 1924 and re-elected the following year, and as a member of the Orgburo, he played an active part in the struggle against the left opposition and the United Opposition. He was overworked, and reached a degree of strain that made life with him more and more difficult. He died on 20 July 1926 of a heart attack that struck him in the middle of a particularly turbulent meeting of the Central Committee.

Who was this man Dzerzhinsky, whose name became, during the 1920's, the synonym of terror, who was the bogeyman of Western public opinion? Not only in bourgeois eyes, but also for the socialists, left-wingers included, Dzerzhinsky was hateful; the Austrian socialist Oskar Blum, compared the echo of his name with the spirit of Banquo in *Macbeth*.[1] For his friends, however, Dzerzhinsky was the very typification of Bolshevism, firm, hard and uncorrupted, acting only in the service of his revolutionary ideals. His personal diary and letters which appeared a few years ago show the 'Red hangman' as a complex figure, capable of great tenderness towards children and simple folk, believing in friendship and torn apart as well as utterly convinced by the necessity of the tasks he had to accomplish.[2] It was not mere chance that he was appointed head of the Cheka: he had asked for this 'dirty work himself, out of masochism as much as out of the spy-mania that haunted him— he could see Okhrana men everywhere. Although he thought him excessively harsh, Lenin was convinced of Dzerzhinsky's integrity and blind obedience to Party discipline, and thus entrusted him with this responsibility. With death in his heart he was prepared to strike down all those the Party considered its enemies—even if they were his friends. Radek, who belonged to the opposition in 1926, said this on learning of the death of a man who had been his comrade and adversary for many years: 'Felix died just in time. He was a dogmatist. He would not have shrunk from reddening his hands in our blood.' But nobody in the opposition doubted Dzerzhinsky's 'uprightness'.[3]

G. H.

[1] O. Blum, *Russische Köpfe* (Berlin, 1923), p. 103.
[2] *Dnievnik. Pisma Rodniym*, 2nd ed. (Moscow, 1958).
[3] V. Serge, *Memoirs of a Revolutionary*, p. 221.

ADOLF ABRAMOVICH IOFFE (literary pseudonym: V. KRYMSKY)
(autobiography)

I was born on 10 October 1883 in Simferopol (Crimea), the son of a wealthy merchant. I was still studying in a Gymnasium at the end of the 1890s, when Russia witnessed an upsurge in the labour movement in general, and strikes in particular, and when the well-known persecution of students began. Nevertheless I joined the revolutionary movement and the RSDRP. As a result of this, by 1903, when I left the Gymnasium, I had become 'politically unreliable' and I could not enter a single Russian university. Therefore, I went abroad to study in Berlin where I entered the Medical Faculty, continuing at the same time my studies of the social and political sciences and participating in both the German and the Russian SD movements, as a member of the auxiliary RSDRP group in Berlin.

In 1904 I was instructed by the Central Committee to convey litera-ture to Baku and to conduct propaganda there. I joined the Baku SD organisation, but I had to leave Transcaucasia in the same year to avoid arrest, and I was sent to Moscow for the same sort of work. I was soon exposed there, too, so I took refuge abroad, where I arrived immediately after the events of 9 January 1905. I straightaway returned to Russia and took part in the Revolution in various towns, first in the north and then in the south. I was in the Crimea at the time of the Potyomkin mutiny and I subsequently arranged the escape from the Sebastopol military prison of K. Feldman, one of the mutineers. After this, I again had to take refuge abroad. In Berlin, after the Stockholm Party Congress, I was designated one of the four members of the first 'Foreign Bureau of the Central Committee of the RSDRP'.

In May 1906, on a directive from the Imperial German Chancellor von Bülow, I was expelled from Germany as an 'undesirable alien'. I left to go back to Moscow, but as I was being hunted by the police there I was again obliged to emigrate, this time to Zurich, where I entered the Law Faculty, maintaining at the same time my revolutionary and Party activity. I returned to Russia in 1907, only to be forced to emigrate in 1908. I settled in Vienna, where Trotsky and I began to publish our *Pravda*. On behalf of the editorial board, I visited all the Party organisations in Russia in 1910. I made a similar trip in 1911 and in 1912, when an organisational commission was set up to summon an all-Party congress, I was given a seat on it to represent the *Pravda* group and its editors. In this capacity I made another clandestine tour of Russia to urge the calling of this congress. During my stay in Odessa in

1912, I was arrested with the whole of the local Party organisation.

In the absence of material proof, I spent ten months in solitary confinement and was then sentenced to administrative exile in Tobolsk province in the far north for four years. Following the arrest in Alexandria in Egypt of the editor of the journal *Moryak*, with whom I had been in correspondence as co-editor of *Pravda*, and the discovery of letters signed by a V. Krymsky in the journal's archives, proof that Krymsky and Ioffe were one and the same person could be established to the satisfaction of a court. Consequently, in 1913 I was rearrested in Siberia and accused under Article 102 of being involved in the affair of the 'Black Sea Union of Sailors'. In court I admitted my membership of the Party but, in view of the recent outbreak of war and leniency in sentences, I was not condemned to hard labour but to exile for life in Siberia, together with deprivation of all the civic privileges to which I had been entitled by birth. I was not, however, exiled. On the basis of the papers from the trial, an indictment for membership of the Party was drawn up and I was transferred to the hard labour block. In 1916 I appeared in court for the second time, and in view of my earlier confession of Party membership, I was again sentenced to exile in Siberia. The place chosen was Kansk district, Yeniseysk province, and as a result of the shortage of doctors caused by the war, I was compulsorily appointed head of the hospital at a mica mine in the very heart of the taiga. From Siberia I continued to contribute to various illegal papers. As soon as rumours of the 1917 Revolution reached me, I left the mine and, after a short stay in Kansk to organise revolutionary activity there, I left for Petrograd.

There, Trotsky, myself and some others began to produce the paper *Vperyod*. Then I represented the Bolsheviks successively on the Petrograd city Duma, the Petrograd Soviet, the VTsIK, and the Constituent Assembly (as member for Pskov); I was a participant in the 'Democratic Conference' and the 'Pre-Parliament'. At the sixth Party Congress in July 1917, I was elected a member of the CC of the RSDRP(b) and then, after its change of name, of the RKP(b). During the October rising, I was chairman of the Military Revolutionary Committee. When the latter was abolished, transferring its powers to the Council of People's Commissars, I was sent to Brest-Litovsk as head of the peace delegation. I concluded and signed the armistice with Germany, Austro-Hungary, Turkey and Bulgaria, but after the German ultimatum I refused to sign the peace treaty, declaring that this was not an agreed peace but a dictated peace, which must be resisted with all available means. At the end of the Brest negotiations, I was Commissar for Foreign Affairs and Social Security, and then I was sent as envoy to Berlin. There I held talks with the German government and concluded an additional agree-

ment supplementing the Brest peace treaty. Next I undertook negotiations with Turkey. I took an active part in the preparations for the
German revolution and on 6 November 1918, three days before the
rising, the whole embassy and I were expelled from Germany.

After the trimph of the German revolution I made contact with the
new German government and the Berlin Soviet of Workers' Deputies
from Minsk and Borisov, where our train was held up, but I did not
succeed in returning to Germany. When the All-German Congress of
Workers' and Soldiers' Deputies was convened, I was sent as head of the
VTsIK delegation, but we were not allowed into Berlin. After this, I
was dispatched to Lithuania and Byelorussia as a member of the CC to
direct Party work there and further the formation of a Lithuanian-
Byelorussian republic. Immediately before the occupation of Vilno by
the Poles, I returned to Moscow.

Soon I was sent to the Ukraine in my capacity as member of the
Defence Council and Commissar for Soviet Socialist Inspection. With
the capture of Kiev by Denikin, I retreated with the army and other
members of the Council to Chernigov, whence I returned to Moscow
after the whole of the Ukraine had been overrun by Denikin and
Petlyura. I was directed to Petrograd to organise the newly formed
Rabkrin in accordance with my plans and methods. I also joined the
Petrograd Party Committee, and during the advance of Yudenich and
the Estonians, I was a member of the Council for the Internal Defence
of Petrograd. When Yudenich had been routed, I was sent to Yuriev to
conclude a peace with Estonia. Within a short space of time, I also
headed delegations to discuss peace terms with Latvia, Lithuania, and,
in 1921, Poland. When they had all been agreed, I was sent to Turkestan
as Chairman of the Turkestan Commission of the VTsIK and the
Turkestan Bureau of the CC.

I toured the whole of Turkestan, Bukhara and Khorezm before
being recalled to Moscow and dispatched to Genoa as a presidium
member of the Soviet delegation. When talks there were ended, I was
made Ambassador Extraordinary to China and Japan, and led the
delegation which negotiated with Japan in Ch'ang-Ch'un (Manchuria).
This was concluded despite serious illness on my part, and I returned to
Peking for talks with the Chinese government. Then Viscount Goto, a
member of the Japanese House of Lords and Mayor of Tokyo, invited
me to Japan ostensibly for medical treatment, but in fact for diplomatic
reasons. At first I had unofficial conversations with him, and then official
ones with Kawakami, a representative of the Japanese government. My
health at this time deteriorated to such an extent that I was obliged to call
a halt to these talks and return to Moscow. There I fell gravely ill and

in spring 1924 I was taken to Vienna for treatment. When I had recovered somewhat, I was sent to London as a presidium member of the Soviet delegation, and after a first agreement with Great Britain had been signed, I was left in London to prepare a second. Then I was appointed Plenipotentiary in Vienna.

During the whole of my Party and revolutionary career, I have contributed to a large number of Party newspapers and journals, and edited some of them. I have also written a few pamphlets, of which the chief ones are: *Local Self-Government, The Collapse of Menshevism, The Foreign Policy of the Soviet Government, The Peace Offensive, The Genoa Conference, From Genoa to the Hague, The Last Utopian,* and *England Today.*

Ioffe was a son of the upper Crimean bourgoisie, a member of the Karaite sect, and a brilliant intellectual who at a very young age already had behind him many years as a militant and many positions of responsibility. He had, moreover, donated his entire inheritance to the Party. From 1908 he belonged to the small group of Trotsky's disciples, and he helped the leader publish *Pravda* in Vienna; Ioffe also financed the newspaper in part.

Afflicted with nervous disorders and suffering from violent attacks of neurasthenia, Ioffe was treated in Vienna by the psychoanalyst Alfred Adler. Trotsky took a great liking to him and did all he could to give him confidence in himself. He returned to Russia in 1912 to carry out secret work, but was arrested and deported. He was not freed until the February Revolution. Ioffe had never been a Bolshevik but joined the Party as a member of *Mezhrayonka* and went straight to the top leadership.

The thankless task of negotiating the peace treaty of Brest-Litovsk with the Germans fell to him. He did it reluctantly out of discipline. At the CC meeting in January 1918 he was the only one who instead of abstaining voted against Lenin's motion in favour of resuming talks despite the ultimatum. Nevertheless, Trotsky managed to win him over to the position that Soviet power must not be jeopardised for the sake of a hypothetical German revolution. Thus Ioffe resumed the Brest-Litovsk talks and brought them to their conclusion. Ioffe's talents as a diplomat, which Lenin appreciated highly, were thenceforth apparent. His nervous illness seemed to disappear; as his friend Trotsky said, the Revolution 'did much more than psychoanalysis to liberate Ioffe from his complexes'.[1]

Ioffe was chosen as the first Ambassador to Germany. For the Bolshevik government, this was a post of strategic importance: the chances of

[1] Trotsky, *My Life,* p. 220.

world revolution depended on Germany. He took up his post on 20 April 1918. In May he transmitted to the German government the Soviet proposal for economic and political negotiations. The economic negotiations had no great outcome, but on the political front, however, Germany, who wished to diminish her isolation in the world, accepted an alliance with the Soviet Union, which was duly signed by Ioffe on 27 August 1918.

In Berlin Ioffe acted in the interests of world revolution. He directed both revolutionary proganada and political and financial aid to the German revolutionary movement. The German government was justifiably afraid that the Soviet Embassy was becoming a centre for revolutionary propaganda. On 6 November Ioffe was obliged to leave his post in Berlin and diplomatic relations were broken off. Upon his return he declared with pride: 'I too have helped within my own means towards the victory of the German Revolution.'

The most diverse tasks then fell to this 'always meticulous' man.[1] He was an organiser and political commissar entrusted with special missions in various fields, but above all remained one of the builders of the Soviet diplomatic corps: the name of Ioffe is connected with all the major points in its history, his signature is to be found beneath every important treaty.

This kind of life once again wrecked his health. When his illness no longer permitted him to take up diplomatic posts, he was appointed Rector of the Chinese University in Moscow. The Party's internal crisis only worsened Ioffe's nervous state—for he was above all a political man. Diplomacy, like any other public service, represented in his eyes a mission to accomplish but not a career.

He had 'a bearded, Assyrian face, powerful lips, and eyes that disconcerted the newcomer, so severe was their squint', according to Victor Serge.[2] Ioffe found enough time to write, to reflect and to pronounce on the major problems of his day. He remained a faithful supporter of Trotsky, and for a short period recommenced his collaboration with him. He was Trotsky's deputy on the Glavkontseskom.

The way he ended his life bears the mark of this unconditional loyalty. His illness (polyneuritis had made him a semi-invalid), and Trotsky also, prevented him from becoming as deeply involved in the opposition struggle as he would have liked.

That is why he planned, after Trotsky's expulsion from the CC and then from the Party, to give his death a political significance. He committed suicide on 16 November 1927. He left a farewell letter to Trotsky

[1] See Fischer, *The Soviets in World Affairs*.
[2] op. cit., p. 182.

– his political testament – in which he encouraged him to persevere in a struggle he considered a just one, to 'follow the example of Ilyich', and to acquire the qualities which had been the secret of his victory: 'intransigence, obstinacy'. His funeral was the pretext for the last public demonstration of the opposition.[1]

G. H.

[1] ibid., pp. 229–30.

ALEKSANDRA MIKHAILOVNA KOLLONTAI

(autobiography)

The first woman to join a government and the first woman representative and Ambassador Extraordinary of her country.

I was born in 1872 and grew up in a land-owning gentry family. My father was a Russian general, and Ukrainian by birth. My mother was a native of Finland and came from a peasant family. I spent my childhood and youth in St Petersburg and Finland. As the youngest in the family, and moreover the only daughter (my mother had been married twice), I was an object of special concern for all our numerous family with its patriarchal traditionalism. I was not allowed to go to a Gymnasium for fear that I should meet 'undesirable elements'. At sixteen I passed the school-leaving certificate and began to attend private courses and lectures given by professors of history and literature. I was also forbidden to go to the Bestuzhev lectures. I studied a great deal, mainly under the guidance of the famous literary historian, Viktor Petrovich Ostrogorsky. He considered that I had literary talent and urged me to enter journalism. I married very early, partly as a protest against the will of my parents. But three years later I separated from my husband, the engineer V. Kollontai, taking my little boy with me (my maiden name is Domontovich).

By this time, my political convictions had already begun to take shape. I worked in a number of cultural and educational societies which then (this was in the middle of the 1890s) bore the character of a cloak for clandestine ventures. Thus while working in the 'Mobile Museum of Educational Textbooks' we made contact with prisoners in the Schlüsselburg fortress. Our work in the educational society, and the lessons we gave to the workers, provided us with the opportunity for rich, personal contact with the latter. In addition we arranged charity evenings to raise funds for the political Red Cross.

1896 was the decisive year in my life. In the spring of that year I visited Narva and the famous Kremholm textile works. The enslavement of the 12,000 weavers had a shattering effect on me. At that time I was not yet a Marxist and was more inclined to Populism and terrorism, but after my visit to Narva, I set about studying Marxism and economics. The two first legal Marxist journals, *Nachalo* and *Novoye Slovo*, were launched at that time, and they opened my eyes. The path for which I had been searching with particular insistence since Narva, was found.

The famous strike of textile-workers in 1896 in St Petersburg also greatly contributed to a clarification of my political views. 36,000 workers, male and female, were involved, and E. D. Stasova, myself and many other comrades organised collections and help for the strikers. This visible sign of the growing consciousness of the proletariat, for all its servitude and lack of rights, finally decided me to join the Marxist camp. I did not as yet, however, undertake any literary activity in this field, nor did I take any active part in the movement. I considered myself insufficiently prepared. It was in 1898 that I wrote my first article, 'The Foundations of Education according to Dobrolyubov'. It appeared in the September edition of the journal *Obrazovaniye* which at that time still bore a pedagogical character, but which later became one of the most restrained legal organs of Marxist thought. Its editor was A. Ya. Ostrogorsky. On 13 August of the same year, I went abroad to study social and economic sciences.

I entered the university in Zurich to work under Professor Herkner, whose book on the labour movement (in its second edition) had interested me. A characteristic feature was that the deeper I delved into the laws of economics and the more I became a true 'orthodox' Marxist, the more my professor and tutor moved to the right and the further he departed from Marx's revolutionary theory, so that by the fifth edition of his book, he had become a real renegade. This was that strange period when the German Party saw the emergence of tendencies such as 'practical conciliationism', opportunism, 'revisionism', all deftly initiated by Bernstein. My worthy professor echoed Bernstein and praised him to the skies. But I resolutely sided with the 'leftists'. I became a passionate supporter of Kautsky, devouring every edition of his paper *Neue Zeit* and Rosa Luxemburg's articles, especially her pamphlet *Social Revolution or Social Reforms*, where she demolished Bernstein's time-serving theories.

On the advice of my professor and armed with introductions from him, I set off for England in 1899 to 'study' the English labour movement, which was supposed to convince me that truth was on the side of the opportunists, and not the 'leftists'. I had an introduction to Sidney and Beatrice Webb themselves, but after our first conversations I realised that we were not talking the same language, and I set out to see the labour movement for myself without their guidance. What I saw convinced me that they were wrong. I realised the acute social contradictions existing in England and the impotence of the reformists to cure them by trade union tactics or by the famous 'settlements' such as Toynbee Hall, the co-operatives and clubs, etc. I returned from England even more persuaded of the correctness of the 'leftists' and the 'true' Marxist, and I went not to Zurich but to Russia. I had made contacts with underground militants and I wanted to try my hand at the real thing, to apply myself to the struggle.

When I had left Russia in 1898, all the *avant-garde* of the intelligentsia and students had been Marxist-inclined. Their heroes were Beltov, Struve and Tugan-Baranovsky. A fierce struggle was taking place between the Populists and the Marxists. The up-and-coming elements – Ilin (Lenin), Maslov, Bogdanov and others – were providing a theoretical basis for the tactics which had been formed underground by the SD Party. I returned with the optimistic hope of finding myself among like-minded people, but the Russia of autumn 1899 was not the Russia of previous years. The honeymoon unity between legal and underground Marxism had come to an end. Legal Marxism was openly turning to the defence of large, industrial capital. The 'left wing' was going underground, defending with ever increasing determination the revolutionary tactics of the proletariat. The passion for Marx was replaced among students and the intelligentsia by a no less ardent passion for 'Bernsteinianism' and revisionism. Nietzsche began to come into fashion with his 'aristocracy of the spirit'.

I remember as if it were yesterday an evening arranged in the flat of E. D. Stasova's father to raise funds for the political Red Cross. Struve gave a lecture on Bernstein. It was a 'select' audience including many underground activists, and yet Struve's lecture received sympathetic, even fulsome praise. Only Avilov spoke against him. All the leading lights and 'names' of that period supported Struve. I took the floor, although this was granted reluctantly, as to someone little known. My defence of the 'orthodox' (leftists) was too heated. It met with general disapproval and even an indignant shrugging of the shoulders. One person declared it was unprecedented impudence to speak against such generally accepted authorities as Struve and Tugan. Another thought that such a speech played into the hands of the reactionaries. A third believed that we had already outgrown 'phrases' and must become sober politicians. [. . .] During this period I wrote articles against Bernstein, about the role of the class struggle, and in defence of the 'true' Marxists for the journal *Nauchnoye Obozreniye*, but the censors indicated in red and blue pencil that my articles were unsuitable for publication.

Then I decided to devote myself to research in economics. My links with Finland were still strong. The Finnish people were suffering a black period of violence and oppression under the Governor, General Bobrikov. The independence of this small people had been shaken to its foundations. The constitution and laws of the country were being blatantly infringed. A struggle was in progress between the Finnish people and the Russian autocracy. Both intellectually and emotionally I was wholeheartedly on the side of the Finns. I saw in Finland the growing but scarcely recognised strength of the industrial proletariat. Noticing the signs of sharpening class contradictions and the formation of a new, workers' Finland in opposition to the nationalists, bourgeois parties – whether pro-Swedish, pro-Finnish, or in favour of the Young Finn movement – I helped the Finnish comrades to organise their first strike fund. My articles about Finland appeared in 1900 in the German economic journal *Soziale Praxis*, as well as in *Nauchnoye Obozreniye* and *Obrazovaniye*. One article, a concrete, statistical analysis, was carried in *Russkoye Bogatstvo*. Simultaneously during the years 1900–3, I collected material for my large economic and statistical work on Finland, which had the innocent title of *The Life of Finnish Workers*. Naturally, these years were not solely devoted to literary and scientific work. I had also to undertake underground activity, but here I remained more on the fringe —organising circles beyond the Nevskaya Zastava, compiling appeals, storing and disseminating underground literature, etc.

In 1901 I went abroad. I met Kautsky, Rosa Luxemburg, the Lafargues in Paris, and Pleknanov in Geneva. An unsigned article by me about Finland appeared in *Zarya*, and another article appeared under the pseudonym 'Elena Malin' in Kautsky's *Neue Zeit*. Since then I have remained in regular contact with foreign comrades. At the beginning of 1903 my book *The Life of Finnish Workers* was published—an economic analysis of the state of Finnish workers and the development of Finland's economy. Written in the Marxist spirit, it was greeted sympathetically by the underground militants and disapprovingly by many legal Marxists.

In 1903 I made my first speech at a public meeting organised by students on St Tatiana's day, where I contrasted the idealist philosophy with the socialist one. In summer 1903 I went abroad again. This was the time of peasant rebellion in Russia, and the workers in the south were rising. Heady ideas were abroad. Two antagonistic forces were coming into ever more bitter conflict: underground Russia marching towards the Revolution, and the autocracy stubbornly clinging to power. Struve's *Osvobozhdeniye* group occupied an intermediate position. Many of my close friends were going over to *Osvobozhdeniye*, considering pure socialism a utopia, given the Russia of that time. I had to make a clean break with recent comrades-in-arms and like-minded associates. Among socialist *émigrés*, the arguments were no longer between Populists and Marxists as before, but between Mensheviks and Bolsheviks. I had friends in both camps. I was closer in spirit to Bolshevism, with its uncompromising belief in revolution, but the personal charm of Plekhanov restrained me from condemnation of Menshevism.

On my return from abroad in 1903, I joined neither of the Party groupings, offering to be used as an agitator for proclamations etc. by both factions. Bloody Sunday, 1905, found me on the street. I was going with the demonstrators to the Winter Palace, and the picture of the massacre of unarmed, working folk is for ever imprinted on my memory. The unusually bright January sunshine, trusting, expectant faces . . . the fateful signal from the troops drawn up round the palace . . . pools of blood on the white snow . . . the whips, the whooping of the gendarmes, the dead, the injured . . . children shot. . . . The Party Committee had been very wary and mistrustful of the demonstration of 9 January. At specially organised workers' meetings, many comrades had attempted to dissuade workers from participating, seeing in it a 'provocation' and a trap. I thought that we had to go. This demonstration was an act of self-determination by the working class, a school of revolutionary activity. And I was inspired by the decisions of the Amsterdam Congress on the question of 'mass actions'.

After the January days, underground work went forward with new energy and strength. The Bolsheviks in St Petersburg began to publish a clandestine paper (the name of which I forget), for which I not only contributed articles but also did technical work. Of the proclamations I wrote during this period, a particularly successful one was directed against the idea of a *Zemsky Sobor*[1] and in favour of a Constituent Assembly. Having maintained my close contacts with Finland, I now actively assisted the co-ordination of the efforts of the Russian and Finnish SD Parties to strike a blow against Tsarism.

I was one of the first women socialists in Russia to lay the foundations of an organisation for female workers, arranging special meetings and clubs for them, and moreover from 1906 I defended the idea that the organisation for female workers should not be separate from the Party, but that inside the Party there should be a special bureau or commission to ascertain and defend their interests.

I worked with the Bolsheviks until 1906, when I split with them over the questions of workers' participation in the first Duma, and the role of trade unions. Between 1906 and 1915, I allied myself with the Mensheviks, and since then I have been a member of the Bolshevik Party. In 1908 I emigrated to escape from two court cases: I was accused of organising female textile-workers, and of calling for armed insurrection in the pamphlet *Finland and Socialism*. I remained a political *émigrée*

---

[1] A national gathering found in medieval Russian history, at which peasants brought their petitions and complaints to the 'little father' in Moscow. In the nineteenth century, the summoning of such a body was mainly advocated by some Populists.

until 1917, that is the first bourgeois revolution. Whilst abroad, I immediately joined the German, Belgian and other Parties, and I was a militant agitator and writer in Germany, France, England, Switzerland, Belgium, Italy, Sweden, Denmark, Norway and the United States (1915–16).

During the war, I was arrested in Germany, deported to Sweden, and again arrested for anti-militarist propaganda. Nevertheless, I consistently advocated support for the Zimmerwald Union (against the second International) and for internationalism, in Norway, in Sweden, and in the United States, where I had been invited by the German group in the American Socialist Party. Thus my underground work also served Russia. Returning to Russia in 1917, I was elected the first female member of the Petrograd Soviet Executive Committee, and then of the VTsIK. I was arrested with other Bolshevik leaders by the Kerensky regime, and only released just before the October Revolution on the insistence of the Petrograd Soviet. I was elected to the Bolshevik CC and stood for the seizure of power by the workers and peasants. In the first Bolshevik revolutionary cabinet I was People's Commissar for State Assistance. From the moment of my return to Russia, I worked for the organisation of women. From 1920 I directed the Party section dealing with female labour. During my period as Commissar for Social Security, I published decrees, introducing maternity and child protection and benefits.

I was Plenipotentiary and trade representative in Norway from May 1923. From March 1924 I was Chargée d'Affaires there, and from August Minister Plenipotentiary and Envoy Extraordinary.

My major theoretical socialist and economic works are the following: *The State of Working Class in Finland* (1903), *The Class Struggle* (1906), *The First Workers' Calendar* (1906), *The Social Foundations of the Female Question* (1908), *Finland and Socialism* (1907), *Society and Motherhood* (600 pages), *Who Needs the War ?* (which sold in millions of copies), *The Working Class and the New Morality*. In addition to this, I have written a large number of articles, case histories of sexual problems, and all sorts of agitational literature directed mainly against the war and in favour of the emancipation of female labour.

Aleksandra Kollontai specialised in questions of sexuality and women's liberation, and she has left her name in history as one of the inspirers, together with Shlyapnikov, Kiselev and Medvedev, of the Workers' Opposition (1919–22). Her Granat autobiography does not make the slightest allusion to this. This autobiography is no doubt also one of the most unselfconscious and revealing of the period in which it was written:

a long pre-history followed by a few discreet lines on the years after 1917.

In 1912 Kollontai was one of the leaders of the anti-Leninist August bloc, but from 1915 to 1917 (when she joined the Bolshevik Party) she was one of Lenin's few faithful adherents, and he wrote to her frequently. Upon her return to Petrograd immediately after the Revolution, she opposed the majority line on critical support for the Provisional government; and when, on 4 April, Lenin delivered his historic speech to the conference of bemused Bolsheviks, Kollontai was alone in speaking out in favour of the leader. A ditty went round Petrograd at that time:

> Though Lenin gives a tweet
> Kollontai follows suit.

At the time imprisoned by Kerensky, Kollontai was elected *in absentia* to the CC at the sixth Congress. Her prestige was at that time so high that on 5 October 1917 the CC elected her to membership of the Programme Commission—a commission entrusted with the task of refurbishing the Party's programme, which Lenin thought out of date. She figured at the head of the Bolshevik list of candidates (third name from the top) for the Constituent Assembly. Jacques Sadoul saw her at that time and found the Bolshevik Egeria of free love very beautiful, and extremely eloquent.

Moved more by sentiment than by rational motives, she rallied to the left communist group during the discussions on the Brest-Litovsk peace terms, and declared to the seventh Congress, 'If our Soviet Republic must perish, others will carry the banner forward'. This frenetic romanticism cost her her seat on the CC, to which she never returned.

Nevertheless she retained a certain amount of prestige, and when she joined the Workers' Opposition in 1920 she brought to the group the weight of her name and her talents as a writer. Early in 1921, she drew up a pamphlet entitled *The Workers' Opposition*, but it did not reach a wide public. In it she defined the problems which had led to the creation of the Workers' Opposition: 'The cardinal point in the controversy between the Party leadership and the Workers' Opposition is this: to whom will the Party entrust the construction of the communist economy? To the Sovnarkhoz, with all its bureaucratic departments, or to the industrial trade unions?' She placed this problem in the context of a general analysis of the dangers of the Party's fossilisation, and she brutally stated that 'to rid Soviet institutions of the bureaucracy that lurks within them, the Party must first rid itself of its own bureaucracy'.

At that time Bukharin first saw in Kollontai traces of 'disgustingly sentimental catholic bestiality'.

She was one of the 'twenty-two' members of the Workers' Opposition who protested to the Comintern, and the CC tried to have her expelled at the eleventh Congress in March 1922. Stalin tried out a 'device' on her, which he later used abundantly: to detach her from the Opposition – and indeed she did break with it – he sent her abroad as a diplomat. From then on she made a diplomatic career: from 1923 to 1925 she led the Soviet Legation to Norway, from 1925 to 1927 to Mexico, then again to Norway from 1927 to 1930, and from then until 1935 to Sweden. In 1927 she wrote a novel, *Love Affair*, in which some have seen a fictionalisation of the alleged relationship between Lenin and Inessa Armand, and a weapon in Stalin's battle against Krupskaya, who still preserved in her links with the opposition. In 1930, it was she who handed Stalin's ultimatum to the Swedish government, who were willing to grant Trotsky a visa. In 1945 she retired, and she died peacefully on 9 March 1952, in Moscow. She was the only major figure of any of the oppositions whom Stalin did not exterminate.

J.-J. M.

KARL BERNHARDOVICH RADEK
(autobiography)

I was born in 1885 in Lvov, eastern Galicia. I lost my father when I was four years old and was brought up by my mother, a primary school teacher, in the town of Tarnow, western Galicia, where I attended the Gymnasium. All my mother's family were self-taught people with a passion for culture. Since Polish literature was Catholic and clerical, the source of education for her family, as for all Galician Jews, was classical German literature, with its universal, humanitarian ideas.
[. . .]
But at school I soon fell under the spell of Polish literature and history. Polish patriotism captivated me despite its Catholic wrapping. I embraced it and, until I was thirteen, I was not only a Polish patriot but even had a leaning towards Catholicism. I was impelled to study social questions in order to discover the reasons for the division of Poland and the means of reuniting it. Old democratic and patriotic literature, which I read, represented the reasons for Polish decline as lying in the rule of the gentry and indicated that Poland's future was linked with the international revolutionary movement. I witnessed the grinding poverty of our family – mother had to feed and educate my sister and myself on a pittance – and the penury of the craftsmen living round about us. When I was ten, I heard from an old farm-hand the story of the peasant rebellion of 1846. [. . .] From him I received my first invigorating whiff of a large revolutionary movement and I began eagerly to observe what was happening among the peasantry. [. . .]
Whilst at the Gymnasium, I began to attend clandestine meetings with a group of hatters. They belonged to an all-Austrian union which distributed literature in German among its sections, and they kept their social democratic literature in a cupboard in the room of the Jewish baker where they gathered. There I found Kautsky's *Erfurt Programme*, Bebel's *Woman and Socialism*, Lassalle's speeches, and Mehring's *The History of German Social Democracy*. For the rest of the year I neglected my school work and read this literature day and night. When I had assimilated the rudiments of socialism, I naturally set about spreading propaganda in the Gymnasium, where there was a tradition of illegal organisations. I myself belonged to a patriotic organisation whose immediate goals were beyond me, but which sent us boys out late at night to the cemetery so as to test our strength of character. [. . .] Later, when some socialist pamphlets found their way into my hands, I set about forming new socialist circles. They attracted roughly twenty people including the now well-known Polish actor Stefan Jaracz, and Marian

Kukiel, the Polish military historian and Commandant of the Military Academy of liberated Poland. Socialism was identified in our eyes with the striving for an independent Poland. We heard nothing of the Social Democratic Party of Poland and Lithuania, which had been crippled by arrests in 1896 and only began to make itself felt again in 1902–3. Patriotism, democracy, socialism – the title of a collection of articles by Boleslaw Limanowski, the veteran of Polish patriotic socialism – these three words summed up our political ideas. [. . .]

After being expelled from the Gymnasium for the second time in summer 1901 for subversive activities, I devoted myself to the organisation of workers. Two or three months later, I left for Krakow and persuaded Haecker, the editor of the Krakow paper *Naprzód*, to come and give a public speech to us. I owe a great deal to Haecker. [. . .] It was from him that I learnt, in an understandably distorted form, of Rosa Luxemburg's position on the Polish question and that Zygmunt Żulawski, one of the young members of Galician social democracy, supported her. I hastened to make the acquaintance of Żulawski, who soon came to occupy the post of secretary of the growing trade union movement in Tarnow, and it was from him that I received the first literature by social democrats in the Kingdom of Poland,[1] the first numbers of the splendid Marxist journal *Przeglad Socjaldemokratyczny*, published by Adolf Warski, Rosa Luxemburg and Tyszka. This journal, and in particular Warski's articles, had a stunning effect on me. From them I learnt how Polish Marxists posed the question of a programme for the Polish movement and how they made a clean break with the ideology of Polish patriotic socialism. I spent the whole year reading Marxist literature; the first volumes of the works of Marx's youth had then appeared, published by Mehring, and they introduced me to the laboratory in which Marxism was born. I was also involved in practical work among bakers, hatters and construction workers. In summer 1902 I passed the school-leaving examination and then took my first literary steps. I wrote three articles: a study for young people of historical materialism printed in the socialist youth magazine *Promien* ('The Ray'), an article on the position of bakers in Tarnow in the paper *Naprzód*, and an article on the excellent book by Max Schippel, *The History of Sugar Production*. I found a complete edition of the scientific journal of German social democracy in the house of a lawyer called Simkhe, and I read it number by number.

In autumn I went to the university of Krakow, where I decided not so much to study law as to win over Galician social democrats to a con-

[1] The name given to that part of Poland ceded to Russia at the Congress of Vienna in 1815.

sistently Marxist policy. I was due to achieve this with Z. Žulawski, who incidentally has now become Chairman of the Central Commission of Polish Trade Unions and a deputy in the Sejm, thus rejecting this task completely and showing his true colours as a member of the PPS and an enemy of communism. Despite my views, I was added to the editorial board of *Naprzód* for as Daszynski, the Galician social democrat leader, laughingly said, radicalism is a short-lived childhood malady, and everyone begins his Party career with the conviction that Party history is going to start with him. This year, spent in dire poverty, energetic thought and work among the Krakow workers, completed the first period of my life. I became acquainted with Felix Edmundovich Dzerzhinsky, whose revolutionary fervour, comradely directness and cordiality hastened my development, and it became clear to me that the gains of social democracy in a *petit-bourgeois* country with no industrial proletariat are not easily achieved and that it would be more productive to work in the Polish Kingdom, but that for this I would need serious preparation. Therefore, after clashes with Haecker whom I attacked at a public meeting, I left for Switzerland without a kopeck in my pocket, but with the hope of supporting myself by contributing articles to a Marxist weekly called *Glos* which appeared in Warsaw and in which Adolf Warski was the leading figure. I made my debut in this paper in 1904 with an article about the development of the peasant movement in Galicia, and then articles by me on the Western labour movement and reviews of books on the Polish economy and the international labour movement began to be featured every week. I entered into a correspondence with Rosa Luxemburg and was enormously proud when Warski entrusted me with the translation of Kautsky's manuscript introduction to a new edition of the *Communist Manifesto*.

In autumn I set off for Switzerland, leaving unpaid debts in Krakow but with my head full of faith in the future. When I arrived, I threw myself into study and the labour movement. [. . .] The *émigré* cell of the Polish and Lithuanian Social Democratic Party, which I joined, brought me into contact with the Russian labour movement. It was included in the Federation of Russian Social Democratic Organisations and through it I came to know a number of Russian SDs. Zinoviev was studying in Berne at that time, and Medem, a well-known member of the Bund, was also there. It was there that I first heard Lenin speak at a meeting, though I did not understand a word of what he said, and there that I first heard Plekhanov, who made little impression on me. [. . .]

The Russian Revolution broke out and I longed to go back to Tsarist Poland for grass-roots Party work. Even in 1904, whilst still a member of Galician social democracy, I exchanged letters with Rosa Luxemburg and collaborated on the *Volkszeitung* which she published in Poznan. Now I approached her with a proposal for a trip to Poland. She at first suggested I should work abroad for the Party literary centre and soon I received an invitation to Berlin. I was not destined to stay there long. But during the few weeks that I did spend over literary work in libraries, I looked closely at workers' meetings and organisations, with deep emotion made the acquaintance of Kautsky, and strengthened my links with *Die Leipziger Volkszeitung*, published by Mehring and Jaeckh. I had made contact with the latter from Switzerland, when I had sent him material on the Polish participants in the first International.

The day arrived when I crossed the frontier with a false passport, not knowing a word of Russian. The first person I met was Dzerzhinsky, the second Leon Jogiches (Tyszka), the main leader of our Party. I was immediately assigned to the editorial staff of the central Party paper, participated in the publication of the first legal Party daily, *Trybuna*, and threw myself into propaganda work among the Warsaw working masses. It was the first time that I had had to deal with the proletariat of huge factories. I made speeches to thousand-strong meetings, saw how the masses were thriving on the revolutionary struggle, and shook off the dust of SD traditions. Warsaw was an excellent school. If direct participation in the mass revolutionary movement was in itself sufficient to upset all that I had learnt in the school of German social democracy, this process was all the more fruitful since it involved the closest collaboration with such outstanding revolutionaries as Rosa Luxemburg, who had just arrived in Warsaw, Tyszka and Warski. I was most strongly influenced by Tyszka, who was the best editor I have ever met. [. . .] He and Rosa Luxemburg were soon arrested, together with Warski; only Marchlewski, Malecki and I remained on the paper. Simultaneously, the electoral campaign for the first Duma began. A group of workers and I had to 'borrow' the printing-presses of bourgeois papers to ensure publication of our clandestine central paper. [. . .] At the same time, we had to speak at legal meetings called by bourgeois parties. Our Party not only boycotted the elections, but also broke up electoral meetings, often by force of arms.

In March or April 1906 I was detained in Warsaw, but since I was picked up at random in the street – 'I didn't like the look of him' – the comrades were able to bribe my release. Two weeks later I was again arrested. This time I was held for six months, which I spent quite agreeably in the Pawiak prison, learning Russian and reading Lenin, Plekhanov and Marx's *Theory of Surplus Value*, which had just been published by Kautsky. In prison I wrote my first article for *Neue Zeit* (the theoretical organ of German social democracy) about the problems of the trade union movement in Poland, and I was terribly pleased when I received the edition of Kautsky's journal with my article in it. On leaving prison, I was assigned by the Party to the Central Trade Union Commission: I edited its paper, and helped lead a series of strikes.

Thanks to the Russian which I had learnt in prison, I began to find my bearings in the arguments inside the Russian Party. Our Party largely steered clear of them. In general we supported the Bolsheviks, above all in their opposition to the Menshevik tendency towards coalition with the liberal bourgeoisie – in Poland liberalism was insignificant – but we undoubtedly underestimated the revolutionary role of the peasantry, being influenced by Polish conditions where the kulak still played a central part in the peasant movement. My experience of trade unions had strengthened my interest in the daily life of the working class and their immediate struggle for an improvement of their position. In spring 1907 I was again 'put inside', being straightaway transferred from Lodz to the 'Tenth Pavilion'[1] of the Warsaw citadel. [. . .]

In winter I was deported to Austria, and on orders from the Central Committee, I immediately made my way via Berlin to Terijoki where Warski and Tyszka were living after escaping from prison, where Dzerzhinsky was due to arrive, and where a large part of the Russian CC was centred. There I became more closely acquainted with the Russian leaders for the first time. We issued the central Party organ from there but only stayed for a few months. Police conditions forced the Polish CC to transfer us abroad. In spring 1908 Tyszka and I set off via Sweden for Berlin, where the central Party paper, the theoretical journal *Przeglad Socjaldemokratyczny*, and a number of other publications, were being edited. I helped in this work, but it did not occupy all my time, and I began to be a permanent contributor to the German left-wing social democratic press, involving myself fully in their movement.

This was 1908, the year of the Balkan crisis. A new Moroccan crisis was approaching and Stolypin's Russia adopted an active policy in the Balkans, Constantinople and Persia. A revolution took place in Turkey, and international politics became the centre of attention. I had become greatly interested in it even earlier during the Russo-Japanese war. Now I devoted all my energies to the study of contemporary imperialism and I followed its growth in the world's press. I began to write daily about international political problems for *Die Leipziger Volkszeitung*, for *Volksstimme* of Frankfurt, for the Bremen Party newspaper, for *Vorwärts* (the central organ of German social democracy), for *Neue Zeit* (its theoretical journal), and for the Polish theoretical organ *Przeglad*.

[1] The political prison.

[. . .] I was compelled to occupy myself in detail with the colonial practice of European powers so as to refute those reformists in the Party who wanted it to join in the race for colonies. By the end of 1910 I had formed the conviction that faced by the threat of imminent war, radical social democracy ought to move from protests against capitalism in general directly to mass preparations for the revolutionary struggle.

During all these years, I carried out grass-roots propaganda and agitation among the German workers and I was very closely connected with the most militant sections of social democratic youth. Therefore the question of the struggle with imperialism immediately became identified for me with the question of the struggle to change the character of the German and international labour movement. What was needed was agitation for a general strike and the use of extra-parliamentary tactics. After moving to Berlin for personal reasons, and then to Bremen for two years, I had the opportunity of bringing my ideas on these topics closer to those of Rosa Luxemburg and the Dutch Marxist, Anton Pannekoek, and of checking them against the daily practice of the SD Party. German social democracy appeared to me as something completely different from what Russian and Polish revolutionaries imagined it to be, judging it only by Congress decisions and writings. [. . .]

In our lively discussions, which were reflected in the press, we expressed the conviction that the seizure of power by the proletariat was impossible without the destruction of the bourgeois state (Kautsky stigmatised this idea as 'anarchist' in a polemic with Pannekoek). But although we were now at the heart of the question of the dictatorship of the proletariat as a stage of transition from capitalism to socialism, we did not examine this idea further.

The period 1910–13, the time of the creation of left-wing radicalism in German social democracy, was for me extremely hectic. I wrote daily articles for the popular newspapers of Bremen and Leipzig. In addition, I compiled a twice-weekly bulletin on world politics for the Party press which was reproduced in fifteen papers. In 1912 I published a work on German imperialism which attempted to show its historical line of development and raised the question of a socialist revolution. Our struggle inside German social democracy led to a split between the centre, headed by Kautsky and Bebel, and the left, radical wing, the predecessor of the present Communist Party. Apart from Rosa Luxemburg and Pannekoek, those most closely involved in this were Clara Zetkin, August Thalheimer, Brandler, Walcher, Frölich and Pieck, all now members of the German Communist Party. We were linked not only by militant comradeship, but also by personal friendship. Whilst the nucleus of this party was being formed around us, the left-wing radicals, our hatred grew not only for the right-wing leaders, but also for the centrists. With every day that passed, we felt more keenly that we were not on the same road. But, finding a ready response in the industrial centres of Germany, we were convinced that the working masses would easily overcome the resistance of trade union and Party bureaucrats when, as the class struggle sharpened, they finally joined the movement. For that reason it never entered our heads that a split in the Party was a necessary condition for the triumph of the coming German revolution. [. . .]

My friend Thalheimer edited a Party organ in Göppingen in Wurtemberg. Göppingen, a small town with a rapidly developing metallurgical industry, was with Stuttgart the centre of the radical movement in southern Germany. Both the Stuttgart and Göppingen papers were completely under our control. The leadership of Wurtemberg social democracy relied on organisations in the non-industrial areas and was in endless conflict with these two radical groups. To bring the struggle to a successful conclusion, it decided to wring the neck of the Göppingen paper, which despite its small size was one of the staunchest organs of the left-wing radicals. So it made use of the fact that the Göppingen leaders had, through ignorance of the laws, committed a number of offences in setting up the press, for which they could be hauled before the courts. Under German law, co-operatives could only incur debts up to a fixed percentage of their capital. The printing-press, which was run on a co-operative basis, had greater debts than the law allowed and was in financial difficulties, as were many other Party presses. Thalheimer had not the slightest idea of this. Whilst he was on leave and I was deputising for him, the Wurtemberg leaders suddenly presented an ultimatum. They agreed to pay off the debts on condition that the paper was merged with reformist ones and that Thalheimer was dismissed. Should the paper not agree, the Wurtemberg CC would refuse any further assistance, and this would lead to bankruptcy and a charge of fraud. When I learnt all this, I recalled Thalheimer by telegraph. We mobilised the Party organisation and appealed to the all-German CC, not knowing that all this had been staged with the knowledge of Ebert, the second Party Chairman. Ebert arrived to resolve the matter with Braun, the present Prime Minister of Prussia.

At the joint session of the leaders of the Göppingen organisation and the representatives of the all-German and Wurtemberg CCs, we demonstrated that this was blackmail: the financial difficulties of the paper were being exploited to hand it over to opportunists. Then Braun and Ebert declared that they had come to settle the conflict, but since we were not responding, they would suspend the sitting. They refused to allow the facts we had established to be placed on record. But the Göppingen engineering workers barred the doors with tables and announced to Ebert that they would not let him out until this was done. Furious, he shouted: 'The boil of left-wing radicalism in our Party is ripe for lancing, and this we shall do.' The Göppingen organisation would not risk the complete collapse that would have undoubtedly ensued if its leaders had been sentenced for fraud, and so it submitted. It fell to Thalheimer and myself to carry on the struggle. All means were used against us, beginning with the fact that I, a foreigner, and moreover one who wandered from town to town for political reasons, did not pay regular Party dues, and ending with the allegation that as a result of the split in the Polish and Lithuanian Party, Unschlicht (the present Vice-Chairman of the RVS) and I had been expelled from the Party by the main leadership. (It was true that the Party opposition in Poland, led by Hanecki, Unschlicht, Malecki, Dombrowski and myself, had clashed with the main leadership, headed by Warski, Marchlewski and Dzerzhinsky, but it had not been over a question of principle; rather it was about organisation—it was a rebellion by the mass of workers, inspired by the Revolution, against the *émigré* centre which did not realise that one of the consequences of revolution is great autonomy for the workers.) Citing my expulsion from Polish social democracy, the German leadership announced that it no longer considered me a member of its Party. At the Chemnitz Party Conference, it played an excellent trump card: it derided this obscure personage of foreign extraction who dared to accuse the German CC of corruption. I was not, however, abandoned by the Bremen workers who, under the leadership of my friend Johann Knief [. . .] and Anton Pannekoek, defended my right to direct their paper, and for many years the Bremen Party organ presented a sight unparalleled in the labour movement: a man who was excluded from two parties clarifying not only general political questions, but also all the problems of Party tactics in one of the best Party papers. Soon a special commission of the Russian SD Party cleared me of all reproaches hurled in the heat of the Polish factional struggle, and I could have achieved at the next German Party Congress the honour of rejoining the Party, if history had not developed in such a way that it was no longer an honour to be a German social democrat. On 1 August 1914 the world war broke out and German social democracy sided with imperialism.

I was in Berlin at the time. From the moment of the assassination of the Austrian archduke it had been clear that we were on the brink of war. The weeks preceding the outbreak saw a furious campaign in the Bremen paper. Knowing that we should soon be silenced, we did everything to impress our cause on the workers and to urge them to fight against the threat of war. We formed a small group in Berlin under Liebknecht's leadership, which strove to foment demonstrations and to provoke clashes with the police, so as to force the masses to intensify their efforts. The very fact that the brutal Berlin police did everything it could to avoid confrontation, clearly indicated that the government was bent on war. When the declaration came, the workers who were called to arms were disoriented. The Party was silent. The ale-houses were full of cannon-fodder trying to drown their anxiety. We radicals dashed about like madmen, cursing the Party for its failure to give the signal even for mass demonstrations. The most pessimistic feared that the SD bloc in Parliament would abstain, but not even the wildest pessimist imagined that it would vote *for* credits. When, on the evening of 3 August, a deputy, Henke, informed me as he left a meeting of the parliamentary group that they would vote for war credits, we immediately agreed that he should vote against and that I would write a declaration before the following morning to explain the motives for this vote. He would then attempt to rally a few left-wing deputies round this declaration. I was completely stunned, and it was only on the way back to the suburb where I lived that I grasped what had happened—a whole epoch in the labour movement had come to a shameful end. When I handed my outline declaration to Henke next morning, I could tell from his face that he would not swim against the current. Liebknecht, whom I had also met on 4 August, explained why he had decided not to oppose the motion: in his opinion, the government would very quickly proceed to a persecution of the Party, and then the whole Party would present a united front against the war. I could no longer believe this. The social democratic press was no more than a stinking cesspool poisoning the workers. It went over *en bloc* to the service of imperialism.

For the first few days, I, like many other comrades, had the feeling that there was no point in writing. Had forty years of socialist propaganda not been able to save even the leaders of social democracy from that fateful decision ? But, naturally, this mood could only last for a short while. I resumed my activities and, despite censorship, began to expose the true nature of the war in the Bremen paper. I was greatly helped in this by a detailed knowledge not only of imperialist books and pamphlets, but also of the German military journals, which boasted how well German imperialism had prepared for the war. [. . .]

The split in the Polish organisation in 1912 had estranged me from Rosa Luxemburg. But I maintained the closest of relations with Liebknecht and Mehring, and they kept me informed of the beginnings of her group, which later grew into the Spartakus League. I also coordinated my activities with theirs. Since I was closest to the north-western organisation, I made it my task to gather the revolutionary forces in Hamburg, Bremen and associated towns. In Bremen, despite the fact that Paul Frölich and Johann Knief had been called up, the nucleus of the old Party group was wholly committed to us. Henke, the local deputy and editor of the Party paper, did not always stand firm under pressure from the trade union bureaucracy, but he had not yet split with us and the paper was under our control. The organisation in Hamburg was entirely in the hands of the right-wingers, but Dr Laufenberg, the historian of the Hamburg labour movement and a man of great influence, as well as a young agitator called Wolfheim, full of the ideas of the American 'Industrial Workers of the World' organisation, were both active among the rank and file. I met both of them in Bremen in September, and we decided to undertake publication of propaganda pamphlets directed against the war. Laufenberg was mistrustful of Rosa Luxemburg's theoretical position and did not want direct links with her group, but he pledged himself to co-ordinate our actions through me. In Berlin there existed a private school for Marxist propaganda, directed by a very eccentric, but very steadfast man called Borchardt. Before the war he had published a popular, propaganda news-sheet, *Lichtstrahlen*, which had been widely circulated among the working rank and file. Without hesitation, he put the school and the paper at the service of the anti-war group. Whilst pretending to lecture on the history of English imperialism to hundreds of workers, I in fact outlined the theoretical foundations for our struggle against Scheidemann's treachery. The car hooters that signalled the approach of several automobiles during these lectures, made the audience think that we would be taken directly from there to the hospitable premises of the Berlin police on the Alexanderplatz. My work could not remain secret for long. [. . .]

I wrote many letters to my old friend Konrad Haenisch, one of the best men in the radical movement who, after the first few weeks of war, had gone over to the patriotic 'socialist' majority. I attempted to dissuade him, and our correspondence fell into the hands of the Hamburg reformists, who had it printed as a pamphlet and distributed it throughout the organisation. The atmosphere deteriorated. Liebknecht persuaded me to go to Switzerland to improve our links with the Italian communists and the French internationalists.

This I succeeded in doing, and I came to an agreement with Robert Grimm, editor of the Party organ *Berner Tagwacht*, about a secret exchange of letters between us and correspondence for his paper. He put his daily entirely at the disposal of the German opposition and we agreed that it should be distributed throughout Germany until the government banned it. I also met Angelica Balabanova, who lived in

Switzerland to keep open communications with the Italian CC. I could not trace Vladimir Ilyich – on his release from the Austrian prison, he had retreated into the mountains[1] – but the manifesto which he released in the name of the CC had an enormous impact on me with its incisive statement of the problem. I was in full agreement with its assessment of the war and of the International, but being still under the influence of the state of German social democracy, I considered that the path to civil war was still a long one, and that it was premature to raise the question of a split. Trotsky, who was then in Zurich, agreed with me on the latter point, but was very optimistic as regards the prospects of revolution, and he reproached me for pessimism in a lecture which I gave to the Union of Foreign Workers in Zurich. I also had long conversations with Pavel Borisovich Akselrod, who, being an opponent of the policy of the SD parties, found a thousand explanations for it which, in reality, tended to defend patriotic 'socialism'. After gathering all the documents unknown in Germany, I returned at the moment when the German Reichstag was meeting for the second time.

Now Liebknecht decided to vote openly against war credits and to make a suitably revolutionary declaration. Mehring and Rosa Luxemburg believed that he should do this only if a few other left-wingers joined him. They feared that if he voted alone, this would dispirit the masses by demonstrating his complete isolation. But of the people on whom one might have relied, Lensch deserted to the patriotic 'socialists'. Hope remained only for Rühle and Henke. It was my task to persuade the latter. Liebknecht and I met him, and Liebknecht read out a plan of his declaration. Henke began to make objections. Liebknecht immediately agreed to entrust me with the formulation of the declaration, promising to accept it if Henke would do the same. I returned home and set about my task. The three of us met again in Josty's Café a few hours before the Reichstag session of 2 December, and the other two declared themselves pleased with my outline. Nevertheless, Henke announced that he would not vote against the credits and was quite open about his motives for this decision: the trade union bureaucracy in Bremen had grown stronger, there were still no signs of movement among the workers, he was a family man and could not take risks. When Liebknecht replied that a few children could not determine a revolutionary's position, Henke angrily retorted that it was easy for him to talk since he was financially independent, but in any case he doubted whether even Liebknecht would go alone against the Party. Liebknecht made no answer. We set off for the Reichstag. And I watched from the gallery as

[1] Radek's information was incorrect. Lenin was freed from detention following the intervention of Victor Adler and was allowed to leave Galicia.

Liebknecht rose to throw down his lone challenge to the imperialist world.

All the press started buzzing. They began to depict him as a madman. Even those so-called left-wingers who had not been able to bring themselves to join his protest began to hiss in the corners. But everything that was alive and revolutionary in the Party raised its head. The struggle had moved out of conspiratorial gatherings and Party circles into the open. A banner had been raised around which the workers could unite. The correspondence which I sent secretly to the Bremen paper and which was published under the pseudonym 'Parabellum' attracted the attention of the social democratic and bourgeois press, for they wore an external sign of the consolidation of the opposition, and they openly developed its ideology. Speculation in the SD press about its author and nods in my direction raised the question as to whether it was worth risking arrest, whether it would not be wiser to attempt to create a conspiratorial base for the opposition in Switzerland. The comrades expressed themselves in favour of the latter course and I made my way there.

This time I found Vladimir Ilyich and Zinoviev at once. We established unity on all basic points; disagreement came only over the slogan for national self-determination. As for the open proclamation of the split, Lenin considered it a tactical question that could not be decided in isolation from the strength of the opposition in each country. I settled in Berne, where I gave lectures on imperialism at the Party school, wrote for the Berne and Zurich Party organs, as well as for the Bremen paper and Borchardt's *Lichtstrahlen*, and organised clandestine communications with Germany through my wife who was a doctor in the Moabit Hospital in Berlin. Daily contact with Lenin and discussions with him finally convinced me that the Bolsheviks were the only revolutionary party in Russia, and as early as the International Conference of Women in April 1915, I helped in the struggle against Clara Zetkin's centrist policies. At the same time we worked together among the young people who published *L'Internationale de la Jeunesse*, and among the Swiss social democrats.

When Trotsky, Balabanova and Robert Grimm took the initiative in preparations for the Zimmerwald Conference, contact had already been established with part of the German left, the so-called north German left-wing radicals, the Swedish left, and part of the Swiss left. My wife, who had arrived for a few weeks in Switzerland, took back with her to Germany an invitation to the conference. We made very careful preparations. I wrote some theses which were subjected to rigorous criticism by Lenin; he insisted that they should be of an agitational nature and extremely concise. There were, however, no disagreements on matters of principle.

When the conference assembled, the following spectrum of opinions was present. The right wing was represented by the German centrists led by Ledebour. The centre consisted of the French, the Italians, Kolarov for the Bulgarians, Rakovsky, Trotsky, Martov, the Spartakus group led by Meyer, and Lapinski from the left wing of the PPS. On the left flank were our group with Lenin and Zinoviev for the Bolsheviks, Berzin on behalf of the Letts, myself for the regional Polish SDs, Borchardt for the German radicals, Nerman and Höglund on behalf of the Swedes, and Fritz Platten for the Swiss left-wing social democrats.

I was entrusted by our group with the opening speech. A reply was made by Ledebour who was later pilloried by Lenin and Zinoviev. The clash concerned two questions—the necessity of voting against war credits, and the urgent need to abandon propaganda circles for mass street demonstrations against the consequences of war with the aim of expanding the struggle into one against the war itself. To defend our point of view, we delegated Lenin to represent us on the commission. Despite the inadequacy of the resolutions adopted by the commission, we decided to sign its appeal unanimously, believing that the moment for a break with the centre would only come when the labour movement had acquired a much broader base. After the conference was ended, we held our own conference of the Zimmerwald left, at which we decided to publish this appeal with a rider sharply criticising its half-heartedness, and to create our own organisation with myself as secretary. The action fund of this organisation was set up in the following way. Vladimir Ilyich contributed twenty francs on behalf of the Bolshevik CC, Borchardt another twenty francs in the name of the German radicals, and I borrowed ten francs from Hanecki to contribute for the Polish social democrats. The future Communist International, therefore, had fifty francs at its disposal to conquer the world, but ninety-six francs were needed to print a pamphlet about the conference in German. So forty-six francs had to be borrowed from Shklovsky, a manufacturer of mineral salts, who employed Zinoviev and Safarov. We regained this sum from the sale of our pamphlet. The Zimmerwald left operated in complete harmony, combating centrist elements in all countries. Its secretariat distributed circulars on all changes in the position and tactics of the centrists. These were compiled by me and, after they had been critically examined by Lenin and Zinoviev, I copied them out by hand and hectographed them. We could not as yet afford the luxury of a typewriter. During this time *Lichtstrahlen* was appearing daily, and we had in it a legal organ with a large circulation in Germany. In 1916 our friends in Bremen collected 200 roubles in subscriptions from workers to publish a small journal called *Arbeiterpolitik*, half of which I wrote in Switzerland; Zinoviev, Kollontai, Bukharin and Evgeniya Bosch were among the Bolsheviks who also contributed. [. . .]

At the Kienthal Conference in 1916, we were already an important force. The prolonged war had led everywhere to a shift to the left [. . .]. In Poland, our organisation was engaged in a heroic struggle against the German occupation, whilst in Germany, despite the arrest of Liebknecht and Rosa Luxemburg, the Spartakus League was swelling into a genuine movement. In France, Monatte and Rosmer had supplanted the more moderate Merrheim. We had succeeded in making contacts inside America. In England, the opposition of the working class had sharpened. Thanks to these developments, we were able at Keinthal to impose on the former Zimmerwald participants our anti-pacifist position and to parry attempts at holding negotiations with the second International. The Spartakus representatives and those from the Italian CC voted with us on a whole series of fundamental questions. After the conference, at a session of the Zimmerwald Bureau, we made a direct attack on Robert Grimm who, as Secretary of the Zimmerwald alliance, was conducting an opportunistic policy in Switzerland. Through the Zimmerwald left, Bolshevik ideological influence was spread to all countries.

After the Kienthal Conference I moved to Davos, from where I maintained communications with Ilyich and Germany. Lenin was in direct communication with France, England, America and the Scandinavian countries. We often met when he stopped to see us on journeys from Berne to Zurich. In Zurich, he made Bronsky and myself keep in touch with Swiss workers, considering that even the most left-wing of the Swiss Party leaders were waverers.

One day over dinner in the Basle Sanatorium in Davos, between the meat course and the dessert, a Swiss doctor informed me in his nasal voice that agency telegrams about a revolution in Petrograd had been pasted up in the town. This was said with such equanimity that neither I, nor Paul Lévi who was my guest, believed him. Nevertheless, we were seized with apprehension and, without waiting for coffee, ran into town, where we read the first agency telegrams. When we returned home, Bronsky telephoned me and asked us to come and see Vladimir Ilyich immediately. There was no train until the following day. Vladimir Ilyich met us with his mind made up about two things: we had to break with Zimmerwald and return to Russia. On the former question, in spite of his arguments that to remain in Zimmerwald would mean giving the impression of a bloc with the Mensheviks, Zinoviev and I won the following concessions: not to sign any joint declaration with Martov, but not to leave Zimmerwald either. As for the second question, on instructions from Ilyich, Lévi and I asked the *Frankfurter Zeitung* correspondent, whose name was Datmann or Dietmann, to sound out the German envoy as to whether Germany would agree to allow some Russian *émigrés* to pass through Germany in exchange for a corresponding number of prisoners of war. Soon we heard that the German Ambassador was ready to discuss this question. Then Martov and I gave Robert Grimm a free hand in the negotiations. But his report on them convinced us that this ambitious politician might become embroiled in general political discussions. Therefore we declined his services and entrusted further conduct of the negotiations to Platten, who conscientiously saw them through to the end. All the tales about participation by Parvus in these talks have no basis in fact. His attempts to intervene were rejected by Lenin, which does not exclude the possibility that the German government asked for his opinion. The legend of the 'sealed train' is equally without foundation. The train was not sealed at all—we merely pledged ourselves not to leave the coach. Platten dealt with communications with the Germans. As for me, being an Austrian subject and moreover barred from Germany (my wife had just been arrested), I used a false passport to cross to Stockholm without the knowledge of the German authorities. I remained there with Hanecki and Vorovsky as CC agent in charge of communication abroad. This ushered in a period of activity encompassing only a few months but full of extremely interesting episodes.

In Stockholm, an international atmosphere had sprung up with the outbreak of the Russian Revolution. It was taken by German social democrats as an opportunity to negotiate about peace. Within a short time, all their attempts at making contact with the Kerensky regime, the Mensheviks and the SRs were concentrated there. The Danish social democrats led by Borberg acted as their assistants. The Executive Committee of the first Congress of Soviets sent representatives in the shape of Rozanov and Meshkovsky. In their turn, the social democrats of the *Entente* countries employed as their agent Branting, the leader of Swedish social democracy.

The International Bureau of the second International began to stir and its chief, Huysmans, set up his office there. Preparations began for the summoning of the Stockholm Conference of the second International. Delegations arrived from all countries. There were Austrians, under the leadership of Renner and Victor Adler, who was seriously ill; there were Hungarians led by Kunfi; there were Belgians. We attempted to forge links with the leftist elements in all these delegations. The most amusing incident concerned the Austrian delegation. The honourable Renner had brought in his case letters from Austrian comrades sympathising with us. Unknown to him, one of the letters contained the information that he had been granted a secret audience by the Austrian Emperor immediately before his departure. We hastily printed this news, to Renner's great discomfiture.

The man who made the most profound impression of me was the Belgian leader, De Brouckère, whom I had known before the war as one of the best left-wing Marxists, and who now could talk and think of nothing except war to the end. Kunfi told us of the revolutionary situation in Hungary. He was the only social democrat who believed in an imminent revolution in Central Europe. It was the independent German social democrats who cut the most pitiful figure. They professed to be very revolutionary but were afraid of giving more concrete information about the position in Germany. We naturally drew closer to the Spartakus League which was represented by Fuchs, and to other like-minded groups, who corresponded with us secretly. Johann Knief, who had gone underground and was scouring the country, managed to transmit to us news of the revolutionary movement in Germany which we telegraphed to *Pravda*, to the great joy of Vladimir Ilyich. For the information of the Western European social democratic press, we began to publish a twice-weekly hectographed bulletin entitled *Correspondence from Pravda*. Great use was made of this in the workers' press. Soon it was superseded by the weekly *Vestnik Russkoy Revolyutsii*. Both the bulletin and the *Vestnik* entailed great difficulties. Not only were our resources very meagre, which forced us to print these publications in a primitive way (the whole technical staff consisted of Hanecki's wife and mine), but we were deprived of news, for the Petrograd censors would not allow the Bolshevik press to reach the outside world. Hanecki, however, soon discovered that this ban did not apply to papers printed in Finland and we were able to receive not only *Tiomes*, the organ of the Finnish Party, but also *Volna*, the Helsinki Bolshevik paper. As the latter consisted largely of reprints from *Pravda*, we were supplied with all essential information. [. . .]

The Zimmerwald Conference was due to take place in September. We made thorough preparations for it so as to do battle with the Mensheviks and force the Zimmerwald parties into taking a definite position on the struggle between the proletarian and *petit-bourgeois* tendencies in the Russian Revolution. Ermansky and Akselrod spoke for the Mensheviks. Our delegation consisted of Vorovsky, Hanecki, Semashko and myself. The argument was embittered mainly by Akselrod's open defence of the disgraceful measures taken against us by the Kerensky regime. With his back pressed tight against the wall, the leader of the German independents, Haase, attempted to shift the discussion to the question of whether we accepted the use of violence against other socialist parties. We made it perfectly clear that if we came to power, we would both admit and practise violence with regard to other would-be socialist parties who betrayed the Revolution. Thus the delegates were asked whether they would link themselves with the *petit-bourgeois* parties who used violence against the fighters of the proletarian revolution. We were supported not only by the Spartakus representatives but even by old Ledebour, who could not stomach Haase's argument and spoke openly in our defence. The conference ended by adopting a resolution calling for mass revolutionary support for the Russian Revolution. It must be mentioned that Vladimir Ilyich was insisting in his letters from Petrograd on a split with the Zimmerwald parties, believing that it was time to lay the foundations of the third International. We could not decide on this step, which we thought premature.

As the struggle in Petrograd reached its climax, we spent sleepless nights awaiting news of the outcome. This arrived late one night, and towards morning the Hungarian journalist Gutman brought us the telegraphed version of Vladimir Ilyich's speech at the opening of the second Congress of Soviets. Hanecki and I immediately prepared to leave, but we were detained by a telegram informing us that a representative of German social democracy was on his way to see us. This representative turned out to be none other than Parvus, who passed on assurances that the German social democrats would immediately enter the struggle for peace with us. He privately declared that Scheidemann and Ebert were ready to call a general strike if the German government, under pressure from the military, did not agree to an honourable peace. We openly printed an account of these talks in the Swedish Party paper, and Hanecki and I set off for Petrograd, armed only with a document from Vorovsky certifying that we were members of the Foreign Bolshevik Bureau. Not knowing who was in control of the frontier, we sent a Finnish comrade ahead to transmit information we had collected about the uproar caused by the October Revolution. He returned with the news that the frontier was in the hands of our comrades, and we crossed at night. We found an ardent and devoted young sailor called Svetlichny from the *Respublika*, who immediately put us in touch with Helsinki, since there was a railway strike in Finland and it was impossible to proceed without permission from the strike committee. When we had obtained a special train, we invited some Russian workers to join us from Gaparanda—they had arrived from America and were waiting for an opportunity to travel further into Russia. On the way, we read the Petrograd bourgeois press which exaggerated dissensions in the Bolshevik CC. It was with a very heavy heart that we drew into Petrograd, but when we saw from the carriage window detachments of Red Guards doing rifle practice, we went wild with joy. We reached Smolny as if in a dream and within a minute were in Lenin's office.

The ten years I have since spent in the ranks of the Russian Revolution are too fresh for me to be able to give a coherent account of them. I will limit myself, therefore, to listing the basic episodes in my work. No sooner had I arrived in Petrograd than I was sent back to Stockholm for preliminary talks with Riezler, the German emissary. After this, I accompanied Trotsky to Brest-Litovsk. When the talks broke down I was appointed a member of the Petrograd Defence Committee. After the Brest treaty had been signed, I directed the Central European Department of the Commissariat for Foreign Affairs and the External Relations Department of TsIK.

At the outbreak of the German revolution, Rakovsky, Ioffe, Bukharin, Sokolnikov and I were sent as the VTsIK delegation to the first Congress of German Soviets. I was prevented from entering the country legally, so I travelled illegally. I helped to organise the first Communist Party Congress in Germany, and after the assassination of Rosa Luxemburg and Liebknecht, I remained secretly in Berlin as one of the Party leadership. Arrested on 15 February, I languished in prison until December. Nevertheless, I succeeded in issuing seven small pamphlets on topical questions of the German labour movement, in being an active leader of the German Communist Party, and in establishing and strengthening relations with the Austrian and British labour movements. I also achieved a better understanding with Talat Pasha, Enver Pasha, oriental specialists in German political circles, and the former Foreign Minister Hintze. When released from prison, I returned to Russia via Poland, on the basis of an agreement concluded between Pilsudski and the Soviet government.

In March 1920 I was appointed Secretary of the Comintern. I was one of the chief organisers of the Comintern's second Congress, where I presented a report. After this I was sent to the Polish Front as a member of the Polish Revolutionary Committee.[1] Defeat found me in Siedlce. Then Zinoviev and I arranged the first Congress of the Peoples of the East, where I made another report. In October 1920 I returned clandestinely to Germany to be present at the Congress which was due to endorse the union of the left-wing independents and the Spartakus League.

---

[1] In fact, Radek was not a member of the Polish Revolutionary Committee, which was composed of Dzerzhinsky, Marchlewski, Felix Kohn, Unschlicht and Prountiak.

In January 1921 I devised the tactics of the united front[1] with a so-called 'open letter'. On my return, I presented a report on tactics to the third Comintern Congress, and at the fourth Congress I made a speech about united fronts and workers' governments. In 1922 I led the Comintern delegation at the Congress of the Three Internationals. At the end of that year, I was sent as Chairman of the Russian trade union delegation to the Hague Congress on the dangers of war. In early 1923 I was dispatched to Oslo to forestall a split in the Norwegian Communist Party. Having done this, I went to Hamburg as an observer at the Congress of the second International. I participated in the campaign against the seizure of the Ruhr and in the Leipzig Congress of the German Communist Party. I returned to Russia but in October was directed by the Comintern to give guidance in the forthcoming rising. I arrived on 22 October after the start of the retreat, and I approved this decision of the German CC. On my return to Russia, I sided with the opposition during the discussions of 1924. At the thirteenth Party Congress I spoke out against the impending change in the Comintern's tactics. I was excluded from the CC after being a member since 1919. At the fifth Comintern Congress I denounced the planned changes in its tactics and was expelled from its Executive Committee.

During all the years of the Revolution, I was a contributor to *Pravda* and *Izvestiya*. I wrote mainly on foreign policy and the international labour movement. Collections of my articles and extracts from my pamphlets can be found in: *Five Years of the Comintern* (two volumes); *The German Revolution* (three volumes); and articles on current international politics form the volume entitled *The Year 1924*. Part of my pre-war works were published in German in 1920 under the title *In den Reihen der russischen Revolution*. Since 1925 I have been Rector of the Chinese Sun Yat-Sen University, and I am one of the editors of the *Large Soviet Encyclopedia*.

The brilliant, noisy Radek (born Sobelsohn) made himself noticed well before 1914 in international socialist circles for his extremist positions and outrageous radicalism, and for the scandals he unleashed in his native land, Poland, and in his country of adoption, Germany. His autobiography gives the measure of his character: loquacious, extremely intelligent and sharp, unstable, clever and opportunist, leaving in the shade without a scruple that which does not flatter, and choosing the events in his life which show him off to advantage. He turns to his own

---

[1] Radek transformed this into the 'Schlageter tactics', after the name of a German killed by French occupation troops, which unleashed the fury of the nationalists. These tactics led to 'National Bolshevism' in Germany.

profit the scandals he caused, and presents himself as a victim of the opportunist and centrist leaders of the German social democratic movement—which is not entirely without foundation. But the leaders of the German left—Rosa Luxemburg, Clara Zetkin, G. Ledebour, hated him quite as much as he hated them. Although Rosa Luxemburg's rupture with Radek was not unconnected with the split in the Polish Party in 1912, it was all the same a reflection of her lack of esteem for a man who had been accused of theft, in Poland in 1908. Radek caused much ink to be spilt in 1912–13, moreover, not only about this alleged theft but also about the Göppingen affair.[1] He succeeded none the less in having a grand jury assembled, known as the 'Paris Commission', which absolved him of all the charges, and he also gained the support of Lenin, Trotsky and Karl Liebknecht.

With his audacity and lack of scruple, he soon took upon himself to move in the highest circles of the international socialist world. He was not afraid of the authorities, and he spared no one – not even Kautsky, or, on the left, Lenin – in his violent attacks. Radek left no one indifferent to him, and the enemies he gained were fierce enemies. On the other hand, the disputes he stirred up lent him a certain charisma in the eyes of the German left, who took him as one of their theoreticians. He was an inexhaustible publicist and a man of encyclopedic knowledge, picked up in the course of his multifarious and heterogeneous reading. He had put all his passion into the study of Marxism and of international problems. He and Pannekoek were the leaders of the Bremen radical group.

During the war he remained the spokesman of the extreme left and untiringly pursued his constant activity as a publicist from Switzerland, where he had taken up residence. It was at that time that he drew closer to Lenin, at whose side he took part in the Zimmerwald Conference, where he put forward the extremist resolution. He began to make his place in the Bolshevik group while at the same time remaining a militant worker in the German workers' movement. In 1916, he and Paul Levi attempted to create within it a pro-Bolshevik splinter. In 1919 he expressed his attachment to Germany in an autobiographical letter: 'If I follow my inclination, I feel more connected to the German working class than to the Russian. I think in German words and my feelings are expressed by German poets.'[2] His activities were not approved of by the traditional left wing of the German social democratic movement and he had to overcome Clara Zetkin's hostility in order to be able to take part in the Kienthal Conference. A year later, at the third Zimmerwald

[1] See J. P. Nettl, *Rosa Luxemburg*, vol. 1 (Oxford, 1966).
[2] Unpublished letter, Hoover Library, Stanford.

Conference held in Stockholm between 5 and 12 September 1917, he and Hanecki were representing the reunited SDKPiL.

At the end of November 1917 Radek returned to Moscow and took up an important position at the Commissariat for Foreign Affairs, in the Smolny Palace, where he was in charge of international propaganda.[1] He was succeeded in this post by Béla Kun. The British diplomat R. Bruce Lockhart, who was in daily contact with him, described him thus:

A little man, with a huge head, protruding ears, cleanshaven face (in those days he did not wear that awful fringe which now passes for a beard), with spectacles and a large mouth with yellow, tobacco-stained teeth, from which a huge pipe or cigar was never absent, he was always dressed in a quaint drab-coloured Norfolk suit with knickers and leggings. . . . He looked like a cross between a professor and a bandit. . . . He was the virtuoso of Bolshevik journalism and his conversation was as sparkling as his leading articles. Ambassadors were his game and Foreign Ministers his butts. . . . He was a Puck full of malice and with a delicious sense of humour. He was the Bolshevik Lord Beaverbrook.[2]

Lenin relied on Radek's energy and knowledge of German affairs, and so he took part in the Brest-Litovsk talks. In March 1918 he returned to Narkomindel, and became head of the Central Europe section. He was entrusted with fraternisation propaganda aimed at the German army, and with the recruitment of revolutionary militants among the prisoners of war. When he tried to get into Germany in December 1918 to attend the Congress of German Councils as the official delegate of the Soviets, he was turned back at the frontier, but succeeded in smuggling himself over the border. As a delegate of the Bolshevik Party, he took a hand in the creation of the German CP and succeeded in reuniting the Spartakists and his reticent friends from Bremen. Rosa Luxemburg required some convincing, however, before she would accept collaborating with Radek. His awareness of the situation in Germany made him realise very quickly that any attempt to seize power would end in failure, and that was why he tried to hold back the over-enthusiastic Liebknecht. After the assassination of the latter and Rosa Luxemburg, Radek himself was arrested in February 1919, and spent eleven months in the Moabit prison, the 'political chamber' where he played the double role of adviser to the leader of the German CP, Paul Levi, and semi-official

[1] E. H. Carr, *The Bolshevik Revolution*, vol. 1 (Macmillan, 1950).
[2] R. Bruce Lockhart, *Memoirs*, p. 255.

representative of the Bolshevik Government to German politicians and military chiefs.[1]

1919 marks the peak of Radek's career: at the eighth Congress of the Russian CP he was elected *in absentia* to the CC, and on his return to Russia he took on the secretaryship of the Comintern. He was deprived of this post in 1920, for he and Paul Levi had taken a stand against the decision of IKKl to invite to the second Congress of the Comintern the left-wing members of KAPD. Nevertheless he was elected a member of IKKI by the same congress and at the following congress he was elected to the 'small commission' of IKKI (to become the Presidium), where he remained until 1924. Upon his return from Germany in 1921 he became a convinced opponent of Levi. In 1922 he and Bukharin led the Comintern delegation to the conference of the three Internationals in Berlin, that is to say of the second and third Internationals and of the 'Vienna Union'.

He was in Germany on three occasions in 1923: at the KAPD Congress in February; at the Congress of the second International in Hamburg in May, where his main concern was to extricate the KAPD from its complicated situation *vis-à-vis* the Comintern (in Zinoviev's absence, Radek went to Moscow to persuade Stalin of his point of view, and the demonstrations planned for July were cancelled, which Radek approved *post facto*, being hostile to any kind of *putsch* politics); and he was in Germany again in October, directing, apparently against his better judgement, the Comintern team which was entrusted with the job of preparing for the insurrection. The lack of support for the KAPD and Hitler's Munich *putsch* reduced his efforts to naught.

In the Comintern, Radek's cleverness became legendary from this time on. He was more of an improviser than a theoretician, his mind was cynical and sarcastic: as the Austrian socialist Oskar Blum once remarked, 'the whole world was for Radek a large colonial problem'[2] Balabanova had known him well since the Zimmerwald Conference, and described him thus:

> Radek was to me a strange psychological phenomenon, but never a puzzle.... Today he would prove that the events on various fronts had to be so and so; tomorrow, just when the contrary had happened, he would attempt to prove that it could not have happened otherwise.... He was ... a strange mixture of amorality, cynicism and of spontaneous appreciation for ideas, books, music and human beings.[3]

---

[1] O.-E. Schüddekopf 'Karl Radek in Berlin', *Archiv für Sozialgeschichte*, vol. 2 (1962), pp. 87–166.
[2] *Russische Köpfe*, p. 87. [3] A. Balabanova, *My Life* (London, 1938), p. 246.

Victor Serge, on the other hand, found him 'monkey-like, sardonic and droll . . . realistic to the point of cruelty'.[1] It was however Trotsky who drew the subtlest portrait of Radek in an article published in May 1929:

> Radek is indisputably one of the best Marxist journalists in the world. . . . He has an ability to react with exceptional speed to new phenomena and tendencies, even to the first symptoms of anything new. . . . But his journalistic strength is his political weakness. Radek exaggerates and goes too far. He measures in yards where he should be looking at inches—and thus he always finds himself either to the left or the right (more usually the right) of the correct line.[2]

The direction of Radek's thought, none the less, always remained to the left. In 1918 he was a left-wing communist and never hesitated to express opposition, although he did perform opportune about-turns. He advised Lenin against the march on Warsaw in 1920, and in 1923 he was a member of the opposition and adhered to the 'Declaration of the 46' by a personal statement. His stands lost him his post in the Comintern in 1924, and he was made responsible for the failure of the Comintern's tactics during the German revolution, which was all the more convincing since he had been in a position to evaluate the situation accurately. Although he belonged to the left opposition, Radek continued to oscillate from right to left. He tried several times, between 1924 and 1926, to reconcile the left opposition with Stalin. He remained basically hostile to Zinoviev, his most bitter enemy. Thus in 1925 he came out against the formation of the United Opposition and sought to persuade the left opposition to form a bloc with Stalin against Zinoviev.

At the thirteenth Congress of the Russian CP he was not re-elected to the CC and in 1926 he was relegated to the directorship of the Sun Yat-Sen University in Moscow. Radek had studied the Far Eastern question and had definite views on it, as on the specific nature of the Chinese revolution. His thesis was that China had no feudal system and no landowning caste, and that consequently the agrarian revolution should be directed not against the impoverished gentry but against the bourgeoisie. China was not ripe for a proletarian revolution, but on the threshold of a democratic revolution of which the aim should be the establishment of a democratic dictatorship. He thus tolerated the alliance of the Chinese CP with the Kuomintang. But as early as 1926 he noticed a change in the attitude of the latter party. He warned the Politburo and demanded a

[1] op. cit., pp. 108, 137.
[2] In *Contre le courant*, no. 31–2 (10 June 1929), p. 4.

change in its China policy—but in vain. Once again, however, events proved him right. He then sought to place the critique of the Comintern's China policy at the centre of the United Opposition's struggle (he had joined this group despite his mistrust and aversion for Zinoviev). The columns of *Pravda* and *Izvestia* were thenceforth closed to him, and in May 1927 he was relieved of his duties at the Sun Yat-Sen University.

In December 1927, at the fifteenth Congress, he was expelled from the Party with seventy-four other members of the opposition and exiled to Siberia. He threw himself impulsively at first into ultra-leftism, then made an abrupt about-turn. In July 1929 he joined Preobrazhensky and Smilga to lead a group which published a declaration supporting the struggle against 'rightist opportunism' and condemning all splinter groups, as well as repudiating Trotsky. He was readmitted to the Party and rallied to Stalin. He then became director of the CC's information bureau, which meant in effect that he was Stalin's personal adviser on foreign affairs, as well as one of the best-known commentators in the Soviet press on international political questions. In 1936, he and Bukharin collaborated on the drafting of the Soviet Constitution. During that year, he and Pyatakov demanded the death sentence for Kamenev and Zinoviev, but by the end of the year he too was arrested and accused of maintaining secret relations with Trotsky, and of having formed a 'reserve centre' to take over from Kamenev and Zinoviev. At his trial, which began on 23 January 1937, he maintained an extremely ambiguous attitude. He was both insolent and cynical, but it was not clear whether he was insisting on incriminating himself and other potential victims (Tukhachevsky, for example) or whether he was trying to discredit the procedure of the trial and the regime in general. On seeing Radek leave the courtroom, someone said: 'He's a devil, not a man.' He was sentenced to ten years' imprisonment.

It is not known when he died, but it is assumed that he was murdered by his co-prisoners in 1939 or thereabouts. According to a different story, he may have stayed in Moscow after his sentence, and continued to work on *Izvestia*, before dying of a heart attack while being evacuated to Kuibyshev during the German offensive in 1941.[1]

G. H.

[1] For a critical analysis, see W. Lerner, 'The Unperson in Communist Historiography', *South Atlantic Quarterly*, LXV, no. 4 (autumn 1966), pp. 438–45.

KHRISTIAN GEORGIYEVICH RAKOVSKY
(autobiography)

I was born on 1 August 1873 in the Bulgarian town of Kotel. As early as the first half of the nineteenth century, Kotel had become an important economic and political centre. The family into which I was born belonged to the most prosperous class in town. My father engaged in agriculture and trade, and for the sake of the latter spent a few weeks in Constantinople every year. He was a member of the so-called 'Democratic Party', was noted for his inquisitiveness, had received a Gymnasium schooling and knew Greek. None of this, however, was of any benefit to me in my future development.

It was different with my mother. She came from a family which had played a vital part in the political and cultural history of the Bulgarian people. From it had come Captain Georgy Mamarchev, a former officer in Dibich-Zabalkansky's Russian army, who had made the first attempt at a concerted rising against the Turkish yoke. The rising was crushed and Mamarchev arrested. He was exiled to Asia Minor, and then to the island of Samos, where he died. He was the uncle of the famous revolutionary figure Savva Rakovsky, who dominated the Bulgarian political and cultural scene from 1840 until 1867. Whilst in Rumania in 1841, he had raised a partisan detachment to invade Bulgaria. He was arrested and sentenced to death, but escaped to France. An amnesty gave him the opportunity of returning to his native town, but not for long. Soon both father and son were flung into the Constantinople prison. The vengeance of their political opponents was also heaped on the now defenceless family, including my mother who was still then a girl. The family were excommunicated and forbidden all contact with neighbours, so that when there were no matches, at a time when a fire was lit by bringing embers from next door, they had to pay for the political sins of their father and brothers by starving and freezing. Although I reached the age of awareness many years after Savva Rakovsky's death, the reminiscences of my mother and grandmother were still sufficiently vivid to stir my imagination.

From early childhood I conceived a strong and passionate sympathy for Russia—not merely because the revolutionary activity of my grandfathers and uncles had been mainly connected with Russia, but also because I had witnessed the Russo-Turkish War. I was not more than five then, but the dim vision of Russian soldiers marching through the Balkans became imprinted on my childish memory. Our house was one of the best in town and therefore became the quarters of high-ranking officers. I met General Totleben, the architect of the siege of Plevna. I met and accompanied Prince Vyazemsky, one of the commanders of the Bulgarian militia division, who was later nursed for more than forty days in our house after being wounded. Among the officers there were also people in contact with underground organisations, and there was a legend in our family that they kept saying, 'We are liberating you, but who will liberate us?' The war upset our family life as well: our estate was inside Romania, and we all had to be evacuated to Romanian Dobruja.

I received my initial education in Kotel, and continued it in Dobruja under my mother's supervision. I spent the last year of primary school in Varna, and then went to the Gymnasium there. It was the period when even the youngest students were passionately interested in politics. I, too, began to take notice of social questions. In 1887 the political ferment at the Gymnasium came to a head, aided by discontent with a few teachers. A riot erupted, which it took a company of soldiers to suppress. I was one of those arrested and excluded from all Bulgarian schools. I spent one year in my father's house in Mangalia, reading indiscriminately everything that came to hand. In 1888 I was given permission to attend a Gymnasium again, and I went to Gabrovo, where I entered the fifth form. I spent less than two years here, for before the end of the sixth form I was again excluded from all Bulgarian schools, and this time it was for good.

It was in Gabrovo that my political ideas were moulded and I became a Marxist. My mentor was Dabev, one of the veterans of the Bulgarian revolutionary movement. Balabanov, a friend of mine who subsequently died a tragic death in Geneva, joined with me in publishing a clandestine, hectographed newspaper called *Zerkalo*, in which there was something of everything: Rousseau's educational ideas, the struggle between rich and poor, the misdeeds of teachers, etc. We also obtained a few illegal publications printed in Geneva and translated into Bulgarian, which we distributed among the peasants. Whilst still in the fifth form, I had stood up in the church at Kotel and preached about the 'first Christian church of St James'—in other words about Christian communism. But in general our activities were confined to the Gymnasium.

In autumn 1890 I set off for Geneva to enter the medical faculty. I chose medicine because we imagined that it would enable us to meet the people directly. At that time we only knew of individual influence. We still did not think of activities on a mass scale. It seemed to us that the regime of the Bulgarian dictator, Stambulov, would last for ever.

During the first few months after my arrival in Geneva, I became acquainted with the Russian political *émigrés* and, in particular, the Russian social democratic circles. A little later, I met Plekhanov,

Zasulich and Akselrod, and for many years their influence on me was decisive. I spent three years in Geneva, from 1890 to 1893. Although I enrolled as a student and even took the examinations, I was completely indifferent to medicine. My interests lay outside the university. I quickly became involved in activity among the Russian students, and directed Marxist self-education circles with Rosa Luxemburg, who lived for a short while in Geneva.

I did not confine myself, however, to purely Russian concerns. Together with other foreign and Russian comrades, we organised the socialist elements among the Geneva students. We also developed links with socialist students in other countries, particularly Belgium, where the first International Congress of Socialist Students was held in the winter of 1891–2. I did not succeed in attending this congress myself, although I corresponded with the organizers. Yet all the prepratory work for the second congress, which took place in Geneva, devolved in effect upon me. On all the most difficult problems, I consulted Plekhanov. I was also in touch with the Geneva and French labour movements. In Geneva I was close to the Polish and Armenian revolutionary circles as well, but my main preoccupation was with Bulgaria. I translated Deville's book *L'Évolution du Capital*, adding a long introduction which contained an analysis of economic relations in Bulgaria. Later, we edited a Bulgarian journal in Geneva, which in name, format and external appearance was a direct imitation of the Russian *émigré* journal *Sotsial-Demokrat*. But this was understandable since Plekhanov was also the inspiration behind our journal. I translated a number of his articles directly from the manuscript. When the first Marxist journal, *Den'*, was launched in Bulgaria, and the first SD weekly paper *Rabotnik* was founded, as well as *Drugar* ('Comrade'), I became a permanent contributor to them all, but particularly to the latter. Sometimes half an edition would be filled with my articles written under various pseudonyms. In 1893 I was a delegate to the Socialist International Congress in Zurich. This Geneva period in my life strengthened my Marxist convictions and my hatred for Russian Tsarism.

Whilst still a student in Geneva, I visited Bulgaria more than once to give a series of lectures attacking the Tsarist government. In 1897, when I graduated from the university, a book of mine was published in Bulgaria entitled *Russiya na Istok* ('Russia in the East'), which for years to come provided ammunition not only for the Bulgarian Socialist Party against Russian Tsarism, but also for all so-called russophobe tendencies in the Balkans. I was following Plekhanov's dictum: 'Tsarist Russia must be isolated in its foreign relations.' But the Bulgarian bourgeois press had already drawn attention to me during my first visits to Bulgaria. The russophile papers had waged a campaign against me while I was still a student. In autumn 1893 I entered the Medical Faculty in Berlin with the aim of acquainting myself more closely with the German labour movement. There I wrote articles on Balkan affairs for *Vorwärts*. I also joined the clandestine, socialist student groups and became particularly close to Wilhelm Liebknecht. Through him, I met the other leaders of German social democracy. He had a great influence on me, and we corresponded until 1900. He was greatly interested in the Balkans, and the Russian, Polish and Romanian revolutionary movements. In Berlin all my political life was centred on the Russian colony. This was the time of the flowering of Russian Legal Marxism. The Russian colony lived on arguments: about Populism and Marxism, about the subjectivist school and about dialectical materialism. But I also became involved in more specialised debates (for example against the Zionists).

After six months in Berlin I was arrested, and deported a few days later. I spent the summer term of 1894 at the Medical Faculty in Zurich, in which town P. B. Akselrod was also living, and the winter of 1894–5 in Nancy. I maintained contact with the Bulgarian movement and corresponded with Plekhanov and V. A. Zasulich, the latter living in London.

The last two years of my student career were spent in Montpellier. Besides associating with Russian and Bulgarian students, I also began to draw closer to the French socialists and to collaborate on the Marxist journal *La Jeunesse Socialiste*, edited in Toulouse by Lagardelle, as well as on the daily organ *La Petite République* when it passed under the control of Jules Guesde. The debate among Russian students in Montpellier revolved around the same topics as in Berlin. In addition, the Zionists here had many followers, against whom I waged an unceasing campaign. I was also a member of a French student circle and spoke at closed workers' meetings. Even in Nancy I had been kept under observation by the French police and as a result of this I could not, of course, expand my activities.

The end of my student days coincided with events that burst upon the European political scene: the rebellion in Armenia and on the island of Crete. In a series of articles I attempted to draw the attention of the French Socialist Party and the French proletariat to the advisability of interceding on behalf of the Armenians, Cretans and Macedonians. I believed in general that ignorance and a lack of understanding of Eastern questions were one of the defects of the international socialist movement, and I devoted a report to this problem which I presented on behalf of the Bulgarian SD Party at the London International Socialist Congress in 1896. It was subsequently reprinted by Kautsky in *Neue Zeit*.

I concluded my medical education with a doctoral dissertation on *The Causes of Criminality and Degeneracy*, in which I essayed a Marxist approach to the subject. It caused a sensation among students and professors which was echoed in the local press and, later, in specialist literature throughout the world.

It was in Montpellier that I began to take a closer interest in the Romanian labour movement. Although I was technically a Romanian citizen, I only came into formal contact with Romanian comrades at a late stage. I also began writing articles in French for some Poles from the PPS whom I had come across at the London International Socialist Congress. Of the other revolutionary parties, I was particularly drawn towards the Armenians, with whose Secretary I had been closely connected whilst still in Geneva.

In 1893 I had the good fortune to see and hear Engels in Zurich. We maintained an occasional correspondence when I was in Geneva— he sent a letter to our Bulgarian *Sotsial-Demokrat*. Subsequently I always approached him through V. A. Zasulich, for whom he had a deep love and respect.

When I graduated from the university in 1896, I was confronted by the question: what now? I had mainly worked for the Bulgarian Socialist Party but, on the other hand, I was a Romanian citizen. Yet my greatest wish, which was strengthened by the fact that I had married a Russian girl from Moscow, E. P. Ryabova, a revolutionary Marxist and a close friend of Plekhanov and Zasulich, was to work for the cause in Russia.

After visiting all the main centres of Bulgaria, where I read reports on various topics, and after passing a qualifying examination so that I could practise medicine in Bulgaria if the need should ever arise, I decided to settle temporarily in Romania as a stepping-stone on the way to Russia. In addition I was due for military service, and after taking preliminary medical examinations in Bucharest, I was enlisted as a doctor in the medical corps. In February 1899 I received two weeks' leave and went to St Petersburg, where my wife was already living. At this time the Russian Legal Marxist press had acquired its own journal, *Nashe Slovo*, later *Nachalo*. An article by me on political parties in Bulgaria was featured in the first of these under the *nom de plume* 'Radev'. A bitter polemic was then being waged in St Petersburg between Marxists and Populists. I used my stay to speak on the same subject at one of the branches of the Free Economic Society. Since I did not conceal my name, it was not difficult for the police to trace me. But by the time they had learnt my address, I had already left.

Military service did not interfere with my literary work. I continued diligently to provide contributions for Bulgarian socialist journals. The Party organ was no longer *Den'* but *Novoye Vremya*, a monthly edited by Blagoev. Besides this, I published in Bulgarian a book entitled *On the Political Significance of the Dreyfus Case*, as well as a polemical pamphlet against spiritualists called *Science and Miracles*. I recast my doctoral dissertation, turning it into a popular book which was actually passed by the Tsarist censorship under a new title, *The Hapless Folk*, and with the signature of a female doctor, Stanchova. It also appeared in Bulgarian, but with the name of its true author. At the same time I was preparing a book called *Contemporary France*, which had been commissioned by the *Znaniye* publishing house in St Petersburg.

During my short stay in the capital, I had counted on meeting Lenin, who was then in Pskov, but this was not to be. My military service ended on 1 January 1900. Once divested of my officer's uniform, I could openly express my views in the Romanian socialist press and at a workers' meeting in Bucharest. But I did this only to become aware of the utter decline of the labour movement following the betrayal of its leaders, who had deserted *en bloc* to Bratianu's Liberal Party. As I was longing to return to Russia, however, my activity in Romania was limited to this one speech. Whilst I was still in the country, I acted as a forwarding point for a voluminous correspondence between, on the one hand, Zasulich and Plekhanov, and on the other the St Petersburg Marxists. Zasulich herself came to Romania before I left—I supplied her with a Romanian passport in the name of Kirova so that she could cross into Russia, and I intended following her a few months later. By that time, the dispute had already begun between Bernstein's followers, in particular Struve, and the revolutionary Marxists. Plekhanov was especially incensed by the desertion of his close comrade. He wrote to me in Romania, saying that a bloc must be formed even with Mikhailovsky against Struve, and suggested that on my arrival in St Petersburg I should help him collaborate on *Russkoye Bogatstvo* under the name 'Beltov'.

When I reached St Petersburg, I discovered that Struve had veered sharply to the right. He bitterly reproached Zasulich for returning to Russia since, if discovered, she might compromise her 'friends'. This greatly distressed her, for she had been very attached to him since 1896 when he had stayed for a few weeks in London after the end of the International SD Congress. Things developed to such a pass that while Mikhailovsky, Karpov and Annensky, not to mention our Marxists (Tugan-Baranovsky, Veresaev, Bogucharsky, etc.,) would meet her in my wife's flat, Struve for a long time refused to see her.

As for Plekhanov's plan of contributing to *Russkoye Bogatstvo*, we discussed it in the Russian circle and rejected it as unsuitable. We thought it would be more advisable for him to write for *Zhizn*, published by Posse and Gorky.

I myself was extremely happy to be in St Petersburg. I inhaled great gulps of winter air and dreamt of prolonged activity in Russia. With my wife and some comrades (including A. N. Kalmykova and N. A. Struve, who was further to the left than her husband), we drew up plans for propaganda among workers and students. Very soon, however, I was ordered to leave Russia within forty-eight hours. This expulsion upset all my plans. I had no desire to return to the Balkans, for the closer I came to the Russian revolutionary movement, the more my interest in the Balkans decreased. It was suggested that I should go to Revel under police supervision and wait for a boat, which I did, accompanied by my wife. It was there that I completed *Contemporary France*, which was published under the pseudonym 'Insarov' (a name chosen for me by my St Petersburg friends).

Among those who were directly involved in efforts to win an extension of my stay in St Petersburg was N. I. Gurovich, who subsequently proved to be an *agent provocateur*. Before my departure, he assured me that, thanks to his connections at court (either with the brother or the brother-in-law of Baron Frederichs), he was convinced he would be able to arrange my return within a short period of time. He repeated this when he came to Paris in summer 1900, and his assertions about the possibility of my return became more frequent. Finally, he asked me for money 'to bribe the relatives of Baron Frederichs'. Of course, this was no problem and I was soon back in Russia. Before I left, I enrolled as a student at the Law Faculty in Paris, thinking that, after all that had happened in St Petersburg, I would not be able to remain there long and that I would have to return to France.

In St Petersburg it was like a desert. After the student disorders of spring 1901, a large number of propagandists had been banished from the capital, among them many Legal Marxists. The only link which remained for me was with the clandestine world, where Lenin's pamphlet *What is to be Done?* soon became the main topic of discussion.

I redoubled my collaboration on the 'thick' Russian journals, which continued until 1904, mainly under the pen names of 'Insarov' and 'Grigoriev'. But this still could not satisfy my longing for real activity, and after the misfortune of my wife's death I returned to Paris in 1902, where I began to sit law examinations with the intention of settling there, adopting French citizenship, and taking a militant part in the revolutionary movement.

It was at this time that I practised medicine freely for the only time in my life. I was a doctor for six months in the village of Beaulieu in the department of the Loire. I formed political as well as professional ties with the peasantry, particularly after an official banquet where I made a speech which greatly displeased the Senators and Deputies present. It was suggested that I should stay in Beaulieu, but the death of my father in summer 1903 forced me to return home. From that moment, I reverted to work with the Balkan parties, especially the Romanian labour movement.

During the winter of 1903–4 I returned to Paris, and I was there when the Russo-Japanese war broke out. I was one of the speakers at a huge meeting attended by representatives of all the revolutionary parties. My speech earned the reproaches of the chairman, my mentor Plekhanov, for its defeatist spirit. He had come to Paris before the declaration of war to give a paper, and as he was then expelled from the country, we had to prevail upon Clémenceau to intervene and obtain a temporary entry visa. I remember how, on the day following the meeting, Plekhanov, Jules Guesde and I were lunching together, and Plekhanov complained of my defeatism. Jules Guesde sententiously replied: 'Social democracy can never be anti-national.' Many a time after this Plekhanov reminded me of this phrase. Three months later I returned to Romania, and then to Bulgaria, where the split between the *tesnyaki* (those wanting a tight Party structure) and the *shirokiye* (who wanted a looser structure) was an accomplished fact. I sided firmly with the *tesnyaki*.

In the same year I attended the International Socialist Congress in Amsterdam, where I had mandates from the Serbian as well as the Bulgarian SD Parties. I was actively involved in the deliberations of the commission on tactics. Whilst I was in Amsterdam, I was invited by the Russian delegation to address a workers' meeting about the assassination of Plehve.

I returned once more to Romania, where the events of 9 January 1905 roused the working class. We founded the weekly newspaper *România Muncitoare* ('The Workers' Rumania'), which gave birth to a political organisation with the same name. Unlike the dissolved Romanian SD Party, which had mainly consisted of intellectuals and members of the *petite-bourgeoisie*, we paid the greatest attention to the formation of trade unions so as to provide a proletarian base for the SD Party. It was an extremely opportune moment. The working class readily responded to the call of *România Muncitoare*. The strike movement grew to such an extent that even the Bucharest police asked us for help in organising their strike. More and more trade unions came into being. Both capitalists and the government were taken completely by surprise, and the first strikes were ended quickly and successfully. But the employers retreated only the better to prepare a counter-attack.

The years 1905 and 1906 were marked by acute class conflict in
Romania. The press of all shades of opinion saw me as the inspiration for
this movement, and by concentrating their campaign against me, a
foreigner by birth, supposed that they could discredit the whole labour
movement. Two events infuriated the Romanian government and ruling
classes even more: the arrival in Constanza of the battleship *Potyomkin*,
and the peasant rebellion of spring 1907. The government suspected a
hidden motive behind the appearance of the *Potyomkin* and my help in
organising its sailors—that of using the latter to provoke a revolution
in Romania and thereby further the revolution in Russia. We, however,
set ourselves the more modest goal of politically educating the *Potyomkin*'s crew. Between the ship's arrival and the peasant rebellion, there
occured another event which put the government even more on its
guard. A ship loaded with arms from Varna (dispatched by Litvinov, as I
later learnt), and bound for Batum, ran aground on the Romanian coast
and was seized by the authorities. I had a meeting with the crew, among
whom was the Bolshevik delegate Kamo. I learnt from him that it was a
case of treachery, as the captain himself had turned the ship towards the
shore. But whatever the reason, this extremely valuable cargo of at least
50,000 rifles, formally destined for the Macedonian revolutionary organisation in Turkey, was now in the hands of the Romanian government. The press began to claim that it had really been intended for a
rising in Dobruja and pointed a finger in my direction.

In February 1907 the peasant rebellion broke out. It was directed at
first against Jewish tenants in northern Moldavia and was prompted by
the antisemitic outbursts of Romanian liberals and nationalists. After
plundering the Jews' farmsteads, however, the peasants turned on the
Romanian tenants and then the landlords. The position became critical.
The whole country, that is all the villages, was engulfed in the flames of
the rising. The government massacred peasants and demolished villages
with artillery. Its second action was to take rapid reprisals against the
labour movement, which had kept the town authorities on constant alert
on the eve of the peasant rising. So as to render the movement harmless, a whole series of measures were taken in the towns: searches, confiscation of socialist newspapers, closure of trade union premises, and the
arrest of workers' leaders. I was the first to be detained. This was soon
followed by the blatantly illegal act of deportation. For the next five
years, the class struggle of the Romanian workers raged around the question of my return, which they had set as a practical objective. From exile
I continued to participate in the leadership of the Romanian labour
movement and to write for Party and trade union organs, in addition to
producing pamphlets and the SD journal *Viitorul Social*. I also pre-

pared two books: one in Romanian, *From the Kingdom of Arbitrariness and Cowardice*, and one in French, *La Roumanie des boïars*. The first was intended for the Romanian workers, the second for the information of socialist parties and public opinion abroad, but both dealt with the persecution of Romanian workers and peasants.

I returned secretly to Romania in 1909. I was arrested and deported without a trial. I resisted and a free-for-all ensued until I could be bundled into the carriage. At the border, the Hungarian authorities refused to admit me, and I was shuttled backwards and forwards like a parcel between the two countries until finally, after diplomatic negotiations between the Romanian and Austro-Hungarian governments, I was allowed into Hungary. Both my comrades and I had been counting on a series of prosecutions against me which they could use for agitation in the workers' organisations. Even earlier, in March or April 1908, the Romanian government had brought two charges against me in my absence. In doing so (and in order to justify my deportation, since there was no law in Romania which empowered the government to deport its own citizens), it resorted to unbelievable legal chicanery, and did not even shrink from fabricating evidence against me. We struggled to have my case tried while I was in the country, but the government preferred to let me go free abroad, rather than hold me in prison and try me, thus providing a weapon which could be turned against it and the bourgeoisie.

Although the fact of my arrest had been withheld, it nevertheless found its way into the papers, whereupon the government categorically denied it. The Romanian working class, which knew from experience that the government was capable of all sorts of illegality, saw its attempt to conceal my arrest and my non-admittance into Hungary as an indication of its criminal intentions towards me. Their indignation grew until on 19 October 1909, after a remark by Bratianu reported in the evening papers that he would 'rather destroy me than let me back into Romania', they organised a street demonstration which ended in a bloody battle with the police. Apart from the dozens of injured, roughly thirty workers were arrested, among them the leaders of trade union and political labour movements, who were beaten up in the Bucharest police cellars the same night. All these outrages provoked protests not only inside Romania – in working-class areas both large and small, and in the bourgeois-democratic press – but also abroad. The conflict between the government and the workers became more acute. There was an unsuccessful attempt on Bratianu's life, in which it transpired that even the police were implicated. This attempt was the signal for new repressions against the workers and for emergency laws banning strikes and suspending the right of association. The government could no longer remain in office and it departed, cursed by the workers, to be replaced by a Conservative government headed by Carp.

In February 1910 I secretly re-entered Romania. This time I managed to reach the capital and, after contacting the comrades, I gave myself up to the judicial authorities. Yet again the government preferred to pack me off abroad rather than open wide the gates of prison. Since I was barred from entering Hungary, it twice tried to hustle me across the Bulgarian border and failed. The way was still open for them to deport me to Russia, but they could not resort to this, and only the sea was left. I was put aboard a steamship, armed with a Romanian passport, and sent off to Constantinople. Here too, however, I was arrested after a few days by the Young Turk authorities on the demand of the Romanian police, but the intervention of Turkish socialist deputies released me from prison. I arrived in Sofia and organised the daily socialist newspaper *Napred*, the main task of which was opposition to the bellicose Bulgarian nationalism which was inciting war in the Balkans. Of course, I became a target for all Bulgarian nationalists.

In the meantime, a change in my favour was about to take place in Romania. The main enemy of the labour movement was the Liberal Party, which represented not only landlords and tenant capital, but also most industrial capital. After a few concessions to the peasants, which brought a little calm to the villages, the conservatives decided that for the time being they need not fear fresh outbursts from the peasantry and that the labour movement could be of use to them in their struggle with the liberals. Whatever the reasons, after my second return and second deportation, the conservatives declared that they were ready to allow a review of my case. The decree on my exile was rescinded and a special court restored my political rights. This was in April 1912.

We were not fated to enjoy for long the period of 'peaceful' party organisation. In autumn 1912 the First Balkan War broke out, and not a year had passed after its conclusion before the omens of world-wide conflict could be read by all. From August 1914 until August 1916, when Romania entered the war, its SD Party had to sustain a very hard struggle. We had to defend the country's neutrality against two pro-war parties—the russophiles and the germanophiles. The argument was not confined to unprecedentedly bitter polemics in the press, at meetings and street demonstrations. It occasionally assumed more tragic proportions. In 1916 a massacre of workers took place at Galatzi, in which eight people were killed. I was arrested and accused of organising an 'insurrection' against the authorities. This provoked an outburst of indignation among the workers. A general strike was declared in Bucharest, which threatened to spread to the whole country. The government was obviously afraid of sparking off disorders on the eve of war and freed me, as well as the other arrested comrades.

During the period 1914–16, my activities were not limited to a struggle with the Romanian bourgeoisie and landowners. As a member of the Romanian Central Committee, I did everything in my power to build up contacts with those parties, groups and individual comrades abroad who remained faithful to the precepts of the International.

In April 1915 I was invited by the Italian Socialist Party to an international anti-war meeting in Milan. On the way home, I broke my journey in Switzerland to meet Lenin and the Swiss workers' party. Even before this, I had been in contact with Trotsky who was then editing *Nashe Slovo* in Paris, and for which I also wrote. These discussions and meetings ended in the summoning of the Zimmerwald Conference.

During the preceding summer, a conference had met in Bucharest of all the Balkan socialist parties with a platform based on explicitly internationalist and class principles. Consequently the party of the Bulgarian Social Democratic opportunists (the *shirokiye*) was excluded from the conference. A 'Revolutionary Balkan Social Democratic Labour Federation' was formed, comprising the Romanian, Bulgarian, Serbian and Greek parties. A Central Bureau was elected, and I became its Secretary. Thus even before the Zimmerwald Conference, the Balkan parties had indicated their implacable hostility to imperialism.

I participated in the Berne Conference of Zimmerwald delegates in spring 1916, where I spoke with Lenin at an international workers' meeting. But I did not have an opportunity of attending the Kienthal Conference, since Romania's borders had been closed in readiness for war. Hostilities commenced in August 1916, and within one month I was under arrest.

The Romanian government dragged me with it when it retreated from Bucharest to Iassy, where I was freed by Russian troops on 1 May 1917. The first town which I visited after my release was Odessa. Here I began my struggle against the war and 'defencism', and I continued this campaign after arriving in Petrograd. Although I had not yet joined the Bolshevik Party and I disagreed with them on some points, I was threatened with deportation if I continued my activities.

During the Kornilov days, I was hidden by the Bolshevik organisation at the Sestroretsk cartridge factory, and from there made my way to Kronstadt. When Kornilov had been defeated, I decided to go to Stockholm, where a conference of the Zimmerwald left was due to meet. I was still there when the October Revolution broke out. In December I was in Petrograd, and at the beginning of January I left for the south as an organiser and Commissar for the Sovnarkom of the RSFSR, escorted by a detachment of sailors led by Zheleznyakov. I spent a certain time in Sebastopol and after organising an expedition to the Danube to fight against the Romanians who had already occupied Bessarabia, I accompanied it as far as Odessa. Here a Supreme Autonomous Collegium was set up for the struggle against counterrevolution in Romania and the Ukraine, and as its Chairman and a member of Rumcherod (the Central Executive Council of Romanian Soviets), I remained in Odessa until the town was captured by the Germans. Thence I went to Nikolaev, the Crimea, Ekaterinoslav (where I attended the second Congress of Ukrainian Soviets), Poltava and Kharkov. After my arrival in Moscow, where I spent no more than a month, I departed for Kursk with a delegation which was to hold peace talks with the Central Ukrainian Rada. There we learnt of Skoropadsky's *coup d'état*. We concluded a ceasefire with the Germans, who were continuing their offensive, and then the Skoropadsky government proposed that we should go to Kiev. Here the task of our delegation was to explain to the workers and peasant masses the true policy of the Soviet government, contrasting it with the policies of Skoropadsky, the Central Rada, and the other agents of German imperialism and the Russian landlords. In September, I was sent on an emergency mission to Germany to continue negotiations with the German government about a peace treaty with the Ukraine.

From there, I was due to go to Vienna, where a republic already existed, and whilst in Berlin I received the agreement of the Austrian government, whose Foreign Minister at that time was the leader of Austrian social democracy, Victor Adler. But the German authorities refused to allow this. Indeed, I was soon expelled from Germany with Ioffe (our Ambassador), Bukharin and other comrades. We were still on our way to the border under German escort when, at Borisov, we received news of the German revolution.

Shortly afterwards, the TsIK included me in the delegation which was to attend the first Congress of German Soviets of Workers' and Soldiers' Deputies—the other members being Marchlewski, Bukharin, Ioffe, Radek and Ignatov. We were detained, however, by the German military authorities in Kovno and after a few days' 'imprisonment' sent back to Minsk. After a short stay there, and also in Gomel, where German control was tottering, I arrived in Moscow. I was summoned from there by the Ukrainian CC to become President of the Provisional Revolutionary Government of the Workers and Peasants of the Ukraine. The third All-Ukrainian Congress of Soviets was convened in March 1918 and there I was elected Chairman of the Ukrainian Sovnarkom. I held this post until mid-September at first in Kharkov, then in Kiev and, after the evacuation of Kiev, in Chernigov.

In mid-September I went to Moscow and, whilst retaining my chairmanship, I was also put in charge of the Political Directorate of the RVS of the Republic. I directed this institution until January during the dark days of the thrusts by Denikin, Kolchak and Yudenich.

When Kharkov was liberated from the Whites, I was soon designated Chairman of the Sovnarkom of the Ukrainian Soviet Republic and member of the RVS of what was then the South-Western Front. Here we had gained the advantage against Denikin and were now conducting the war with the Poles. Subsequently, this area was renamed the Southern Front and its RVS was led by the late M. V. Frunze, whose colleague I remained. I held the chairmanship of the Ukrainian Sovnarkom simultaneously with the chairmanship of other bodies: the Extraordinary Commission for the Struggle against Banditry, the Emergency Sanitary Commission, the Special Commission for Fuel and Food, and the Ukrainian Economic Council. I remained continuously in the Ukraine until July 1923, with the exception of the period when I accompanied Chicherin, Litvinov and others to the Genoa Conference.

In July 1923 I was named Plenipotentiary in England, where I conducted negotiations for the recognition of the Soviet Union by the British government. Later I headed the Soviet delegation which concluded the well-known agreements with MacDonald, only to see them repudiated by the new Conservative government.

From London I directed talks with Herriot, and then with Herriot and de Monzie, which led to the recognition of the Soviet Union by the French government. Since the end of October 1925 I have been Ambassador in Paris.

Since 1918 I have been a member of the TsIK, at first of the RSFSR and then of the USSR, and I was a Presidium member until 1925. Since 1919 I have also had a seat on the CC of the RKP. Until 1924 I was a member of the following Ukrainian bodies: the TsIK, the CC and the Politburo.

Khristian Rakovsky enjoyed international notoriety and authority before 1917, and brought to the Russian Revolution all his militant fervour and experience, his stature and talents, his courage and clarity; his view of affairs, moreover, was on a European level, and profoundly internationalistic. He was Bulgarian by birth, Romanian by nationality, French by education and Russian by his relations, feelings and culture; and he was characterised by a subtle mind, a 'profound nobility of soul' (Trotsky) and a wide culture combined with great efficiency, little taste for violence and a very special regard for human relationships.

The essential aspects of his life are presented in the following words, spoken at his trial in 1938: 'Citizens, since my earliest youth I have carried out my duties as a soldier in the fight for the emancipation of labour with honesty, loyalty and devotion.' Everywhere his eventful life took him, he played an active part in workers' movements: in Bulgaria, where he was one of the pioneers of socialism; in Russia, where he became the *enfant chéri* of the *Osvobozhdeniye Truda* group leaders, Plekhanov and Vera Zasulich; in France, where he acquired a following among the supporters of Jules Guesde; and in Romania, where from 1905 on he became the leader of the reawakening workers' movement. He was involved at various times in all the branches of these parties' internal life, from practical organising to major political decision-making. Rakovsky's autobiography, centred as it is on his involvement in the Russian movement, gives but a pale image of the multifarious sides to his eventful life. His rich and colourful existence was affected, down to his choice of profession, to his revolutionary faith and socialist beliefs, by his endless peregrinations and by his multiple activities, which also made him, according to Trotsky, 'one of the most truly international figures in the European socialist movement'.

Rakovsky was an untiring propagandist, a learned essayist and a highly talented polemicist: his works number several hundred pamphlets, articles and studies. His writings and speeches have appeared in many languages and in countless papers and reviews. He sought not effects but effectiveness, and was not averse to using anonymity, or many different pseudonyms, even when circumstances did not demand such discretion. Rakovsky dealt with all manner of questions, from Marxist theory to history, philosophy and art, down to the practical details of the workers' struggle. In Bulgaria he was one of the best-known Marxists of his day, and according to D. Blagoev, his historical works and philosophical polemics 'constituted a remarkable weapon in the theoretical and practical struggle against the adversaries of socialism, of which the most vulgar and fierce were the russophiles'.

His role in Romania was similar; there, he centred his writings mainly on the theoretical and practical problems of the workers' movement. In Russia, the lengthy studies which he published in the major reviews of the period showed him to be extremely knowledgeable about France. As Anatole de Monzie remarked about a book published by Rakovsky (in Russian) under the title *Contemporary France*, 'this work is evidence both of impeccable erudition and of warm sympathy for the

Third Republic'—though in fact, the sympathy was for French republican and democratic traditions.

In France and Germany he was a permanent contributor to most of the major socialist organs of the day, and he specialised in Balkan affairs and their problems with regard to peace. It must be remembered that Rakovsky's most original contribution before 1914 was his study of the question of nationalities in the Balkans. He was a bitter opponent of all forms of nationalism and elaborated a socialist solution to the problem which launched the struggle for a federation of Balkan democratic republics.

His writings and his predominant role in Balkan socialism were not, however, the sole sources for his international notoriety. While he was still a student, he was one of the promoters of the International Socialist Students' Assizes. He was a familiar face at international socialist congresses from 1893 on. He was a delegate to the ISB, and was entrusted by the International, at the time of the Balkan crises, with confidential missions aimed at ending divergences and co-ordinating socialist action in the dangerous 'powder-house of Europe'. He was the bogeyman of all Balkan governments, and had his card in the files of all the police forces in Europe. He was expelled seven times—from Germany, from Russia, and most frequently of all, from Romania. Each time, he took refuge in France, and in 1901 he thought of naturalising. In France, his strong personality, his eloquence and subtlety, his manner and bearing, his whole style of life not only conquered many socialists, but won over a number of politicians of various shades of opinion. In Paris, too, he formed the friendship which was to concern every aspect of his subsequent destiny: in 1903, he met Trotsky. Trotsky's visit to Romania as a war correspondent in 1913 served to strengthen the links that became active collaboration after the outbreak of world conflict. Rakovsky gave financial support to Trotsky's paper, *Nashe Slovo*, and the two worked together on the same platform amongst the internationalists. Rakovsky was keenly active in support of Balkan neutrality, and he attempted to regroup all the socialists from the neutral countries and to work out a common platform for action. Using the social democrats as a go-between, Germany attempted to make use of Rakovsky's neutralist propaganda. First Parvus, then Südekum came to Bucarest to win over to their cause the author of the celebrated reply to Charles Dumas, which had savagely criticised the *Union Sacrée* in France. Rakovsky's criticisms, coming from a known francophile, offended French socialists, who gave credence to the violent smear campaign launched in France by the Romanian right wing which accused him of being a German agent. Rakovsky had taken part in the first anti-militarist and pacifist congress in Milan in spring

1915, and he was also one of the moving spirits of the Zimmerwald Conference, where he supported Trotsky's theses and was on the commission which drew up the resolution.

In the years 1915–16, Rakovsky found himself under a considerable amount of attack: on the left, Lenin accused him of centrism, found his position harmful and declared there was no common way with men of Rakovsky's sort; on the right he was the bogeyman of the Bulgarian and Romanian nationalists—and the latter threw him into prison as soon as Romania entered the war. A little pamphlet denouncing the 'crimes of the Romanian oligarchy' and published in Paris by the Committee for the Resumption of International Relations was dedicated to 'Comrade C. Rakovsky, the valiant leader of Romanian social democracy, who, after having been insulted, outraged and calumnied during two years of chauvinistic lunacy, now has to atone in jail for the crime of not having wished to renounce his ideals'.

Rakovsky was freed in May 1917 by Russian soldiers on the Romanian Front who had been won over to the Revolution, and he then put himself at the service of the Russian Revolution. He joined Martov's internationalist group. At that time he differed from the Bolsheviks on fundamental questions, and he kept his earlier reservations about Lenin. The two men had known each other personally since 1900, but after the schism in 1903 Rakovsky had withdrawn from the Russian revolutionary movement and had not made a public issue of his hostility towards Lenin. He simply ignored him while keeping up a close relationship with Plekhanov, Akselrod and other Menshevik leaders. Their meetings and talks with Lenin during the war, in Switzerland, did not bring any real change in their relationship. It was Trotsky's influence that made Rakovsky change his attitude and join the Bolsheviks on the eve of the October Revolution. Thenceforth he was entrusted with missions of ever greater importance, and the main theatre of his activities during the Civil War was the Ukraine. He was given the hot seat in this critical area because of his political stature, which was called for by both the military situation and the divergences between the Ukrainian communists. Only Rakovsky could rise above the crowd and arbitrate between the two hostile and warring factions, namely the left-wing communists, known as the 'ultra-internationalists', and the Ukrainian communists, or Separatists.

Thus in the summer of 1919, the Politburo dismissed the military leaders on the Ukrainian Front after a military defeat, but did not extend this measure to Rakovsky because 'he was a great political figure'. During the Polish campaign, Lenin sent Rakovsky and Smilga as political commissars to Tukhachevsky. It was strange that Rakovsky, one of the founders of the Comintern, was not called to play his part as a leader of that organisation like other foreign communists, but served the cause as a member of the CPSU in the Soviet Federation. At the third Congress of the Ukrainian Soviets, he was appointed President of the Council of People's Commissars. As head of the USSR's second republic, with the most wide-ranging authority, Rakovsky 'was to exercise all his talents—administrative, legal, medical, pedagogic and economic'. He was a member of the Russian CC until 1925, and took an active part in the major struggles and divergences in the period 1921–3. He supported the confederate principle in the construction of the Soviet Union, and fought Stalin's policies of russification and his plans for centralisation. At the thirteenth Congress, he attacked him forthrightly. Rakovsky's work on the question of nationalities, his own unimpeachable internationalism and the position he held lent his views great weight and made him a considerable opponent for the General Secretary. The question of nationalities was however only one side to their differences. With his critical mind and attachment to the principles of workers' democracy, Rakovsky was one of the most active and distinctive figures in the left-wing opposition, led by his old friend Trotsky.

In July 1923 he left his post in the Ukraine to take up a diplomatic career. Indeed, nobody seemed better qualified for this than Rakovsky, for the main objective of Soviet diplomacy was to break down the isolation of the USSR. In summer 1918, he had been entrusted with the task of arranging a truce with the Ukrainian Rada; he had like Ioffe and Bukharin been one of the delegation that went to Berlin; and it was Rakovsky who had concluded the agreement with Lithuania. In the context of the year 1923, however, his transfer to the diplomatic service was only a clever manoeuvre to get him out of the way. He was a member of the Soviet delegation at the Genoa Conference, and in 1923 was made Ambassador to Britain. In 1925 he was put in charge of the Paris Embassy. He carried out his ambassadorial duties with ingenuity and gusto.

Despite his being far away, he remained active in the opposition. He was recalled to Moscow in 1927, where he continued the struggle and involved himself in all the activities of the opposition. At the fifteenth Congress, he acted as spokesman for the indomitable oppositionists. On being asked to yield to the CC, he gave this reply, which demonstrates well the courage, obstinacy and generosity of his character: 'I am beginning to be an old man. Why should I spoil my autobiography?' He was expelled from the Party with the other oppositionists, and deported first to Saratov then to Astrakhan; but he continued none the less to lead the opposition and to draw up his political writings in the form of letters. With his lucid mind he made a penetrating analysis of the decadence of

Soviet power in an article known in English as 'The Occupational Hazards of Power'. Rakovsky signed the opposition declaration at the sixteenth Congress, remaining unshakable even after the mass capitulation of 1929. He was sent to Barnaul, in Kazakhstan, as a minor official in the Gosplan, but still remained firm: he composed critical analyses and sent them to the CC. Stalin's entourage did not publish these works, but had to take them into account; Molotov himself took on the task of refuting them in the newspaper *Bolshevik*. Rakovsky's health was ruined by the Kazakhstani climate and in 1932 rumours reached Europe that he had died.

In April 1934 Rakovsky capitulated. It was out of conviction that he did what neither intimidation nor the harsh conditions he endured in detention had been able to force him to do. He considered that the international situation threatened the Soviet Union, and that in these conditions he had no alternative but to rally to the leadership. Stalin gave Rakovsky's letter enormous publicity and did not try to hide his satisfaction at this turn of events. He had succeeded in checkmating a man whom he found especially odious, who enjoyed a reputation for integrity and independence, and who was to cap it all the best friend Trotsky had.

Rakovsky then found himself entrusted with a Red Cross mission to Japan which turned out to be a frame-up. He was arrested and charged with espionage; with Bukharin, Rykov and Krestinsky he was one of the main defendants in the third and last big Moscow trial which opened on 2 March 1938. Rakovsky was the eldest defendant to appear before Vyshinsky, the judge, but he was a broken, exhausted old man. What had been a slanderous implication about Rakovsky during the First World War became the main charge against him: that he had been a German spy since 1914. At the time of the trial, Rakovsky was a veteran of fifty years standing in the ranks of revolutionary socialism, and his disciples included every important figure in the socialist movement of the Balkans; among them was Georgui Dimitrov, General Secretary at that time of Comintern. He was sentenced to twenty-five years imprisonment and died in a concentration camp, probably in 1941.

Rakovsky's sentence was first and foremost a way of getting at Trotsky. It was both a political and moral execution. Rakovsky's name was struck out of the history of the USSR and only very recently has it reappeared in the histories of the Bulgarian and Romanian workers' movements; yet a so-called 'historical school' in the West still repeats the slanders of the Romanian chauvinists of 1915 and the insinuations made by Vyshinsky.

G.H.

LARISSA MIKHAILOVNA REISNER

Larissa Mikhailovna Reisner, the daughter of the communist professor M. A. Reisner, was born on 1 May 1895 in the Polish Kingdom in Lublin, where her father was lecturer at the Pulawy Agricultural Institute. She spent her childhood in Germany and went to primary school in Berlin and Heidelberg. There she grew up in an atmosphere dominated by her father's connections with *émigré* Russian revolutionaries and the leaders of German social democracy. These years sowed the seeds of a lifelong attachment to German culture, and a few years spent in Paris with her parents widened the scope of her cultural interests.

She went to school in Russia just after the suppression of the 1905 Revolution, and already at the Gymnasium she displayed her literary abilities and revolutionary temperament. She took to literature at an early age, and a strong formative influence was a friend of her parents, Leonid Andreyev, who guided her through literary history. He did not, however, greatly influence her ideas, as can be seen from the drama *Atlantis* which she wrote at the age of seventeen and which was printed by the 'Shipovnik' publishing house in 1913. The theme of this drama was the attempt of a man to save society by personal sacrifice. The sources from which she drew material for the play – including Pellman's *History of Communism* – clearly indicate the nature of her ideas at that time.

From the very beginning of the war she was acutely distressed by the collapse of international social democracy and the Russian intelligentsia's conversion to chauvinism. She fully agreed with her parents' split with Andreyev on these grounds. For Professor Reisner it was unthinkable that one should hold aloof from the anti-war campaign and this impelled him to publish the journal *Rudin*, which both by outspoken articles and brilliant caricatures of the deserters to the patriotic camp represented a graphic protest against the war by an isolated, intellectual, revolutionary group. The moving spirit behind *Rudin* was Larissa, who printed in it not only brilliant, well-turned verses, but also a whole series of pungent sketches. At the same time, she shouldered the burden of arguments with the censorship and the raising of funds. When the latter ran out, *Rudin* had to close, and Larissa began to contribute articles to Gorky's *Letopis*. In 1917, even before the Revolution, she became associated with workers' circles. The February Revolution set her immediately among the opponents of a coalition with the bourgeoisie. A telling pamphlet against Kerensky printed in *Novaya Zhizn* provoked not only a broadside from the bourgeois press but even frightened the editorial board of Gorky's journal. She also became involved in large-scale workers' organisations and educational circles among the Kronstadt sailors.

The October Revolution met with a ready response from her. During the first months she was busy preserving works of art, not in the spirit of a protector of the old against barbarians, but in order that the best of our cultural heritage should be saved to inspire the creators of the new culture. The outbreak of civil war destroyed all the attractions of this work. She longed for direct combat, and Sviyazhsk, near Kazan, where the Red Army was being forged in its struggle with the Czechs, saw her in the front line with a rifle in her hand, as veterans of this campaign recounted.[1]

Similarly she later participated in the whole campaign of the Volga flotilla. A veteran of these battles and former Tsarist officer, F. Novitsky, has told[2] of the respect this young revolutionary earned among experienced soldiers by her intrepidity in the most dangerous situations. After the defeat of the Czechs and the liberation of the Volga, it was inconceivable that she should be separated from the Red Navy, and she was named one of the Commissars on its Staff. Her enthusiasm and sensitivity, allied with her imperturbable and clear-headed reasoning, enabled her to win the respect of top-ranking Tsarist officers like Admirals Altvater and Berens who, after joining the Soviets, needed a dynamic person to help them identify with the Revolution.

When our flotilla was again pressed into service against Denikin, Larissa saw action with it from Astrakhan to Enzeli. After the end of the Civil War, she lived in Petrograd and attempted to study at first hand the life of the working masses in a factory. She was driven to the verge of despair by the Kronstadt rebellion and the beginning of NEP and, full of unease about the future of Soviet Russia, she went to Afghanistan as wife of the Soviet Plenipotentiary there, F. F. Raskolnikov. In Kabul, she did not remain a mere spectator of the diplomatic struggle between the Soviet representatives and British imperialism. She sought the most active involvement by ingratiating herself with the Emir's harem, since it played an influential role in Afghan politics. From the vantage-point of Afghanistan, which was considered an Indian outpost by the British, she was able to make a study of Britain's policy in India and the Indian nationalist movement.

When she returned from Kabul in 1923, she published *The Front* and *Afghanistan*. *The Front* will always remain one of the most brilliant literary portrayals of the Civil War. It is remarkable for the sensitivity and attention with which the author observes not only the heroes and

[1] See e.g. A. Kremlev, *Krasnaya Zvezda* 14 February 1926.
[2] *Izvestiya*, 12 February 1926.

leaders of the war, but also the masses who were directly responsible for victory.

In October 1923 she went to Germany with a dual goal. Ostensibly she would evoke for the Russian workers the civil war which was in the offing there as a result of the economic chaos and the seizure of the Ruhr by the French. At the same time, in case of a seizure of power in Saxony, she was to serve as liaison officer between the local German social democratic organisation and the Comintern representatives in Dresden. Events in Saxony, however, did not develop as had been hoped. After the defeat there, life in Berlin became extremely difficult and she helped to ascertain the moods of the people for the Comintern men who lived as a tight, conspiratorial group. She stood in queues of unemployed at labour exchanges and in front of shops; she went to factory assemblies, social democratic meetings, and hospitals; she participated in the first demonstrations we managed to organise despite the dissolution of the Communist Party by the government.

At the first news of the Hamburg rising she hurried there, but it was a short-lived affair and she only arrived after it had been crushed. She collected details of the heroic resistance of the Hamburg proletariat from the families of fugitives, and she found her way into the court-rooms where summary justice was meted out to the vanquished. She had her material checked by outstanding participants in the rising, re-turned to Russia, and wrote *Hamburg at the Barricades*, which was printed in the first number of the journal *Zhizn*. It is a unique work of its kind, for neither the Finnish uprising[1] nor Soviet Hungary[2] has pro-duced its like. The German censorship and the imperial court banned the German edition of the book and ordered it to be burnt. An aesthete protested against the ban in the liberal *Frankfurter Zeitung* in view of the book's great artistic merit, but the class-ridden legal system of the German counter-revolution knew what it was doing in destroying the book which preserved the spirit of the Hamburg uprising for the German proletariat.

Hardly had she recovered from the harsh conditions of the con-spiratorial life she had had to lead in Hamburg, than she was off to the Urals to study the living conditions of the proletariat there. This trip not only fulfilled a literary goal. She had already had her doubts about NEP and now she set them against real life. In the backbreaking labour

---

[1] The uprising by Finnish socialists took place on 28 January 1918. It was crushed with the help of a German expeditionary force in April and May 1918, the final remnants surrendering on 4/5 May.

[2] The Hungarian Soviet Republic was formed in March 1919 and was sup-pressed by foreign intervention the following July.

of the engineering workers and the masses, and in the work of administrators scattered in settlements throughout the Urals, she found the
answer to the question as to whether we are building socialism or
capitalism. She returned full of faith in our future and threw herself
into a study of our economic construction. She tore herself away from
her books to visit the Donbass and the textile region. Her book *Iron,
Coal and Living People* depicts the Russian proletariat at work. From the
artistic point of view it is remarkable for the fact that Larissa, who had
grown up among the Acmeists and had had a very refined style, was now
beginning to write more simply and straightforwardly for the sake of
the working masses. This was not artificial vulgarisation but the fruit of
the greater *rapport* with the workers which she achieved during her trips
as a propagandist with the Moscow garrison.

In 1925, ill with malaria since the Persian expedition, she set out for
treatment in Germany, but even illness could not prevent her from contacting the Hamburg proletariat. She slipped away from the malaria
hospital to take part in a demonstration by the Hamburg communists,
and after recovering slightly she toured Germany, studying the conditions of the working class and the social changes which had resulted
from stabilisation. She not only visited the workers' quarters, the
barracks of mass poverty, but also found her way into the Junkers
technical laboratory, the Krupp offices, the huge Ullstein newspaper
plant and the coal mines in Westphalia. Her book *In the Country of
Hindenburg* is not merely a number of artistic sketches, but a masterful,
large-scale socio-political canvas painted by someone deeply sympathetic
to the struggle of the working class.

As soon as she finished this work, she set about examining material
on the Decembrists. Her sketches of Trubetskoy, Kakhovsky and
Shteingel evoked warm praise from the best Russian Marxist historian
and also represented the peak of her artistic achievement. She never saw
these works in print. She contracted typhus at a time when her head was
full of plans for a book about the life of the Urals workers at three
periods in history: during the Pugachov revolt, under capitalism and
then under Soviet power. She also had in mind a large-scale book on the
history of the proletarian liberation movement. Her body had been so
ravaged by malaria that it was unable to withstand the illness, and on
9 February 1926 she passed away in the Kremlin hospital. She was on the
threshold of a great creative career.

In her died a valiant communist who had been directly involved in
the liberation struggle and whose lot it had been to write a vivid evocation of it. In her died a communist deeply attached to the Russian working class, but who was also able, thanks to her great culture, to become

associated with the revolutionary movement in East and West. In her, lastly, died a profoundly revolutionary woman, a precursor of the new human type which is born in the throes of revolution.

K. Radek

In the words of Lev Nikulin, 'Nature gave her everything: intelligence, talent, and beauty.' She was indeed of an uncommon stamp, and her destiny was far from ordinary. She was a Commissar in the Fifth Army—the army of Ivan Smirnov, Putna and Tukhachevsky, the army that repulsed the Czechoslovaks in their wanderings towards Moscow, which held back Kolchak, shook him badly and retook Siberia. She was a Commissar on the General Staff of the Red Fleet, and a member of the Red Fleet's expedition from Astrakhan to Enzeli. She was the wife of Fyodor Raskolnikov, Vice-President of the Kronstadt Soviet, first Soviet Minister Plenipotentiary to Afghanistan (she left him, however, on their return from that country). She was sent by the Russian CP's Central Committee to Saxony in 1923, was a belated but enthusiastic witness of the Hamburg insurrection, that unfortunate twist to the failed German revolution of 1923; and she died of malaria in 1926 at the age of thirty-one. Even in her death, Larissa Reisner belonged to the realm of legend: for she contracted the disease in Persia, and died of it at about the time when many men, such as Lutovinov, who could not stand the contrast between the days of revolution and civil war and the rule of the Central Committee, where Stalin was still apparently only *primus inter pares*, were committing suicide. Raskolnikov, a morbidly jealous husband, had treated her roughly, and she became Radek's companion.

Larissa Reisner was, then, a character of some stature. Radek's biography gives her life its true dimension, for it recounts a destiny rather than a mere life. It is significant that Radek, whose style is frequently so verbose, fantastical and humorous, should have given here only a concise outline. The biography can be complemented with what Trotsky wrote in *My Life* (though there are, as can be seen, two small inaccuracies in it):

> Larissa Reisner occupied an important place in the Fifth Army, as she did in the Revolution as a whole. This beautiful young woman, who had dazzled many a man, flew over events like a flaming meteor. With the looks of an Olympian goddess, she combined a brilliant and subtle mind with the courage of a warrior. When Kazan was occupied by the Whites, she disguised herself as a peasant and got into the enemy camp to spy on them. Her bearing, however, was too extraordinary, and she was arrested. A Japanese officer in the espionage section

interrogated her. During a break in the interrogation, she succeeded in slipping out by the door, which was not properly guarded, and disappeared. From then on she worked in reconnaissance. Later, on board warships, she took part in the fighting. She has written essays on the Civil War which will stand as pieces of literature. She has described with no less brilliance the industries of the Urals and the workers' uprising in the Ruhr. She wanted to see everything, to know everything and to take part in everything. In a few short years she became a writer of the first rank. Having passed unharmed through the trials of fire and water, this revolutionary Pallas was abruptly carried off, in the calm of Moscow, by typhus: she was not yet 30.

A participant in and witness of many of the decisive events of the Revolution, Larissa Reisner will remain in history as an observer. Radek is right to insist that *On the Front* is one of the best works to come out of the Civil War. These 130 pages are far more effective than volumes of history in evoking the war, from Kazan to Petrograd. That is true to the extent that the selection of works published in the USSR in 1965 contained a very mutilated version of *On the Front*: the original is too close to the truth.

J.-J. M.

MIKHAIL NIKOLAYEVICH TUKHACHEVSKY

Mikhail Nikolayevich Tukhachevsky was born in 1893, the son of a landowner who was reduced to poverty before the 1905 Revolution. He received his initial education at the First Gymnasium in Penza and then the Tenth Gymnasium in Moscow.

Having an innate leaning towards military affairs, he decided to enter the Cadet Corps. He was exempted from the first six classes of the First Moscow Military School after passing an examination, and in autumn 1911 he entered the seventh form, graduating one year later. From there he went to the Alexander I Military Academy, successfully completing his studies in 1914. On the declaration of the imperialist war, he was commissioned into the Semyonovsky Regiment of the Imperial Guard as a second lieutenant and went off to war.

In 1914 he saw action at Lublin in Galicia, at Ivangorod and Krakow. In 1915 he fought at Lomja, and on 19 February he was captured during a German attack. He made five attempts at escape, covering in all nearly 1,000 miles on foot. Finally, in October 1917, he succeeded in crossing the Swiss-German border, after which he returned to Russia where he was promoted company commander.

Tukhachevsky joined the RKP(b) on 5 April 1918, and his work in building up the Red Army began during the first days of its existence. He also made a name for himself as a strategist. Many large operations were carried out under his leadership, and his revolutionary biography is most closely connected with heroic struggles on all fronts.

During spring 1918 he worked for the Military Department of the VTsIK and inspected many Red Army formations. In May 1918 he was appointed Military Commissar for the Moscow region. Then, on his own request, he was dispatched to the Eastern Front to take command of the First Army. The build-up of the regular Red Army was at its most critical stage. During the Muraviov mutiny in July, Tukhachevsky was arrested by the latter and only escaped execution thanks to some quick-witted Red Army soldiers who realised the situation.

During this period of organisation, plans were laid for an operation to break through the Czechoslovak front at Simbirsk. This was accomplished on 12 September by units of the First Army under Tukhachevsky's command. Then followed a drive at the enemy's rear in Syzran and a rapid advance on Samara, in which Khvesin's Fourth Army also participated as it advanced from Saratov. Later came the Buguruslan and the Belebey operations.

In December 1918 Tukhachevsky began preparations for the Orenburg campaign, but then he was appointed Deputy Commander of the Southern Front and soon Commander of the Eighth Army. With the latter he advanced as far as the northern Donets River after which, in March, he was transferred back to the Eastern Front to command the Fifth Army during our retreat to the Volga. This army was included in Frunze's Southern Group offensive, and Tukhachevsky mounted the Buguruslan, Bugulma, Menzenlinsk and Birsk operations.

The situation on the Eastern Front was critical and the Urals had to be crossed. Tukhachevsky carried out a bold manoeuvre, electing not to go by the Ufimsk-Zlatoust road, but to make a wide detour along the Yurezan river valley towards Zlatoust with the main force of his army whilst protecting his left flank with an auxiliary operation against Krasnoufimsk. It was a complete success and opened up the way to Siberia for the Red Army.

Later followed the Chelyabinsk and Kurgan operations, as well as the strategic retreat to the river Tobol. By redoubling the efforts of the Fifth Army and mobilising the local Siberian inhabitants of the Chelyabinsk and Kurgan regions, a new campaign was planned, this time against Omsk. It was distinguished by its rapidity of advance—between 14 October and 14 November the troops covered up to 400 miles, that is an average of thirteen miles per day. This operation ended in the complete rout of Kolchak's troops. Tens of thousands of prisoners were taken, and Kolchak's army effectively ceased to exist as an organised force. To ensure the final elimination of the enemy, a relentless pursuit was immediately set in train, aided by close collaboration from the Siberian Red partisans.

At the end of November, Tukhachevsky was transferred to the Southern Front as Commander of the Thirteenth Army, but before he could take up this position he was made Commander of the South-Eastern (Caucasus) Front to cope with fresh instability on the rivers Don and Manych. He arrived there on 3 February. By 14 February he had already reorganised and regrouped the troops and launched the decisive advance. On 26 March Novorossiysk was captured, after which Denikin's army disintegrated.

In April he was preparing to mount an operation in support of the newly established Soviet authorities in Baku, when he was summoned from Petrovsk to Moscow to take charge of the Western Front. On 14 May came the first advance. This overran the Polotsk base which was later used as a springboard for further attacks. The second phase of the offensive began on 4 July and within one month our troops had advanced from the Berezina to the Vistula. There, as result of a failure to co-ordinate the tactics of the armies of the Western and South-Western

Fronts, the Poles inflicted a serious defeat on the former. A new offensive could not be mounted for lack of supplies and so the armies of the Western Front fought a slow and stubborn retreat as far as the present Polish-Soviet border.

The result of the 1920 campaign was the liberation of Soviet Byelorussia. In autumn 1920 Tukhachevsky crushed the Bulak-Bulakovich invasion. In March 1921 he was appointed Commander of the Seventh Army to suppress the Kronstadt mutiny, which was accomplished on 17 March. In May of the same year he took command of the troops in Tambov province to quell the long-drawn-out Antonov rebellion. There he introduced new methods of co-ordinating military activities with the consolidation of local Soviet authority, and the rising was crushed methodically in accordance with a forty-day timetable.

In autumn 1921 Tukhachevsky was made Head of the RKKA Military Academy. In January 1922 he took over command of the Western Front. In spring 1924 he was promoted Deputy Chief of Staff of the RKKA, which post he held during the army reorganisation. In 1925 he was appointed Commander of the Western Military District and also a member of the RVS of the USSR. In November he was made Chief of Staff of the RKKA. He combined this work with the post of chief tutor in strategy at the Military Academy, directing the training of top-ranking officers. He has been a member of the General Staff since 1920.

In 1921 and 1922 he was elected to the VTsIK, has been a member of all convocations of the TsIK, and was a member of the Belorussian TsIK in 1924 and 1925. He was chairman of the commission which drew up the RKKA Field Service Regulations. He has also written works on military science.

G. Novikov

Tukhachevsky ranks with Gamarnik, Frunze and Yakir as one of the finest examples of military leaders engendered by the Civil War: he was a fiery orator, a captain with daring and sometimes adventurous views, and a military theoretician with exalted, sweeping ideas. He came out of the First World War with the rank of lieutenant, joined the Bolshevik Party in April 1918, and was sent in June to the Eastern Front where he took command of the First Army, and then at the end of the year to the Southern Front to command the Eighth Army. He began to show his mettle in March 1919 when he was sent back to the Eastern Front to take command of the Fifth Army. Kolchak was only 85 kilometres from Kazan, 100 km from Simbirsk and 85 km from Samara. Under Tukhachevsky's command, the Fifth Army pierced Kolchak's lines, crossed the Urals and poured into Siberia. Order No. 167 dated 7 August 1919, from the RRVS, attributed this success to the 'clever command of Army Leader Tukhachevsky. . . .'

From then on Tukhachevsky began to work out a 'Marxist' military theory, the 'Proletarian Concept of War', together with Frunze, the former commander of the Southern Group on the Eastern Front, with Gusev and a few others. The theory was marked by hostility towards the Tsarist military experts, by the necessity for the emergence of Red Commanders, the development of a mobile partisan war, by tactics systematically based on constant and total offensive, and finally, the last stage, by the constitution of an international revolutionary military General Staff.

These ideas were part of the Polish campaign of June–August 1919: an astounding advance, given the limited technical means at its disposal, took the Red Army to within 30 kilometres of Warsaw: but faced with an Army without reserves, with wretched air support spread out over 200 km of front, weakened by lack of discipline in the command of the South-West Front (Stalin and Yegorov), the Poles were saved by the 'miracle of the Vistula'. In a long report which he drew up in 1923, Tukhachevsky analysed in a cool and sober manner the reasons for this defeat, but declared none the less that a Red Army victory would have sparked off a European revolution. . . .

In March 1921, he organised the liquidation of the Kronstadt revolt, and in May 1921 he organised the repression of the peasant riots in the Tambov region.

He then began a military 'career' which was to take him to the heights of glory and to the depth of ignominy. Novikov has set out the first steps in Tukhachevsky's fall. . . . He remained head of the Red Army's General Staff until May 1928, when he was appointed Commandant of the Leningrad district forces. In June 1931 he was appointed Director of Munitions in the Red Army and then Vice-Commissar for Defence and Vice-President of the RRVS. He remained in the first of these posts until May 1936 and in the second until May 1937.

At that time he supported a systematic modernisation of the Red Army, while Voroshilov, who was to become his hierarchical superior, was still dreaming of cavalry battles; in 1930 Tukhachevsky turned directly to Stalin to impose modernisation plans blocked by Voroshilov and the General Staff. At the end of 1931 he insisted on the need for developing armoured divisions; and in February 1934 he emphasised the importance of the air force. In May 1932 Stalin gave his approval to some of these points.

It seems that Tukhachevsky was 'opposed' to the total subordination of the military apparatus and, among other things, of the army's Intelligence Service, to the apparatus and Intelligence Service of the GPU. Barmin saw him in 1934–5 and noted 'his broad masculine face, his calm assurance and attentive way of speaking'; but he also noticed the deferential tone of voice with which he punctuated his telephone conversations with Voroshilov, saying 'at your orders, Kliment Yefremovich'. And Barmin adds: 'Other observations led me to the conclusion that his will had weakened and that in this vast system of bureaucracy, he too had become a functionary.'

In any case he was not spared in the purges. In January 1937, Radek made an unmistakable allusion to him at the second Moscow trial. The man who has been presented as a Napoleonic conspirator (but all that he seems to have had in common with Bonaparte was his sharp glance and military talent) 'waited' for his arrest. He and seven colleagues were arrested on 8 June 1937, tried *in camera* by a nine-man tribunal, and sentenced to death for high treason on behalf of Nazi Germany. Stalin had his entire family wiped out, and interned his youngest daughter, not twelve years old. Marshal Tukhachevsky was rehabilitated after 1956. Two volumes of his works have since been published in Moscow. . . .

J.-J. M.

MIKHAIL SOLOMONOVICH URITSKY

Mikhail Solomonovich Uritsky, the son of a Jewish merchant, was born in 1873 in the town of Cherkassy. At first he was brought up by his mother (his father died young), in a strict, religious atmosphere, and he studied the Talmud. But then under the influence of his sister he became fascinated by Russian literature. He entered the Cherkassy preparatory school, went on to the Belaya Tserkov Gymnasium, where he lived in great poverty, supporting himself by giving lessons, and then entered the Law Faculty of Kiev University.

Uritsky became involved in the revolutionary movement at an early age and organised an SD circle while still in the Gymnasium. In 1897, when he graduated from university, he volunteered for military service but after only eight days was arrested on a charge of membership of the SD Party. That was the beginning of a number of years in prison or exile. Exiled first to Yakutsk province, he returned to revolutionary activity in St Petersburg under the pseudonym of 'Dr Ratner'. He was soon rearrested, being deported to Vologda and then Archangel provinces. After a short time came freedom, then arrest, prison, exile and finally emigration.

After siding with the Menshiviks at the time of the Party split, he adopted an internationalist position on the outbreak of war and collaborated with Trotsky on *Nashe Slovo*, where he proclaimed his determined opposition to the war. He returned to Petrograd after the Revolution and joined the Bolsheviks. He was immediately given responsible tasks and elected to the Central Committee. In October 1917 he unhesitatingly spoke in favour of a rising against the Kerensky government and took the most active part in its overthrow as a member of Military Revolutionary Committee. After this he was appointed Commissar in charge of the Constituent Assembly. An opponent of the Brest peace, he nevertheless submitted to the decision to sign the treaty for the sake of Party discipline. Appointed head of the Petrograd Cheka, Uritsky waged an unremitting campaign against counter-revolution. He was killed on 30 August 1918 by the student A. Kanegisser.

With his pince-nez and broken neck, Uritsky looked the perfect intellectual. He and Volodarsky, both members of *Mezhrayonka*, shared the honour of being considered by the SRs as the most execrable representatives of Bolshevism; as a result, he was assassinated by one of them on 30 August, the same day that some SR Pimpernel attempted to murder Lenin.

Uritsky made Trotsky's acquaintance in 1900 during the first deportation, on the banks of the Lena. He remained his friend until death.[1] A Menshevik from the schism in 1903, he associated himself with Trotsky, outside splinter groupings, in 1905, and in 1910 was a member of Plekhanov's so-called 'Party Mensheviks'.

On his return to Russia immediately after the February Revolution he joined the *Mezhrayonka* (he did not join the Bolshevik Party straight away, as his anonymous biographer would have us believe). If one is to believe Sukhanov, Uritsky first supported unity between all socialist splinters and even proposed on the evening of 17 March that a workers' delegation, complete with military band, should meet Tseretelli, declaring that 'Tseretellis don't come every day'.

Then he changed rapidly. In August he joined the Bolshevik Party, like all members of the *Mezhrayonka*, was elected to the CC and during the October discussions held reservations about the lack of practical preparedness, but none the less supported the move to insurrection. For this he was chosen, on 16 October, as one of the five members of the RVS nominated by the CC to go on to the Petrograd Soviet RVS. He played a major role in the RVS and sometimes signed its documents under the style of 'president'.

During the discussion of the Brest-Litovsk peace terms he was one of the most consistent left-wing communists, one of the four who refused right through to vote for the Brest treaty terms. He reproached Lenin with 'seeing things from Russia's point of view, not from the international point of view'. He stated, 'After having taken power, we have forgotten about world revolution. [. . .] Our capitulation to German imperialism will retard the awakening Western Revolution.' At the seventh Congress of the Bolshevik Party he proclaimed: 'A defeat could promote the development of a socialist revolution in Western Europe much more than this obscene peace.' At the same Congress Lenin accused him to taking his criticisms from left-wing SR newspapers.

Granat's biographer praises Uritsky's discipline on this occasion. He is rather overstating himself. In fact, Uritsky was the most extreme of the left communists. On 23 February it was he who read to the CC the declaration of the left communists who were resigning from their positions in Party and Government. Uritsky left his post as a member of the inner cabinet of People's Commissars, as well as the CC, where he remained to the end the most virulent spokesman of those who had resigned. He demanded the right for the left wing to propagandise within the Party, even after the signature of the peace treaty. He was one

[1] Trotsky called him 'my old friend' when recalling their meeting in 1917. It was not a phrase he much used.

of the three editors of the left-wing communist splinter weekly, *Kommunist*, launched in Petrograd in February 1918. At the seventh Congress it was again Uritsky who read out the declaration of the left communists who refused to enter the CC and even to participate in the elections. Elected an alternate member of the CC, he, with Bukharin and Lomov, refused to work on it. Many months passed before Uritsky 'submitted'.

After being appointed President of the Petrograd Cheka, he responded with firmness to the left-wing SR insurrection. The SRs took their revenge and assassinated him on 30 August. Although he appeared to feel a strong antipathy towards Stalin, whom he had attacked several times in the CC and at the seventh Congress, where he opposed his appointment to the Programme Commission, Uritsky was left a small place in official Soviet history. But this man, whose religious upbringing no doubt made him give his political principles a rigorous moral value, has remained in the chronicles of the revolution only as a fervent internationalist with no face and no voice.

J.-J. M.

V. VOLODARSKY (pseudonym of MOISEY MARKOVICH GOLDSTEIN)

V. Volodarsky was born in 1890 in the locality of Ostropol, Volhynia province. He came from a poor Jewish family. Under the impact of the agrarian agitation of 1905 he joined the revolutionary movement, participating first in the 'Small Bund' and then 'Spilka' (the Ukrainian SD Party). He composed and printed illegal appeals, as well as holding short meetings. After entering the fifth form of the Dubno Gymnasium, he was expelled one year later for 'political unreliability'.

In 1908 he was clapped in prison but soon released. From 1908 until 1911 he was active as an agitator in Volhynia. In 1911 he was arrested and deported to Archangel province for three years. He used his enforced idleness to study for the school-leaving certificate; he passed the examinations and then in 1913 returned home under an amnesty. Police persecution, however, drove him abroad. He went to Philadelphia in the United States, where he found work as a cutter in a garment factory. He joined the International Trade Union of Tailors and became a militant agitator, propagandist and journalist, at first among workers in Philadelphia and then in New York. He was a most active collaborator on *Novy Mir* with Bukharin and Chudnovsky.

After the February Revolution he returned to Russia, soon joined the Bolshevik Party, and gradually rose to the first rank of Party activists, at first working as a district agitator, and then as chief agitator for the Petrograd Committee. He was elected to the Presidium of the Petrograd Soviet and, after the October Revolution, to the Presidium of the VTsIK, taking a direct part in the congresses of soviets. He was sent by the Party to the Ukraine to attend the Congress of the Army of the Romanian Front, and on his return he was entrusted with the editorship of the Petrograd *Krasnaya Gazeta*. With the formation of the Petrograd Commune, he was elected Commissar for Press, Propaganda and Agitation. On 20 July 1918 he was murdered on his way to a meeting.

In 1920 a collection of his speeches was published.

This 'pale, tall young man with a bad complexion and glasses' (John Reed) is today thoroughly forgotten. The SR assassins who shot him down on 20 June 1918 blocked his path to history in which he was destined to play more than a minor part.

At the age of fourteen he was already a militant, at eighteen a professional revolutionary agitating in Volhynia. From his youth, Volodarsky was distinguished for his talents as an orator, which served him well in the American Clothes-Workers' Union and Socialist Party, of which he was a member during his exile in the United States (1913–17). He returned to Russia in April 1917 and promptly joined *Mezhrayonka*. He did not wait for the merger to come about (in August) but joined the Bolshevik Party in May. The Party badly needed agitators, but only had a handful—Zinoviev, Slutsky, Kollontai, Chudnovsky, Lunacharsky. Volodarsky was elected to the Petrograd Committee as soon as he joined the Party, and then to the *Ispolkom*. He was responsible for the Peterhof-Narva area, which included the huge Putilov works and its 30,000 metal-workers—the spearhead of the capital's proletariat. In a few weeks Volodarsky won Putilov over to the Bolsheviks. 'From the moment he set foot in Narva district', the worker Minichev recounted, 'the ground began to shake under the feet of the SR gentlemen at Putilov, and after two months or so the workers followed the Bolsheviks'. At the time of the July days, Volodarsky's speech to the *Mezhrayonka* conference was instrumental in preparing the merger with the Bolsheviks.

He had less success on 3 July when the CC gave him the task of persuading the First Machine Gun Regiment not to demonstrate. . . . During the July-August repression, the Petrograd Committee relied heavily on Volodarsky. Boris Ivanov writes: 'Volodarsky now carries almost single-handed the tasks of propaganda and agitation in quasi-illegal conditions'. But he put on an assured front. At the Petrograd Conference on 16–20 July he maintained that the demoralisation was a shallow, passing mood, and opposed the liquidation of the slogan 'All Power to the Soviets' which Stalin had proposed.

He was deeply involved with the masses among whom he plunged each day; and as one of the leading Bolsheviks in the Soviet, coming behind Trotsky and Kamenev, he expressed the people's fear of decisive action by opposing the move to insurrection. 'We must know that once in power we shall have to lower wages, increase production, introduce terror. . . . We do not have the right to refuse these means, but neither should we hasten to use them.' And he added: 'Only a revolutionary explosion in the West can save us.' He suggested putting the question to the Congress of Soviets. Once the decision for insurrection had been taken, however, he fought for its success. *The History of the Russian Revolution*, 'edited under the supervision of M. Gorky, V. Molotov, K. Voroshilov, S. Kirov, A. Zhdanov and J. Stalin', pays Volodarsky the following tribute: 'On the tribune one could see more frequently than the others the slender figure of Volodarsky, one of the best Bolshevik agitators. He was a passionate speaker and very popular with the workers and soldiers.' Before contradictory meetings with the Mensheviks or the SRs, the Petrograd Committee's telephone never stopped ringing: 'Send us Volodarsky. There'll be a lot of people at the meeting.'

He was a member of the Soviet TsIK elected on 26 October, and one of the fiercest opponents of the conciliators—led by Zinoviev and Kamenev, who had been his political ally until very recently. Volodarsky led the fight, at the all-night meeting of the TsIK on 1 November, against the 'coalition government'. He succeeded in getting his motion passed *nem con.* . . . Entrusted with preparing the Constituent Assembly elections in the capital, he declared to the Petrograd Committee on 8 November, 'If the Constituent Assembly does not have a Bolshevik majority, then we shall have to make ready for a third Revolution'.

In the following months he fell from public view somewhat. Profoundly hostile to the Brest-Litovsk agreement, remaining a 'left-wing communist' to his fingertips on this issue (although never included by historians in their lists of left-wing communists of the period) he abstained out of a sense of discipline from any splinter activity. He remained silent. On the Petrograd Soviet Executive Committee he remained silent, in working sessions as in plenary sessions of the Soviet; and on the TsIK he remained silent, going so far as to abstain on a vote on the peace treaty on 24 February. On 25 February, at the Petrograd Soviet, the left-wing SR Frishman described the Bolsheviks as 'traitors to the revolution'. Volodarsky jumped up, delivered a flamboyant speech which concluded with these words:

> I declare in the name of those opposed to the peace terms: we accept this treaty, however ruinous, however annexationist, we shall sign it and march at your sides, at the sides of those who did not fear to take on an enourmous responsbility in order to save the fate of the revolution. [. . .] we shall march forward beneath this heavy cross on a road of thorns towards socialism.

Hardly had he resumed his place in the front rank of the Petrograd Bolsheviks than he was killed, one evening in June, on his way to a meeting. He was not yet twenty-eight years old and according to Boris Ivanov, 'He had no private life. He lived alone in order to give himself more completely to the Revolution'. He was a popular figure and the Bolshevik leaders in Petrograd, much to Lenin's indignation, had to calm the communist workers in the former capital to prevent them from replying to Volodarsky's assassination with a wave of mass terror.

J.-J. M.

List of Periodicals

BEDNOTA (The Poor) — Popular peasant daily newspaper, published by the Central Committee of the RKP(b), 27 March 1918 to 31 January 1931

BOLSHEVIK — Twice-weekly, theoretical paper published by the Central Committee of the RKP(b) from 1924

BORBA (Struggle) — (1) Bolshevik daily, legal. Published in Moscow from 27 November [NS 10 December] to 6 [NS 19] December 1906. 9 issues
(2) Trotsky's newspaper, Petrograd, from February to July 1914

BORBA PROLETARIATA (Struggle of the Proletariat) — Organ of the Caucasian Social Democratic Labour Movement, Baku 1905

BYULLETEN OPPOZITSII (Opposition Bulletin) — Trotskyite. Paris, July 1929 then New York, August to October 1939

DEREVENSKAYA BEDNOTA (The Country Poor) — Peasant daily published by the Central Committee of the RSDRP(b), Petrograd 1917; merged with DEREVENSKAYA PRAVDA (Country Truth) to form BEDNOTA

DNI (Days) — Daily, then weekly, edited by A. F. Kerensky, Berlin then Paris, 1922–8

DRO (Times) — Caucasian Bolshevik daily, Tiflis, 11 March to 15 April 1907. 31 issues

EKHO (Echo) — Legal Bolshevik daily, Petersburg, 22 June [NS 5 July] to 7 [NS 20] July 1906. 14 issues, replacing VPERYOD

GOLOS (The Voice) — = NASHE SLOVO, Paris, issues 6–108; 18 September 1914 to 7 January 1915

GOLOS PRAVDY (Voice of Truth) — Published by the internationalist social democrats, Paris, 1 May 1917

GOLOS SOTSIAL
DEMOKRATA
(The Social
Democrat Voice)

Organ of the Mensheviks in exile, Geneva-Paris, February 1908 to December 1911. 26 issues

GUDOK (The
Siren)

(1) Legal Bolshevik daily, published by the Oil-Workers' Union, Baku, 12 April 1907 to 1 June 1908. Replaced by the Menshevik BAKINSKY RABOCHY (The Baku Worker)

(2) Soviet railway-workers' daily, first issue 11 May 1920

ISKRA (The
Spark)

The first underground Marxist paper for all Russia, December 1900. Published in Leipzig, Munich, London, Geneva; became Menshevik from issue 52 (19 October [NS 1 November] 1903)

IZVESTIA
(The News)

General political daily published by the Soviet TSIK. Sub-title varied frequently. First issue 28 February [NS 13 March] 1917

KAZARMA (The
Barracks)

Underground social democrat paper, Petersburg, February 1906–7. Bolshevik as from issue 4. 43 issues in all

KIEVSKAYA
MYSL (Kiev)
Thought)

Liberal bourgeois daily, Kiev, 30 December 1906 to January 1918

KIEVSKIE
OTKLIKI
(Kiev Echoes)

Legal semi-Marxist paper, Kiev, 1903.

KOMMUNIST

(1) A review founded by Lenin and published by the editors of SOTSIAL DEMOKRAT in Geneva, 1915. Sole double issue brought out for the Zimmerwald Conference

(2) Left-wing communist daily, then weekly, Petrograd then Moscow, March 1918. 4 issues

KRASNAYA
GAZETA (Red
Gazette)

Organ of the Leningrad city soviet, January 1918 to 1939

KRASNAYA
ZVEZDA (Red
Star)

Daily paper published by the Ministry of Defence, Moscow. First issue 1 January 1924

KRASNAYA NOV
(Red Earth)

Literary, artistic and scientific review, Moscow, June 1921 to August 1942. From 1934, organ of the Union of Soviet Writers

LEIPZIGER VOLKSZEITUNG (Leipzig People's Paper)	Organ of the left wing of the German social democratic movement; daily from 1894 to 1933. From 1917 to 1922, was the organ of the USPD, but came under the control of the social democrat majority in 1922
LETOPIS (The Chronicle)	Monthly, founded by Gorky and the internationalist social democrats, Paris, December 1915 to December 1917
LUCH (The Ray)	Legal Menshevik daily, Petersburg, September 1912 to August 1913, then August 1913 to August 1919 (under Dan and Martynov). Supplanted in July 1913 by ZHIVAYA ZHIZN then by NOVAYA RABOCHAYA GAZETA
METALLIST (The Metal-Worker)	Organ of the Metal-Workers' Union, Petersburg 20 August [NS 12 September] 1906 to 12 [NS 25] June 1914. In 1913, turned Bolshevik
MIR BOZHI (World of God)	Popular monthly review of art, literature and politics 1892–6
MOLODAYA GVARDIYA (Young Guard)	Popular monthly review of literature, art and politics 1922–41
MORYAK (The Sailor)	All-Russian Sailors' paper, Vienna, 1911–13. 14 issues
MYSL (Thought)	(1) Legal Bolshevik monthly review of philosophy, society, economics, Moscow, December 1910 to April 1911. 5 issues (2) SR daily, Paris, 15 November 1914 to 14 March 1915, then weekly, Geneva, 20 June 1915 to 2 January 1916
NACHALO (The Beginning)	(1) Legal Marxist organ, Petersburg, 1899. 5 issues in 4 (2) Continuation of GOLOS and NASHE SLOVO, 30 September 1916 to 24 March 1917. 147 issues
NASHE SLOVO (Our Word)	Continuation of GOLOS, 29 January 1915 to 15 September 1916. Internationalist social democrats
NAUCHNOYE OBOZRENIYE (Scientific Review)	Petersburg 1894–1903. Weekly to 1897, then monthly
DIE NEUE ZEIT (New Times)	Theoretical review of the German social democratic movement, Stuttgart, 1883–1923
NOVAYA EPOKHA (New Epoch)	Continuation of NACHALO (2), Paris, weekly then daily, 5 April to 3 May 1917

NOVAYA ZHIZN (1) The first legal Bolshevik daily; Petersburg,
(New Life) 27 October [NS 9 November] to 3 [NS 16] December
1905. 28 issues
(2) Internationalist Menshevik daily, Petrograd,
April 1917 to June 1918

NOVOYE SLOVO Legal Marxist literary and scientific monthly, Peters-
(New Word) burg, 1894–7

NOVY MIR Organ of the internationalist social democrats, New
(New World) York, 1911–16. Weekly

OBRAZOVANIYE Monthly, Petersburg, 1892–1909. From 1905 to
(Education) 1907, close to Legal Marxism

PRAVDA (Truth) (1) Daily, published by the CC of the RKP, Petersburg, 22 April [NS 5 May] to 5 July 1913. Became
RABOCHAYA PRAVDA from 13 July to 1 August 1913,
then SEVERNAYA PRAVDA from 1 August to 7 September 1913; then PRAVDA TRUDA (11 September to
9 October 1913); ZA PRAVDU (1 October to 5 December 1913); PROLETARSKAYA PRAVDA (7 December
1913 to 21 January 1914); PUT PRAVDY (22 January
to 21 May 1914); RABOCHY (22 April to 7 July 1914);
TRUDOVAYA PRAVDA (23 May to 8 July 1914). 346
issues. Resumed in 1917, at first under title PRAVDA,
then after the July days as LISTOK PRAVDY (6 [NS 19]
July); RABOCHY I SOLDAT (23 July [NS 5 August] to
10 [NS 23] August 1917); PROLETARY (13 [NS 26]
August to 24 August 1917); RABOCHY (25 August
[NS 7 September] 1917); RABOCHY PUT (3 [NS 16]
September 1917). As from 27 October [NS 9 Nov-
ember] 1917: PRAVDA. Transferred to Moscow on
3 March 1918
(2) Paper published by Trotsky; Geneva, Lvov and
Vienna, 3 October 1908 to 23 April [NS 6 May] 1912

PROLETARY (1) Central organ of the RSDRP, Geneva, 14 [NS 27]
(The May to 12 [NS 25] November 1905. 26 issues
Proletarian) (2) Underground Bolshevik paper founded after the
fourth Congress. Published by the Moscow and
Petersburg Committees of the RSDRP; Finland,
Geneva, Paris, 21 August [NS 3 September] 1906 to
28 November [NS 10 December] 1909. 50 issues
(3) See under PRAVDA

PROLETARSKAYA
REVOLYUTSIYA
(Proletarian
Revolution)

Historical review published by the Marx-Engels-Lenin Institute, Moscow, 1921–41. 132 issues

PROSVESH-
CHENIYE (En-
lightenment)

Legal, social, political and literary monthly; theoretical organ of the Bolsheviks; Petersburg, December 1911 to June 1914

PUT PRAVDY
(The Way of
Truth)

See under PRAVDA

PRZEGLAD
SOCJALDEMO-
KRATYCZNY
(Social-Demo-
cratic Review)

Published by the Polish social democratic movement, Krakow, 1902–4, 1908–10; articles by Rosa Luxemburg

RABOCHAYA
GAZETA
(Workers'
Gazette)

(1) Underground organ of the Kiev social democrats, issue 1: 22 April, issue 2: 20 December 1897. Declared the RSDRP's official organ at the first Congress at Minsk. Issue 3, prepared at Ekaterinoslav, never appeared

(2) Underground Bolshevik paper, Paris, 30 October [NS 12 November] 1910 to 30 July [NS 10 August] 1912

(3) Popular daily, published by the CC of the RKP, Moscow, 1 March 1922 to 30 January 1932. 98 issues

(4) Central organ of the Menshevik RSDRP; Petrograd, 20 March to 30 November 1917. Succeeded by LUCH, ZARYA, KLICH, PLAMYA, FAKEL, MOLOT, MOLNYA, SHCHIT and NOVY LUCH from 2 December 1917 to 22 February 1918

RABOCHAYA
MYSL (Workers'
Thought)

The 'economists'' paper, Petersburg, Berlin, Warsaw, October 1897 to December 1902. 16 issues

RABOCHEYE
DELO (Workers'
Cause)

(1) Underground journal of the Union of Struggle for the Emancipation of the Working Class, Petersburg, 1895

(2) Review published by the Union of Russian Social Democrats in Exile, Geneva, April 1899 to February 1902. 12 issues

(3) Trade union weekly, Moscow, 1 May 1909. Succeeded by VYESTNIK TRUDA and NASH PUT

RABOCHEYE ZNAMYA (The Workers' Flag) — Regional Party organ, Moscow 1909

RABOCHY (The Worker) — (1) Underground paper published by the CC of the RSDRP, Moscow, August to October 1905. 4 issues
(2) Central organ of the RSDRP, Petrograd, succeeding PROLETARY; 25 August [NS 7 September] to 2 [NS 15] September 1917. 12 issues

RABOCHY I SOLDAT (Worker and Soldier) — See under PRAVDA

RABOCHY PUT (Workers' Path) — See under PRAVDA

RUSSKAYA GAZETA (Russian Gazette) — Popular paper published by Trotsky and Parvus, Petersburg, 1905

RUSSKOYE BOGATSTVO (Russian Wealth) — Populist literary and scientific monthly, liberal from the 1890s. Petersburg, 1876–1918

SAMARSKY VYESTNIK (Samara Messenger) — Daily, Samara, 1893–1904. Published some Marxist articles

SEVERNY VYESTNIK (Northern Messenger) — Monthly political and scientific review, Petersburg, 1885–8

SOLDATSKAYA PRAVDA (Soldiers' Truth) — Published by the military organisation of the RSDRP(b)'s Petrograd Committee; Petrograd, 1917 to 1918

SOTSIAL-DEMOKRAT (The Social Democrat) — (1) Literary and political review of the Osvobozhdeniye Truda group, Geneva 1890–3. 4 brochures
(2) Underground organ of the CC of the RSDRP; Petersburg, 17 September to 18 November 1906. 7 issues
(3) Underground central organ of the RSDRP; Russia, Paris, Geneva; February 1908 to January 1917. From 1910, Bolshevik
(4) Daily published by the Moscow Region Bureau, then by the RSDRP(b)'s Moscow Committee; March 1917 to March 1918. 246 issues

SOVREMENNIK (The Contemporary) — Literary and political review, Petersburg, 1911–15

SPARTAK (Spartacus) — Fortnightly review, published by the left-wing Bolshevik splinter of the Social Democratic Party's Moscow Committee. May to October 1917. 10 issues

SVOBODNOYE VOSPITANIYE (Free Education) — Monthly pedagogical review, Moscow, 1907–17

VYESTNIK TRUDA (Workers' Messenger) — Daily, Moscow, 1909; continuation of RABOCHEYE DELO; succeeded by NASH PUT

VOLNA (The Wave) — Legal Bolshevik daily, Petersburg, 26 April to May 1907. 25 issues

VOPROSY STRAKHO-VANIYA (Questions of Insurance) — Legal Bolshevik weekly, Petrograd, October 1913 to March 1918

DER VORBOTE (The Herald) — Theoretical review, organ of the Zimmerwaldian left; published in German, Berne, 1916. 2 issues

VORWÄRTS (Forward) — Central organ of the German social democratic movement, Berlin 1876–1933

VOSTOCHNOYE OBOZRENIYE (Eastern Review) — Literary and political weekly, Petersburg then Irkutsk, 1882–1906

VPERYOD (Forward) — (1) Underground Bolshevik weekly, Geneva, 22 December 1904 [NS 4 January 1905] to 5 [NS 18] May 1905; succeeded by PROLETARY. 18 issues
(2) Organ of the Petrograd Internationalist social democrats, 15 June to 15 September 1917
(3) Menshevik social democrat paper, Moscow, March 1917 to May 1918
(4) Legal Bolshevik daily; Petersburg, 26 May [NS 8 June] to 14 [NS 27] June 1906. 17 issues; succeeded by EKHO
(5) Collection of articles by the VPERYOD group, organ of the left-wing Bolsheviks. Paris, 1910 11. 3 issues
(6) Organ of the VPERYOD group; Geneva, 25 August 1915 to 1 February 1917. 6 issues

YUZHNY
RABOCHY
(Southern Worker)
Illegal social democrat newspaper, published by a group of the same name; Kremenchug, Smolensk, Kishinyov, etc., January 1900 to April 1903

ZA PARTIYU
(For the Party)
Paris, April 1912 to February 1914. 5 issues. (Plekhanov, Lyubimov, Vladimirov)

ZARYA (Dawn)
Scientific and political Marxist review; Stuttgart, 1901–2, 4 issues. Published by the editors of ISKRA

ZVENO (The Link)
International socialist review; Petersburg, May to September 1906

ZVEZDA (The Star)
Legal Bolshevik paper (see under PRAVDA). Petersburg, 16 [NS 29] December 1910 to 22 April [NS 5 May] 1912

Abbreviations, Acronyms, Organisations

AGITPROP	Agitation and Propaganda	A department of the Central Committee Secretariat
AVIAKHIM	Obshchestvo sodeystviya aviatsyonno-khimicheskomu stroitelstvu v SSSR	Society for the Advancement of the Aviation and Chemical Industry in the USSR (1925–7). In 1927 became Osoaviakhim
BUND	General Union of Lithuanian, Polish and Russian Jewish Workers	Founded in 1897, joined the RSDRP at its first Congress, left it at the Second and rejoined after the Fourth Congress in 1906
CHEKA	See under Vecheka	
COMINTERN	Third International, or Communist International	First Congress: 2–7 March 1919. Dissolved on 10 June 1943
DUMA	House of Representatives	Set up in Tsarist Russia as a consequence of the 1905 Revolution. First Duma. April–July 1906; second Duma: February–July 1907; third Duma: 1907–12; fourth Duma: 1912–17. Also the name of pre-revolutionary municipal councils
GLAVISKUSSTVO	Glavnoye Upravleniye po delam Iskusstva	Central Directorate for Artistic Affairs
GLAVKONTSESKOM	Glavny Kontsessionny Komitet	Chief Concessions Committee

GLAVREPERTKOM	Glavnoye Upravlenie po Kontrolyu za Zrelishchami i Repertuarom	Central Directorate for Theatres and Entertainments
GKO	Gosudarstvenny Komitet Oborony	Government Defence Committee
GOSPLAN	Gosudarstvenny Plan	State Planning Commission
GPU	Gosudarstvennoye Politicheskoye Upravlenie	Government Political Administration. A political police force set up in 1922 to replace the Cheka; itself replaced by OGPU from 1922 to 1934. Then came under the NKVD; today comes under the KGB
GUBKOM	Gubernsky Komitet	Province Committee
GUS	Gosudarstvenny Uchony Soviet	State Academic Council (1919–33)
IKKI	Ispolnitelny Komitet Kommunisticheskogo Internatsionala	Executive Committee of the Comintern
ISB	Internationai Socialist Bureau	
ISPOLKOM	Ispolnitelny Komitet	Executive Committee
KD(KADETS)	Konstitutsionnaya Demokratiya	Constitutional Democracy, founded October 1905
MEZHRAYONKA		Inter-district social democratic organisation, created in Petersburg in 1913. Joined the RSDRP(b) at the Party's sixth Congress
MOPBR	Mezhdunarodnaya Organisatsiya Pomoshchi Bortsam Revolyutsii	International Revolutionaries' Aid Organisation
NARKOMINDEL [NKID]	Narodny Kommissariat Inostranikh Del	People's Commissariat for Foreign Affairs
NARKOMNATS	Narodny Kommissariat po Delam Natsionalnostyey	People's Commissariat for Nationalities
NARKOMPROS	Narodny Kommissariat Prosveshcheniga	People's Commissariat for Education

NARODNAYA VOLYA	The People's Will	A Populist secret society, founded 1879, decimated by the Tsarist authorities after the assassination of Alexander II in 1881
NEP		New Economic Policy
NKVD	Narodny Kommissariat Vnutrennykh Del	People's Commissariat for the Interior
OKHRANA		Tsarist political police
ORGBURO		Organisational Bureau
OSVOBOZH-DENIYE	Liberation	Liberal group, with paper of same name, published between 1902 and 1905 under direction of P. Struve. The group later formed the nucleus of the Kadets
OSVOBOZHDENIYE TRUDA	Workers' Liberation	The first Russian Marxist group founded by G. Plekhanov, Geneva 1883
POUM	Partido Obrero de Unificación Marxista	Non-communist Marxist group founded by Nin and Maurin
PPS	Polska Partia Socjalistyczna	Polish Socialist Party, founded 1892, originally to promote Polish independence. Split between right and left wings in 1906. During the war, the left merged with the SDKPiL
PROFINTERN	Profsoyuzny Internatsional	Red International of Trade Unions
PYATYORKA		Name of the RVS set up on 10 [NS 23] October 1917 by the Central Committee, to become part of the Soviet RVS and run the practical side of the Revolution
RABKRIN	Narodny Kommissariat Rabochey i Krestyanskoy Inspektsii	People's Commissariat for Workers' and Peasants' Control

RADA		Pre-Soviet Ukrainian councils
RKKA	Raboche Krestyanskaya Krasnaya Armiya	Workers' and Peasants' Red Army
RKP(b)	Russkaya Kommunisticheskaya Partiya (bolshevikov)	Bolshevik Party, from 1918 to 1925. Formerly RSDRP(b). From 1925 to 1952, renamed VKP(b); from 1952, became KPSS (= CPSU)
RSDRP	Russkaya Sotsial-Demokraticheskaya Rabochaya Partiya	Russian Social Democratic Workers' Party. Founded 1898 at Minsk Congress, split at second Congress into Bolshevik and Menshevik factions. Bolshevik faction became RKP at sixth Congress in 1918
RSFSR		Russian Soviet Socialist Federal Republic
RRVS	Respublikansky Revolyutsionny Voyenny Soviet	Revolutionary Military Council of the Republic
RVS	Revolyutsionny Voyenny Soviet	Revolutionary Military Council
SDKPiL	Socjaldemokracja Królestawa Polskiego i Litwy	Polish and Lithuanian Social Democratic Party
SEMYORKA		Name of the political buerau set up by the Central Committee on 10 [NS 23] October 1917 to control the political side of the Revolution
SOVNARKHOZ	Soviet Narodnogo Khozyaistva	Council of the People's Economy, created by decree on 5 [NS 18] December 1917
SOVNARKOM	Soviet Narodnykh Kommissarov	Council of People's Commissars

SPILKA		Ukrainian social demo-cratic group, associated with the Mensheviks and founded towards the end of 1904. From 1907 existed as a number of small groups. Published *Pravda*, which was transferred to Vienna and came under the control of Trotsky and Ioffe
STO	Soviet Truda i Oborony	Labour and Defence Council
TSEKTRAN	Tsentralny Komitet Obyedinyonnogo Professialnogo Soyuza Rabotnikov Zheleznodorozhnogo i Vodnogo Transporta	Central Committee of the United Trade Union of Railway and Waterway Transport Workers. Created September 1920
TSENTROBALT	Tsentralny Komitet Baltiskogo Flota	Central Committee of the Baltic Fleet
TSIK	Tsentralny Ispol-nitelny Komitet	Central Executive Com-mittee, elected by the Congress of Soviets
TSKK	Tsentralnaya Kontrolnaya Kommissaya	Central Control Commis-sion, instituted by the Central Committee of the RKP(b) in June 1921 to direct the Party purges
UNION OF RUSSIAN SOCIAL DEMOCRATS IN EXILE		Created in Geneva, 1894, at the instigation of the OSVOBOZHDENIYE TRUDA group. Broke with it in April 1900
UNION OF STRUGGLE FOR THE EMAN-CIPATION OF THE WORKING CLASSES		Marxist working-class circles in Petersburg united by Lenin in autumn 1895. Similar union in Kiev, March 1897
UKSSR		Ukrainian Soviet Socialist Republic

URAVNILOVKA		An egalitarian economic and social theory, considered under Stalin to be a *petit-bourgeois* reactionary leftist deviation, and ascribed to supporters of Trotsky, Zinoviev, Kamenev and then to the trade union leader Tomsky
USSR		Union of Soviet Socialist Republics
VKP(b)	Vserossiskaya Kommunisticheskaya Partiya	All-Russian Communist Party. Formerly RKP(b)
VNESHTORG		Commissariat for External Trade
VTSIK	Vserossisky Tsentralny Ispolnitelny Komitet	Central Executive Committee of the All-Russian Congress of Soviets. Became the Presidium of the Supreme Soviet
VECHEKA	Vserossiskaya Chrezvychainaya Kommissiya po Borbe s Kontrrevol-yutsiyey i Sabotazhem	Better known by the name Cheka, Extraordinary Commission for the Struggle against Sabotage and Counter-Revolution. Instituted 7 September 1917. In 1922, became GPU
VTSSPS	Vsesoyuzny Tsentralny Soviet Profsoyuzov	All-Union Central Trade Union Council
ZAKKRAIKOM	Zakavkazsky Kraikom	Transcaucasian Regional Committee
ZEMSTVO		Local administrative authority, instituted in 1864, with control over local economic matters, but coming under the province governors and the Ministry of the Interior

Index of Names

Names are listed alphabetically and references given under 'main' or most commonly known names, with 'second names' (pseudonyms or original names) following in brackets. Numbers in bold type refer to sections principally dealing with the person in question, numbers in italic refer to passages written by the person.

General Index